UNDERSTANDING PUBLIC COMMUNICATION

Richard L. Weaver, II
Bowling Green State University

PRENTICE-HALL, INC. Englewood Cliffs, New Jersey 07632

Library of Congress Cataloging in Publication Data

Weaver, Richard L., II
  Understanding public communication.

  Includes bibliographical references and
indexes.
    1. Public speaking. I. Title.
PN4121.W3472 1983   808.5'1   82-13153
ISBN 0-13-936740-3

Editorial/production supervision: Richard Kilmartin
Cover design: Maureen Olsen
Cover photo: Goffery Gove, The Image Bank
Manufacturing buyer: Edmund W. Leone

Printed in the United States of America

10 9 8 7 6 5 4 3 2 1

ISBN 0-13-936740-3

Prentice-Hall International, Inc., *London*
Prentice-Hall of Australia Pty. Limited, *Sydney*
Prentice-Hall Canada Inc., *Toronto*
Prentice-Hall of India Private Limited, *New Delhi*
Prentice-Hall of Japan, Inc., *Tokyo*
Prentice-Hall of Southeast Asia Pte. Ltd., *Singapore*
Whitehall Books Limited, *Wellington, New Zealand*

To

Florence B. Weaver

*with whom
I first publicly communicated*

CONTENTS

PREFACE   ix

ACKNOWLEDGMENTS   xi

one

GETTING STARTED: YOUR FIRST SPEECH   1

Analyzing the Audience 3   Finding Appropriate Material 6   Organizing the Material 10   Choosing the Language 15   Learning to Use Nonverbal Communication 16   Presenting the Message 18   Summary 20   Note 22

two

UNDERSTANDING THE PROCESS: CONCEPTS AND ELEMENTS   23

Axioms of Communication 24   Elements of Communication 27   A Model 43   Summary 46   Notes 47

three

LISTENING: LEARNING, DISCOVERING, AND IMPROVING   48

Learning More About Communication 49   Discovering More Information 50

Improving Your Ability to Listen 51   Why Don't We Listen? 54   Improving Our Listening Skills 56   Summary 63   Notes 65

four

ANALYZING THE AUDIENCE: IDEA ADAPTATION   67

Need for Audience Analysis 68   What Do We Want to Analyze? 69   How Do We Analyze the Audience? 76   What We Do with the Information 79   How Do You Know If You Have Been Successful? 88   Summary 90   Notes 90

five

IDENTIFYING APPROPRIATE MATERIAL: SPEECH SUPPORT 92

The Structure of Arguments 93   Logical Support: Data 96   Emotional
Considerations 104   Catalog of Needs 105   Personal
Considerations 111   Summary 114   Notes 115

six

LOCATING SOURCES: LIBRARY USAGE 117

Find a Specific Purpose 120   The Library: First Stop—Card Catalog 124
The Library: Second Stop—Periodicals 127   Finding Statistics 131
Government Documents 132   How Much Is Enough? 134   Summary
136   Notes 137

seven

ORGANIZING THE MATERIAL: ARRANGEMENT AND OUTLINES 138

Outlining 139   The Body of the Speech 139   The Introduction 152
The Conclusion 155   Transitional and Internal Summaries 158
The Outline 160   Summary 165   Notes 165

eight

CHOOSING THE LANGUAGE: WORD SELECTION 167

The Nature of Language 168   Language Choices 175   Improving Our
Language Use 187   Summary 189   Notes 190

nine

USING THE BODY: NONVERBAL COMMUNICATION 192

The Nature of Nonverbal Communication 193   Nonverbal Choices 201
Improving Our Nonverbal Communication 212   Summary 213
Notes 214

ten

FOCUSING YOUR ENERGY: DELIVERY 216

Anxiety 218   Preparation and Practice 229   Summary 232
Notes 232

eleven

STYLES OF PRESENTATION: DELIVERY 234

Memorized Delivery 235   Manuscript Delivery 237
Impromptu Delivery 240   Extemporaneous Delivery 244
Building Credibility 246   Memory 250   Summary 252   Notes 253

twelve

SEEKING UNDERSTANDING: INFORMATIVE SPEECHES 254

Informative Speeches 255   Ways to Increase Understanding 263   Visual
Aids 266   Answering Questions 271   Summary 273   Notes 275

thirteen

CHANGING ATTITUDES: PERSUASIVE SPEECHES 276

Your Potential Persuasive Impact 276   Types of Persuasive Speaking 279
Propositions 281   Influencing Attitudes 285   Persuasive Organizational
Patterns 288   Persuasion and Ethics 294   Summary 295   Notes 296

fourteen

SPEAKING TO CONVINCE: REASONING LOGICALLY 297

Definition 297   Principles of Reasoning 298   Kinds of Reasoning 301
Summary 309   Speaking to Persuade Using Logical Arguments 309
Note 312   Resources 312

fifteen

SPEAKING FOR SPECIAL OCCASIONS: SOME DIFFERENT SITUATIONS   314

Introductory Speeches   316   Presentations   318   Acceptances   319
Tributes, Farewells, and Eulogies   321   The Speech of Entertainment   323
Summary   326   Notes   327

appendices

SAMPLE SPEECHES

A: INFORMATIVE SPEECHES   331

Vitamins—Take Them or Leave Them   331   Caffeine   334   Notes   336

B: PROPOSITION OF VALUE: PERSUASIVE SPEECHES   337

Violent Cartoons   337   Sexual Harassment: The Boss's Filthy Little Perogative
Is Finally Being Exposed   339   Notes   341

C: PROPOSITION OF POLICY: PERSUASIVE SPEECHES   342

Just Don't Sit There—Exercise   342   Off-Campus Housing   345
Notes   348

D: SPECIAL OCCASION SPEECHES   349

Commencement Speech   349   Note   351

GLOSSARY   353

NAME INDEX   359

SUBJECT INDEX   363

PREFACE

At all points in the development of this book, I was careful to keep the student in mind. I wanted a readable book full of practical and, where possible, research-based suggestions and ideas. To be useful, a book must be enjoyable to read, but it also must be of help.

The writer of this book is not only a writer, he is also a teacher. This book is designed to be an extension of that teaching function. But in addition to writing and teaching, the author is also a lecturer. In the past eight years alone, he has talked to more than 25,000 students. This has served as a unique opportunity to practice most of the ideas and suggestions put forth in this book in realistic, student-related situations. This lecturing perspective adds a practical dimension.

The teacher using this book will find an instructor's manual of tested ideas and suggestions to accompany it. This manual includes activities, exam questions, and additional bibliographical sources for each chapter—all in a form convenient for duplication and immediate distribution.

Writing this book continually reminded me of the first course in public communication I took. It was a required course in the pre-medical program at the University of Michigan. It was that one course, and that one instructor (Dr. Roger Sherman), that initiated a change in directions for me. That one public-communication course resulted in a change in career orientation. This is just one example of how meaningful and significant such a course can be. For this author, it was perhaps *the* most meaningful and significant course in my entire educational program!

Public communication courses touch all of us because communication is such an integral part of our society and of our lives. To understand public communication is not just to be an effective speaker, it is, indeed, to increase our effectiveness as a consumer of communication as well. It is knowledge essential to living—a basic survival skill. Thus, when I get excited in the book about communication—even trying to emphasize and underscore particular ideas—you will understand the basic philosophy from which I operate.

I hope you enjoy reading the book and using some of the suggestions I have made as much as I enjoyed writing it and offering the suggestions. My feeling is that we can all improve, grow, change, and develop. None of us is "there" (wherever "there" is!) yet. So what I have tried to do is to suggest that the time is now and the best teacher is yourself. That is why I have included so many "Try This" exercises throughout the book—as self guides. I hope you will use this book as a guide to help you improve or, perhaps, to move in a new direction. I think

that if you take it seriously, it can be one of the most interesting and exciting
excursions of your educational career. It was for me. Please read it, and have fun
with it.

Dick Weaver

ACKNOWLEDGMENTS

Increasingly I have come to appreciate the value of writing acknowledgments. It is the very least I can do to express feelings that should be expressed in so many other ways but often are not. It makes one realize one's indebtedness, or, to put it differently, how much one's ideas, and even life, is intimately bound to the ideas and lives of others.

My first acknowledgment is to my reviewers. As I write this, I know not who you are; but I know very clearly the contributions each of you has made. I have become involved with your perceptions and responses—even wrestled with your ideas and suggestions. In working through the manuscript each time, I confess that I have not always uttered flattering comments on your observations; but I have tried—sometimes desperately—to be fair and thorough in my decisions to change or not to change accordingly. A special thanks, then, is due Nancy Arnett (Brevard Community College), Richard Katula (University of Rhode Island), Wil Linkugel (University of Kansas), Stephen Lucas (University of Wisconsin), Richard Rea (University of Arkansas), and Bruce Wagener (Indiana University). Your time and effort are greatly appreciated. Where the manuscript was strengthened because of your observations, thank you. Where there are yet weaknesses, I take full credit, and only ask that you write to me with your further comments and suggestions.

Writing is part of my teaching. As a teacher and writer, I am always growing—changing. But I need feedback. That is how I can become better at what I do. And you—the reader—can be of help, if you'll write. When you find confusion, or when you have suggestions, I ask that you write to me. This kind of author-reader dialogue is no less important than any in-class teacher-student dialogue. If you have never before written to an author of one of your books, here is a formal invitation.

My colleagues at Bowling Green continue to be supportive and understanding. Allen White, the Director of the School of Speech Communication, Donald Enholm, former Chair of the Interpersonal and Public Communication Program Area, and James R. Wilcox, current Chair, Raymond K. Tucker, the late Delmer Hilyard, John T. Rickey, Nelson Ober, and to my newer colleagues, too, Dorothy Williamson-Ige, William and Pamela Benoit, and Timothy Stephens, I want you to know that I appreciate having you as colleagues. It is a pleasure working with you. It is just such an environment that helps fire the imagination.

The graduate students with whom I have had contact at Bowling Green have also been a source of help and inspiration. Too numerous to mention all of them, I select those with whom I have had closer contact because of their association with the basic-communication course as representative. Thanks, then, go to Jim Clymer, Leslie Young, Paul Fritz, Glenda Hodges, Cynthia Berryman-Fink, Rick Armstrong, Jan Patterson, Patti Sabath, as well as Melanie Mumper and Robert Duran.

To my more than 25,000 students in the basic course—who shall remain nameless—I want you all to know that you, too, make my work worthwhile. Without your stimulation and commentary, my job would not be as fulfilling, fruitful, or complete. You have served as a testing ground and sounding board for many of the ideas found herein.

To the members of my classes in public speaking, who have no idea the extent of the influence they provided, a sincere debt of appreciation is due. These students offered the original motive for this work. We were searching for a textbook that would be workable for us.

In addition, the final work on this manuscript was completed while I served as a Visiting Professor at the University of Hawaii-Manoa. For their helpful advice, assistance, and understanding, a very special mahalo to Donald W. Klopf, Chairperson of the Department of Speech, and in alphabetical order, Ethel S. Aotani, Ronald E. Cambra, John B. Davis, Lauren E. Ekroft, David D. Hudson, Michael R. Neer, Kazuo Nishiyama, Wayne H. Oxford, Clay Warren, and Bernadine T. Yim.

For their reading of and recommendations on Chapter 6, "Locating Sources: Library Usage," I want to thank Melville Spence and Tim Jewell. Their suggestions helped assure me that the information in that chapter was accurate and current.

For her excellent job in typing the rough draft of this manuscript, a big thank you to Judy Harris. For their love and inspiration, thanks too, to Jim and Pat Angel, Wayne and Carol Canary, Howard and Bonnie Richardson, Jim and Judy Harris, Bud and Jacque Morris, Kelii and Estie Gross, Wayne and Marilyn Meeds, Mike and Anita Siler and Robert and Barbara Cool. One could not ask for a finer group of friends.

For helping duplicate the materials, I am indebted to Gloria Gregor and Mary Lou Willmarth. Dedicated, warm, and supportive does not do justice to their full, continuing contributions to my writing efforts. It is a pleasure knowing and working with you.

But most of all to my family, I express my very humble and sincere debt of gratitude. I think they understand now the passion that drives me. But I am not certain they appreciate some of the sacrifices that follow from this commitment. For Andrea, my wife, whose responses often grace these pages in either subtle or blatant fashion: she *is* my inspiration. And for Scott, Jacquie, Anthony, and Joanna, you have my thanks for putting up with a daddy who "is writing."

Dick Weaver

one

GETTING STARTED

Your First Speech

Before you have a chance to read and absorb what is written in all of the following chapters, you are likely to be asked to present a public speech. The ideal situation would be to make reading of this book a prerequisite to getting into a basic public speaking course, but since that is unlikely to happen, this chapter will highlight a few of the most important fundamentals for getting started. It will allow you to get your feet on the ground. Then you can read these fundamentals in more detail and depth and at a more leisurely pace.

TRY THIS 1

You haven't even had time to get into this chapter and already you are being asked to stop and try something. Can you believe it?

Rank your fear of each of the following items by placing a number before each item, using the number 1 to represent that which you fear the most, and so on through number 10.

_____ Death	_____ Speaking before a group
_____ Insects and bugs	_____ Sickness
_____ Deep water	_____ Heights
_____ Flying	_____ Loneliness
_____ Dogs	_____ Financial problems

After you have ranked each of these fears for yourself, you may want to check on p. 22 of this book to see how 3,000 U.S. inhabitants responded to these items in 1973 when asked: "What are you the most afraid of?"

Knowing a few fundamentals will help you approach your first speech calmly and rationally. Some people experience apprehension at the thought of having to give a speech. This is a normal response. Confidence comes from knowing what we are doing and preparing well. If certain procedures are called for, confidence comes from knowing that we have followed them to the best of our ability. That is all that can be expected of us—to do our best. Success is within our reach, and we can all achieve it.

This chapter is designed to get you started. Because the ideas in it will be discussed in depth later, it provides only a skeleton, a brief outline of what will follow. No matter when you are asked to give a speech, no matter where, no matter on what topic, and no matter why, you will face essentially the same problems. Whether you are to give a speech before your church congregation a month from now or before your classmates tomorrow, whether you speak in a lecture hall that seats three hundred or in a classroom that seats thirty, whether you talk on "Problems Youth Face" or "Causes of the American Revolution," and whether you try to convince an audience that youth should be taken seriously or try to enlighten them on the forces that provoked the Revolution, you will be faced with similar problems, and these problems can be resolved. There are ways of approaching a speech that will help, whatever the situation.

Although each speech situation is different from any other, all contain similar elements—or variables—that allow us to generalize from one situation to another. Many variables are involved. A variable is something that is subject to

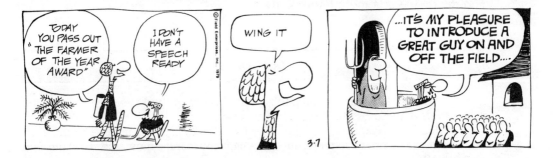

THE WIZARD OF ID by Brant Parker and Johnny Hart. By permission of Johnny Hart and Field Enterprises, Inc.

change. To succeed in public speaking we must recognize the important variables and control them.

What are some of the variables? The main headings of this chapter identify the *major* variables; within each of these are many other variables. But do not think of these as minor variables—many of them, by themselves, can determine the success or failure of your public communication effort. For example, *presenting the message* may be considered a major variable, and it certainly is an important element; however, any of the variables within this category, such as rate, volume, or eye contact, could significantly affect the outcome of your speech. Rate, volume, and eye contact cannot be labeled minor variables by any means.

The actual number of variables involved in any communication situation is infinite. Communication concerns what goes on in people's minds. Each person thinks differently from others and thinks about different things. This alone makes variables in public communication quickly shifting, flexible, sometimes elusive, and directly relevant only to the specific, exact situation.

The major procedures that will help you get started in public speaking are (1) analyzing the audience, (2) finding appropriate material and locating sources, (3) organizing the material, (4) choosing the language, (5) learning to use nonverbal communication, and (6) presenting the message. These are precisely the concepts treated in Chapters 4 through 10. If you find that you need more details or a fuller explanation of any of these areas *now*, refer ahead to the appropriate chapter. It is better to spend a little more time now, if needed, to acquire a firm base than to waste important practice time because of a lack of understanding.

ANALYZING THE AUDIENCE

After the speaker, the audience is the most important variable in any public speaking situation. You do not give the same kind of speech to different audiences. If the audience changes, you automatically change the speech. The speech will change whether you control it or not, since different audiences will perceive the same message differently. Seldom, if ever, will you get the same response to the same speech. The more a speaker can *control the difference* between a message given to one audience and the message given to another audience, the more likely the message the audience receives and interprets will be similar to the one the speaker wants them to receive and interpret. The key is to control the message.

Public communication is the attempt by a communicator to evoke in receivers (the audience) the meaning that the communicator intends. The communicator can achieve this by adapting the message to the audience's needs and desires. A message that is not closely tied to their specific interests (however these are defined) is likely to be lost because of lack of interest or misunderstanding. Messages can be interpreted by audience members only if they are listening.

This fact, then, dictates the speaker's first job as the initial public speaking assignment is approached. What are the needs and desires of your audience? To answer, you must ask several other general questions:

1. How old are the audience members?
2. Are they male or female?
3. What values do they hold?
4. What interests them?
5. Why are they here?
6. What are their expectations for the situation or occasion?
7. What previous knowledge do they have?
8. What do they expect to hear you say?
9. How is the environment likely to affect them?

Ideally we would want to go beyond these general questions and find still more specific answers about what they need or desire, but at this early stage we must make inferences and assumptions. Although at times we may know our audience quite well before making our first speech to them, at other times we will know little about our audience at this point; obviously, as our information about our audience increases, our inferences and assumptions become more factual.

To give a good speech at this early stage you must start inferring right away.

TRY THIS 2

Position yourself where you can see many people coming and going in a relatively short span of time. A bus, train, or air terminal is recommended, since in these locations you will most likely find a wide variety of people.

Using only age, sex, and dress, derive inferences or assumptions about people's values and interests. Strive to determine one person's needs and desires, and when you have analyzed this person move on to another. Then answer the following questions:

1. Did you find this easy or difficult?
2. How accurate do you think you were?
3. Did you find any common needs or desires that people generally or people of specific age groups seemed to have?
4. How does this exercise relate to audience analysis for an early speech assignment?

This is not intended to be busy work. Audience analysis must sometimes be based on just such inferences and assumptions. We derive values and interests—inaccurate as they may be—from such nonverbal cues as age, sex, and dress. As we get to know others better or perhaps the closer to our own age they are, the more accurately we can predict their values and interests. Beginning to think about such things is one way to initiate the process of audience analysis.

Assess the demographics of your potential audience. Demographics, the vital pieces of information about an audience, would include such data as average age, income, and education. You might even write down in your notebook the assumptions you make on the basis of such data. Be as specific as possible. You are trying to determine how best to approach them, persuade them, and interact with them.

At the risk of being stereotypical about age, but not purposely prejudicial, allow me to suggest several topics that may be related to age, simply to raise awareness. If your listeners are generally young (eighteen to thirty-five), you can assume that their interests include education, money, success, adventure, and recreation. If your audience is generally middle-aged (twenty-five to fifty), you can assume interest in job security, raising children properly, holding a family together, and establishing meaningful friendships. If listeners are older (fifty to seventy), they may be interested in Social Security, treatment of the elderly, coping with leisure time, and travel. These suggested topics are purposely general. The point is that needs and interests are often related to age. But topics can best be determined by looking at specific audiences and situations. Certainly, interests overlap; for example, travel and recreation would appeal to all age groups but an approach appropriate for senior citizens might have little appeal for high school seniors.

Audience analysis helps us discover audience interests. But as we do so, we accomplish several other things.

We narrow our range of topics.   Although we may find thermal dynamics fascinating, our audience might not share our interest. Although we might welcome the challenge of making a remote topic interesting, in the public communication classroom it is better to keep the challenge within our capabilities—at least for our early speeches. Why make our early efforts more difficult than they need be?

We streamline our research and investigation efforts.   By knowing our audience's interests we can select appropriate facts, examples, opinions, and illustrations as we develop our topic. In putting together a speech on fraternity activities, for example, you would want to cite activities of fraternities that have chapters

FUNKY WINKERBEAN by Tom Batiuk. © 1978 Field Enterprises, Inc. Courtesy of Field Newspaper Syndicate.

on your campus. Why do unnecessary research? Knowing one's audience interests helps to channel our energies.

   We increase the probability of success.   If we have an opportunity to analyze our audience in advance to determine their interests, we would be silly to deny or disregard our results. Even a cursory or superficial analysis is some help. The more we know about our audience, the more we are forced to think deeply and comprehensively and the better we are able to answer the question, "What are the *best* methods or resources available to gain success?" Those resources may come from the library, other people, or ourselves.

FINDING APPROPRIATE MATERIAL

Most of us are not experts. We could, very likely, say something on any topic but would soon run out of anything to say. Our base of information is limited; we must go well beyond the information we already possess.

   True, not all speeches are "research" speeches. Some speakers may simply wish to tell a story—a narrative speech. Some may wish to present a process—that is, tell how something is made or manufactured. Some may give descriptive speeches, drawing a mental picture for the audience, characterizing an activity, or making a report. Some may give speeches of definition, using precision and detail to explain or interpret a sharp demarcation or to specify something precisely. In such speeches research and personal information are both valid, depending upon the speaker's analysis of the situation.

   But what is our goal? In searching out information—whether research-oriented or personal—we are looking for material that will hold the attention of the audience while we achieve our purpose. Thus, *appropriate* information is that which is appropriate to (1) ourselves, (2) our situation, (3) our audience, and (4) our message.

   One should try to determine the knowledge level of the audience. What the audience knows or does not know about the topic—as indicated by your analysis—will determine what material should be included or omitted. Also, their knowledge level will determine the kind of support you will require and the organizational strategy you should use.

Appropriateness To Self

The more information you already have on a topic, the less you must seek from other sources. Try to find a topic about which you are already knowledgeable or that you have a genuine interest in pursuing. You are not always granted unrestricted latitude in choosing topics for speeches. In many life situations—business is a good example—topics are dictated by the total setting. Consider your personal resources. Think about your own interests, beliefs, feelings, and desires. Ask yourself these questions:

- On what topics do you already have some information?
- In what areas are you interested?
- What things concern you that also concern others?

As you begin to probe your background and experience base, recall your actual life experiences. Think about what you have seen and done. Your past employment may spark an idea, as may your hobbies, special interests, or skills. Think about books and articles you have read, other courses you are taking, or beliefs you have formed. Have you engaged in any group discussions, interviews, or plays that provoked an idea? How about a lecture, documentary film, or news report you may have heard?

If you have been in a hospital lately, the experience could easily evolve into several topics:

- Volunteer service
- Hospital bureaucracy
- Reasons for malpractice suits
- Hospital costs: realistic or a rip-off?
- Isolation in a sanitary box
- Care and treatment of invalids
- What it takes to be a nurse or doctor
- Medication: needed or unnecessary?
- Reducing the cost of hospital care
- Story of an operation

Giving a speech that encompassed all of these would be impossible. It would be long, confusing, and superficial. But any one could be developed into a reasonably brief and interesting speech, one likely to relate to one of your audience's interests: the desire for good health or the need for affordable health care.

TRY THIS 3

Take the general subject of *education* and list as many specific topics as you can.

Notice how a broad topic can generate many different areas of interest, each capable of stimulating a speech. Narrowing a topic is important; otherwise, the speech becomes general and superficial. The broader your chosen topic, the less depth you can provide to your audience in the allotted time.

Probes for topics, if they have positive results, will make the whole process of speech development and presentation easier. The motivation for speaking becomes more internal—within you—and less external—from your instructor. You will like what you are doing! For an early speech select a topic that will be fairly easy or convenient to research, if research is required. Find a topic with many sources of information. Library books, newspaper and magazine articles, and resource people will be your primary sources. A topic on which you could get no information would be inappropriate for you.

Appropriateness To Situation

Appropriate also means appropriate to your situation. Admittedly, your classroom is not a street corner in downtown Chicago, but it is a *real* location with *real* people who will *really* listen to you. Some people look at the entire classroom scene as artificial. Such a perception will affect your motivation to speak. It will not only hinder your own psychological set (how you approach the speech) but also affect the audience, since they are likely to detect your attitude.

Why go into a speech situation thinking that it is not real? That you are just filling an assignment? That no one really cares about your speech except the instructor? To believe in the reality of this situation can ignite the spark that creates the raging fire. These people before you can and will listen, react, and do what you ask of them if you are effective—and effectiveness is within your reach!

The public speaking classroom is a unique and positive situation. Students will hear and see a variety of speaking styles, and they will learn about new and interesting topics. They will also have the opportunity to hear speeches critiqued. In this give-and-take atmosphere designed to increase student effectiveness, everyone will find many ideas they can put to immediate use. Students learning from one another is an important function of classroom activity.

One aspect of the classroom situation is unusual: You will probably give several speeches before the same audience. The impression you make in your early efforts is likely to carry over to later efforts. Remember the cliché, "first impressions are lasting." Make an effort to avoid errors of judgment now that might affect later speeches. Do not, for example, choose superficial or trivial topics. Avoid off-color humor. And maintain a good reputation by giving thoughtful, well-planned addresses in a serious, forthright manner.

CONSIDER THIS

The double difficulty in communicating is that while it is impossible to communicate adequately, it is equally impossible *not* to communicate. (Just as refusing to make a decision is a decision.)

SOURCE: From STRICTLY PERSONAL by Sydney J. Harris. © 1979 Field Enterprises, Inc. Courtesy of Field Newspaper Syndicate.

Appropriateness To Audience

Your audience analysis should be a major consideration in your choice of a topic. If you probe your own background and come up with no topic, then begin scanning periodicals, always keeping your audience in mind. You are not speaking just to hear yourself talk. Your audience is your focus, and you want a significant, relevant, and interesting speech. Ask yourself:

- What topics are currently in the news?
- On which topics would I like more information?
- On which topics can I best exhibit my own feelings and convictions?

If you are still without a topic, you can browse through a recent issue of *Reader's Guide to Periodical Literature*. Since it catalogs current articles by subject, when you find a suitable subject, you also have a list of popular, easily accessible magazines with information on your topic. Newspapers, as well as books located through your library's card catalog, may be used to secure further information.

TRY THIS 4

Set aside one page in your notebook for listing possible speech topics. As you discover topics, write them down—do not trust them to your memory. Often an idea that is not written down is lost. You must be receptive to insights as they occur. Remember the saying: "Today comes but once and never waits, so live today as if tomorrow were already here." Plan for your future. Since you will be giving several different speeches, build up a supply of possible topics well in advance. One topic may lead to another; one idea may stimulate another; one area of interest may be subdivided into several speech topics. Begin now by writing ideas that might form the basis of a speech.

If your audience is the same age as you are, they will probably have interests similar to your own. Think about your hobbies, experiences, travel, upbringing, friends, reading, unusual occurrences in your life, brothers and sisters, goals, things considered "bad" or "wrong" in our society, articles you have read, classes you have taken, things you want to do, beliefs, values, needs, hopes, and dreams.

Appropriateness To Message

Perhaps the overall guideline for finding material is to select a topic that your audience will be interested in, and then carefully and precisely narrow it to fit the available time limit. Try not to cover too much in your speech. Be succinct by using just enough information—facts, examples, statistics, opinions, and illustrations—to do the job. This should be ample for an early effort. Your audience will want to know exactly what you are talking about, why you are telling them about it, how you know so much about it, why you care, and what difference it makes.

As you discover material, always considering the audience as you decide what to keep and what to discard, also keep in mind the thesis of your message. The thesis serves as a rallying point for speech material. It is the position you are advancing and will support in your speech. Thus, all your material should directly contribute to that position; anything that does not should be discarded.

Above all, keep in mind the need for clarity and simplicity. Complexity confuses. Since intelligibility must be an overriding goal, remember the K.I.S.S. fomula: Keep It Simple and Straightforward. Narrowing a topic helps keep it

THE WIZARD OF ID by Brant Parker and Johnny Hart. By permission of Johnny Hart and Field Enterprises, Inc.

simple. Because the process of narrowing a topic may be difficult or new, let me offer two specific suggestions:

1. Try to find the part of a topic that most interests you. For example, within the broad topic of college life, you might find your attention drawn to the Greek system. But you may not be interested in all aspects of the Greek system. Rather, your concern may be how sororities are run—or, to narrow the topic still further, the administration of your own sorority.

2. Think about your specific audience. You could call them your *target audience.* This is a specific, relevant, and identifiable group. It may be parents and prospective parents, taxpayers, or those who own or know someone who owns guns for speeches on, respectively, "Parent Effectiveness Training," "Tax Increases," or "Gun Control." If it is your public speaking class, ask yourself, "Would they want to hear a speech on "How Sororities Are Run"?" Would you? Your target audience will include both men and women; you had better include fraternities in the topic. "Administration" of something—anything—sounds dull. How about another context? How about showing how fraternities and sororities are run in the context of a recruitment drive for members? Would your target audience be interested in this topic? Perhaps, but you will have to make it interesting with stories of personal experiences, the experiences of friends, and any other interesting examples.

ORGANIZING THE MATERIAL

Idea structuring is a matter of managing substance. Once we have the material, we must find ways to organize it clearly, accurately, and completely for presentation to an audience. The content is the substance of the speech; how it is organized is the methodology. Methodology is the focus of this section.

There is nothing magic about organizing a speech. Sometimes the organization will evolve naturally from the topic or from your specific purpose. To find a speech purpose early is like discovering that guided tours are available for a region you thought you would have to investigate alone. Like a guide, a speech purpose helps direct the speaker to the most important points of interest. It directs attention to a particular end. Not only will it help you see what is most important, it will also guide you in organizing the material.

To find your specific speech purpose, ask yourself, first, if your general purpose is to inform, persuade, or entertain. Having determined the general purpose, you can then narrow it down and derive the specific purpose from it. The general purpose is usually extended to include the specific purpose. Here is one example:

- To *inform* my audience that daydreams can be both an emotional and intellectual resource
- To *persuade* my audience to increase their capacity to daydream
- To *entertain* my audience with descriptions of the daydreams of famous people

Not only is the general purpose included within the specific purpose, but so is mention of the audience and a *specific* statement of the topic, or thesis.

TRY THIS 5

From the following list of possible speech topics, compose a specific purpose for (1) a speech to inform, (2) a speech to persuade, and (3) a speech to entertain.

adultery	deity	ignorance	pornography
afflictions	despair	imagination	power
athletics	divorce	inferiority	prestige
atrocities	eating	jargon	profit
bargains	education	justice	proficiency
blunders	evil	juveniles	quality
bosses	failure	labor	radio-television
business	falsehoods	language	records
cars	friends	leisure	safety
careers	gas	leniency	Satan
celebrations	government	love	sex
clothing	gratitude	music	speech
comfort	greed	myths	science
communications	habit	nature	teaching
crime	health	obscenity	technology
death	honesty	poetry	transportation
debt	hygiene	population	wealth

Next, elaborate your specific purpose to include a statement of organized content—that is, expand your statement to include the major points or assertions of your speech. Doing this will help to guide your organizational approach when preparing the actual speech. You will have the major points of the outline so that the research, organization, selection of materials, and even the presentation can be aimed at the specific audience, guided by the specific purpose.

If you choose the specific purpose "To increase audience understanding about the demise of our space program," your organizational scheme would probably follow a time (chronological) sequence. If you were speaking on the specific purpose "To inform my audience of what makes people criminals," your information might indicate some major reasons for criminal behavior such as parents, environment, peers, and opportunity. Each of these could become a major topic (topical sequence) for your speech.

Of still greater value would be an elaborated specific purpose. With it you could test the quality and relevance of the materials and, eventually, the success of the speech. The purpose statement would reflect the major points or assertions in the speech. For example, using one of the specific purposes from above, an elaborated specific purpose might read, "To inform the audience, who will be affected by criminal behavior, that the major causes of criminal behavior are parents, environment, peers, and opportunity." This statement in turn will guide your organizational approach. With the major points of the outline included, researching, selecting materials, and even presenting the final product will not only be aimed at the specific audience but also will be guided by the specific purpose.

If you were worried about losing your audience's interest once they realize what you are driving at—for example, donating your body to medical science—you might choose to set up the evidence and arguments first, then toward the end of the speech bring in your conclusion or generalization (inductive sequence).

We organize a speech for several reasons:

1. To help the audience follow it
2. To help us remember it more easily
3. To help us make ideas clear and concise
4. To help us present the information in the least distracting manner (We wish to fight against distraction. Any element that takes audience attention away from our main idea and purpose must be eliminated.)

As you gather your information, look at it in terms of possible organizational approaches. There is no need to make organization a separate process. Also, think of how the information might fit into the three major parts of your speech: introduction, body, and conclusion. You might plan the body first, then plan the conclusion so that it follows directly from the body. After you know what will be in the body of the speech and in the conclusion, you can go back and write or outline a dynamic and interesting introduction.

At this point, plan to cover no more than three major ideas in the body of the speech. Plan to support each idea with no less than three subheads—these will contain your evidence. The basic outline might look like this:

Introduction (written out or outlined)
Body
    I. Main point (full sentence)
       A. Fact (fully described)
       B. Example (enough provided to prompt understanding)

C. Personal experience (described briefly)
II. Main point (full sentence)
    A. Illustration (enough provided to prompt understanding)
    B. Statistic (fully described, with source)
    C. Opinion (fully described, with qualifications of source)
III. Main point (full sentence)
    A. Fact (fully described)
    B. Personal experience (described briefly)
    C. Statistic (fully described, with source)
    D. Opinion (fully described, with qualifications of source)

Conclusion (written out or outlined)

Missing from this skeletal outline are the transitions. A transition is simply a signpost. It tells the listener where you have been, where you are, and where you are going. It may simply indicate that you are moving to the next idea. There is no rule about when a transition must be placed in the outline. The writer must rely on his or her feeling for when something is needed to move the listeners smoothly and easily from one idea or item to another, or from one main point to another. We know from experience that if the transitions are not *written into the outline* they will be forgotten and not used. Transitions are usually needed as you move from the introduction into the body, between the main points, and from the body into the conclusion *as a minimum.* Listeners seem inclined to get lost at these points. Transitions help clear up the confusion. Insert them whenever you think it would help the audience to know where you have been and where you are going. Without these valuable signposts your audience is likely to get lost. With the transitions inserted, the outline given above will now look like this:

Introduction

(Transition, fully written out)

Body
  I. Main point
    A.   (Transitions could also be
    B.   used between these subheads.)
    C.

(Transition, fully written out)

  II. Main point
    A.   (Transitions could also be
    B.   used between these subheads.)
    C.

(Transition, fully written out)

III. Main point
    A.   (Transitions could also be
    B.   used between these subheads.)
    C.
    D.

(Transition, fully written out)

Conclusion

You need not limit yourself to the transitions in the skeletal outline. Whenever and wherever you can help the audience by a quick summary of ideas, a reminder of what you are doing or where you are going, a review of your purpose, it is to your advantage to do so. Seldom, if ever, do speeches suffer from too many transitions.

In organizing our ideas, we often forget that a speech is a one-time event. Readers can always go back and reread a complicated passage. The audience at a speech cannot go back—except in a question-and-answer session—to figure out a confusing idea. When they are confused, their attention span becomes diffused and their interest lags. Even if a question-and-answer session is provided, it may come too late to rescue the listener. It is the speaker's job to prevent confusion. A carefully planned introduction and conclusion can help orient the listener.

The introduction should fulfill the following basic requirements:

1. It must secure the attention of the audience.
2. It must direct the audience to the basic topic to be discussed (unless you are using an inductive organizational pattern with a hostile audience.)
3. It should lead the audience naturally and easily into the speech.

Introductions can serve other functions, and these will be discussed later. The introduction that fulfills these minimum functions will serve your purpose well at this point.

The conclusion should follow directly from the body of the speech. It also has special characteristics that set it apart from the body of the speech:

1. It summarizes the main points of the speech.
2. It reminds the audience of the main thesis or purpose of the speech.
3. It presents the idea or thought that the speaker wants the audience to retain as a final impression regarding the speech.
4. It offers a final plea for action.

Strive to avoid cliché endings such as "I would just like to conclude by saying that ..." or "To end my speech, I just want to point out ..." or "In conclusion, I would just like to say that ..." Instead, use a strong transition: "For these reasons, then, because ..." (and summarize the reasons) or "With this evidence, one can see why it is difficult to deny that ..." Begin and end the conclusion effectively. Remember that your closing ideas are often best remembered by the audience—they are most recent in the minds of your listeners. It is often this final impression that they take away with them. You must make certain it is precisely and exactly the one you intend them to retain.

CHOOSING THE LANGUAGE

Be conversational. Use short sentences and familiar language. This is the best advice that can be given with respect to the language. Often we try to be too formal, or we recite orally the language we have written or found written elsewhere. If we just pretend we are conversing with the audience, our language will be natural and unaffected. The speech must sound like *us* talking—that is the essential criterion.

But a conversational manner cannot be achieved solely through our selection and projection of words. The proper *attitude* toward the communication situation is also necessary. Some speakers, because they perceive the public speaking situation as formal and structured, prepare formal, rigid presentations. It is far more effective to perceive the situation as informal and flexible, as if the speaker were talking to just one person—but extended to the entire audience. This form of communication is sometimes referred to as *extended conversation.*

TRY THIS

In each case below, rephrase the statement to make it sound as if *you* were talking. Change and reword as necessary.

1. I do not believe that book would suit my interests.
2. I am generally not inclined to indulge in such behavior.
3. Although I believe in the philosophy, I hardly find it manageable on a practical level.
4. I believe that I am not up to such activity as far as my physical stamina is concerned.
5. I can not actually say that it was bad, it's just that I did not particularly care for it.

Did each statement become shortened?

Did you use contractions?

Were words changed to make them suitable to your own vocabulary?

Did some examples seem more like *you* talking than others, or were they all a bit foreign to you?

Do you know of anyone who actually talks like this—that is, like these examples?

There is a difference between written language and spoken language. There are also distinct differences between one person's way of saying something and another's way of saying the same thing. The language you use in public communication should be your own. It should be easy, natural, and comfortable. The more the language you plan to use conforms to these three characteristics, the less you will have to worrry about the language of your speech. It will become an automatic outgrowth of the ideas you plan to share and your own personality.

You may have heard a preacher who speaks very effectively extemporaneously—using just notes to give a sermon prepared beforehand. Yet when this same preacher tries to read a piece of prose or poetry, the words are strained, stumbled over, and difficult to understand. Some people can speak fluently in front of an audience but have difficulty reading a speech word for word. Here are several suggestions that can help you with your *language* as you start preparing your speech:

1. Avoid slang, technical jargon, and words that are unfamiliar. If you must use unfamiliar words, rehearse them until you feel comfortable pronouncing them. Be sure to define any words that may be unfamiliar to your audience.

2. Present your ideas from a key-word outline using different language each time you say them. Know your ideas, not the exact words to explain the ideas. It is best to avoid memorizing.

3. Be natural. Be yourself. Don't be formal. The audience wants to see and hear *you* in your speech, and if the language you use is not your own, the real you is unlikely to show through.

4. Avoid using the language that you find in articles and books, except for brief quotations. Such language is intended to be read, not heard. Besides, it's *not* yours!

The real key to being conversational is to have full command of the ideas. Know the ideas you want to share so well that you do not have to worry about them. If they are well organized, they should flow naturally and hang together tightly. Let the actual words you want to use to express those ideas come naturally at the time of delivery. When ideas flow smoothly, you appear relaxed, direct, spontaneous, unrestrained, and thus effective.

The goal in our choice of language, as in other aspects of speech development, should be to select words that enhance our ideas and make certain that what is said in no way detracts from our main intention—getting the audience to grasp our ideas. When we concentrate on the idea, the language will come—especially if we are genuinely and sincerely committed to the idea.

LEARNING TO USE NONVERBAL COMMUNICATION

Sincere commitment to an idea can be conveyed by effective use of your body. Remember that *everything* you do before, during, and after the speech should enhance your message. In your early efforts, you may forget that exhibiting anxiousness, uncertainty, and unwillingness to give the speech while still seated before you get up to deliver the speech, will have a negative effect not only on this effort but on later efforts as well.

Place a checkmark by each characteristic that reflects positive behavior before getting up to give a speech:

_____ Shuffling feet	_____ Putting head on desk	_____ Listening to speaker
_____ Sitting calmly	_____ Looking at ceiling	_____ Perspiring
_____ Maintaining alert posture	_____ Looking uncomfortable	_____ Exhibiting spurious mannerisms
_____ Combing hair	_____ Stacking note cards	_____ Reading text
_____ Twiddling thumbs	_____ Rehearsing speech	_____ Adjusting clothing
_____ Keeping feet on floor	_____ Being organized and orderly	_____ Going to bathroom
_____ Shaking knees	_____ Slouching in chair	_____ Having upset stomach

The point of this list is to call your attention to the things many speakers do, subconsciously or inadvertently, before giving their speech. The more aware we are of our behavior, the more effectively we can control it and make it reflect a positive mental attitude.

Your body should reveal the following characteristics to positively reinforce your message:

Alertness	Command or commitment
Strength (assertiveness)	Directness
Calmness or relaxation (as appropriate)	Genuineness or sincerity

Any use of the body that does not convey these characteristics or that distracts from them will undermine your effectiveness.

In addition, your body should directly reinforce your message. If you are talking about a sad topic such as death or tragedy, your body should reveal that same sadness. You should be sincere in all your reactions, but your message should dictate your mood and approach. Imagine your reaction to a speaker who is relating various ways that snowmobilers have been killed—such as being decapitated by an unseen barbed-wire fence—if he is having trouble explaining the various ways without laughing uproariously. If you talk of hate and you do not reveal hate, your audience will be getting a double message and will find it difficult to know which message—the verbal (language) or nonverbal (body cues) —to believe.

A novice speaker can also reveal his or her lack of expertise, inexperience, or questionable motivation after giving the speech. You may have seen a speaker do one of the following things after a speech:

Shake his or her head in bewilderment (or astonishment—it's over!)

Look to the heavens (ceiling) for a sign

Sigh deeply and appear pleased that it is over

Deliver the last line of the speech while walking (or running) to his or her seat

Drop all the note cards in the wastebasket, thus assuring us "That's it!" or "It's all over, thank heavens!"

The speaker should finish the speech while in front of the class, collect the notes with directness and efficiency, and, making no distracting movement or motion, proceed directly to his or her seat in the spirit dictated by the subject of the speech, the mood established, and the audience response. It is this straightforward and determined image that reinforces and enhances the content.

In talking about using the body, it was not my intention to suggest that all nonverbal cues are body cues. There are also vocal nonverbal cues (how the words are said, not the words themselves). These are called paralinguistic cues (paralanguage). A speaker's attitude may be revealed paralinguistically. For example, you can detect a speaker's sincerity from his or her voice. Those who are really troubled will sound troubled. If they say they are troubled but do not sound as if they are, audience members may doubt their sincerity. Paralanguage includes vocal quality: your vocal range, rhythm, articulation, and resonance. Even lip control may affect your vocal quality. Paralanguage also includes other vocalizations such as laughing or crying, inhaling, exhaling, yelling or whispering, coughing or clearing the throat, sneezing or snoring, and moaning or groaning. There are also vocalized pauses marked by variants of *uh-huh, ah, um,* or *uh.* A speaker's paralanguage should be controlled so that it (1) does not distract from the content and (2) provides reinforcement of the content. Control of paralanguage also contributes to the impression of a conversational approach.

PRESENTING THE MESSAGE

The same advice given for your use of language is relevant here: Be conversational. How do you act when you are talking with another person? What are the characteristics of an effective conversational style? They can be listed very simply as: (1) eye-to-eye contact, (2) a relaxed and informal approach, and (3) natural gestures.

TRY THIS 8

Recall a recent lengthy conversation you have had with a close friend. Answer the following questions about that conversation:

1. Did you look your friend in the eye?
2. Did you have trouble finding words for your ideas?

3. Did you talk about things you knew about?
4. Did you worry about the impression you were making?
5. Were you conscious of your friend's reactions?
6. Were you nervous?
7. Was your language informal?
8. Did you use any technical language or jargon?
9. Did you use some clichés? worn-out phrases? "hip" or "jive" talk?
10. Did your conversation have any effect on your friend? How do you know this?

Begin thinking about the way you talk to other people. When you start thinking about the impression you are making and the results you achieve, you can begin to focus on the ways you can control the impression you make and gain the results you want. As you realize that the methods can be changed to suit the person, the message, or the situation, you will become aware of alternative strategies and approaches. Since no two situations are identical, having a range of alternatives enables you to be flexible and adaptable.

Presentness describes the attributes of a natural conversational style. Presentness is your ability to be yourself in a speech situation—to be genuinely, sincerely, and uniquely *you.* When you demonstrate presentness, you allow your real self to show through. Your audience comes to know you better because they see you and hear you before them. "Presentness" also refers to your mental set as you conceptualize the "being" of the speaker-audience relationship. There is something more—something almost intangible—that goes beyond the visible, mechanical behavior that occurs in a speech situation. It is a feeling; it is a unique union of speaker and audience; it is an unprecedented combination of variables. The very *opposite* of presentness is:

—Offering façades
—Reading others' words

SHOE by Jeff MacNelly. Reprinted by permission of Tribune Company Syndicate, Inc.

—Fulfilling an assignment just to get it over with
—Neglecting what you are doing or saying
—Revealing fake emotions, attitudes, or feelings

Effective delivery aids in conveying ideas. Once speakers have analyzed their audience, selected an appropriate topic, committed themselves to that topic, framed a specific purpose, found ideas and materials they want to share, organized that information into an effective format, and summoned up the energy, enthusiasm, and desire to share those ideas with others, the delivery follows naturally. Otherwise, it is a sham; it is decoration, a show, a vacant exercise!

The desire to convey ideas to others will provide the motivation to do a good job. Some rules, hints and suggestions to help you do this are:

1. Make minimal use of a lectern.
2. Try to limit your use of notes.
3. Move, but not excessively, in front of the class.
4. Consider the possible use of a visual aid.
5. Make meaningful gestures with arms and hands.
6. Practice making effective facial gestures.
7. Maintain direct eye-to-eye contact with class members.
8. Display enthusiasm, energy, and animation—a desire to do a good job.
9. Practice effective reception and use of feedback from the audience as you are talking.

SUMMARY

Not all the ideas that can and will help you be a success have been included in this first chapter. For that we will need the entire book. But these ideas should help you get started and make your first effort a satisfying prelude to your future successes. To make sure you have grasped the essentials, the following questions review the key ideas from each of the major steps in speech preparation covered so far:

1. What are the needs and desires of your audience?
2. How can you both hold the attention of your audience and achieve your purpose?
3. Can you find a topic that will interest your audience and carefully and precisely narrow it to fit the time limit?
4. Can you let your audience know what you are talking about, why you are talking about it, how you came to know about it, why you care about it, and what difference it makes?

5. Can your audience follow your information?
6. Will the audience remember it clearly and concisely?
7. Have you eliminated any distracting elements?
8. Have you incorporated natural transitions to help the audience see how the items of information follow and relate to each other?
9. Does your introduction fulfill the basic characteristics?
10. Does your conclusion fulfill the basic characteristics?
11. Is your language conversational? It is simple and familiar?
12. Are you being yourself? Are you using your own words and letting them come naturally?
13. Do your words in any way distract from the content?
14. Do you and your actions reflect alertness, calmness, strength, commitment, directness, efficiency, and sincerity?
15. Do your body actions reinforce your message?
16. Have you done anything before, during, or after the speech that would reflect negatively on your interest in or motivation for this speech effort?
17. Are you able to be yourself in this speech situation?
18. Have you summoned up the energy, enthusiasm, and desire to share your ideas with your audience?
19. Can you use the other delivery tools to help enhance the effect you want to have on your audience?
20. Have you developed a positive frame of mind toward the whole speech situation?

Speaking is a human experience, and all speaking should be characterized by one overriding, all-important, superpurpose. That is, every speech that is given, for whatever specific purpose, should also include a higher, more encompassing reason for its existence. Commit this superpurpose to memory and use it as a focal, unifying, central thesis for every speech you give. This can provide the spark that lights the fire that releases the burning desire to speak. Remember that—

All speech should serve to maximize human potential: to help others become what they can become.

1. Have you pushed the frontiers of knowledge?
2. Have you challenged what we already know?
3. Have you made us think beyond the superficial? beyond the obvious?

Stand for something; believe in something; commit yourself to something, and you can and will make a difference.

Answer To Try This 1[1]

1. Speaking before a group	6. Sickness
2. Heights	7. Death
3. Insects and bugs	8. Flying
4. Financial problems	9. Loneliness
5. Deep water	10. Dogs

NOTE

[1]David Wallechinsky, Irving Wallace, and Amy Wallace, *The Book of Lists* (New York: Bantam Books, 1978), pp. 469–470. Citing the *Sunday Times* (London), October 7, 1973.

two

UNDERSTANDING THE PROCESS

Concepts and Elements

In the first chapter I offered a brief look at the variables or components of a speech effort—just enough to get you started. Now we begin a closer scrutiny. In this chapter I will present the basic concepts and elements of the process. *Concepts* are broad generalizations regarding human communication behavior. *Elements* are basic, essential parts of the communication process. When you have mastered these first two chapters, you will have established a solid foundation from which further inquiry, understanding, and work can proceed.

You have been asked to give a speech in one of your classes on a topic about which you have considerable information. This assignment is not an uncommon one; you are likely to face it again and again—not just in classes, but also in committees, organizations, societies, clubs, businesses, churches, and schools. Success in such efforts can lead to better grades, positions of leadership, promotions, visibility, increased income, influence, and a happier, more rewarding life.

Although the topic, the audience, and the situation may differ among speech events, a number of similarities occur. Certain basic concepts and elements are common to most speech communication situations. An understanding of the nature and function of the basic concepts and elements may help you become a more effective communicator.

I want to discuss the concepts first. Before turning to a discussion of elements, it is advisable to have some understanding of the larger framework into which they fit. The broad principles of communication that are offered first have been labeled *axioms*. Understanding these axioms will give us greater control of the communication event.

As the basic concepts and elements are presented, you should realize that to separate them is artificial. They *always* interact. It is the blend of the whole that counts. A parallel can be found in trying to evaluate a piece of music played by an orchestra. We can examine the parts played by the violins, the trumpets, or the percussions, but in the final analysis, we want to know how all the instruments blended together to produce the piece. When we applaud the conductor, it is for his or her ability to create the blend. We applaud him or her as representative of each of the parts. The communicator is like the conductor. He or she strives for a successful integration of concepts and elements, but examining them separately is like examining the parts played by various instruments. We can find out where problems lie, or we can find out how to improve the whole effort, but we can never really evaluate or appreciate the whole by examining only the parts.

AXIOMS OF COMMUNICATION

Axioms—or widely accepted propositions or truths—serve as another way of viewing and understanding the process of communication. These axioms appear to govern communication situations and events. To understand the axioms will give us greater control of the event. If we intend to increase understanding, we would like to know that understanding will be increased. If we want to change a belief, we would like to know that it will be changed. If we seek to get action, we would like some assurance that action will be taken. There are several basic principles or axioms; these operate in most speech communication situations.

We Cannot Not Communicate[1]

All of the speaker's behavior has message value. He or she cannot turn off communication. Whether talking or silent, active or inactive, quiet or loud, a speaker is sending messages. Communication cannot be turned off like tap water. When we accept this fact as reality then we have to view our communication as multifaceted or multidimensional. There are many facets, many dimensions. The communication process is fluid, not static, and all factors help reinforce or qualify the others.

Our Communication Has Both Content and Relationship Aspects

We often see communication as content or information—what we want our audience to understand. But as we stand before an audience, more is occurring as a result of what is being said or conveyed. Whether or not we recognize it, whether or not we can control it, or even whether or not it is perceived similarly among audience members, a relationship dimension is also conveyed. By how we handle ourselves, our message, and our audience, we define a relationship between ourselves and audience members. We say, but not usually in so many words, "This is how I see myself," or "This is how I feel about what I am saying," or "This is how I see you," or "This is how I see you seeing me," or "This is how I feel you feel about my message."

Seldom do we convey all of these attitudes consciously. We may, indeed, not even be fully aware that we are doing so. The more spontaneous, forthright, and sincere the speaker, the more the control of the relationship dimension will fade into the background. Audience members may still perceive it, but they will be less concerned about it when they perceive the speaker in a positive, healthy light.

When control is especially important, speakers will attempt to control the impressions they want the audience to receive: They will practice *impression control.* When speakers attempt to give overt signals about how they see themselves, how they feel about their message, how they see their audience, how they think the audience sees them, and how they think the audience feels about their message, they are engaged in another communication process, called *metacommunication.* They are engaging in overt or subtle communication about the communication. The speakers are, in a sense, providing directives. These may be obvious signals such as saying, "I see my role in this as important because . . . " or "What I have to say today comes from the very bottom of my heart." Or the signals may be less blatant, such as the speaker's simply revealing sincerity or emotion.

CONSIDER THIS

We are in constant communication with each other, yet we are almost completely unable to communicate *about* communication. (And until we can, most verbal disputes cannot be resolved on the communicative level.)

SOURCE: From STRICTLY PERSONAL by Sydney J. Harris. © 1979 Field Enterprises, Inc. Courtesy of Field Newspaper Syndicate.

Every communication has both dimensions. The relationship dimension helps clarify the content dimension. Because it serves to tell the audience how better to interpret or understand the content, it is metacommunication.

There Are Two Modes to Every Communication

Most communication has both a verbal and nonverbal mode. Some things, such as information or content, are best expressed verbally; others such as relationship, are best expressed nonverbally. If I have facts, statistics, and other evidence to share, I use the verbal mode. If I have feelings and emotions that I want to reveal, I use the nonverbal mode. However, neither mode is limited exclusively to a particular type of communication. There is carry-over between the two.

The most effective communication exists when our verbal and nonverbal communications agree, but sometimes our posture, gestures, facial expression, voice inflection, or rhythm contradicts our verbal message. This causes incongruency, or a mixed message. But because it is generally easier for a person to lie verbally rather than nonverbally, an audience is likely to place its faith in nonverbal cues. When judging the sincerity or insincerity of human attitudes, the audience will tend to ignore a speaker's words, relying instead on nonverbal signals to reveal underlying attitudes. It should be clear at this point that the content aspects of a communication are revealed verbally, whereas the relationship aspects are generally revealed nonverbally.

The Relationship Between the Speaker and the Audience Will Be Based on Equality or Difference

Think about giving a speech before your classmates. Essentially, you are one of their equals, thus the relationship between you and them may be considered *symmetrical,* or equal. When a relationship is considered symmetrical, the speaker and audience mirror each other's behavior. One is not considered better or stronger than the other—only equal.

Imagine speaking before a group of faculty or a group of high-school students. In both cases, there is a difference between you and your audience. The faculty are likely to be older and more experienced than you, high-school students, younger and less experienced. When there are differences between the speaker and audience, the relationship is considered to be *complementary.* It is much easier to determine complementarity when an audience is homogeneous.

A relationship that begins as symmetrical does not always remain that way. In some cases, the speaker would want to build credibility and expertise that distinguishes him or her from the audience. A speaker may want to be seen as a person with a special viewpoint, a higher level of knowledge, more evidence, better background, or some other unique contribution or distinction. On the other hand, some speakers may well want the opposite to occur. They might want to establish likenesses or similarities between themselves and their audience. The purpose is to move from a complementary relationship toward a more symmetrical one—even though we may not succeed in reaching total equality. These relationships may be viewed as poles that appear on a continuum—a continuum that results from the use of such words as *differences* versus *similarities* (see Figure 2–1).

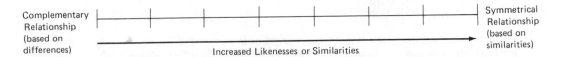

Complementary Relationship (based on differences) — Increased Likenesses or Similarities — Symmetrical Relationship (based on similarities)

Figure 2–1

The relationship between speaker and audience is likely to shift as an experience or event develops. The audience's perception is likely to, and does, change as a result of a speech. The situation is never static. This works to the speaker's advantage if he or she wants to effect a complementary change, as noted above. It can also work to his or her advantage if he or she wants to establish a symmetrical relationship. For example, a politician may develop a relationship of farmer talking to farmer. Even though the politician may develop this relatonship, the audience may continue to see this farmer as a shifty politician.

There is nothing inherently good or bad, strong or weak, in complementary relationships. But it is important that the speaker understand that they exist. To know how extreme audience impressions are, or how intense, also helps— especially if the speaker plans to shift these impressions. How much background information is needed or how much evidence should be shared bears directly on how much time a speaker must devote to this aspect. For some speakers this axiom may be very important; for others it may be irrelevant. How it affects your efforts will depend on your goals.

ELEMENTS OF COMMUNICATION

Six basic elements of communication are: (1) speaker, (2) message, (3) audience, (4) situation, (5) noise, and (6) feedback. How important any element is will be determined by the particular communication situation. As we discuss each element remember that our purpose is *not* to perfect it for its own sake. Rather, our goal is the all-important product or outcome. We want to make certain that our audience understands our message. When the audience accurately understands what we have said, we have acheived what we call *fidelity.* The proper blend of the above elements assures fidelity. The higher the fidelity, the greater the accuracy between the message sent and the message received. Accurate understanding is a prerequisite for any other kind of effect we may want to achieve. If our audience does not understand, it is unlikely that anything other than confusion will follow.

Speaker

As speaker, you are the conductor of the communication situation. You are also the originator of the message. Because of the influence you have over many of the other elements in the process, your other roles include coordinator, director, and guide. It is also the unique characteristics that make you who you are that help to make the message a creative extension of you. Many people do not realize their own creative potential.

Our speech is the most practiced creative effort we engage in. To do anything that limits our contribution will limit our creativity. On the other hand, anything that we can do to enhance our effort will help to guarantee that our role as speaker will be effective—that it will not distract. Of course, there is no *sure* guarantee.

What are the things that limit speakers? That is, what may speakers do that would inhibit their effort? They may not be prepared. They may read their material. They may dress or act inappropriately. They may use weak language (or language not their own). They may not offer significant, relevant, or interesting information. They may not offer anything of themselves; for example, what personal insight or viewpoint are they offering? Or, they may stumble over words, use inappropriate nonverbal cues, or speak in a monotone. And these are only a few possibilities.

To help improve on these weaknesses and to solve these problems is what much of this book is all about. It is important to realize the significance of speakers as originators of the message. They must cast ideas in as clear, appropriate, and vivid language as possible in order to facilitate fidelity.

Because it is impossible to know or anticipate all the possible factors that are going to affect a speech effort—even in a classroom—speakers will benefit by doing everything possible to eliminate distraction. Distraction is created when the attention of any member of the audience is diverted from speakers' messages. Effective speakers, then, must strive to eliminate—or come as close as possible to eliminating—*distraction.* Think of the potential for distraction in the six areas above!

Have you ever tried to listen to a speaker and to concentrate on the message when the person came across as unprepared? Have you ever tried to listen to a speaker who was reading to you? "I couldn't listen, she was so boring!" you might say. If you, as an audience member, find yourself looking at the speaker's mismatched colors, a pendant the speaker is wearing, or mud on the speaker's shoes, you are being distracted from the message—even if only momentarily. The speaker's use of jargon, slang, or "gutter" language may distract you; so may information you find irrelevant or simply dull. Or possibly an idea or example the speaker cites causes you to think of something else.

TRY THIS 1

Next time you listen to a speaker, list, if you can, anything about the speaker that called your attention away from his or her message. Each time you find your mind wandering from the message, record the distraction.

After compiling such a list, answer this question: "How would you behave, if you were the speaker, to overcome these distractions?" Be specific.

If you knew in advance that you were going to be distracted while listening to a speaker, what precautions might you take to limit or eliminate such distraction?

To eliminate distraction when you are the speaker, you must carefully plan your entire speech effort, anticipating possible problems. We cannot predict all the problems that might occur, but here are a few examples of what you could experience:

1. Location. You are going to speak somewhere other than where you had planned. The place is not set up as you had envisioned.

2. Situation. It is hotter or colder, or lighter or darker, than you anticipated. (One speaker tried to establish "mood" in an auditorium by turning down the lights—then did not have enough light to read his notes.) Also, unusual events or occurrences may have affected the mood of the audience, for example, a student strike, a suicide, a bad administrative decision, a canceled concert.
3. Audience. There are more or fewer people than anticipated. They are less interested or more interested in your topic than you predicted.
4. Message. It is longer or shorter than planned. It lacks attention-holding material (the audience is bored). It is not responsive to a change in current events.
5. Speaker. You are feeling ill. You are excited. You are tired, unmotivated. You have a sore throat.

There is no way to anticipate all possible problems, but the harder you try, the more likely that you will handle those that arise successfully. Speaking skill grows with experience, thus you view each communication experience in retrospect. After each effort, analyze and evaluate what happened. How did you feel? What did you do? How might you change your attitude or improve your effort? There is no better evaluation than your own. Even the comments of others will make little difference unless you integrate them—that is, incorporate and use them— in your next speech. Although the suggestions may originate with others, they become your own as you choose to use them—as you choose to become more effective because of them.

TRY THIS 2

On the premise that "the unexamined life is not worth living" and thus, the unevaluated speech is not worth giving, please engage in the following self-analysis throughout the remainder of this public communication class.

1. List the comments you receive from both the class and the instructor. (This should be done for every speech you give.)
2. List what you need to do to improve.
3. Devise specific plans for improvement. Tell in detail how you could integrate each of these suggestions or comments listed in the two items above.
4. What improvements or changes have you made since your last speech?

There is perhaps no more practical, on-going, systematic, and valuable critical evaluation advocated in this textbook than this. This may be the most important and significant activity you perform in this class if you take it seriously and do it thoroughly as constructive self-criticism based upon both class and instructor comments.

Message

The next interacting element, and the one over which the speaker has considerable control, is the message. The message is the carrier of freight—idea substance. When we think of the message, however, we should not limit ourselves to the verbal portion—the words—of the communication. The nonverbal—that not represented in the speaker's language—is also important, as is the interaction between the verbal and the nonverbal.

Again, the speaker must fight distraction, and retain control over the communication. A message can easily become distorted and confused. Even the simplest messages can be misunderstood; thus, the more complex the message, the more likely that confusion will occur. Audiences do not hear precisely what we say—whether it be verbal or nonverbal.

One way to prepare for potential distortion as you plan your message is to anticipate it. If you know, for example, that the audience is likely to become confused, you should strive for exceptional clarity and precision. Your goal is accuracy in understanding—*fidelity*.

What can you do in the planning stage to help achieve fidelity? First, ask questions of yourself, your material, and your language. Challenge them. Assume there will be problems and misunderstandings rather than the opposite. Second, incorporate special mechanisms for adding clarity *as you plan the speech.* Write them in your notes. Do not assume you will remember them when you deliver the speech if you have not written them beforehand. Such special mechanisms include transitions, internal summaries, relating ideas to main thesis, and repetition and rephrasing—redundancy.

Finally, to achieve fidelity, try to let your ideas and the way you phrase those ideas be a natural extension of yourself. The more natural the ideas and language, the more likely you are to be clear. Using the ideas and phrasing of others tends to distort what you say because you do not have the same frame of reference as others. Also, an easy and comfortable approach as you plan the message will allow an easy, comfortable adjustment if things do not go as planned.

Adopting a natural approach also helps to counter the idea of a speech's being formal and cold. An informal warmth that allows the speaker's personality to shine through is the preferred approach. It is effective because it is engaging.

The importance of the message cannot be overemphasized. When people think of public communication, they often focus on the delivery or presentational aspects—people *speaking* to other people. This emphasis or orientation tends to place the other elements, including the message, in a secondary position.

Think about "giving a speech." Your first thought is usually *not* the message. The message is almost an incidental element—"Oh, yes, I need something to talk about, don't I?" The suggestion here is that the message is indeed important. Without it, nothing else matters.

To focus on the message and how it relates to the speaker, audience, and situation is to focus on the content. Message elements that relate to the language of the communication include the material, evidence, body of knowledge, or substance of the communication. The message also determines the way the material is organized and the language—or words—of the communication.

To believe that if we control the substance, organization, and words of a communication, we control the message is to deny the importance of two other factors; namely, nonverbal communication, and the way the audience interprets the message. Messages involve what we say in words and what we say without words. Although we cannot—and do not—completely control what we say without words, at least we can exert greater or more conscious control if we realize the existence and importance of our nonverbal messages. Their *potential* impact is tremendous—sometimes greater than the impact of the verbal message.

But how do we control nonverbal message elements? What would we control if we could? The list is almost unlimited and includes anything to which an audience member could or would attend:

1. The manner in which a speaker gets to or from the front of the audience
2. The mood the speaker creates
3. The nonverbal cues the speaker reveal (eye contact, facial expression, gestures, body movement, posture)
4. The way the speaker presents the verbal message (the way the words are stated)
5. The dress—or clothes—of the speaker
6. The attitude of the speaker toward the audience (his or her concern, involvement with, and relationship to them)

CONSIDER THIS

Communication is sometimes thought of as a loop: sender, medium or channel, message, receiver, and—it is generally, though not always, desired—feedback. But most people are more interested in the sending and message aspects of the communication act. Too often, the audience is thought of only as a commodity to be measured by polltakers, those witch doctors of modern America. The generally insipid quality of television programming is one result of this preoccupation with measuring mass audiences.

Communication means picking up the phone, dialing, and listening to what the other person has to say, and not just impressing him with the force of one's own argument. Despite the staggering output of words, spoken and written communication remains a rather rarely practiced art.

SOURCE: "Sharing Ideas," *The Blade* (Toledo, Ohio), October 12, 1978. A newspaper account of syndicated columnist Sydney Harris's speech to the Toledo Town Hall Series audience. Reproduced with permission.

When it is said that an audience listens to a speaker, it is easy to think of them listening *to the words* being spoken. But, when you think of it—picture yourself *listening* to someone—you never listen just to the words. Even when all you can hear is the words (as when listening to a radio commentator), you still listen to the way the words are said. You strive to put the words into a larger context. You also listen with your mind, heart, and imagination.[2]

Listeners do not want to know only what is said. They want to know how the speaker really thinks or really feels, and they make these judgments from any available cues. These cues become part of the message. Thus, listening really involves receiving a total impression. A message, then, is not confined to words, to the way the words are said (vocal communication), or to other nonverbal cues. It is, indeed, the interaction of all these elements.

What makes the message element even more difficult to understand, however, is that although the impression the speaker intends to convey (the message he or she constructs and delivers) is important, still more important is the meaning the audience gains as a result of it.

Meaning is in people. The meaning in the mind of the speaker—the one he or she wants the audience to understand—is not necessarily the meaning the audience constructs from the verbal and nonverbal communication it receives. The verbal and nonverbal elements are simply vehicles the speaker uses to stimulate, evoke, or call forth meaning in the minds of the listeners. And it is the meaning that results in the listeners' minds that concern us. This is what results in understanding. One author on language states it this way, "the meaning of a linguistic form appears to be the total disposition to make use of and react to the form."[3]

There are, then, two kinds of meaning, each is a function of the people involved in the communication. There is *intended* meaning—that which resides in the speaker. And there is *received* meaning—that which is evoked or called forth in the listeners' minds by the speaker's messages. It is the received meaning that results in comprehension (making sense of what the speaker said) and retention (being able to recall what the speaker said after a period of time). See Figure 2–2 for an illustration of the normal filtering and reduction process that occurs from the conception of a message to its receipt by the audience. Notice that in Step 4 the audience received only one of the three elements coming to them but added a unique second feature of their own. This may have been a combination of other elements or entirely fabricated.

When we look at a message, then, as something that crosses between a speaker and an audience, we are *not* examining meaning. We are simply looking at symbols—verbal and nonverbal elements—that are specifically designed (that is the *desire*) to evoke in the audience the same meanings they have for the speaker. A word is a symbol because it represents something else. You can talk about a table, and the word table represents the object. Nonverbal cues are also symbols. Eye contact, for example, can be symbolic of concern or sincerity. Eye contact can represent either the speaker's concern for the audience or sincerity of purpose. It can be symbolic of still other things. Communication is often referred to as symbolic interaction because it involves the give-and-take between people through the use of symbols. All the symbols that can be listed are message parts.

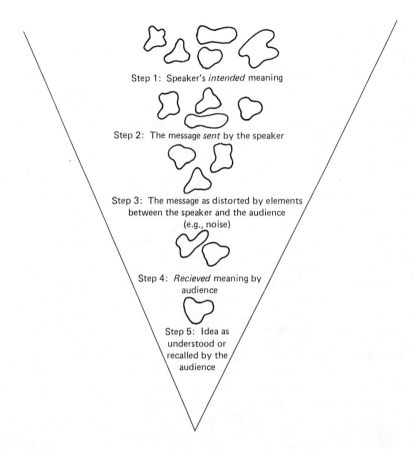

Step 1: Speaker's *intended* meaning

Step 2: The message *sent* by the speaker

Step 3: The message as distorted by elements between the speaker and the audience (e.g., noise)

Step 4: *Recieved* meaning by audience

Step 5: Idea as understood or recalled by the audience

Figure 2–2

TRY THIS 3

When listening to a teacher, minister, lecturer, or other speaker, notice and list the kinds of things—the factors—that become part of the message for you. Every time you attend to some part of the performance, performer, or situation—even to the way he or she parts his or her hair—make a note of it. Record too, if you can, how often this happens.

After having done this, put yourself in the speaker's position. If you were to control all the factors you have listed to reinforce and promote your overall purpose, what would *you* do differently than this speaker? Could you control all the factors to which you attended? Would you want to if you could? What might happen if you tried to control them all?

Did you notice through all this how complex a message can become? How many different messages do you think there were? How many of these do you think the speaker consciously recognized?

Audience

If the message component of the communication process is complex, understanding the audience is even more so. We are dealing with those who receive our message—or, at least, those to whom we are speaking. Whether they are truly recipients is often difficult to determine. It would certainly be helpful to know if audience members really understood a message (that is, heard the meaning the speaker intended) after it was delivered. Often, as speakers, we must do everything in our power to make this happen and then assume, after the speech, that it has. Since we cannot get into the heads of the audience members, we must engage in some guesswork.

The guesswork involved in our relationship with the audience does not occur only after the speech. Actually, we begin making assumptions as we anticipate a speech event. Just as individuals are unique and complex, so are audiences —but more so. No longer do we have a simple combination of individual uniquenesses; we also have the effect of audience members on one another. The sum of the effect is greater than a mere sum of the parts.

We said earlier that no speaker has total control over any speech effort. A speech communication situation is a relationship or interaction between speaker and audience. Because we cannot get into the heads of audience members, we cannot control what they perceive, understand, or retain. Thus, some aspects of the speech situation must be left to chance. As speakers we must try, as it were, to call the appropriate play. As quarterbacks, we must try to make certain that all the players on our team—the elements of the speech communication event over which we have control—are in their appropriate places. With the snap of the ball, we attempt to follow the action prescribed in the play we called —realizing of course that we must adjust our play to the positions of those people we face. If we are skillful, adaptable, and energetic enough—and if we have correctly identified and responded to the positions of those who help determine our success—we may achieve our goal. But as in any game much of our success is determined during the actual confrontation—it depends on how the game is played.

This is not to suggest that speechmaking is a game, any more than life is a game, but there are similarities. For example, the more strategies we can devise in playing some games, the more options we have. Having alternatives means that when something goes wrong, or when something is not working as planned, we can shift to another strategy or approach. Also, as in most games, there is an unknown element. There is no guarantee of success, but it is clear that the more solid the foundation the better the chances that the superstructure will be sound.

When we anticipate a speech event—such as being asked to give a speech in a class (the example we used to open this chapter)—we can find out certain things about our audience that will help us. Mentioned in the last chapter were such features of our audience as:

age	interests	attitudes
sex	knowledge	beliefs
occupations	expectations	needs

The reason these features are obvious—and they may *not* be!—is that classes generally are fairly homogeneous—that is, made up of people with the same or similar features. A class of all freshmen or all sophomores is more homogeneous than a class with a mixture of undergraduates.

The more homogeneous an audience, the easier it is to determine important features and plan an approach that best conforms to or complements (builds off) these features. What is the point to this? The point is that any effective speech is designed with a specific audience in mind—what we referred to as a "target audience" in the last chapter. Just as a teacher would not give the same presentation to a junior-high-school audience as to a high-school audience, a speaker must plan an approach that is carefully geared or adjusted to the specific audience. A business executive speaking on company assets would very likely give one speech to company employees and a quite different one to stockholders. These two audiences have access to different kinds or levels of information and thus would require different approaches.

If the audience will be a class that you are enrolled in, the job of analyzing your audience is easier. If you can be honest and objective, you yourself can answer questions about the audience. Think seriously about the message you intend to give to this class. Would you want to listen to it if another class member were delivering it? Does it appeal to your needs and desires? Would it satisfy, complement, or add to your knowledge base? Would it meet or challenge your expectations? If you answered any of these questions negatively, I would seriously question whether the message you intend to give is appropriate.

CONSIDER THIS

Many deaf people work or come in contact with people who have had little or no previous contact with deafness. Here are excellent suggestions for hearing people from Dr. Leo E. Connor, executive director of the Lexington School for the Deaf, Queens, N.Y.

- It is important to have the deaf person's attention before speaking. He may need a tap on the shoulder, a wave of the hand, or another signal that you wish to communicate.
- Speak slowly and clearly, but don't exaggerate and overemphasize. This distorts lip movements and makes speech reading more difficult.
- Try to show facial and body expression when you speak.
- Not all deaf people can read lips, even the best speech readers miss many words. Therefore, if the deaf person does not reply or seems to be having difficulty in comprehending, rephrase the thought rather than repeating it exactly.
- Look directly at the person while speaking. Even a slight turn of your head can obscure the deaf person's vision. Other distracting factors include beards and mustaches.

- Don't be embarrassed about communicating with paper and pencil. Getting the message across is more important than the medium used.
- Establish eye contact. It helps convey the feeling of direct communication. Don't restrict conversation to business matters. Deaf people have feelings and opinions. Humor, gossip, and small talk help everyone relax.

Many deaf children attend regular schools where teachers and hearing students have to learn communication techniques. This mainstreaming is much easier with deaf students who have learned to speak, rather than relying solely on sign language. The most important advice for those who hear is to remember that deaf people can speak. Deafness is not muteness.

SOURCE: Ann Landers, "How to Communicate With the Deaf." Reprinted by permission of Ann Landers and Field Newspaper Syndicate.

The problem of analyzing an audience found to be highly heterogeneous —consisting of dissimilar people—is more complex. The greater the mix, the greater the challenge for the speaker. As an extreme example, imagine a speaker asked to give a speech on the topic, "Permissiveness in Raising Children" to an afternoon group that includes children, adults, and even some older folks whose children have already grown up and left home. The speaker's task would be less challenging if the group were composed of parents of elementary-school or of preschool-age children. Better focus and depth could be provided.

The problem is that one of the speaker's responsibilities is to try to appeal to all members of the audience. And as an audience becomes more heterogeneous, the speaker's message must attempt to satisfy a broader group of people.

Speech communication assumes some identification between a speaker and an audience. If there is no identification, time is wasted. The audience may question the purpose of getting together and may also express doubts about the expertise or credibility of the speaker. Since we try to avoid such circumstances, as speakers we must try to develop a clear, well-defined, and meaningful relationship. Understanding the importance of the audience is part of this process.

To relate to an audience is not always an easy process. The more an audience can identify with—achieve sameness or unity with—a speaker's ideas, the more they are likely to understand those ideas. Thus, one of the speaker's goals should be to present ideas with which audience members feel some closeness. Examples and illustrations should be those that touch their lives. The stronger the identification, the more likely success will occur (see Figure 2–3).

Often, at the beginning of a speech, audience members may see themselves as having little in common with the speaker (see Figure 2–4). Note that speaker and audience ideas (values, beliefs, attitudes, needs) overlap very little. The speaker, wanting to increase audience understanding, will attempt to develop and illustrate *commonalities*—things with which the audience can immediately identify. Imagine yourself listening to a speaker who is successfully developing such comonalities. You might respond (to yourself, of course) with "Oh, yeah!" or "That's right!" or "I believe that too!" (Figure 2–5).

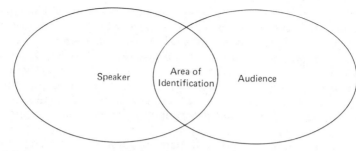

Figure 2–3

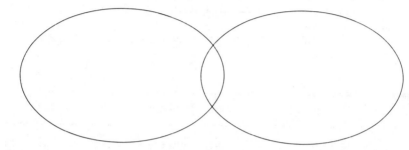

Figure 2–4

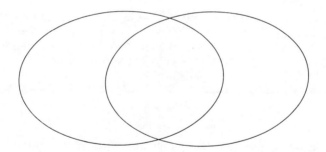

Figure 2–5

Each time you discover similarities between your ideas and those of the speaker, the area of identification grows larger. It is impossible for this overlap to be complete, but we may perceive it as being more complete than it really is. We hear the speaker's theories and philosophy, and perceiving them as similar to our own, assume that many or most of the speaker's other ideas are also similar. This is a halo effect that occurs when we, as listeners, make projections: Because there is agreement in one or two areas, we assume (project) agreement in others. This can also happen on the negative side as we perceive disagreement on one or two issues and assume it on more.

The use of identification is a procedure very close to that used by a successful salesperson. Salespeople are trained to gain positive responses from those with whom they speak. An encyclopedia salesperson might say, "You do believe in the very best education for your children, don't you?" How could a parent possibly say no to that? Then the salesperson works closer and closer to a sale by adding other questions like, "I'm sure you think that any investment you could make that will help your children do better would be worthwhile, don't you?" A parent might respond with, "I do want to help my children do well!"

The suggestion being made here is *not* to become adept at sales techniques, but rather to get on the same wavelength as your audience members—to get them to identify with you and your ideas. This concept, once again, reinforces the importance of the interaction of elements. It is not the speaker, the message, or the audience that determines success, it is the unique coming together of all three that counts.

Speakers have a number of major problems in relation to this element—the audience—of the speech communication event. Some common problems are: failure to consider the audience at all; ignoring specific audience traits or features; unwillingness to adapt to the characteristics discovered; lack of ability to adjust to changes or misjudgments that may occur or have occurred; and the inability to establish identification.

TRY THIS 4

In listening to teachers, lecturers, and other speakers, pay close attention to the way they adapt to their audience. What processes or methods do they use? Were they successful?

The next time you are speaking—even if it is just to one or two others and not to a larger group—notice the way you make your message specifically appropriate to them. What adaptations do you make? How specific are these? Do you do this often? Could you do this better? How might you improve?

Situation

Communication does not occur in a vacuum. For every communication a situation or environment can be specified. A speech occurs somewhere, and *where* can affect what happens. In fact, location can shape the communication more than most people realize. A classroom situation, by its very nature, causes one set of expectations in the audience; a church or synagogue creates quite different expectations. To counter such anticipations is not always easy. If a speaker must deviate from the expected norm, he or she might be well advised to select another more appropriate location.

Another element that affects the speech situation is time: *when* a speech is given. Teachers, for example, sometimes complain about classes at 8:00 A.M. or 4:00 P.M. They find it difficult to maintain student interest at those times. Crossing the mealtime hours can also prove difficult—or at least more challenging.

But timing does not simply refer to time of day; it also refers to the sequence of events. Often, we have no control over this sequence, as when a speech advocating a change in the legal drinking age or legal voting age is scheduled on the same day that the state legislature approves the change. Timing can also work to the speaker's advantage, as when a long-scheduled speech on the need to develop better control over nuclear power plants falls on the day after a plant has experienced a breakdown.

The situation often determines the frame of mind—or mind set—of audience members. On the first warm, bright, spring day, everyone is happy and lively. To attempt to counter this mood with a somber and serious speech makes the speaker's job more difficult. This is not to suggest that it cannot be done—just that it is difficult. It is often better to point out the problem to the audience, so that they recognize you are aware of it, and then proceed with your speech as planned.

Part of the situation, too, is the *channel* through which messages and feedback must pass between speaker and listener, as if in a loop. The channel is often determined by the situation. Sitting at home listening to a speaker on television tells an observer about the twofold channel involved: (1) the television medium, and (2) the distance between the television and the listener. This would be a one-way channel—not a loop. A third aspect of that channel might be identified—the distance between the speaker and the microphone, or how far the message travels before it can be considered part of the medium. Although channels are important, as the differences between radio, television, telephone, public-address system, and air would indicate, they are part of the situation. Most speakers (especially early in their speaking experience) experience channels dictated by the particular classroom environment, and as a part of the communication loop.

Just as analysis and knowledge of the audience is important, so is analysis and knowledge of the situation. Not to know about the situation in advance may create a situation in which a speech is unimportant or irrelevant. Also, it may result in a speech that is not as sharp or focused as it might be. It could result in a speech that makes no sense at all. When the situation and the speaker, or the situation and the message, or the situation and the audience are not synchronized, it can cause audience members to question other factors, such as the overall worth of the ideas, the support or evidence provided, or once again, the credibility—or worthiness—of the speaker.

TRY THIS 5

Below are different speech situations. How might a speaker adapt to each of these to prove his or her awareness of its importance? What might a speaker *say*, for example, that would cause the audience to realize that he or she is aware of the uniqueness or peculiarity of the situation?

1. A speaker speaking on "Elements of Success" just after the college or university football team has won an important game
2. A speaker talking about "The Effects of Television" just after a rating service has announced that a recent show was the most watched show in history

3. A speaker who thought the speech was to be given in a small, comfortable lounge but suddenly found the site had been moved to an auditorium in order to accommodate a larger audience
4. A speaker who knew the speech was to be recorded on audiotape, but on arriving, found three cameras set up to record it via videotape
5. A speaker planning to speak on "How to Get the Most Happiness Out of Life" on the day when a prominent statesman dies suddenly.

Noise

Noise is also present in every communication situation. It can be found in two forms: (1) physical, or external, noise and (2) psychological, or internal, noise. Although the first, caused by elements in the situation, is part of the situation, the second is not. The second occurs in the minds of the people communicating; it may result from distracting elements in the situation, but this is only one of many possible causes.

Physical noise, the most obvious kind, can most often be controlled. If there is noise in the hall outside the classroom, we close the door. If there is noise outside the window, we close the window. If members of the audience are noisy, we either wait for the confusion and noise to subside or ask the members to quiet down. Sometimes speakers become so preoccupied with the speech they plan to give that they pay little attention to obvious physical noise. Since noise has the potential of disrupting and distracting the audience, the speaker should try to reduce its impact—or potential impact—before beginning the speech.

Psychological noise is more elusive. It is difficult both to recognize and to control. It is also difficult to judge its intensity. Psychological noise is *anything* that occurs to the people involved in the communication that is not directly relevant to the message the speaker is sending. It could be said that psychological noise is essentially mental distraction. In a speech situation, it can disturb both the speaker and the receiver. For example, if, as you were speaking, you thought to yourself, "I wonder if they're listening," or "I wonder if I look all right," or "I sure am having trouble using my notes," or "I could use a drink of water right about now," you, as a speaker, would be experiencing psychological noise.

For the speaker, however, the mental noise that distracts listeners' attention is most important. If the noise is excessive, it will be impossible for the audience to receive the symbols you intend them to receive. They are distracted —not listening. Imagine, for a moment, all the things to which you could attend —that you could think about—while listening to someone else speak. The list is very likely infinite. For most students, this experience is real and immediate: They engage in the practice every time a teacher drones on: what they did last night, how they did on a recent exam, what they are planning for tonight, why a certain person does not understand them, and many other preoccupations. Often psychological noise is composed of numerous such distractions, and our minds hop rapidly (every three to eight seconds) from one idea to another and back again. Such a barrage of psychological noise can result in the audience members' hearing little or nothing of what the speaker says.

A speaker can compensate for physical noise—even if it involves changing the location—but compensating for psychological noise is more difficult. The best advice is to make the primary stimulus before them—*your* intended message—as powerful and interesting and all-encompassing as you can. This will not only cause audience members to attend to you, but it is more likely that when their minds wander, they will come back to your message rather than finding another competing stimulus.

How to make a message powerful and interesting should be a continual concern of the speaker. Many workable methods will be discovered as we find support for our speech, as we organize the ideas, as we choose the language, and as we present our ideas to the audience. The point to note here is the importance of discovering and using these techniques. If you do not, the speech can fall flat, and you, as the speaker, may stand back and objectively (in retrospect) *not* discover the cause of the problem. It may well be that the audience's psychological noise was so intense that it drowned out your ideas. It is wise to try to predict this intensity, but it is also wise to understand that it cannot be fully predicted.

TRY THIS 6

Next time you listen to a dull speaker, analyze what happens to your mind as you listen. Write down *all* the things you think about while he or she is talking. The reason for using a dull speaker is that you are unlikely to listen, anyway, and this "TRY THIS" offers an opportunity to use what would otherwise be wasted time in a constructive manner.

Another reason for trying this with a dull speaker is to illustrate how far and fast your mind can wander. The speed and breadth of its dimensions is simply amazing. Dull speakers provide better stimuli for mental meanderings than interesting ones. When you are bored with what you are hearing, it is a common phenomenon to turn your attention to something more stimulating.

Feedback

Have you ever sat in the audience before a speaker or lecturer and wondered why in the world you were there? If you and everyone else left, would the speaker or lecturer even notice? Would he or she go on talking as if nothing were amiss? Some speakers give this impression, most usually because they lack experience or skill. A seasoned speaker or lecturer is not only aware of feedback—the response he or she gets from the audience—but also knows how to adapt the message to acknowledge the response or to compensate for a lack of response.

Feedback is an essential part of any in-person public communication event. Obviously, in radio and television broadcasting, feedback is one of the items missing. To be aware of the response one gets from the audience, involves being sensitive to such cues as eye behavior, posture, drowsiness or alertness, scuffling of feet or changes in body position, movement of the head in agreement or disagreement, and audience members' being easily distracted by physical noise. The speaker must attempt to gauge audience receptivity to the message.

CONSIDER THIS

Drawing a sharp distinction between information (the telling of what has happened or is happening) and communication (why something has happened or is happening), he implied that we talk to, at, down, over, across, past, and against—but communicate only when we talk "with."

"Every major crisis in human history is no less and no more than a breakdown in communication," he said.

Information, Mr. Harris stated, can be transmitted in a monologue, but communication calls for response, for a dialogue. The real communicator must do more than preach and be persuasive.

Communication is more than the sending back and forth of signals, he said. Communication is "a joint activity—exploring, comparing, evaluating, creating ideas, interests, feelings—for the basis of all true communication is shared feeling and interest."

Communication is real, Mr. Harris stated, only when meaning is explicit, when feelings and interests are shared, when there is a person-to-person basis, and when there is adequate feedback. It is mutual exploration of minds which ultimately should lead to the concepts that bind us together more surely than those that divide us.

SOURCE: Boris Nelson, "Talk With Each Other, Harris Says," *The Blade* (Toledo, Ohio), October 6, 1978. A report on a speech syndicated columnist Sydney Harris gave to the Toledo Town Hall Series audience. Reproduced with permission.

To acknowledge feedback is to be aware of the human element in communication: There is somebody out there—not just three walls and a bunch of unoccupied chairs or desks! But to acknowledge feedback is not enough. One must also use feedback to guide future speaking—that is, to adjust the communication that directly follows the feedback. What adjustments can be made?

1. You can add more interesting or lively material to stimulate audience attention.
2. You can add another example to make a point more precise or clear.
3. You can add an internal summary to remind the audience where they have been and to tell them again where they are going.
4. Information or examples can be deleted to shorten the speech and limit the boredom.
5. You can assume the feedback is positive and proceed on track. One need not assume that changes are necessary.

This kind of feedback discussed above is the most obvious kind, but it is not the only kind. Another kind of feedback bears directly on the one mentioned above. We use the past in the present to predict the future. Past experience is feedback, in that we use it—if relevant—to predict the future and to gain the outcome we desire.

If you have ever given speeches before, you will use that experience— what you did then—to help you now. Your purpose is to increase the audience's understanding, to change their beliefs, or to get action. To do this, you draw on the past, in the present, to try to secure or guarantee your goal.

If we can increase our alternatives, enlarge our past experience, and expand our repertoire of possible behaviors, we will have more resources to bring to bear on any situation, thus improving our chances of success. The future becomes more promising. We are always feeding back what we know from the past to more successfully move forward.

TRY THIS 7

Think about that speech you are going to give in class. How many classroom speeches have you ever given? Can you remember them vividly? Can you recall any strengths or weaknesses from those efforts? Make two short lists, one labeled "Strengths" and one labeled "Weaknesses." List as many features as you can recall in each column. Do not limit this to one speech, but think about every speech you have ever given.

If you were asked to do this assignment right now, your lists might look something like this:

Strengths	*Weaknesses*
uses illustrations	speaks too fast
well-organized	tries to include too much infor-
spontaneous	mation
conversational approach	uses jargon (technical terms)
sense of humor	tends to be sarcastic

A MODEL

The six elements—speaker, message, audience, situation, noise, and feedback— make up the basic ingredients of every speech situation.[4] But they are not inde- pendent of each other. Rather, they are all interdependent—interlocked, but not interlocked like links in a chain, with the speaker linked to the message, the message to the audience, and so on. They are each interlocked with all others. We can visualize this by viewing the speech communication event as a transaction (Figure 2–6).

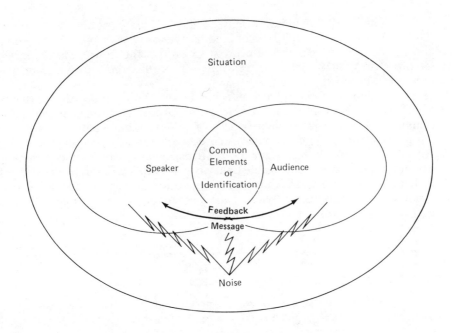

Figure 2–6

Speaker and audience are tied together through a common situation. How much communication occurs depends, in part, on the common elements shared by the speaker and the audience. The speaker sends the essential message and through the same channel receives feedback (an audience message). Noise, the distracting element, affects speaker, audience members, and the message. To visualize communication in this way helps us to see that no part stands by itself, that changes in one element affect other elements, and that a concern for becoming a better or more effective communicator requires improvement or adjustment in several different areas—not just in the speaker or in the message sent.

Another important feature of this model is that when we communicate, we form an impression or image of the audience, and we communicate with that image. The audience, likewise, forms an image of the speaker, and responds to that image. Since we can never know all there is to know of an audience, nor them of the speaker, we guess; the guesses we make congeal (come together) to form an image—an overall impression. The more accurate the image, the more likely we will be able to create or effect identification as speakers. This image formation is important because it emphasizes the psychological nature of communication. We are not dealing with realities, for the most part. Our concept of the audience, as speakers, is really a construct—something that we assemble in our minds. This is one characteristic of the transactional nature of communication. The model presented is a transactional one.

Now I want to take the same model as presented in Figure 2–6 and add a number of components that will help explain the variables presented there. Notice that the model is the same; I have simply provided more explanation, while trying to keep it as clear and simple as possible.

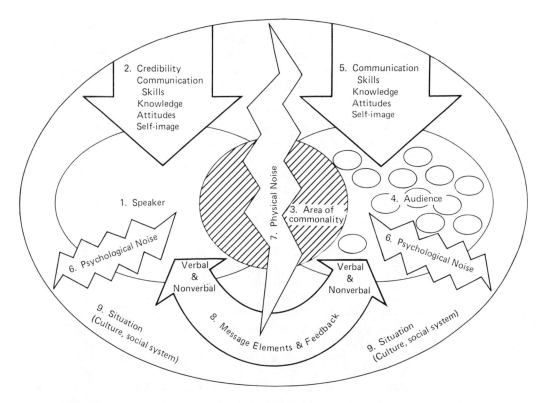

Figure 2-7

I have numbered the various components of the model so that I can briefly identify each and conveniently refer to it.

1. Speaker—the originator of the message. We can assume that means you.
2. Factors that affect the kind of message you develop and present. *Credibility* concerns your status or image with this audience, on this topic, at this time—how believable are you? Your *communication skills* include everything from your ease and experience with audiences to your verbal articulation and vocal inflection. It is a broad category that simply suggests some people are more skillful than others. *Knowledge* refers to all the information you possess—not just the knowledge on this topic alone. *Attitudes* refer to your mental state as well as your feelings and emotions toward life, the audience, public communication, and to the topic itself. *Self-image* refers to both your conception of yourself and your role.
3. Area of shared experience and knowledge through which you establish identification with audience members.
4. Audience—the receivers of your message, and the providers of verbal and nonverbal feedback (8)—primarily nonverbal feedback.

45

5. Factors that affect the way audience members receive the speaker's message. They vary between audience members. The *communication skills* include their backgrounds in public communication—their perceptiveness of speaker effectiveness or ineffectiveness. Also, their *listening skills* would be part of this category. The description and effect of their *knowledge, attitudes,* and *self-images* would be similar to those presented in (2) above. Realize that how much knowledge they have, the attitudes they hold, and the feelings they have about themselves will affect their receptivity to the message.
6. Psychological noise—everything that occurs in the people's minds that is not directly connected with the message. It could be considered internal, mental distraction.
7. Physical noise—external distraction. It usually originates in the situation and has a direct, negative effect on both the message and feedback.
8. Messages and feedback. These flow both ways between speaker and audience, although in a public-speaking situation you expect the primary or essential message to flow from speaker to audience and feedback to flow from audience members to the speaker. Messages and feedback can be verbal and nonverbal.
9. The situation—the whole cultural system in which this communication takes place, the specific social system, and the very particular communication environment (e.g., the classroom). The situation governs the communication that takes place by established *norms*—principles of right action that guide, control, and regulate acceptable behavior.

SUMMARY

To understand the process of speech communication, you must recognize the basic concepts and elements of the process and understand how they interrelate. You also need a way of visualizing the whole process—a framework. The goals of this chapter have been: (1) to introduce concepts, (2) discuss elements, and (3) present a model. Our purpose has been to expand and show relationships among the material offered in Chapter 1.

The four axioms of communication were presented first:

1. We cannot not communicate.
2. Our communication has both content and relationship aspects.
3. There are two modes to every communication.
4. The relationship between the speaker and the audience will be based on equality or difference.

The basic elements of the speech communication process are the speaker, message, audience, situation, noise, and feedback. Although each element is important, it is the interaction of the elements that creates the dynamic, ongoing process that is totally unique each time it occurs.

The framework discussed for looking at the relationship of the elements indicates how closely they are interlocked. Changes in one part cause changes in others. Although speaker and audience are in a physical relationship with each other, it is the mental image each has of the other—part of the meaning derived from the whole event—that is important. What occurs in a speech communication situation is a result of the changes that occur in people's images.

The design of this chapter has been to introduce the student to basic speech communication concepts and elements, as well as some of the basic vocabulary. Many items presented in skeletal form here will be fleshed out in later chapters. To improve in communication, to analyze it, and to talk maturely and reasonably about it, we must be able to dissect the process. Although dissection is largely an artificial and academic procedure, it does help direct growth, development, and progress. We need methods that are controlled, structured, guided, and personal to move in a specific direction with both purpose and energy.

NOTES

[1] These axioms have been adapted from Paul Watzlawick, Janet Helmick Beavin, and Don D. Jackson, *Pragmatics of Human Communication: A Study of Interactional Patterns, Pathologies, and Paradoxes* (New York: W. W. Norton & Co., 1967), pp. 48–71.

[2] Gerard Egan, *Encounter* (Belmont, Calif.: Brooks/Cole, 1970), p. 248.

[3] Roger Brown, *Words and Things* (New York: Free Press, 1958), p. 109. Copyright © 1958 by The Free Press, a Division of Macmillan Publishing Co., Inc.

[4] Development of this model of communication grew out of the work of Dean C. Barnlund. See his "A Transactional Model of Communication," in Kenneth K. Sereno and C. David Mortensen's *Foundations of Communication Theory* (New York: Harper & Row, Pub., 1970), pp. 83–102.

three

LISTENING

Learning, Discovering, and Improving

Of the first six chapters of Thomas Gordon's bestseller, P.E.T. (*Parent Effectiveness Training*),[1] four are devoted to listening. Gordon's point is that we go from infancy to adulthood without learning how to listen effectively, and yet listening is the key to understanding others. Gordon says that when we listen empathically to another person, we not only get to understand him but also, in his words, we come "to appreciate his way of looking at the world—in a sense," he says, the person who does this sucessfully "*becomes that person* during the period of putting himself in his shoes."[2]

In a public communication course we can learn and practice the skills of effective listening. Our purpose could be to become more effective parents, but that goal is a bit removed from our current interests. Instead, we might establish several more important goals for effective listening:

1. To learn more about the art of effective public communication
2. To discover more about a variety of different topics and issues
3. To improve our ability to concentrate, analyze, and evaluate

We will examine these goals in more detail to see the way they can affect our lives and our immediate success or effectiveness in this course. In the discussion of communication thus far, I have focused more on the speaker than on the listener. Discussion of either speaker or listener, however, must not be done in isolation. In focusing on the total act of public communication, one must look at both speaking *and* listening. It would be even better to view the two processes joined as a result of the transaction—that unique interaction that occurs between speaker and audience as each constructs images of the other and responds to those impressions. As we look at listening, remember that neither speaking nor listening can be considered apart from the total transaction.

CONSIDER THIS

"It takes two people to say a thing—a sayer and a sayee," Samuel Butler observed. "The one is just as essential to any true saying as the other."

We are all "sayees," but most of us accord little thought to performance in this vital role in human affairs. We confuse hearing with listening, believing that, because hearing is a natural function, then listening must be effortless.

According to Dr. Harrel Allen, American speech communications expert, it is anything but. "Listening is energy—your heart speeds up, your blood circulates faster, your temperature goes up."

So, listening is a kind of activity. Those who aspire to be good listeners must turn it from an unconscious activity to a conscious one.

SOURCE: From *The Monthly Letter* (January 1979), published by The Royal Bank of Canada.

LEARNING MORE ABOUT COMMUNICATION

We sometimes forget that we can learn about public communication by simply paying attention. In looking at and listening to others we can mold our standards of excellence. Our personal experience very likely will make a longer-lasting impression on us than any words written or spoken by others. To repeat once again an idea mentioned earlier, the best teacher of communication is oneself. We pick and choose those elements of communication that we find effective. We discard those deemed weak, and incorporate and practice those considered strong. This is the primary justification for including a chapter on listening early in this book. Although it might appear obvious that we learn by listening, imagine the impact of this idea on one who did not find it obvious. If he or she did not realize the value of listening until halfway through the course, valuable opportunities would have been lost.

The point is, and it can be as serious as you want to consider it, pay attention. What you have to gain may be your success in public communication! Listening *can* make a difference.

Andre Gide once opened a lecture by noting: "All this has been said before, but since nobody listened, it must be said again."

Nobody listened. How often is this the case, and how often must messages be repeated because they were not heeded in the first place.

In business, family, and other personal relationships, the failure to listen properly is responsible, at the very least, for an enormous waste of time.

Yet, scant attention has been paid in the past to the listening side of communication.

SOURCE: From *The Monthly Letter* (January 1979), published by The Royal Bank of Canada.

TRY THIS 1

At your very next opportunity to hear a public communicator, begin to listen for your own personal benefit. Ask yourself these questions.

1. What was so effective that I would like to be able to do it myself?
2. What was so weak (ineffective) that I would *not* want to do it myself?

In your notebook make a list of strengths and weaknesses. Continue the list throughout this course. You will be amazed at how much room to grow such a list can suggest.

DISCOVERING MORE INFORMATION

The discovery of more information is one product of a course in public communication. Life provides the material of creativity. One would be hard-pressed to make an argument for separating the public communication classroom from life! What you listen to and what you learn becomes part of your vast storehouse of knowledge. Notice that I do not say "storehouse of *useless* knowledge," for how can one, at *any* point in time, determine what knowledge will be valuable or useless. The person who is most creative and most entertaining is the one who can bring the most experience, knowledge, and insight to each situation. To accumulate this background requires that we soak up knowledge—grasping at tidbits, absorbing morsels, and pondering over the particles of knowledge we receive. Since it is obvious we will hear more speeches than we will ever give, do not waste this opportunity to enlarge your own knowledge, to expand your storehouse. Don't close your mind to what your peers have to offer you.

TRY THIS 2

The next time you listen to a person speaking, ask yourself these questions:

1. What is being said that I don't know?
2. How does this information affect me?
3. What could I do about this?
4. What difference does this information make?
5. Why is this information important to me? to others?
6. Why is the speaker involved in this? interested in this? concerned about this?
7. How does this information bear on the present? the past? the future?

Challenge yourself with the information you hear. Never let an opportunity pass to respond, absorb, and discover new and interesting insights. These questions are designed to give you reasons for listening—to make listening an effective, worthwhile, and meaningful experience.

IMPROVING YOUR ABILITY TO LISTEN

You may think listening requires little if any ability. After all, you spend more time during an average day listening than speaking.[3] If we are alert, we are listening. Wrong! Listening is a complex, active process, and to improve our ability requires some commitment on our part—a commitment, incidentally, that few are willing to make.[4] It is a commitment that if perfected now can aid us not only during our college career but throughout our lives.

Alertness is definitely part of the process. If we are not alert to a particular sound, we pay no special attention to it, and although it may be noticed, it has no effect. Listening involves not one but several essential parts.[5] The first part is hearing. Hearing is a physical process and unless one is hard of hearing it is a natural process. What happens once the sound is within the system is more important: Hearing is primarily an external process—done with the ears—whereas listening is primarily internal—done with the mind (see Figure 3–1).

The second part of listening is perception. Perception follows the brain's reception of the stimuli from the ears. At the perception stage, you simple screen the messages being received from the message source to determine those of sufficient importance to stimulate your thinking. Perception is a filtering process.

The next part of listening is attention. We do not attend to every sound we hear. Some sounds, obviously, are more important than others; thus, we select for consideration *some* of the sounds we hear. We may have a special concern for that sound—the idea may appeal to us ("Let's go out for pizza"). The point is that we selectively perceive what we want to attend to. We hear what we want to hear, and we make those judgments based on our thoughts and feelings.

Human beings first perceive either isolated sounds or groups of sounds. These must be placed in some order or context to become recognized as meaningful word symbols. If we cannot understand what we hear, we are unlikely to choose that sound (or combination of sounds) to attend to. What we select, then, is based on a complex background of knowledge and experience unique for every individual. It is at this point that symbols are assigned meaning. Your interpretation and evaluation of a set of sounds will be considerably different from that of another person. A music major, for example, might select different sounds to attend to than a fan of rock music, and a person might find a husky, deep, sexy,

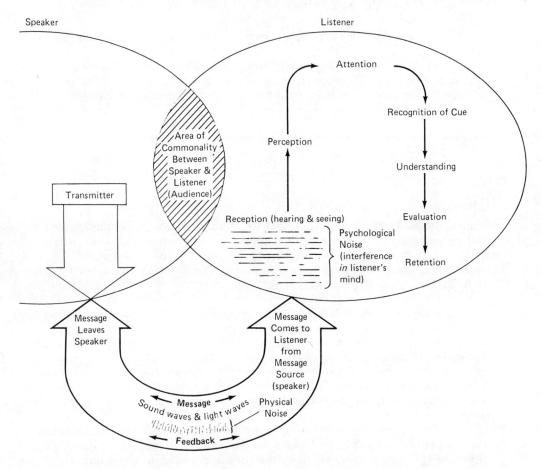

Figure 3–1

male voice of more interest than the voice of a young child. Understanding, then, is the process of attaching meaning to the sound waves that stimulate the sensory receptors of our ears. This meaning attachment occurs at the "recognition of cue" stage in Figure 3–1.

Once you have attached meaning to the sound waves and feel you understand what a message means, then you evaluate it in light of your values, attitudes, and beliefs. Evaluation is sometimes performed prematurely—before all the available information is in. This can lead to invalid evaluations.

Finally, we remember only part of what we listen to. Learning-forgetting curves indicate that 90 percent of the information heard will not be remembered.[6] Usually that which is most important to us is remembered most easily, but this is not always the case. Even if something is important, we may not remember it because:

1. The sounds were transmitted poorly
2. We were not in a position to hear the sounds well
3. We could attach no meaning to the actual sounds we heard (even though we knew by other indicators that they were important)
4. Too much noise interfered with the sounds (both physical and psychological)
5. We were too tired, hurried, harassed, aggravated, or perturbed *to take the time* to make sense of the sounds
6. We were trying to remember too many other things at the same time

Thus, as important as listening is, we often do not listen as well as we should. We have instructors who do not speak clearly; we have seats too close to a door, window, or radiator to hear well; we have problems with jargon and technical terms; we have classmates distracting us just as the instructor is giving an assignment; we have too much on our mind at certain times; we are too sleepy to pay attention; we have just received a grade on a report that is much lower than we expected; we are told too much at one time.

TRY THIS 3

What suggestions would you make to a speaker that would improve your ability to listen, if the speaker gave you the following verbal instructions:

Type it double-spaced with one-inch margins all around and put your name, section number, and date in the upper right-hand corner. Make certain you have a title for the paper; use all the terms we have covered to date, underlining each as it is used and explaining each with a concrete example from your own experience. Be sure to have an introduction and a conclusion, and the body of your paper should include a description, an analysis, and an evaluation. Include at least five sources in your bibliography and put your footnotes at the bottom of the appropriate page. The paper should be at least three pages long, but no more than five pages, and should be submitted no later than the end of this class period one week from today.

Would some of these suggestions be appropriate?

1. Please speak slowly.
2. Could you keep related ideas together?
3. Could you explain what you mean by:
   —*all* the terms we have covered to date,
   —*concrete* examples from our experience,
   —*description, analysis,* and *evaluation,*
   —five *sources,*
   —*bibliography,*
   —*footnotes.*
4. Would you please repeat the assignment so I can be certain I have it down accurately?
5. Could you write it on the blackboard?

WHY DON'T WE LISTEN?

Why we don't listen well, however, often goes far deeper than the reasons just cited. If we need excuses, there are many to choose from, but attitudes and habits are probably basic reasons.[7] Attitudes become barriers to effective listening if we let them. Your attitudes can become a barrier at the perceptual, attention, understanding, or evaluative level. Perhaps that is why their influence can be so pervasive; it can occur at so many points in the listening process. Several examples may illustrate how your attitudes help determine what you decide to listen to. Wouldn't you find it easier to listen to a popular movie star than to an ordinary person off the street? Wouldn't you find it easier to listen to a speech by a person of high reputation and authority than one by an unknown speaker? People's status or visibility will determine our attitude toward them and hence our willingness to listen to them. Do you want your instructor or a classmate to tell you about effective communication? (Maybe that was a bad choice of questions!)

Attitudes affect us in other ways as well. Try listening to someone for whom you have little or no respect, someone you feel is inferior to you or someone unknown to you. Ever wonder why those in high administrative posts often have difficulty listening to advice that comes from below—but not advice from their board of directors? Attitudes can sometimes be a problem when such situations are reversed. We may accept comments, ideas, and suggestions from those for whom we have great respect, from those who are our superiors, or from those about whom we have much knowledge, with little critical judgment on our part. Attitudes, then, can cut off or short-circuit our listening powers.

Habits, like attitudes, also can affect how we listen. Thomas Gordon's concern for the role of listening in parent-child relationships is a concern for breaking habitual listening responses. Because we have never really known what to do, we have done what we felt was best—our only recourse—and in this way a series of undesirable responses have become automatic. Imagine yourself seated in front of an instructor who is droning on and on about something you either already know or care little about. What is your solution? You fake attention and listening while your mind wanders to happier times in the past or in the future. Do you know how to look attentive while your mind wanders? Silly question! Don't we all?

Another habit difficult to break is laziness. Given the opportunity, why exert ourself? Laziness makes public speaking more difficult than it might at first appear. How do we break through listener laziness? If listening requires us to be active when we can just as easily be passive, why be active? It's habitual. We want to be startled, surprised, and amazed. If you can't offer entertainment we'll tune you out. We assume no obligation because the channel selector is in our hands, and we can just as easily switch channels! Kids brought up on *Sesame Street* and *The Electric Company* learn by being entertained. College students often want the same stimulation. Why not? It's exciting and a lot more interesting!

One final hard-to-break habit is fostered by our educational system; it permeates every class where we are examined on content. To pass examinations over content, we must master the facts. This is precisely why some students find application exams—where one must apply the facts—difficult. It is easy to master facts, less easy to apply them. Listening for facts is an essential skill; however, we need to listen with a broader concern in most everyday situations. To fully understand a speaker, we often must know what meaning or shade of meaning is intended, and what attitudes the speaker holds toward the content, the situation, the audience, and himself or herself. We must listen to what is soundlessly said between the words and phrases. To do this we must go beyond the facts.

CONSIDER THIS

In the relatively new discipline called paralinguistics, we are learning how to listen better, not merely to the words, but to the tone, the timbre, the pauses, and the bodily movements that accompany verbal communication. Lacking this skill, speech is a treacherous tutor.

Hans, the famous "counting horse" of the last century, was of course not able to count—but his ability was almost as marvelous. He watched his trainer, and from certain jaw movements imperceptible to witnesses, the horse was able to stop at the correct number.

SOURCE: From STRICTLY PERSONAL by Sydney J. Harris. © 1979 Field Enterprises, Inc. Courtesty of Field Newspaper Syndicate.

Many factors can affect our listening. Not only can we improve our listening ability ourselves, but others can help us too. Listening is often negotiated—that is, when we are having trouble understanding, we seek aid, if the message is important enough to us. If we are carrying on a conversation and trying to watch a TV program at the same time, we may ask someone to turn up the television. If the conversation has become more important, we will disregard the TV program, turn it down, or plan to return to it later. (How much are we likely to miss, anyway?) We may even ask those with whom we are conversing to speak up.

We should, however, take listening seriously and take every opportunity to increase our listening ability.[8] We can become more perceptive and more attentive, and thus we can understand more. We can also increase our skill in describing what we see and hear, analyzing what we see and hear more precisely, and evaluating what we see and hear more accurately. As we improve our ability, we become more responsive to what occurs around us. We are no longer merely passers-by in the process of life; we become immersed in the very process itself. Listening can change the way we are able to respond to all that occurs around us.

TRY THIS 4

Sometimes it is easier to listen if we are listening for specific categories or items. Although some items may not be relevant for every speech, at least we have a specific predetermined means for analyzing or evaluating what we hear. One set that lends itself to most speech occasions is easily remembered because it has been presented in the form of a mnemonic device (the six "S's"). The next time you hear a speech, try applying this series. Listen to determine how well the speaker measures up in each category:

Subject: relevant? significant? interesting?

Sources: what? how many? credible? convincing?

Substance: facts? examples? opinions? personal experience? arguments? strength of ideas? sufficiency?

Structure: introduction? body? conclusion? transitions? flow of ideas?

Style (language): conversational and natural? written or oral?

Symbols: vocal—rate, pitch, loudness, inflection, variety, energy physical—facial cues, gestures, bodily movement, enthusiasm

---

IMPROVING OUR LISTENING SKILLS[9]

Remember how you responded when you drove into a gas station for directions? You wanted very much to get where you were going and you really did not want to stop again. What did you do? You perked up; you prepared yourself to listen; you concentrated. When the message came, you listened intently, deeply. (You may have gotten lost anyway once you left the gas station, but you did listen!)

CONSIDER THIS

Workshops are springing up nationwide to train bartenders and hairdressers as on-the-job counselors to steer troubled patrons away from depression and suicide toward professional help.

There was a time when bartender LeRoy Sunquist preferred not to lend an ear to his customers' woes. And cosmetologist Kathy Spiller used to come home each night with her head ringing with her customers' personal grief. Now they both are willing listeners.

It's partly because of a program that has trained about 115 Southern California hairdressers and about 20 bartenders in counseling skills enabling them to handle crisis situations.

The workshop was launched in 1976 with a $35,000 state Department of Health grant to Crisis House in the San Diego suburb of El Cajon. Participants are now applying their paraprofessional talents in beauty salons and bars throughout California.

Andy Thompson, director of Crisis House's community training program, said that bartenders and beauticians are trained not to give advice or engage in in any form of moralizing.

Instead, they are taught to listen and, when appropriate, refer troubled patrons to agencies dealing with drug and alcohol abuse, mental health counseling, suicide intervention, and family or divorce counseling.

Participants are trained to recognize various suicidal symptoms.

"I had a couple of people who were really on the verge of suicide," the hairdresser said. "But they talked it through and decided there was a lot left to life."

SOURCE: Bob Bast, "Sympathetic Listeners," Associated Press News Service, May 21, 1978.

How you ready yourself for a listening experience is important.[10] It is the first step in developing listening skills.

Prepare yourself to listen. Find a reason for listening. This step is likely to heighten your perceptions and make you more alert and responsive. If for no other reason, listen to increase your basic fund of knowledge. Such listening has been referred to as "enlightened self-interest."[11] There are many other good reasons (see Try This 2) to listen well. If you are not motivated to listen, it is unlikely that you will be able to follow any of the other suggestions.

TRY THIS 5

To determine the difference preparation can make, plan to pay special attention to the conversation you have at dinner tonight. Remember, this one is special—prepare to listen. Then evaluate your effectiveness by answering the following questions:

1. Can you recall the exact conversation? More fully than previous conversations?
2. Did you listen with the same level of concentration as you usually do?
3. What makes you tune in to a conversation in some deeper way? What mental adjustments do you make? What physical adjustments do you make?
4. In what ways did your listening pattern on this occasion differ from the pattern at other dinner conversations?
5. Could you reconstruct rather accurately most of the talk that occurred around the dinner table?

This exercise shows that effective listening requires preparation. It requires effort on your part. It does not happen naturally. It does not take place when you sit back and just let sounds enter your ears. If you do not actually apply yourself to the task, you will not listen effectively.

CONSIDER THIS

It is said that "the mind wanders" while one person hears another talk; actually it darts ahead and off the track like a runaway race horse. This helps to explain why people jump to conclusions. They anticipate what is going to be said instead of following what is being said in the present. In this regard we might do well to remember the admonishment of a rough-and-ready tycoon as he started a meeting; "Now listen slow."

It takes a concerted effort of will to deal with some of the other impediments to listening that clog the mind, the more so since they spring from perfectly normal human feelings.

SOURCE: From *The Monthly Letter* (January 1979), published by The Royal Bank of Canada.

Concentrate on listening. Think about what you are doing. When you concentrate, you are more likely to be more attentive. Concentration is not easy because we think so much faster than we speak; thus, while the speaker is mouthing words, our thoughts move further ahead.[12] We must try to keep our mental energy fixed on what we are doing. We can sometimes do this by asking ourselves questions as the speaker proceeds. We need material to fill the void between his or her speaking rate and our thinking rate:

1. How do the ideas relate?
2. What is the speaker driving at? (What is the speaker's main thesis in this speech?)

3. What is the speaker asking us to believe or to do?
4. In your own words, what is the speaker saying?
5. Do the speaker's ideas make sense? Are they sound?
6. How is this speaker approaching the world?

Try not to be distracted by mannerisms or delivery techniques. Such distractions will lead you away from the speaker's ideas and may cause your mind to wander. The goal of effective listening is better understanding of the speaker's ideas.

CONSIDER THIS

Listening, not imitation, may be the sincerest form of flattery. Most people don't listen. They simple wait out another person's speech or comment, planning just what they are going to say when he stops talking. The result is a series of monologues instead of an exchange of views.

If you want to influence someone, listen to what he says. Don't just sit there alert for the flaws in his argument that you can use against him later. Listen. What is he trying to tell you? What is it that he wants? When he finishes talking, ask him about any points that you do not understand. Then tell him what it is you want and point out the areas where you are in agreement and those where you do not agree. He will be flattered that you have listened intently, that you take him seriously, and that you truly want to understand his position.

SOURCE: Dr. Joyce Brothers, *How to Get Whatever You Want Out of Life* Copyright © 1978 by Joyce Brothers. Reprinted by permission of Simon & Schuster, a Division of Gulf & Western Corporation.

Show alertness and interest. You may wonder how this skill will help you, the listener. It obviously helps the speaker—anyone responds better to an alert and interested audience than to a dull, apathetic one. Concentration, however, is easiest when you are alert and interested. Your mind often assumes a mood consistent with your physical presence. Stand alert and you will feel alert. Walk with your head hung over, back stooped, and dragging your feet and see how you feel. Compare the differences between sitting slumped down at your desk and sitting erect and upright.

One key factor that operates against alertness and interest is impatience. We do not want to wait for a speaker to complete thoughts. We live in a rush, rush, hurry-up world. "Say it, and sit down!" we demand. "Don't waste our time!" We must strive to be patient. It isn't easy, but by being patient, we help assure ourselves that our evaluation of what we hear will be sound and what we choose to retain will be accurate and based on sufficient evidence and information. You will recall that making hasty evaluations was one of the major problems cited at the evaluation stage of the listening process.

Search for the essential message. We have a natural tendency to become distracted. It is natural *not* to enjoy listening to public speeches. Our minds wander at the first opportunity. We must fight this tendency, and the best way to do this is to search for the speaker's essential meaning. Sometimes the message is buried *not* in the words, but in the facial expressions, gestures, or movements. We must search broadly, using hearing *and* seeing, not one *or* the other.

TRY THIS 6

Watch a television show with the volume turned all the way down. Analyze the nonverbal cues. That is, see how much "listening" you can do by examining only what you see.

1. Which cues reveal the *most* information?
2. Which cues are used the most?
3. Which pieces of information are you most certain of—as far as *your* interpretation is concerned?
4. How many different pieces of information can you receive—"listen" to?
5. Is nonverbal "listening" essential to getting the verbal message?

Effective listening involves listening to what is being said both verbally through words and nonverbally through facial expressions, gestures, and body language. When we do not "listen" to the whole person speaking to us, we are missing a very important part of the message.

We should not stop our search once we have found the speaker's meaning. If, for example, the "essential message" is given in the first two sentences of the speech, the next most important question would be, "How is the essential message supported?" or "What are the speaker's major arguments?" or "How is the speaker's message developed?"

Too often people will allow a word, an example, or something the speaker intended as a digression or an aside to trigger a response. One specific word may be enough to set off a chain reaction in the listener's mind. The message is forgotten, main ideas are lost, the speaker's goal or purpose is virtually for naught. One woman listening to a lecture on "Ethics" heard the speaker cite a brief example about the double standard in our society and how the burden of moral decisions often falls on the woman's shoulders. The woman became incensed; she could no longer listen to the speaker's message. She felt that nobody has the right to dictate another person's moral standards. By the end of the lecture she was enraged, but she had confused morals and ethics. The speaker was speaking on ethics and had cited just one example to indicate how we are faced with decisions concerning right and wrong, but the woman took the example and applied it to the whole lecture. Sidetracked by one example, she could not listen closely. We must prevent certain words or examples from leading us away from the message as a whole. We must cut short unnecessary or irrelevant emotional responses—before they have wiped out our ability to listen sanely and rationally.

Keep active.   Nothing says we must sit like bumps on logs while listening. After one public speaker ended an address, she complimented a member of her audience on his *ability as a listener.* She said she really enjoyed talking with him. Why? This audience member was active. He continually provided feedback to the speaker. As a speaker, you appreciate knowing how your message is being received. Am I being clear? Am I being understood? Can the audience follow my train of thought? Without this knowledge, speaking becomes a meaningless and fruitless exercise.

Keeping active can also provide a channel for the energies of audience members. It is not easy to sit still for a great length of time. One member of a congregation suggested to the regular minister that a certain guest lecturer never be invited back again. Why? Because the guest speaker long overstayed his allotted time, and this member of the congregation could not sit still. The problem is universal.

To keep active, turn your energies to providing responses to speakers, for example, smile, nod your head, raise your eyebrows, frown, look surprised or confused, appear doubtful or thoughtful, shake your head, squint your eyes, or shift your body position, when appropriate. These activities, if performed appropriately, are helpful to speakers, for the more information they have, the more likely their message will meet audience needs. This is the basis for effective feedback: the responses listeners give to a speaker and the adjustment the speaker makes to those responses. There is virtually no end to the ways we have of revealing our understanding or confusion, our approval or disapproval, our acceptance or rejection, our surprise or dismay, our appreciation or anger.

Keeping active can also mean planning a specific response. Put yourself on the spot. If you were called on to respond to the content of what this speaker is sharing or has shared with you, how would you respond? This planning can help shape the mode of your listening. If you are confused, you may want to question the speaker. If you want to show that you care or wish to encourage the speaker, you may want to support the comments made. You may want to add an example of your own or suggest ways for putting the speaker's ideas to work. Planning a specific response can be part of keeping active.

Suspend judgment.   Psychologist Carl Rogers noted that we have a tendency to evaluate a message before hearing all of it.[13] Just as we often are sidetracked by a word or idea, we often frame our responses and form our overall evaluation before all the evidence is in. Prejudgments stem from several causes. First, we tend to stereotype according to emotional or psychological sets that are readily triggered. A person says "drug culture" and the words set off a series of responses. Another person says "policeman" or "jail" and another whole set of responses is evoked.

The trigger is pulled and our mind starts conjuring up every bit of associated matter that it can dredge up—related or unrelated at times. Stereotyping also closes our minds to alternatives. We close our minds to new evidence, and because our minds are closed we do not receive the evidence we need to make a complete or proper evaluation. We are prone to find information to support only what we already believe.

Second, before the evidence is in, we are set to disagree. Since we already feel we know it all, we doubt that a speaker could add a new idea to our memory bank in five or ten minutes. Our posture is "You don't (or how could you) know what you're talking about!" rather than "That is interesting; I never thought of looking at it that way." Our mind set is defensive—one of rebuttal and refutation.

Another aid in suspending judgment is to make certain we fully understand the speaker's message before we respond. We should try to pose questions for the speaker to get at those problem areas before taking off on some errant nag headed for a make-believe windmill, thinking it is a battalion ready to obliterate us in full-scale war!

Suspending judgment also means listening to what the other people are *really* saying—and not what we want them to say.[14] We hear what we want to hear and see what we want to see. We are all biased; unless we are willing to exert extra effort to listen with a minimum amount of bias, our judgment will surely be skewed. We cannot eliminate all bias; but we can take precautions—and taking the following precautions requires courage:

1. Can you *really* open yourself to another's ideas?
2. Can you *really* hear attitudes with which you strongly disagree?
3. Can you *really* listen to another person's opinions without allowing your prejudices to interfere?
4. Can you *really* hear values expressed with which you disagree, from people you care for, without being disappointed in them?
5. Can you *really* change your mind as a result of hearing new information on a topic with which you formerly disagreed?
6. Can you *really* appreciate another person's right to be different from you?

TRY THIS 7

Are there people you just cannot listen to? People who put you on the defensive every time you are around them? Are there times when you have simply refused to listen? What factors cause you *not* to listen? List some of them in your notebook.

Can these factors be eliminated? Reduced? Do you *want* to eliminate or reduce them? Can you see advantages in eliminating or reducing them? If you were to go about eliminating them, how would you do it?

Having once gotten lost after asking for directions, are you likely to behave differently the next time you drive into a gas station for directions? Perhaps not, since you are highly motivated to make your best effort in such situations. But we are not always making our best effort when we are listening to our minister preaching, our instructor teaching, a lecturer talking, a businessperson reporting, or a classmate speaking. We *can* improve, but the road to improvement is not easy; rather, it is filled with potholes, detours, and unmarked highways ready not only to upset the unwary but to send them on an unnecessary and wasted journey.

TRY THIS 8

Try to put these six steps into effect. Tune into a radio or news commentary —not just bits and pieces of news but a full 3 to 5 minute commentary on some issue. Listen to the entire commentary without taking notes. Now evaluate yourself:

1. Did you prepare yourself to listen?
2. Did you concentrate on listening?
3. Did you reveal alertness and interest?
4. Did you search for the essential message?
   What was it? Were there any commercials?
5. Did you keep active?
6. Did you suspend your judgment?

Which of these did you have the most trouble doing? Which came easiest to you?

Is listening to a radio commentary the same as listening to a speaker? What are potential differences? Similarities?

SUMMARY

We listen to learn more about the art of effective communication, to discover more information on different topics and issues, and to improve our ability to concentrate, analyze, and evaluate. The process involves hearing sounds, attending to them—this being partially based on our understanding of them—and remembering them. But our considering something important will not, of itself, carry us through the listening process. Barriers occur. Some barriers we can overcome; some we cannot. Perhaps the most significant barriers are attitudes and habits, and recognition of the way they influence our ability to listen is the first step toward diminishing their power over us.

To become more effective listeners we must take the listening process seriously: preparing ourselves to listen, concentrating, revealing alertness and interest, searching for the essential message, keeping active, and suspending our judgment. Think how much we have to learn! If we spend half of our communication time just listening, why shouldn't we turn that half into one of the most useful, interesting, and significant portions? It makes sense. The power is in our hands—or just beyond our ears!

The following form, "Listening to a Speech," is presented here for several reasons:

1. It can serve as a speech critique format.
2. It can help foster discriminating listening.
3. It can serve as an overview of the various considerations that improve listening.

The form can be adapted to various speech situations by adding to or deleting the topics offered. In its present form it is, perhaps, more complete than would be necessary in all situations; however, it should generate insightful discussion about the speech communication process.

LISTENING TO A SPEECH

Subject
1. Did the speaker select a topic of interest to the audience?

Audience
2. Is there evidence that the speaker analyzed the audience (in terms of age, sex, race, religion, attitude, needs, interests, knowledge, size) before giving the speech?

Setting
3. Did the speaker adapt to the speech situation (classroom, lecture hall, or particular circumstances)?

Speaker
4. Were there aspects of the speaker's presence (dress, attitude, demeanor, or overall approach) that added to or distracted from the presentation?

Sources
5. What were the speaker's sources? How did he or she establish credibility on this topic?

Substance
6. Did the speaker appear prepared? Was the material sufficient? Too much? Too little? Did the reasoning appear logical? Easy to follow? Supportive?

Structure
7. Did the speech flow well? Was the introduction effective? Were the main ideas clear? Were ideas tied together well? Was the conclusion effective?

Style-Language
8. Was the speaker's language appropriate, vivid, impressive? Did he or she use an oral (as opposed to a written) style of communication? Did

he or she use slang, jargon, or technical words that distracted? Were there any outstanding strengths or weaknesses in language usage?

Delivery

9. Did the speaker deliver the speech effectively? Did he or she engage in eye-to-eye contact with the audience? Did he or she reveal a positive, supportive mental attitude? Was the delivery spontaneous? Was there enough variety? Did the speaker command the situation?

Memory

10. Was the speech memorable? What would you remember about it? Why? What did the speaker do to drive points home? to emphasize the points to be remembered? to impress ideas on your memory?

NOTES

[1]Reprinted with permission from the book *P.E.T.: Parent Effectiveness Training by Dr. Thomas Gordon, copyright © 1970. Published by David McKay Co., Inc.*

[2]Ibid., p. 58.

[3]Larry Samovar, Robert D. Brooks, and Richard E. Porter, "A Survey of Adult Communication Activities," *The Journal of Communication,* 19 (1969): 301–307.

[4]Carl Rogers is responsible for the concept of active listening. See Carl R. Rogers and Richard Farson, "Active Listening," in *Readings in Interpersonal and Organizational Communication,* Richard Huseman, Cal Logue, and Dwight Freshley, eds. (Boston: Holbrook, 1973), pp. 541–557.

[5]Carl H. Weaver labels the three major steps as comprehension, interpretation, and evaluation. Hearing and attending, however, must precede comprehension. Comprehension (or understanding) occurs only as a result of mentally assigning meaning to words; thus, interpretation is one facet of understanding. Finally, we remember that which was worth to us; thus, evaluation is one facet of the remembering process. See Carl H. Weaver, *Human Listening: Processes and Behavior* (Indianapolis: Bobbs-Merrill, 1972), pp. 144–145.

[6]See Robert R. Bostrom and Carol L. Bryant, "Factors in the Retention of Information Presented Orally: The Role of Short-Term Listening," *Western Journal of Speech Communication* 44 (Spring 1980): 137–145.

[7]Numerous research studies indicate that there are other factors that affect our ability to listen and observe. A sampling of some of these studies includes E. E. Jones and R. Kohler, "The Effects of Plausibility on Learning of Controversial Statements," *Journal of Abnormal and Social Psychology,* 57 (1958): 315–320; R. Leeper, "The Role of Motivation in Learning: A Study of the Phenomenon of Differential Motivation Control of the Utilization of Habits," *Journal of Genetic Psychology,* 45 (1935): 3–40; A. H. Hastorf and H. Cantril, "They Saw a Game: A Case Study," *Journal of Abnormal and Social Psychology,* 49 (1954): 129–134; R. Schafer and G. Murphy, "The Role of Autism in a Visual Figure-Ground Relationship," *Journal of Experimental Psychology,* 32 (1943): 335–343; and Bostrom and Bryant, "Factors in Retention."

[8]For more information on the nature of listening and other studies, see C. William Colburn and Sanford B. Seinberg, *An Orientation to Listening and Audience Analysis* (Palo Alto, Calif.: SRA, 1976); Larry L. Barker, *Listening Behavior* (Englewood Cliffs, N.J.: Prentice-Hall, 1971); and Carl H. Weaver, *Human Listening: Processes and Behavior* (Indianapolis: Bobbs-Merrill, 1972); Andrew D. Wolvin and Carolyn Gwynn Coakley, *Listening* (Dubuque, Iowa: Wm. C. Brown, 1982).

[9]For more information on listening habits, see Emil Bohn and Karen Foss, *Teaching Listening in the Classroom: An Integrated Approach* (Phoenix: Western Speech Communication Association, 1977).

[10]A useful overview of the guides to good listening can be found in Ralph G. Nichols's "Do We Know How to Listen? Practical Helps in a Modern Age," *Speech Teacher* 10 (1961): 118–124. Most suggestions for the improvement of listening owe their formulation to the work of Ralph G. Nichols. Also see Baxter Geeting and Corinne Geeting, *How to Listen Assertively* (New York: Monarch, 1976).

[11]Ralph G. Nichols and Leonard A. Stevens, *Are You Listening?* (New York: McGraw-Hill, 1957), p. 42.

[12]See Ralph G. Nichols, "Listening Is a 10-Part Skill," *Nation's Business,* 45 (July 1957), in *Speech/Communication: A Reader,* 2nd ed. ed. Richard L. Weaver, II (San Diego: Calif.: Collegiate Publishing, Inc., 1979), pp. 266–274, especially pp. 272–274, "Capitalize on Thought Speed."

[13] Carl R. Rogers, *On Becoming A Person* (Boston: Houghton Mifflin, 1971), pp. 331–337.

[14]Research indicates that how you view both the topic and speaker will affect how you understand (and remember) the message. See M. Manis, "The Interpretation of Opinion Statements as a Function of Recipient Attitude and Source Prestige," *Journal of Abnormal and Social Psychology,* 63 (1961): 82–86; L. Berkowitz and R. Goranson, "Motivational and Judgmental Determinants of Social Perception," *Journal of Abnormal and Social Psychology,* 69 (1964): 296–302; and S. Asch, "The Doctrine of Suggestion, Prestige, and Limitation in Social Psychology," *Psychological Review,* 55 (1948): 250–276.

four

ANALYZING THE AUDIENCE

Idea Adaptation

Just for a moment, role play the following situation: You want to go to a movie that has just come to the local theater, but you do not want to go alone. How are you going to convince someone to join you? What methods and techniques would you use to get your roommate or spouse to go? You know this person well, so you could be fairly direct and blunt. Would you use the same methods and techniques to convince your best friend? Instead of suggesting that it is a break from studying or from routine, you might convince your friend that the movie is full of excitement and adventure. If you wanted to invite someone you did not know as well as these others, you might be more logical and convince him or her by telling about the merits of the plot or the quality of the stars of the picture. Would your methods and techniques change if you knew in advance that one of these people had seen the movie before? What if they had previously expressed no interest in seeing this movie?

In each case, the methods and techniques you use to convince the person to go to the movie would probably change—even though changes could be subtle, almost inconspicuous ones. Not only would the information that you share be different, but your relationship with each person is different. A change in the relationship might cause a change in the information you use to convince them. The point is that you make changes in your communication according to the person or persons with whom you talk. This is called *audience adaptation,* and to adapt to different people requires audience analysis.

We are always involved in some form of audience adaptation when we talk with others. Most of this adaptation is casual, unstructured, and unplanned. When and if it works, we feel successful. If it does not, either we dismiss it, or we blame the other person or persons for being unresponsive, unconcerned, or uncaring. We may say something like, "I just can't talk to _____; he won't listen to me," or "_____ sure is in a bad mood today."

Our communication with others could be substantially improved if we were not quite so casual about our audience analysis and if, after a communication, we were to evaluate our effort. We need information to build on, techniques that work for us, and a constant desire to improve. Even more, we need awareness. The more important the communication, the more important it is to get the desired outcome, and thus the more important it is for us to use precisely right methods.

NEED FOR AUDIENCE ANALYSIS

Public communication is little different from interpersonal communication—one person talking to another—when it comes to the need for and importance of audience analysis. The need for analysis cannot be taken casually. You must fully appreciate the importance of its role, its effect on the outcome of the communication effort, and the way it can reinforce or buttress communication. To look at communication only from the speaker's viewpoint, disregarding audience analysis, is *not* to consider all available means to attain a purpose or goal. It is like playing chess or checkers without using strategy. It is like driving to the supermarket without making an effort to find the most direct route.

Although audiences differ, certain aspects of their behavior can be predicted and a speaker can anticipate the probable response when talking to a particular audience. As our predictions move from mere speculation to substantiated analysis and concrete fact, the adjustments we make in our communication to allow for this information will obviously become more accurate and precise, thus making it more likely that we will succeed in obtaining our purpose. We want

THE WIZARD OF ID by Brant Parker and Johnny Hart. By permission of Johnny Hart and Field Enterprises, Inc.

success, and to gain that end we must consider using every technique available —providing, of course, that it is ethical. We do not want to do something that is wrong or that might be harmful to others.

Audience analysis is recognized as an important feature of successful communication, one that can make or break a communication effort. No speaker can be successful unless the audience understands what he or she has to say. Understanding comes about as a result of many different features of the speaker's presentation; most of these bear directly on successful audience analysis.

The main questions involved in audience analysis are these: (1) What aspects do we want to analyze? (2) How do we analyze them? (3) What do we do with the information we discover about the audience? (4) How do we know whether or not we have been successful once we have made the analysis and adapted our material?

WHAT DO WE WANT TO ANALYZE?

The honest answer to the question of what we want to analyze is anything and everything, but that is unrealistic and unreasonable. You see, the more information you have about the people with whom you will be speaking, the better off you will be: the better you can adapt, the better you can understand them, the better you can spontaneously react to unexpected circumstances. More realistically and reasonably, we need to know everything we can know that relates to our communication with them. That also may be a bit unrealistic, since, in many cases, the information we need is difficult to get. Some of it is locked away in the minds of our future audience members, and there is no key!

At times, we get mixed information about an audience. Seldom is an entire audience all of one type. Sometimes we have to decide which people we want to reach with a speech, ready to concede that we will not reach everyone. We call this audience—the specific one we intend to reach—our target audience.

In Chapter 2, some of the more obvious factors that go into audience analysis were mentioned. Not mentioned was the significance of the various findings in each category.[1] Of what use is knowing the age, sex, education level, and knowledge background of the audience—characteristics referred to as demographics? What difference does that demographic information make? Knowledge of this kind can be applied in different ways and at different points in the development of the speech.

Demographics

When we examine demographics, we look at the characteristics of a given group of people. In the following sections, we will look at the variables of age, sex, education, and knowledge background—major demographic variables. In the concluding paragraph to this section, several other variables are also listed.

Age.   Audience age is relatively easy to determine. You want to know the average age of the people with whom you will be speaking. Think for a second about the differences between your ideas and those of your parents—just to get an idea about the influence of age.[2] Would you, for example, say that your parents are more cautious than you? More conservative than you? More pessimistic than you? Are their interests more limited than yours? These generalizations often, though not always, hold true; thus, if you had to address an audience of people your parents' age you would want to take a more cautious position, reveal restraint and conservatism, allow for the more pessimistic nature of audience beliefs, and attempt to meet, satisfy, or at least acknowledge their interests. You cannot expect to talk with such an audience successfully if you make none of the above adjustments. The older audience may not listen; they may not understand; they may not accept. It is likely that they will reject both you and your ideas. In his book on *Rhetoric,* Aristotle made this point clear as early as the fourth century B.C. when he said:

> Now the hearer is always receptive when a speech is adapted to his own character and reflects it. Thus we can readily see the proper means of adapting both speech and speaker to a given audience. [In addressing young men, for example, the speaker should assimilate his character to theirs. Or, again, in pleading for a gift to the poor and ailing, one would appeal to the kindness and generosity of the young, but to the fears and doubts of the old.][3]

For contrast, imagine that the group before whom you are to speak are composed of young children eight to eleven years old. You will be more certain to hold their attention if your remarks are brief, entertaining, animated, and directly relevant to them. A Cubmaster in charge of running a monthly pack meeting found that lots of variety and a fast pace helped to hold the boys' attention. Topics that he found were well received included the use of fire, space, science, adventure, skateboarding, magic, sports, and hobbies.

As another example of how different audiences require different approaches by speakers, think about what *you* would like to hear in a speech. Would these topics hold your attention?

Success	Adventure
Sex	Education
Grades	Getting ahead
Getting a job	Keeping a job

Now consider the topics people in their thirties or forties would like to hear a speech on:

Raising children	Succeeding in business
How to keep the family together	Understanding our economy
Using leisure time	Easing the tax bite

These topics would be likely to change again—probably dramatically—if you considered topics that fifty- and sixty-year-olds might enjoy hearing speeches on:

| Financial independence | How to continue being useful, |
| Maintaining good health | contributing members of society |

People's interests vary with age.

As speakers, it is our responsibility to adapt our message to our audience. Although interests vary with age, two things do not: (1) audiences want us to be well-prepared with intesesting information, and (2) they want us to capture their attention. In general, adapting our message to our audience cannot be done at the last minute. It requires forethought, planning, and imagination. Thus, speakers must be cautious not only in topic selection but in topic development as well.

To bridge the age gap, speakers can emphasize the ways in which they and their audience are similar. They can refer to the interests, concerns, and motives they all have in common. Speakers must always try to capitalize on similarities and common concerns.

TRY THIS 1

You want to give a speech on the topic, "Getting the Most Out of a College Experience." You feel comfortable with this topic not just because you know something about it but also because you feel that already—even at this point in your college career—you are experiencing college to the fullest and you would like to see others get more out of college.

What *specific adaptations* would you make if you planned to give this speech to a group of people

sixteen to seventeen years old?
eighteen to twenty one years old?
thirty to forty years old?
forty to sixty years old?
sixty five and over?

Could the speech be altered to make it appropriate for all of these age groups? Would it be easier to alter or adapt it to some of these groups than to others? Which ages would be easiest? Would *you* be able to give such a speech to all of these age groups?

As mentioned in a previous chapter, an audience composed of a wide variety of age groups is more difficult to address—for obvious reasons. One must choose which approach to use in addressing such an audience. The speaker can broaden the overall appeal, make a barrage of specific appeals to each of the various age groups, or select one specific target audience. The first two approaches reveal concern for the audience, a wide knowledge base, and a desire to affect all audience members. The latter suggests that the message can have its greatest effect if it is directed only to certain members of the audience.

Sex.   Sex has long been recognized as an important variable in communication. Generally the social interests of men and women will be determined by the social roles they play or expect to play. After a certain speech by a male athlete, some of the women in the class were heard to respond, "I have no interest in athletics." Some women might also express a lack of interest in automobile maintenance, gun control, or home construction and repair, but some males have little interest in these areas either. After a woman's speech on Fashion or the ERA, some male members of the audience may respond with a lack of enthusiasm. Although there are significant differences between individual men and women, there are also numerous interests and values that each sex particularly share. An audience's interest in and understanding of any topic cannot be accurately predicted solely on the basis of sex, but it is a factor to be considered, especially when sex is closely aligned with social role. A speech on "Child Rearing" or "Resolving Conflict Within the Family" would make little sense for an audience of independent, single, professional men *or* women.

A speaker may wish to target his or her speech to one sex or the other, but this will not be a wise choice—in most cases—if many members of the opposite sex (opposite from those being targeted) are present. The speech would probably be better received if the speaker were to include both sexes in the target audience. This would likely mean choosing a topic that all members are likely to find interesting, and selecting examples, illustrations, and other supporting material to which all can relate.

Although speakers can probably find topics in which some males or some females have no interest, they should try to avoid reinforcing such sexual stereotypes. Speakers should, however, try to understand the interests, values, and language expectations of the audience, and this includes evaluating similarities and differences between males and females in the audience. Speakers should also remember that in the areas of sexual relations, education, and employment, males and females have grown closer together.

Educational Level.   Education can be a major factor in audience analysis, especially when the level of education is either low, high, or mixed. In a college class, one can depend on his or her own level of knowledge, in general, to be a determiner of beliefs and values. But the more educated the audience, the more likely that the speaker will need to use rational and logical appeals—as opposed to emotional ones—recognize the stability and consistency of the audience's beliefs, values, and attitudes, and consider their knowledge. The higher the educational level, the more background the audience will have on your topic—especially if the topic is oriented toward either current events or experiences that touch their lives. Also, people with more education tend to view issues in shades of gray, whereas people with less education tend to view issues as two-sided—as black and white or right or wrong. Educated people tend to be more pessimistic or fatalistic, and they are more active. They participate in community affairs, and they actively voice their opinions, interests, and reactions.

Knowledge Background.   Although the educational level of a student audience may help to determine how much knowledge background the audience has, you may want more specific information about their level of knowledge. For example, how much do they know *specifically* on your topic? If you choose to talk on a proposal such as a bond issue, it would be useful to know how many other speeches on the issue they might have heard or how much information has been available in the local papers. Must you spend time with basics, or can you get right to the heart of the issue?

Knowing the knowledge background may also reveal prejudices and biases. If people feel strongly for or strongly against your topic, your speech will probably not change their attitudes. It might be better for you to take a different tack—perhaps trying to inform them on some new aspect of the problem—rather than trying to persuade them to change.

Knowing the knowledge background can reveal some members who are strongly in favor of your topic just as it can reveal those who are strongly opposed and those who are neutral or do not care. A homogeneous group is perhaps easier to approach because you have a better idea of what kind of attitudes to expect. Specific suggestions of exact methods and techniques to use are difficult to make because the combination of the various factors, including how extreme the position is thought to be, determines what will or will not work. In general, the speaker might consider the following suggestions:

For audiences strongly in favor of the topic
   A. Impress on them the old truths, and encourage them to act when they have an opportunity to do so.
   B. Urge them to take a very definite and specific action—not just a generalized approach—immediately, or in the near future.
   C. Encourage further or deeper commitment by intensifying their attitudes through emotional appeal and by providing further knowledge. Broaden their base of support.

For neutral or apathetic audiences
   A. Make your approach interesting. This audience may need further information, but they also may need to know how and why the topic affects them. Combine emotion and information.
   B. Strive to avoid any ideas that may alienate this audience. That they are neutral means they could move in either direction. Emphasize and reinforce any ideas with which they already sympathize.

For audiences that are strongly opposed or hostile
   A. This is the hardest audience to approach. Because one speech is unlikely to reverse their attitude or modify their beliefs, your speech should seek to minimize their opposition.
   B. Attempt to meet the chief objections of the audience.[4] Can you admit that there is some merit to their chief objection without being inconsistent?
      1. Such an admission removes a strong competing idea from the audience's mind and allows members to listen better.
      2. It is a compliment to the audience to be told they are right; thus, they are more willing to give the speaker a fair hearing.
   C. Offer the audience new facts or new conditions.

D. Strive to achieve identification by using ideas and opinions that you and your audience share.

E. Offer the audience preliminary explanatory material designed to minimize their opposition and to aid in finding common ground.

Knowing your audience's knowledge background can also reveal their degree of involvement.[5] If speakers want to estimate the level of involvement before a speech, they can judge how closely their topic matches audience needs and interests, how closely it relates to their self-image, how closely it reflects their central values, or how strongly committed they are to the topic. Estimating how involved listeners are during a speech may be easier because of obvious signs, such as listener outbursts and reactions. Audience members may shake or nod their heads, clench their fists, tense their muscles, move nervously, or speak out or yell.

In your audience analysis you may discover that the audience's position on the topic is culturally or ethnically induced. As a speaker, one must be careful not to trespass on traditions—traditions that have grown from the people we have lived with or with whom we have associated. Imagine, for example, a speaker talking on "Investing Your Money" to a group of people from an economically disadvantaged part of town, not realizing that these people have no money to invest. That is like trying to convince students who commute to campus or live in town to change the fraternity or sorority initiation system; most would not care. A black speaker might have trouble getting an audience to identify with him if the audience knew that he had never known poverty, had gone to good schools, and had never suffered discrimination—unless, of course, audience members had similar cultural backgrounds. As another example, one might assume that the profit motive is *the* chief interest of business students. A UCLA study found that a top student concern is to make money.[6] To use such an appeal in a speech could miss the mark, however. If you were speaking to students seeking admission to a business school, appeal to the profit motive might not address the students' primary concerns. It might be better to appeal to their need for intellectual stimulation, early responsibility, and compatibility with fellow workers.[7]

Group memberships may similarly affect audience attitudes and information. Just as belonging to the Elks, Lions, American Legion, or Kiwanis affects the outlook of some adults, so belonging to fraternities, sororities, or being young Christians, young Republicans, or young Democrats can affect student viewpoints. Some informal groups are the occupants of a floor or set of rooms in a dormitory, athletes, the football team, and members of the debate team or thespian's club. The groups to which audience members belong affect their knowledge background because groups often provide well-defined frameworks of the attitudes and behaviors expected of members. These attitudes and behaviors lead to conformity, stereotyping, and group cohesiveness.[8] Members who join groups often adopt the attitude of the group and work for the group's welfare. If they do not accept the group's attitudes, either they do not join the group, they experience frustration within the group, or they withdraw from the group.[9] To earn acceptance and belief, a speaker should attempt to discover the audience's knowledge background.

Several specific areas that might be explored to attain significant information about your audience's beliefs and values have been mentioned. This list is by no means complete, just suggestive. Depending on the circumstances, the vocation, religion, geographical experience, or life style of audience members might be additional considerations. Remember that the purpose of the search is to find guides to the audience's values, attitudes, information, even sense of humor.

TRY THIS 2

What would be your initial assumptions about the attitudes and behaviors of people who belong to any of the following groups?

Catholics	Jewish religion
American Legion	Quakers
Daughters of the American Revolution	Protestants
	Mormons
John Birch Society	Alcoholics Anonymous
Ku Klux Klan (KKK)	Weight Watchers
Baptists	Scouts
Christian Scientists	Jehovah's Witnesses

Logistics

Once you know the characteristics of the audience—what is referred to as demographic information—you must inquire about the logistics. Some have been mentioned before; most are obvious. They are stated here, briefly, as a reminder:

1. Size of audience and seating arrangements
2. Use of (need for) a microphone and PA system
3. Type of hall or room for the speech (setting)
   a. Indoors
   b. Outdoors
4. Lighting
5. Reason the audience has assembled (occasion)
   a. Invitation
   b. Voluntary
   c. Membership requirement
   d. Regular meeting
6. Expected degree of formality or informality
7. Time
   a. Of year (weather conditions?)

b. Of day

c. Allotted for speech

8. Other speakers or the nature of the program
9. Potential noise or distraction
10. Lectern availability
11. Need for blackboard or visual-aids

If the speaker discovers that a public address system or microphones will be used, he or she should allow time to practice using the equipment. Comfort and ease of use result from experience. Public address systems must be adjusted for the appropriate volume. Microphones attached to a lectern limit a speaker's mobility, whereas those that can be worn around the neck—lavalier microphones —allow more freedom of movement. Some microphones do not require an electrical cord, which allows even greater flexibility.

TRY THIS 3

From the following situations, write as many characteristics about the audience as you can derive. Do not worry about whether your characteristics are right or wrong, just write them down:

1. A speaker is addressing the League of Women Voters on "Apathy in Voting Among Students."
2. A speaker is addressing a group of elementary-school students on "Analyzing Advertisements."
3. A speaker is giving a report on "The Political Apathy of Students" to her speech class.
4. A speaker is giving a speech on "The Use of Alcohol on Campus" to a meeting of concerned parents.
5. A speaker is giving a speech on "Legalizing All Gambling" to a group of local ministers.
6. A speaker is giving a speech on "Student Views of Police Officers" to the campus security organization.

HOW DO WE ANALYZE THE AUDIENCE?

How do you find information about the audience? Basically, the same way as you find information that you need about *anything*. First, you ask a lot of questions —beginning with yourself. Always depend on yourself first. People who know a lot are generally those who are willing to ask questions. Our educational system encourages it, for the most part, and one of the essential goals of higher education is to challenge, stimulate, and encourage students to ask questions.

If your audience is a class of which you are a member, you can question yourself—as long as you can be objective about the answers. If you are unsure of your responses, you can question your classmates as well. If you are still unsure, you can pursue one of the other suggestions to be offered.

If the speech is to be before an audience about which you need more information, your host or hostess or the program chairperson will be one of your best resources. Also, trust your knowledge about the audience—any prior experience you may have had with them.

If the audience belongs to or identifies with an organization or association, read the literature of the organization or association: pamphlets, newletters, or journals. What has been written in the newspaper about them? Local libraries sometimes keep files on local organizations and associations. A call ahead might save you a trip, or it might help the librarian make the trip more profitable for you. Armed with enough information, the librarian will often help you with some of the initial searching. Other available information sources may include the local chamber of commerce, local historical society, and other private agencies.

You might also ask the host or hostess for names of potential audience members or an organization membership list. Then, in a written letter or more directly in a telephone interview, you could get some answers to basic questions about your audience.

In addition to audience analysis before the speech, as speakers we must also engage in audience analysis during the speech. We look for clues about the audience's understanding and acceptance of our ideas. Some such feedback is overt and obvious:

> Audience members get up and leave.
> They talk a lot or cough.
> They laugh or respond at appropriate times.
> They applaud, cheer, or shout.
> They shuffle their feet, wiggle, or move in their chairs.
> Audience members fall asleep.

Some feedback may be more subtle, and it may take more concentration to perceive or understand it:

> Audience members stare at you in rapt attention.
> They look you in the eye.
> They sit in front of you in stonefaced silence.
> They frown, smile, or look quizzical.
> They look glassy-eyed, tired, or apathetic. Bored.

Monitoring such feedback is important; more important, however, is our ability to change our message to accommodate it. We may not have any other material. We may not understand the feedback. We may not be flexible and adaptable. The guideline, of course, is to adapt as best we can according to our understanding

MISS PEACH by Mell Lazarus. © 1978 Field Enterprises, Inc. Courtesy of Field Newspaper Syndicate.

of the response. We must also be aware that the feedback we receive may require no adaptation or response at all except to continue as planned. It can tell us that we are right on target.

Using the following Audience Analysis Checksheet will provide a specific, concrete way to make certain that you have covered all the major items in your analysis. Such preplanning will very likely add to the overall impact of your message. It will also increase your confidence; you will feel better about addressing the audience.

AUDIENCE ANALYSIS CHECKSHEET

_____ 1. What is the average age of your audience?

_____ 2. Do you know the sex distribution?

_____ 3. How much education do they have?

_____ 4. How much knowledge do they have of your topic?

_____ 5. How well informed are they generally?

_____ 6. What else do you know about audience demographics?

      a. Occupations?

      b. Religion?

      c. Socioeconomic status?

      d. Cultural or ethnic composition?

      e. Political affiliations?

      f. Group memberships?

_____ 7. Have you all the information you need on the logistics of the situation?

      a. Size of audience?

      b. Seating?

      c. PA system? Microphone?

      d. Type of hall (setting)?

      e. Lighting?

      f. Occasion?

g. Degree of formality or informality?

h. Time?

i. Other speakers?

j. Noise?

k. Lectern?

l. Visuals?

_____ 8. What attitudes do audience members hold (favorable, neutral, or opposed)?

a. Toward you?

b. Toward your topic?

c. Toward the occasion?

_____ 9. Have you made plans to gather information:

a. Before the speech?

b. During the speech?

c. After the speech?

WHAT WE DO WITH THE INFORMATION

This whole process would be a waste of time without some way to put the information to use. Fortunately, the information can be put to clear, purposeful, and immediate use. Effective audience analysis can result in a message that is specifically tailored to an immediate audience and situation. In accommodating a specific audience, a speaker should not blithely dilute the message, betray his or her commitment to truth (as he or she sees it), or court the favor of the audience through unwarranted flattery. Better ways of accommodating audiences are available. The speaker must be alert to the need to be constant—not unbending, but faithful to the decided purpose of the communication effort. This section will explain how audience analysis affects content, evidence, organization, style, and delivery.

Before examining these areas, however, a brief reminder is in order: Our purpose in making use of the information is twofold: (1) to hold audience attention—to make our information interesting and engaging, and (2) to be understood. And we must be concerned about these processes throughout the development of our speech—*not* just in the introduction or beginning portion of the speech. Audience attention lasts a very short time before it shifts to something else. It may last only three to eight seconds and usually no longer than thirty seconds. Also, the span of attention is very narrow; as audience members, we focus on one subject at a time, although we may give others peripheral attention.[10]

CONSIDER THIS

The disparity between speaking and thinking puts the onus on the speaker to ensure that his thoughts do not get lost in the gap between words and thoughts.

Dr. Jesse Nirenberg, a New York psychologist who spent many years studying listening problems, once made the following suggestions for holding a person's attention:

- Always start with the conclusion; never with a question.
- Do not lead up to your main idea slowly; if you do, the listener's mind might have skipped ahead of you by the time you get to the point.
- Translate what you have to say into potential benefits to the listener whenever possible. People will sit up and take notice if they feel there is something in it for them.
- Repeat your point subtly in the course of your delivery, preferably by citing examples that keep the listener from getting bored.
- Avoid pronouns. "What do you think of this?" should be, "What do you think of something specific?" Specifics focus attention.
- Get "feedback" on everything pertinent that you have said by intermittently questioning your listener. By asking questions, you pose problems to be solved which oblige the listener to think about the meaning of what you have to say.

SOURCE: From *The Monthly Letter* (January 1979), published by The Royal Bank of Canada.

The message you have designed for your audience is only one of many stimuli competing for their attention. They may also be thinking of how warm they are, how uncomfortable the seats are, a letter they received in the mail, their plans for the evening, their grades, or a recent party. The real problem becomes how you can make your message compete with all these other stimuli. It *is* possible.

The information acquired through audience analysis should also lead you to realize what modification must be made in the material to gain understanding. To what extent, for example, can you be metaphorical—use figurative language —as opposed to being more direct—expressing yourself without using figures of speech? What arrangements of the material will be clearest? That is, how can the organization of the speech contribute to clear understanding? As each of the following areas is discussed, think of the problems speakers must face with respect to *both* interest and understanding.

Content

The first area of content where audience analysis can have an effect is in the choice of topics. From the following list select the topics that would more likely appeal to an older (fifty and over) audience:

Adventure	Welfare
Job opportunities	Graduated income tax
Astrology	Socialized medicine
Grade inflation	Social Security

Given the age, sex, occupations, and knowledge background of a group of people, such a list of topics can be rather easily constructed. We, as speakers, want to make certain that the topic we select meets the wants, needs, and desires of our audience.

An interesting question arises here: Given a choice of topics that would interest my audience and a choice of topics that would interest *me*, which should I choose? If the question were as clearcut as it sounds here, the answer would have to be that your audience comes first; however, this implies speakers must give themselves to their audience, which is not the case. But think of it in this way: Should you waste the time of your audience by having them listen to material that does not remotely concern them, or is it more important that *you* speak on a topic that concerns you—and your audience be damned?

Actually, a balance is not only possible but is what we must strive for. We must find a topic that we already know about or that we would enjoy investigating, then we must adapt that topic and information to our audience as we develop the speech. For example, take the topic of "success": It could relate to any age group:

- Success to a Boy Scout could mean making money on a fund-raising drive.
- Success to a high-school student could mean becoming more popular or better liked.
- Success to a college student might mean discovering and using better study habits.
- Success to a recent college graduate might mean enhancing his or her career or working life.
- Success to a group of middle-aged people who have families might mean finding economical ways to finance family travel or excursions.
- Success to a group of elderly people might mean finding rewarding ways to make use of their leisure time.

These are general ways to adapt material—a topic and its corresponding information—to a broad range of age categories and to various occupations, educational levels, or levels of information.

TRY THIS 4

State the obvious adaptations that would be necessary if you were to give a speech on "Audience Adaptation in Communication" to the following audiences:

Nurses	Parents
High-school principals	Ministers
Business executives	Used car salespeople
Law enforcement officers	Radio broadcasters
Garden club members	Nuclear physicists

To see how the level of information can affect a presentation, just remember, in your own career, how many different language courses you have had—English, Spanish, French, German, or whatever. A teacher adapts both the material and the approach to the background of the class members. Mathematics, chemistry, physics, or even communication courses are no different. If beginning level communication concepts and principles were taught in a senior level communication course, students would, more than likely, feel cheated and bored. Some teachers survey the students at the outset of a course to determine their background and their purpose for being there, thus gaining a better idea of how to orient the course—or where to begin.

One note of caution should be entered here. The speaker who selects a topic that meets the wants, needs, and desires of his or her audience makes the job of speech preparation and presentation easier. But selecting an appropriate topic alone does not guarantee success. A very strong topic can be handled poorly, and a poorly chosen topic can be handled with effectiveness and precision. Whether or not a topic is well chosen or well adapted cannot be gauged from the choice alone; it can only be judged as a result of the execution—its development. We must see speaker-message-audience-occasion in interaction. The concept of the transaction is again important to keep in mind. The point is, simply, that the beginning speaker brings success into his or her reach at the outset with a well-chosen topic.

Evidence

The evidence of a speech is the proof; it demonstrates the truth and strength of the speaker's ideas. After making certain that the topic is well chosen and appropriately narrowed, you must next select evidence that relates to the audience. As you choose your forms of proof—examples and illustrations, facts and opinions, or statistics and personal experiences—keep your audience in mind. Select the material they can most closely identify with.

The concept of immediacy is important, and it varies for every audience. What is immediate for one group of students may not be immediate for another group. Immediacy means relying on material that directly touches or concerns each member of your audience: events or issues that are near at hand. Discussing theft on this campus, or in this town, is better than discussing it as it relates to other campuses or other towns. The further removed (less immediate) the material is, the less likely it will hold attention.

TRY THIS 5

In each instance below, quickly suggest just *one* piece of material (an idea, example, illustration) that would be *immediate* for each of the audiences mentioned:

1. Avid TV watchers
2. Rock 'n' roll fans
3. New students at a college or university
4. New mothers
6. Science-fiction readers
7. Gardeners
8. Political activists
9. Members of an organization for the promotion of humor

5. Students looking for summer   10. Professional athletes
   employment   11. Professional writers

What was the process you used to discover this thing? How likely is it that what you suggested would be immediate? How might you check whether or not your suggestion would actually be immediate to the particular audience? To which of the above audiences would you find it most comfortable (easiest) to speak?

Perhaps the most outstanding negative characteristic of most public speeches is that they are startlingly unimaginative: They offer nothing new.[11] If you want to make your public speech unique—make it stand out from others—you will place most emphasis on the new, the unusual material. The reason most speeches seldom rise above the average is that speakers do not assume their audience is familiar with the obvious. Speakers often waste time expounding on and further developing common knowledge. Unless this common knowledge is essential to the audience's understanding of your message, throw it aside.

More speakers would become challenged, more speakers would be rewarded, and more audiences would be satisfied, if speakers took it upon themselves to support what could be called a *transcending* purpose or *superpurpose*. In a later chapter, purposes will be discussed. A speaker who wants to increase the understanding of his or her audience, to persuade them, or to entertain them has a purpose in mind. But a superpurpose supersedes—is superior to—all of these. All communication would be improved if speakers thought in terms of a superpurpose: helping others to maximize their potential or helping them become what they can become. Plan to push the frontiers of knowledge. For example, in addition to depending on commonly read newspapers and magazines for information, seek sources your audience would be less likely to have read. Filling in background information only where it is essential, strive to take your audience beyond common knowledge. Remember that a speech is an interaction between speaker-message-audience-situation. The concept of transaction assumes some common base. Use this as a starting point as you provide new insights and information. A speech cannot be a success and the audience a failure: A speech depends on the audience for its success.

The main point, then, is that throughout the discovery process, you must keep the audience in mind. To let them slip from your mind is like forgetting the store where you want to buy a product. You still have the product—what you want to purchase—in mind, but you are going to reduce your effectiveness and possibly not get the best deal by forgetting the particular store where you wish to buy it.

Organization

Audience analysis can also help in the organization of the speech. The age and maturity of an audience, the room and physical conditions (heat and lighting), and the time of day can have an effect on attention spans. Knowing the likelihood of their being distracted may help you determine the need for transitions, internal summaries, and places where you should relate your material back to your thesis. The more distractions, the more frequently you will need to refocus their attention on your speech. The need for repetition can also be affected by these factors.

The knowledge level of the audience can affect how many points you try to cover in a speech. The more points a speaker tries to cover, the more superficial the speech may become. The fewer points, the more depth and substance the speaker can provide, given the same time limit. Thus, if a speaker were talking to an audience with little knowledge of the topic, he or she might choose to provide a brief overview of the problem—just as occurs in many introductory university or college courses—taking many points and covering each superficially, in order to provide a perspective. With that fundamental knowledge present, a speaker can take one, two, or three of the major issues and develop them in depth, as more advanced courses in a discipline would do. A graduate seminar may, indeed, focus on one single, well-defined, and focused issue or topic and develop it in great depth.

Assuming that the Roman numerals are the main heads (major points) in the body of the speech, which of the following two outlines would likely offer an audience greater depth and substance? That is, which would tend to be less superficial?

Outline 1	Outline 2
I.	I.
A.	A.
B.	B.
II.	C.
III.	1.
A.	2.
B.	D.
IV.	II.
V.	A.
VI.	1.
A.	2.
B.	3.
VII.	B.
VIII.	III.
A.	A.
B.	B.

Although it may be obvious that the outline on the left (Outline 1) would be more superficial because numerous main points are presented without support, many speakers will try to cover too much in their speech because they have not taken the time to organize their material. The point, once again, is to keep the audience in mind as you organize your ideas.

Style

The speaker can also use audience analysis to determine the most effective approach to the style or language of the presentation. When a person in communication talks about *style,* he or she is referring to the language—words—the speaker chooses to use. Clarity in a communication results from the choice of words and structure of sentences. For most audiences, the key to clarity is simple sentences and familiar language; however, this can vary with the sophistication of the audience. The greater the sophistication—and by that is meant the knowledge of and experience with the topic as well as education level—the more likely it is the speaker can become more technical, and perhaps more formal: A formal sentence would be one phrased in written style as opposed to oral style. In informal conversation, we often use sentence fragments as well as incomplete and ill-referenced thoughts. We may also use a variety of compound-complex sentences with dangling modifiers, double-referenced subjects and multiple verbs. The more formal a speech becomes, the further it moves from informal conversation. The president of the United States, for example, tends to use a formal style in major policy addresses to avoid the possibility of being misinterpreted. Since the future of our country often rests on his choice of language, a more formal style (written and then read) is required. He uses a less formal style in news conferences.

The best advice for using language effectively is to talk simply and naturally. If audience feedback indicates a need to wake up the audience, use a rhetorical question—a question that does not require an answer. But ask the question as if you care about it and want the audience to mentally think about an answer. This would include questions such as the following:

Do you know what that fact means?
Do you understand how this could affect your lives?
Do you want to know why this is so important?
Now you're probably wondering how you can help in all this.

Also, in your use of language, make certain that you emphasize the important points of the speech. Do not assume the audience will understand their importance just because you said them. Perhaps, the major assumption that disrupts or breaks down clarity of expression is "if its clear to me, it must be clear to you." Often it is not clear. Even the simplest of messages can break down.

CONSIDER THIS

We are so peculiar about words. We know they are our only tools of language, and yet we continue to abuse them thoughtlessly, in a way we would never think of abusing real tools—even though words wrongly used can wreak far more damage than any hammer or chisel or wrench.

We will take a new word and use it to batter a concept to death. Finally, the word is exhausted of legitimate meaning, and we drop it, only to pick up another and misuse it just as willfully or ignorantly.

. . .

Why do we do with words what we are sensible enough to refrain from doing with tools? How can a rational species take a word like "democracy," for instance, and stretch it out to cover such diverse forms of government as the United States, Russia, and China—each proclaiming its sole entitlement to the word, while denying it to the others?

"It all depends on who is to be master," said Humpty Dumpty, "words or you." But, ironically, in trying to be their master, we allow them to master us, and we become the unconscious slaves of words that have slipped their traces and carry us along with them to doomsday.

You, as the speaker, must be the judge of how important it is for the audience to get a particular point, then you must be the judge of the best way to put the point across. This may depend, in part, on how attentive the audience is or on the complexity or simplicity of the point being made. The following methods will help when you are trying to emphasize an important point. They are arranged in a hierarchy with the most important method (most effective) listed first, the second in importance is listed second, and so on:

1. Use an indicator before stating the point.
   "This is the *most important* point I want to share with you . . ."
   "The following idea stands out above all the rest . . ."
   "If you don't understand anything else I have to say, pay attention to this . . ."

2. Use an indicator after stating the point.
   "Now, let me indicate what that point means."

   "This may sound confusing or complex, so let me explain it to you."
   "Notice what I just said."

3. Repeat a point once. This is not a paraphrase. Say the point in exactly the same way twice. More than twice may have a negative effect. Too much of anything can have a negative effect!

Delivery

Delivery, too, can be used to emphasize important points. The first part of the discussion of delivery relates to the three methods of emphasis outlined above. The second part refers to how information from our audience analysis can help determine our approach to delivery.

Two other methods that can be used to emphasize important points utilize delivery techniques. Although not so effective as the first three, they work, and they offer valuable alternatives. The methods are labeled 4 and 5 to indicate their relationship to the three methods previously listed.

4. Speaking slowly can be effective. Here, it is the change in speed of delivery or change in the mood that grasps the attention of the audience and makes the point.

5. Using a pause and a gesture can drive a point home. The timing of the pause and gesture must be accurate. The pause, if you are emphasizing a single word, should occur just before stating the word, and the gesture should occur immediately and exactly with the word: "I want you to notice the [pause] *power* of a strong gesture."[12]

The need for emphasis can often be determined from audience analysis. Being able to use our audience analysis to help determine our approach to delivery is important. Effective delivery reveals action. Activity holds attention. The monotonous speaker who stands rigidly and passively behind a lectern is unlikely to move his or her audience unless the movement is from alertness to sleep. But the exact approach must be tied *to the message.* For example, a speech on automobile deaths should not be delivered in a cheerful, happy, carefree manner. In tying a speech to the situation, one must realize that mood can be determined by events that have gone on before, are going on now, or are planned after the speech. Mood can also be determined by audience expectations. What *should* occur? There is a different mood at a pep rally than at a graduation ceremony, at church than in the classroom. In tying a speech to the audience, you must realize that the audience's age and knowledge background may help determine your delivery approach. The size of the audience may also be significant: Think of the difference between a mass lecture and a seminar of eight students. In tying a speech *to yourself,* make certain your delivery is natural and comfortable. Do not try to be someone you are not; the speech will be strained, unnatural, affected, or even appear false. An effective speech reveals sincerity and concern on the part of the speaker.

TRY THIS 6

What delivery considerations should be made regarding the message, situation, audience, and yourself in each of the following circumstances? Make whatever judgments you wish about the specifics in each instance:

1. A quiz-show emcee
2. An after-dinner speech
3. A classroom lecture
4. A congratulatory speech
5. A graduation ceremony
6. A church or synagogue
7. An awards or honor banquet
8. A funeral
9. A protest march
10. A rock festival (or disco emcee)
11. An announcer at a major sports event

HOW DO YOU KNOW IF YOU
HAVE BEEN SUCCESSFUL?

Think about this question. In *anything* you do, how do you know if you have been successful? You have a gut feeling? That's one way. Other people tell you? That is a second way. You might survey the audience—a third way. Or, if you are asking for action, you may observe to see if the action is taken.

One problem with knowing whether or not you have been successful is that a speech can have short-term and long-range results. Although a speaker may be successful in gaining immediate results, several things may occur as the listener gains greater and greater distance from the speech. The audience members may reassess their position and, perhaps, change it. They may talk to others, who might cause them to accept or reject what they have heard. Or, they may become totally apathetic—although they were excited by the spirit and emotion of the moment, they could become unresponsive and even lackadaisical as the distance from the speech increases.

Immediate results are easier to assess than long-range ones. We hope for long-range effectiveness, but it is never guaranteed and cannot effectively be measured. As distance from the speech increases, the person interested in determining the effectiveness of the speech cannot know what other factors—besides the speech itself—have caused the results. In other words, intervening variables contaminate the results. That is why researchers must be more concerned about immediate outcomes—the here-and-now. Here-and-now results can be measured.

Despite the concern for immediate results, speakers *can* help make the long-range impression more memorable. They must, however, make an impression. One way such an impression can be made is through effective language. Language that stirs up images remains in the listeners' minds longer than language that does not. Effective examples and illustrations make an impression. Those that touch the lives of listeners will be remembered better and longer than those further removed or more abstract. An impression can also be made through effective coverage. Speakers who cover a few points well will be remembered better than those who are too broad, general, or diffuse. Effective delivery is still another technique. Speakers who demonstrate a strong, passionate commitment to ideas are remembered better than those who appear removed, aloof, unconvinced, or uninvolved.

These same characteristics help gain successful immediate results. If you have observed audience reactions, the responses can be a key to determining your success. These audience responses can result in a good gut reaction after the speech is over. The audience nodded or frowned appropriately. They clapped or cheered or laughed at appropriate points. They were alert, involved, aroused, and concerned.

A question-and-answer period after the speech can reveal if everyone really understood your message and if they support your views. If this is not feasible, you can talk informally to members of the audience at the end of your speech. One speaker always made sure his wife was in the audience. Because she could be honest (diplomatic?), she shared with him her reactions and her perceptions of other audience members. One time she said to her husband, "Did you notice Mr. _____ while you were talking? He kept squirming around in his chair hardly able to listen to you." To have someone in your audience who will provide honest feedback and reactions is helpful, but of course not always possible.

Besides asking a few audience members directly, "How did you like the speech?" or "Did you see what I was driving at?" the speaker can, if results are absolutely essential, have the chairperson hand out a survey or questionnaire at some later time to get specific reactions. He or she could also interview members of the audience. One other gauge of success can be whether or not you are asked to speak before this organization again. Successful speakers—those who are not only skillful but well-liked—are in short supply, and many organizations in a community often depend on several speakers who become known for their speaking skills.

However, the question, "How do you know if you have been effective?" cannot be answered solely on the basis of content or effect processes. Another important aspect of postcommunication analysis is applying the results to become a better speaker. After every communication experience, you should ask yourself:

- What did I do in the speaking situation?
- How did the audience respond?
- What should I have done?
- How would I change it in light of the results of performance?
- What can I do now to improve the analysis and speaking process?

The last three questions are the most important, for it is through your answers to these that real learning takes place.

It is easy to become so involved in or so close to a performance that objective analysis and evaluation is difficult or impossible. But objective analysis and evaluation is the basis for growth, change, and development, and personal insight often offers an important starting point. You must attempt to detach yourself from your effort enough so that your accomplishment can be viewed thoroughly and honestly. You might, for example, use the "Listening to a Speech" questionnaire from the last chapter (pp. 64–65) as a beginning point for generating relevant questions on your own performance. It is often useful to write down responses soon after the experience—the sooner the better—so that ideas and suggestions are specific and are not forgotten. Maintaining a "speech file" or log may be beneficial in that all this material can be kept together to be referred to before each succeeding speech effort.

No one but you knows how important or how difficult something you have undertaken is to you. Although success is often determined by other people and their reactions to you or your effort, sometimes the most important successes are internal—as when you tell yourself, "I did it!" To have some record of these successes—especially how and why you succeeded—can be a useful personal teaching technique that will offer valuable instruction on which you can build.

SUMMARY

We approach audiences differently, just as we approach other individuals differently. We do this to make sure that the message we intend is the message they get. The better adapted the message, the more likely we are to be successful.

In this chapter, four questions have been presented and then answered: (1) What do we want to analyze? (2) How do we do it? (3) What do we do with the information we get? (4) How do we know if we've been successful? In answering each question, specific factors were offered. The main point is that the more we know in advance, the better prepared we can be. Speakers need all the information they can get.

Not to be concerned about the audience is to be like the teacher who prepares a lecture and will give it to anyone who shows up—or even if no one shows up! Why should the teacher thus waste her time or the time of her audience members? Effective speech must involve the identities of those communicating. Such communication is based on a transaction—a dynamic *interaction* between speaker, audience, message, and situation. It is the same as an artistic masterpiece, which is an interaction between the artist, the idea represented, the means used to represent the idea (the medium), and the viewer. Music and dance are similar. But speakers are the controlling element in public communication, and much of the success of accomplishing this interaction rests with them and their ability both to analyze the audience and to make effective use of the information they discover.

NOTES

[1]For a more extensive treatment of audience analysis, see Paul D. Holtzman, *The Psychology of Speakers' Audiences* (Glenview, Ill.: Scott, Foresman, 1970); Theodore Clevenger, *Audience Analysis* (Indianapolis: Bobbs-Merrill, 1966); and James W. Gibson and Michael S. Hanna, *Audience Analysis: A Programmed Approach to Receiver Behavior* (Englewood Cliffs, N.J.: Prentice-Hall, 1976).

[2]To see how predictable life stages are and the various values and interests attached to each, from twenty years of age to fifty, see Gail Sheehy, *Passages: Predictable Crisis of Adult Life* (New York: Bantam Books, 1976).

[3]Lane Cooper, trans, *The Rhetoric of Aristotle* (New York: Prentice-Hall, 1960), p. 136. Copyright © 1932, renewed 1960. Reprinted by permission of Prentice-Hall, Inc. The brackets are Cooper's.

[4]See Michael D. Hazen and Sara B. Kiesler, "Communication Strategies Affected by Audience Opposition, Feedback and Persuasibility," *Speech Monographs* 42 (March 1975): 57. After reviewing the ways speakers react to audience opposition, the researchers conclude that the "audience's initial opposition to the communicator's position will be an important factor in determining his strategy."

[5]See Alice H. Eagly and Melvin Manis, "Evaluation of Message and Communicator as a Function of Involvement," *Journal of Personality and Social Psychology*, 3 (April 1966): 483–485; Jonathan L. Freeman, "Involvement Discrepancy and Change," *Journal of Abnormal and Social Psychology*, 69 (September 1964): 290–295; and Joe Ayres, "Observers' Judgments of Audience Members' Attitudes," *Western Speech*, 39 (Winter 1975): 40–50.

[6]*U.S. News & World Reports*, March 22, 1982, p. 16.

[7]*Newsweek*, May 14, 1979, p. 112.

[8]Robert Hopper, *Human Message Systems* (New York: Harper & Row, Pub., 1976), p. 216.

[9]There is a great deal of experimental literature that deals with the effects of group affiliation on individual attitudes. A review of relevant research can be found in Daryl J. Bem, *Beliefs, Attitudes, and Human Affairs* (Belmont, Calif.: Brooks/Cole, 1970), Chapter 7, pp. 70–100.

[10]See Jon Eisenson, J. Jeffery Auer, and John V. Irwin, *The Psychology of Communication* (New York: Appleton-Century-Crofts, 1963). The authors present a summary of research studies and their applications to the speech-building process; see "Psychology of Public Address," pp. 271–309.

[11]See James W. Gibson, "Creativity: The Cornerstone of Speech," in James W. Gibson, ed., *A Reader in Speech Communication* (New York: McGraw-Hill, 1971), p. 166. Also in Richard L. Weaver, II, ed. *Speech/Communication: A Reader* 2nd ed. (San Diego: Collegiate Publishing, 1979), p. 228.

[12]See Ray Ehrensberger, "An Experimental Study of the Relative Effects of Certain Forms of Emphasis in Public Speaking," *Speech Monographs,* 12 (1945): 94–111.

IDENTIFYING APPROPRIATE MATERIAL

Speech Support

Today, anyone can talk on just about anything—as they often do!—and sound fairly knowledgeable. A great deal of information is readily accessible from newspapers, from weekly and monthly news magazines, and of course from radio and television. We are a society generally well informed on most current issues. But this amount of information is quite insufficient when it comes to developing an idea in anything more than a superficial manner; that is, although we can talk about almost anything, our knowledge runs out very quickly. We have, in general, a superficial knowledge, barely able to skim the surface. Public communication requires more knowledge—i.e., substance—than this. We are experts in so few areas that we will have to add considerably to our rather meager information reserves if we are to sound credible to others and have some effect.

As a communicator, you will be judged by audience members on how much you know. A person an audience considers credible—worthy of being listened to—is one who appears to know what he or she is talking about.[1] Speech support is anything your listeners accept as proof. The problem for many speakers, especially youthful ones, is that their youth is a dead giveaway. "Youth" refers to physical age, not outlook. Although credibility that is tied to physical maturity depends on context, often those in their late teens and early twenties experience lack of credibility *because of* their youth. Whether or not you have information, whether or not you are an expert, and whether or not you have something significant to contribute, when an audience notices how young you are, members of that audience are likely to classify you as a person who has little experience, little maturity, and insufficient background, continuity, or perspective. And the conclusion they *can* arrive at is that because of your youth you probably do not know what you are talking about!

Knowing this in advance, we, as speakers, must take quick and effective action to counter such impressions. We can! There are measures we can take that will help us to be taken seriously, that will help us establish expertise, and that will help us make certain that the impression we make on our audience will be strong and memorable. The suggestions are not easy ones; that is, they are not shortcuts. We cannot expect to destroy such impressions as a natural outcome of a situation. It requires work and effort on our part. Nobody says that effective public communication is easy, least of all this author. Too many people equate public communication with a naturally glib individual—a person whose speech is marked by ease and informality and whose content shows little forethought or preparation. A glib person is often characterized as slick, smooth, and superficial. Concerned communicators must strive for more depth and substance. This chapter, more than any other in this book, should help sever this common—but misinformed—relationship between effective public communication and glibness.

In this chapter, the structure of arguments is first discussed. Then three types of speech support will be examined: (1) logical support that derives from the speaker's use of evidence and organizing ability, (2) emotional support that derives from the speaker's use of motivational appeals, and (3) personal support that derives from the speaker's character or credibility. These three types of speech support are most always used in conjunction with each other. Effective speeches usually have either an obvious or implied logical basis.

The material in this chapter rests for its effectiveness on the decisions made as one engages in audience analysis. That is, logical and emotional appeals are not selected for their own sake; the choices are made with reference to the audience, the speaker, the message, and the occasion. We must not lose sight of the interactive nature of the entire communication event.

THE STRUCTURE OF ARGUMENTS

Before discussing logical support, the reader should understand how logical support fits into the structure of an argument.[2] Stephen Toulmin, a British philosopher, in his book *The Uses of Argument,* describes a model of reasoning that emphasizes a logical relationship between the specific evidence one gathers for a speech effort and the conclusions one draws from that evidence.[3] Toulmin labels the evidence *data* and the conclusions drawn from it *claims.*

$$\text{data} \longrightarrow \text{claim}$$

Toulmin also suggests that the data and claim are connected by the *warrant*—the reason why the claim follows from the data.

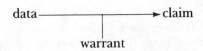

An example will help show how this model of reasoning works thus far. A claim might be made that people need to exercise. The data for that claim would be the numerous reports we can find to suggest that regular exercise is essential to living a healthy, vigorous life. The warrant for this line of reasoning, usually unstated, might be, "People do not think they have the time to exercise," or "People do not know what kind of exercise will benefit them most." Putting this information into the form suggested in the figure above, it would appear like this:

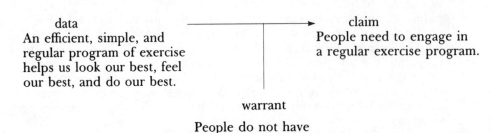

data	claim
An efficient, simple, and regular program of exercise helps us look our best, feel our best, and do our best.	People need to engage in a regular exercise program.

warrant

People do not have
the time to exercise.
or
People do not know
what kind of exercise
will benefit them the
most.

In addition, Toulmin says that a *qualifier* often intervenes between the data and the claim—after the warrant. Qualifiers are simply statements regarding the degree of probability inherent in the claim. To ask, "What is the likelihood people accept the need to engage in regular physical exercise?" is like asking what is the likelihood it will be sunny tomorrow: Remotely possible? Possible? Fairly probable? Highly probable? Virtually certain? In other words, we might rephrase our example to read, "Since an efficient, simple, and regular exercise program helps us to look our best, feel our best, and do our best (data), people will probably (qualifier) see the need to engage in regular physical exercise."

TRY THIS 1

Using the following claims, develop data, warrants, and qualifiers that would be appropriate:

1. The professors at this university are excellent teachers.
2. Bicycles offer the most reasonable alternative to gas-powered vehicles.
3. Violence on television has a direct effect on children.

4. Our values result from the mediated environment in which we live.
5. Students should be given more options for fulfilling basic, required university sequences.
6. Recent trends in music make the music of today more relevant and appealing than that in previous times.
7. Romance novels cater to a special kind of personality.
8. Students of today are lazy and apathetic.
9. Television offers viewers a subjective window on the world.
10. Courses should be taught without textbooks.

But people are likely to see the need only *if* something else occurs—and this "if" Toulmin labels the *reservation*—recognition of possible extenuating circumstances or exceptional contexts in which the claim may not apply: *if* they can be shown that regular exercise does not take much time, or if they are shown some simple exercises they can use regularly. Now Toulmin's model looks like this:

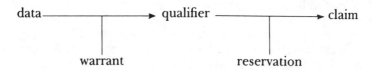

We can apply several essential tests to an argument that is structured like the one above. First, we can ask if the data are true and sufficient in number. Second, we can ask if the warrant—the relationshp between the data and claim—is valid. Third, we can ask about the strength of the qualifier, and, finally, we can ask about the strength of the reservation.

Inaccurate data result in false conclusions. Biased or unrepresentative data may also result in false conclusions. Unacceptable conclusions can also result if the data come from questionable sources.

If the warrant is stated as a yes or no question and cannot be answered yes, then the conclusion is also likely to be false. For example, will knowing that there are exercises that do not take much time and that are simple enough for everyone (me) to understand, make the need to engage in regular exercise easier to accept? If the answer is yes, then the conclusion is warranted if the data are true and sufficient. But if the answer is no, then the conclusion is unacceptable even if the data are true and sufficient.

The qualifier, too, can be challenged. How likely are people to view your data as efficient and simple? How likely are people to see these ideas as beneficial to them? If the answer is a certain no—that these ideas would *not* benefit them—then they are unlikely to accept the need for exercise in their life. If it is likely that the efficient, simple, and regular exercise program you offer saves time—*and* they see it as helping them to look better, feel better, and do better—*then* they are more likely to accept it.

But they might also have reservations regarding the claim. "I get all the exercise I need," or "I'm still young—exercise is for when you get older," or "I lead a very active life; I'm really exercising all the time," might be some common reservations. Others might include, "I have high blood pressure," or "I have heart trouble," or "Everytime I exercise I get sick." You begin to see how reservations can affect your argument.

People could also have reservations about warrants. In our example, an audience member could say, "provided the exercises you suggest are efficient—simple to use," or "provided they really will benefit me." These "provideds" are reservations that tie into the warrants that people do not have the time or that they do not know what kind of exercise will benefit them.

Since reservations are likely to either negate the speaker's claim or seriously reduce the likelihood that it will be accepted, the speaker must be prepared to deal with them when addressing an audience. They can be mentioned and then refuted, or they can be ignored as being unlikely or insignificant. If the data are strong, they are likely to outweigh or counter the reservations audience members may have.

LOGICAL SUPPORT: DATA

Preparation for speechmaking involves the process of finding material, selecting various approaches for using that material, and appealing to the audience. Gathering information is part of this process. The need for engaging in this process is clear. People must be convinced to listen, encouraged to pay attention, assured before believing, and excited or stimulated before acting. The tendency of an audience member is to do nothing before doing something. That is, the rule of least possible effort takes effect if there is nothing present—no other stimulus—to animate, cheer, enhearten, fortify, invigorate, or even inform. This is the purpose of logical and emotional appeals: to arouse, energize, secure belief, or establish understanding.

Regarding the speaker's use of evidence—or data—the most common types will be discussed: facts, examples and illustrations, statistics, opinions, and personal experience.[4] Although it may appear that a certain kind of speech needs more of one kind of data than another—and this certainly may be true—a speech that holds attention is usually that one that depends on a variety of support. A long string of facts, examples and illustrations, statistics, or opinions becomes tedious and dull—boring. The insights shared in the last chapter regarding the concept of attention must not be forgotten.[5] We must have data, for they are the meat of speech communication, but evidence that does not hold attention serves no purpose.

Data, to be perceived as logical and credible, should be part of a larger matrix or background. Part of that background is bodily action—to be discussed in Chapter 9, "Using the Body." Bodily action is used to reinforce, complete, or even substitute for the thought. Vocal action, also to be discussed in Chapter 9, can also influence the thought. A speaker's loudness, quality, pitch, and pacing can influence the kind and degree of thought communicated. Language, to be discussed in Chapter 8, "Choosing the Language," is the primary carrier of thought and, as such, is extremely important. Even the speaker's personality and attitude, discussed in Chapter 11, "Styles of Presentation," can modify the thought. A speaker, too, must not forget the importance of the thought itself, a factor of paramount importance. Another part of the logical matrix has to do with organizing, and that will be discussed later in this chapter.

CONSIDER THIS

A message should be as clear as the precision of language can make it. It should also be as complete as the facts allow.

A basic rule of good communication is never to overestimate the amount of knowledge or information the person on the receiving end possesses. Specialists in various subjects usually are surprised to discover how little other people know—or care—about their fields.

A fine line exists, however, between completeness and superfluity. Too many details can turn off the listener's mind. While it is good to subtly repeat your points to make them understood, to repeat them too often and too obviously is to drive your listener off into a state of ennui.

People tend to talk at greater length than necessary. We might be wise to emulate the thinking of E. M. Forster when he was asked why he had not published a book in the 20 years since he wrote *A Passage to India*. "Well, I hadn't anything more to say," he replied.

SOURCE: From *The Monthly Letter* (January 1979), published by The Royal Bank of Canada.

Facts.   Facts are usually at the core of what we consider to be true. For example, we know that teeth can become decayed: fact. We also know that there is a cause-effect relationship between the amount of sugar consumed and tooth decay, and regularity of brushing the teeth and decay: two more facts. These are bits of truth we know to exist, and their expression can be checked against reality by consulting a dentist, talking to others (those with cavities and those without cavities), using our personal experience, and reading. These facts are well documented in available literature. Anything not disputable is a fact. From research along any or all the lines outlined above, we can prove these facts to be "not disputable." That is, they are pieces of information presented as having objective reality.

TRY THIS 2

Quickly cite as many *facts* as you can on any one of the following topics:

1. Campus rip-offs
2. Sex and violence on television
3. Dormitory food
4. Examination procedures

5. Current movie fare
6. Poorly presented textbooks
7. Campus parking problems
8. Lecturers in basic courses
9. Television programming for children
10. Required courses

A fact is something that has actual existence; that is, it is a piece of information that can be observed or sensed. People are likely to agree on facts because they can be checked.

But there is a difference between facts and inferences. Check your "facts" above to make certain they are not inferences. Inferences are conclusions, judgments, predictions, or interpretations. An inference involves a leap from a fact or group of facts into the unknown and unobserved. More than facts, inferences reflect the habits of thought, personal prejudices, training, and experience of the observer. Facts can be checked by further observation; inferences are more difficult to assess.[6]

Audiences believe us because we offer facts, because we call attention to facts they know to be true, or because of facts that are common knowledge—generally known to be true by all. In any event, facts are at the root of knowledge and belief. In a situation where our intent is to increase the audience's understanding, we simply wish to increase their reserve or repertoire of facts. In a situation where we want them to come to believe something or act on something, we cannot expect them to believe or act unless they have the facts. Examples of this are numerous:

> How could you expect an audience to believe that grades are bad unless they know (1) that grades are given (a fact), (2) that grades cause undue competition (a fact?), and (3) that grades are used to manipulate (a fact?)?
>
> How could you expect an audience to be more energy-conscious unless they were first convinced that there is an energy shortage (a fact?)? (But just being convinced that a shortage exists does not guarantee any perceivable behavior change, anyway.)
>
> How could you expect a university or college to abolish a physical education requirement unless it was proven that it serves *no* purpose (a fact?)?

There are few speeches, indeed, that do not depend on facts as part of the very foundation for gaining understanding, seeking belief, or obtaining action. They are basic and important building blocks.

Examples and Illustrations. Examples are instances or cases in point. A brief specific instance is known as an example; a longer, more detailed, or extended example told in narrative, storylike form is known as an illustration. The three examples above show how facts underlie belief and action. We use examples to clarify a point we have made, to make a point more direct or relevant to an audience, to show how an idea has been or could be put into practice, or to add interest because we know examples help hold audience attention.

If a speaker were talking on the topic of child abuse in the schools, he or she might cite the example reported in the Supreme Court case, *Ingraham* v. *Wright,* where a junior high school student in Florida was pinioned on a table by two assistant principals. While the assistant principals held the boy, the principal beat him more than twenty times with a wooden paddle. The resultant swelling became blood-filled and kept the student in bed, face down, for a week.[7] Although extreme, this example would fulfill all the reasons we gave above for using examples. Speakers must be careful, however, not to select sensational material.

TRY THIS 3

Cite as many personal examples as you can on any of the following topics:

1. Parental discipline that never stops
2. Teacher-student relationships that can be meaningful
3. The value of friendship
4. Accidents that are a learning experience
5. Traveling as education
6. The worth of formal religion
7. Junk food as a diet staple
8. Some of the harm that results from drugs or alcohol
9. What happens when students become irresponsible
10. The value of dreams

Sometimes examples are hypothetical. They are created by the speaker for a specific purpose. If you were talking about a new approach to a problem, it might be difficult to find examples. Under such circumstances the speaker might say, "Now let me show you what could occur if this proposal were adopted." In another instance the speaker might want to provide an example of what a person or thing with a variety of characteristics might look like. He or she could say, "Let's see what a profile of a typical criminal looks like. He is an unskilled male, sixteen to twenty-five years old, poorly educated, from a disadvantaged social class, and severely maladjusted." The speaker could continue by portraying the typical social and cultural characteristics of the neighborhood where this hypothetical person lives.

Illustrations are stories of facts and events. An illustration is a little story within a larger one—the speech as a whole. Illustrations depend on three things for their effectiveness: (1) clearness of the thought, (2) intensity of the emotion, and (3) vividness of the language. They are effective because they portray real people in real situations. Sometimes when an illustration is used, a hush comes over the audience. A speaker talking on hazing achieved such a hush when he used the illustration of John Davies, a University of Nevada at Reno student, who died after a three-day initiation into the Sundowners, an off-campus group.

The speaker was talking about the moral responsibility involved in such situations, and he said that the Washoe County grand jury found the Sundowners Club "morally responsible" for the death of Davies. The speaker quoted the grand jury report that these club members "somehow . . . brought out the worst animal instincts in themselves, becoming unthinking, irrational, and lacking in regard for the law."

To further illustrate his point, the speaker read from the grand jury's report that detailed the three-day initiation spree:

> Five initiates, including Mr. Davies, consumed the following: 16 gallons of wine, 6 quarts of tequila, 4 quarts of gin, 4 quarts of bourbon, 2 quarts of liquor, and 1 bottle of 190-proof Everclear—a preparation used to treat acne.[8]

Examples and illustrations have potential as powerful means of support and are an effective way of making things clear.

Statistics.   Another kind of data that summarizes large bodies of information effectively and concisely is statistics.[9] These are numerical representations of groups of examples or facts. Statistics are powerful because:

1. Numbers carry weight (people respect statistical evidence).
2. To be able to cite statistics adds to the speaker's credibility. (People with numbers at their fingertips are generally highly regarded).
3. They condense much information into a brief space. (People are impressed by the conciseness of a number: what it says.)

TRY THIS 4

Discover at least one statistic on five of the following topics:

1. Traffic fatalities
2. Cheating in college
3. Telephone usage
4. Mass transit
5. Suicide rates
6. Organized religion
7. Grade inflation
8. Overweight people
9. Use of national parks
10. Inflation

Where does a speaker find statistics? Besides the obvious sources of newspapers, news magazines, radio, and television, a speaker might also consult:

Information Please Almanac (1947 to date)
Statistical Abstract of the United States (1878 to date)
World Almanac, and Book of Facts (1868 to date)
Facts on File (1940 to date)

But statistics have another side that is less obvious to many speakers. Although there is magic in numbers, there is also dullness. They must be used sparingly to be effective. Numbers have the capacity to turn off an audience. They are hard to conceptualize. To use a statistic effectively it should be compared with something the audience can visualize. A number will not stand alone. For example, if a speaker simply reported that we, as a nation, produce more than 143 millions tons of household, commercial, and institutional garbage per year, what would that number convey to the audience? Is it impressive? Perhaps, but most people can hardly conceptualize 143 million tons. Even if they were told that we produce more garbage per year than steel (about 126 million tons), it still would not be impressive. But if they knew that we produce enough garbage in a year to fill the New Orleans Superdome from floor to ceiling twice a day, including weekends and holidays, for a full year, they would not only be able to picture this immense quantity, but, better yet, they would have a way to remember it.

A large manufacturing firm advertises that if the cases of ready-to-spread frosting mix they produce in one day were stacked one on top of the other, the pile would be 4,050 feet high. Since it is difficult to conceptualize a pile that high, they add, "This is eight times as high as the Washington Monument."

One other suggestion for using statistics: They should be integrated with other material. Just as historical material can become dull if followed by more historical material, numerous statistics do not wear well on an audience. The beginning speaker should be careful of using material that could bore an audience; he or she needs every possible positive advantage.

But the benefits of statistics should not be underestimated. It is impractical—impossible—to cite every example; better to condense them. For example, a speaker was talking about the fifth most popular sport enjoyed by teenagers—roller skating. She said that more than 28 million people roller skate, that 73 percent of those skaters are under 18, and that 44 percent of all skaters have been skating three years or less, making the point that it is a rapidly growing sport. Her statistics condensed numerous examples into an easily communicated and effective message. Since she was a skater herself, she followed these statistics with personal experience.

Opinions. Opinions are views, judgments, or appraisals about facts, events, or beliefs. A speaker on "Child Abuse in the Schools" might cite three different opinions. When referring to the Supreme Court decision that ruled that corporal punishment in the schools, no matter how severe, does not violate the Eighth Amendment ("cruel and unusual punishment")—a fact—the speaker might cite a *New York Times* editorial:

There is no doubt that corporal punishment is a traditional tool in our culture's education system. But teachers are not in fact reliable instruments of justice. In both theory and practice, therefore, most paddling is an abomination of custom.

The speaker might cite a social psychologist who testified at a Toronto Board of Education hearing on corporal punishment:

> . . . the probability that either an ill teacher or an ill child or both will be involved in an instance of corporal punishment is simply too high to allow it to go on at all.

Dr. Moisy Shopper, a professor of child psychology at St. Louis University School of Medicine, might also be quoted on this topic. He said:

> . . . the same degree of violence that may be bearable for one child can be traumatic for another. But how many teachers and principals know— let alone think about—the specific emotional state of each child being beaten?[10]

The first opinion might be labeled *editorial opinion;* the second *testimony,* since it was given under oath; and the third *expert opinion,* since the person making the statement is an expert.[11] Obviously, the different types—especially the second and third types in this instance—could be combined. That is, an expert could give his or her opinion under oath. *Opinion* is often defined simply as the formal expression by an expert of his or her judgment or advice.

Public opinion results from polling or sampling. A speaker on attitudes toward aging, for example, might state—contrary to youth's impression that the older one gets the more dissatisfied with life one becomes—that in a study at San Diego State University, psychologists found that "older subjects rated their lives as better than younger subjects projected their lives would be at the same age."

Public opinion could be reported on the front runner in a political race, on attitudes toward nuclear power, on inflation, on government infringement of private rights, on morals, on the high cost of higher education, or on almost anything else. Warrants—or the general beliefs listeners hold to be true—can sometimes be determined through public-opinion polls. If available, and if it supports your particular stand, public opinion is valuable because it summarizes attitudes effectively and concisely. But this does not rule out its use when it is contrary to your stand, although it requires a substantial effort by the speaker to prove that, despite public opinion, the speaker's position is actually true or better.

Personal Experience. Personal experience is an excellent source of information. In fact, whatever your topic, you should first discover how much you already know on the topic. Go nowhere and do nothing (as far as discovering source material) until you have plumbed the depths of your own knowledge and background.

But before relying too heavily on this kind of evidence alone, you should recognize some basic disadvantages. As an attention-getter or attention-holder it is effective, but it has two major weaknesses.

First, if you appear young and inexperienced, people may doubt or question your experience. Often, as speakers we simply need more credibility—thus, more substantial information. Personal experience is not weighty nor does it have what might be labeled substantive content. Second, one example or even two may be an exception or exceptions to the rule. That is one reason statistics are so powerful: one number can represent so many cases. The point is, simply, that just because you see two Indians walking in single file does not mean all Indians walk in single file! A personal experience simply carries little logical weight when you are trying to prove something or make a point. Although its emotional weight may be substantial, when making a very important argument it would be wise to seek sources other than, or in addition to, yourself.

CONSIDER THIS

I was amazed—not because of the outburst (these students have their little fits of pique several times a period) but because of the statement: "I don't understand." I was amazed because these students know and understand everything. They understand that *all* teachers are stupid; that *all* classwork is a bore; that *all* assignments are difficult and meaningless; and that the entire educational process is nothing more than a fiendish plot to curb their "free spirits." Up to the moment of this outburst, they had indicated that they knew all the answers to everything. Unfortunately, however, they had never bothered to learn any of the questions.

SOURCE: J. A. Christensen, "The Value of Silence," *Media & Methods,* 15 (January 1979), 27.

The question that grows out of the first major weakness is, "Who are you to say this?" or "Who are you to make this point?" "What is your expertise?" We rely on experts because they are in a position to make an educated judgment. Are you? They have the background and knowledge to put their observations into proper context. Do you? Also, they are relied upon by others to make observations. Credible sources often become credible just because they are readily cited or depended on. Are you?

The point here is not to discourage you from using personal experience, but simply to put it in proper perspective. Such experiences have their place and their value, but they are, perhaps, one of the weakest types of evidence for logically convincing an audience of something. They depend heavily on your own credibility—or how the audience views you.

Most young speakers have had relatively little experience. The older they get, however, the more experience they gain. Some of the most interesting people to listen to are those who have accumulated a vast storehouse of experience. This is, in a sense, a plea for broadening your horizons. It is not difficult to do, but it does take initiative and dedication. *You must want to experience more.* You must energize yourself to move in new directions:

1. Look for new activities.
2. Strive to see familiar things in new ways.
3. Volunteer to take part in new enterprises.
4. Read more and listen better.
5. Strive for more depth and thoroughness—a deeper understanding—of the events you experience.

The use of personal experience may also be a mode of logical support. Although students should be encouraged to rely on their own experience in developing speeches, they should understand that "personal experience" does not parallel and is not discrete from the other categories of logical support. That is, from their personal experience, they may adduce statistics, examples, facts, and opinions to support claims. Personal experience as a category may encompass any of the other categories in this section—depending on how it is used. Its mention here as a discrete category, however, is simply to emphasize its importance and the possibilities for its use.

One note of warning is in order about the use of data. When data are derived from sources other than yourself, a responsible, ethical communicator cites the source. Citing sources when appropriate also adds to a speaker's credibility. Not to cite the source of borrowed ideas is known as *plagiarism,* and it is a factor in public communication. To pass off the ideas or words of another person as your own—without crediting the source—is literary theft, plagiarism. Most plagiarism comes about when the lazy, unimaginative, hard-pressed, or desperate speaker takes another person's speech or adapts a magazine article and then reads it as if it were his or her own. Such dishonest performances cannot be condoned.

EMOTIONAL CONSIDERATIONS

It is impossible to plant an idea in the mind of another person. Simply providing data is also insufficient to win listeners to our point of view.[12] Rather, we must get them to identify with our idea—that is, we must make our idea emotionally attractive to them.[13] This is a common approach. We see it used everyday in commerical advertising. Because advertisers depend heavily on emotional appeals, they use music, attractive models, jingles and slogans, color, personal appeals, and sex—to name but a few of their techniques.

CONSIDER THIS

Ad agencies generally use a transportation theory of communications. They are trying to get information across to people, to sink it into their brains. And they use research to measure what they have implanted in a person's mind. What ad agencies seek to measure after they have produced a commercial, I need to know, in my commercial work, before I start. I do not care what number of people *remember* or *get* the message. I am concerned with how people are affected by the stimuli.

To suggest to speakers that they model their approach or appeal on advertising would be an error. Many advertisers have little or no logical basis for their appeals. It is important for speakers to offer strong, logical support to undergird emotional appeals. An emotional appeal with no logical basis is like a tree full of leaves with no branches or trunk. Logic provides the trunk and branches—the support and system the leaves need.

As early as 1943 Abraham Maslow provided a list of common human needs.[14] It is the appeal to these needs that makes a message relevant. Such appeals tie a message directly to them, cause them to identify with it, and make it fit. Needs are the underpinnings for warrants. That is, general beliefs are often framed as a result of basic needs. Maslow's list provides those kinds of needs or values to which most individuals respond most of the time. These response patterns are general tendencies; that is, most people respond in roughly similar fashion but not identically. They give the speaker a guide for thinking about, planning for, and, finally, appealing to audiences. The primary needs in Maslow's list, indicated by the numbers in the following list, are arranged in a hierarchy beginning with the most basic ones.

CATALOG OF NEEDS

1. Physiological
   a. hunger
   b. thirst
   c. health maintenance
   d. sex gratification
2. Security
   a. freedom from physical danger
   b. avoidance of emotional disturbance
   c. protection from environmental dangers (heat, cold, aridity)
3. Belongingness and love
   a. sense of family or group cohesiveness
   b. love of mate
   c. acceptance by others
4. Esteem
   a. having the respect and admiration of others
   b. exercising power and influence
   c. acquiring self-respect by advancement and effort
5. Self-actualization
   a. full development of capabilities and ambitions
   b. freedom of opportunity for growth[15]

Take a moment to find out which of these needs are most important to *you* (personally) right now. Answer the following questions with respect to Maslow's "Catalog of Needs":

1. Which of the five categories bears most directly on your life at the present moment? That is, which one seems to be the area that currently directs your motivations or energies?
2. Which of the five categories do you feel holds the most importance for you over your lifetime? Which do you hope to fulfill before your life is over?
3. Do you think your responses are similar to those of other people of your age?
4. Are there changes in the needs you consider to be important?
   —from hour to hour?
   —from week to week?
   —from month to month?
   —from year to year?

Maslow's hierarchy of needs indicates that in general people are first concerned about physiological and security needs. Once these are satisfied or fulfilled, people turn their attention to love and belonging, esteem, and self-actualization needs. People have priorities. In most cases, self-actualization—although an important need—would not take priority over the other four needs on the list. It is the first to be released as a need, or put aside, when any of the more basic needs have not been satisfactorily met or fulfilled.

Notice, too, that these are generalities. All people do not necessarily respond in the same way. However, it is amazing how similar human behavior is. Generalizations such as those above help us to understand why people behave, respond, or believe as they do. Accepting this catalog of needs as a series of generalizations, while recognizing that there are exceptions, will help us maintain proper perspective.

The important thing here is not the list of needs but how it can be used. As a speaker attempting to have some impact on an audience, I would want to know how this list could make a difference in my presentation. First, and most important, use of the list calls for audience analysis. A speaker must first know something about the specific audience. It would be fruitless to try to claim that listeners need better health care (maintenance of health—a physiological need) if they felt theirs was very satisfactory. Second, use of the list depends on the topic one wishes to speak on. It might be irrelevant and a waste of time to appeal to either physiological or security needs when one wants to focus on the need for love and belonging and how the erosion of the family is affecting or denying the fulfillment of this need. The speaker might cite the number of unmarried couples living together, women in their early twenties who have never married, households consisting of people living alone, and marriages that end in divorce as proof for the erosion of the family.

A claim about the lack of relevance of education could be developed by using either esteem or self-actualization needs or both. Under esteem needs, the speaker could show how knowledge generates respect and admiration from others. Gaining respect and admiration might be a sufficient warrant. It could also be shown how most people in positions of power and influence have strong educational backgrounds. Education encourages achievement and effort that results in the acquisition of self-respect. Self-respect, too, could be a sufficient warrant. To prove the lack of relevance the speaker would demonstrate how education no longer meets these esteem needs. The speaker could also argue that education lacks relevance because it does not fulfill self-actualization needs: It fails to encourage the development of capabilities and ambitions or to stimulate growth. A combination of these approaches (esteem *and* self-actualization) might also be strong.

If, indeed, these are the needs that cause people to think, believe, or act in specific ways, it is unwise to plan, develop, and deliver messages that fail to utilize this information. Just as we expect and prefer professors to adapt their class and approach to the students—even though some do not relate their material to the needs of students—we must attempt to do the same.

TRY THIS 6

Examine the following list of topics and briefly explain which category of human needs you would use with each topic to appeal to a group of students like yourself:

1. Implementing a rigorous personal exercise program
2. Demonstrating characteristics of the successful business person
3. Revealing the demands of getting along with others (a mate or roommate)
4. Living on the top of a mountain
5. Becoming more assertive
6. Benefiting from traveling
7. Acquiring dates
8. Beginning a new diet
9. Learning how to relax—to relieve tension
10. Trying everything once

Maslow's hierarchy of needs reminds us that audience needs must be in the forefront of our minds as we prepare all aspects of a speech. It neither dictates approaches nor offers arguments; it does provide a framework for determining needs that may be appealed to in a speech. It offers the underpinnings for any consideration of warrants. The hierarchy also helps us understand why a speech that is successful with one audience can fail miserably with another. Warrants not only differ, they also change. For example, a student speech on quality craftsmanship that stimulated students to take pride in their creative endeavors might be well received at 10:00 A.M. or 2:00 P.M., but be poorly received just before noon or dinner when students are hungry and tired—when some of their more primary physiological needs are unsatisfied. In some cases the speaker has little or no control over physiological needs.

The hierarchy also suggests alternatives. Sometimes a speech we intend to give will conflict with an already present need. Imagine trying to claim that audience members should change their majors to realize the full development of their capabilities and ambitions (warrants) to listeners who felt that such a change would result in extreme emotional disturbance (loss of security) or loss of respect from their family (loss of esteem). One would have to counter these losses with strong data—evidence and arguments—while realizing, of course, the high probability of failure. The speaker could admit the possibility of some slight emotional disturbance but minimize it and show how easily it can be overcome. An appeal to the need for esteem could be handled in much the same way: The speaker could show how acquiring self-respect is more important than family, and how familial respect would quickly return once family members realized that the change of the major was definitely wise. Such basic analysis is necessary to make an effective speech. It is so easy to push it aside, believing it is not important or figuring the end product is not worth the effort—and then wondering why a speech failed to appeal to an audience.

To help make motivational appeals more accessible and attractive, we will briefly examine some motives for action and indicate the kinds of audience analysis that can be done prior to a speech. It is assumed, at this point, that the speaker has a proposition—a specific claim—and knows why listeners should accept it—sufficient warrants.

Although this list of motives is brief and incomplete, it includes some of the most powerful reasons why people do what they do. They will increase their understanding, believe, or act if doing so in some way affects their wealth or power, if it makes them more a part of a group, if it is something they can use, if it brings them pleasure, or significantly adds to their knowledge.

Wealth. People generally want to make and save money. This motive grows out of the esteem need. The greater the wealth, it is felt, the greater the esteem. Does your proposition relate to wealth or to material goods? Can it help listeners gain money, save money, or get more for what they have? Since time often relates directly to money ("time is money"), a saving of time may save money; thus, relating a proposition or proposal to the time factor may relate to wealth. Notice how one speaker works in an appeal to our interest in money:

> Another example of the extent to which we have moved away from a free society is the 40 percent of our earnings, on the average, which is co-opted by the government. Each and every one of us works from the first of January to late in April or May, in order to pay governmental expenses, before we can start to work for our own expenses.[16]

Power. This is also an esteem need. It is egoistic in that it relates to individual self-interest. Does your proposition affect the independence, achievement, recognition, self-regard, or dominance of audience members? For many people, their personal worth is dependent on having power over their own destiny, or having power over others. It is important, too, that such power be recognized.

If the speaker's proposal will diminish or take power away from the listener, some form of compensation must be offered. Since power is a strong motivator, audience members will turn away from a proposal that suggests a possibility of reduced power. A substitute for the lost power must be offered to motivate the audience.

Notice the appeal to power that this speaker makes in talking to fathers at an Ohio Chamber of Commerce meeting:

> Dad must be awesome if he's going to preserve what he's been working for all these years. The dad who comes home drunk from the bar or country club may be a little frightening, but he'll never be awesome. The dad who boasts about how he outwitted the Highway Patrol or cheated on his income tax will have a hard time making any mileage. Dad must be an awesome thing. Dad must be something to push against, not a feather pillow.[17]

Conformity. Belongingness and the need for love are strong sources of motivation. People need to be liked, to be part of the group, to fit in. Comfort and security results from belonging to a group. Conformity is the basis for the propaganda technique known as "the bandwagon"—when a speaker demonstrates or asserts that everyone is doing it and therefore they too should. Children reveal their effectiveness with this technique when they tell their mother, "Everyone else has one," or "All the kids are going." Will your proposition cause audience members to be better liked? Will they become part of a group by supporting your ideas?

A former President added two sentences to a speech he gave that reflects this desire for conformity: "We have lost faith in joint efforts and mutual sacrifices. Because of the divisions in our country many of us cannot remember a time when we really felt united."[18]

Practicality. Is your proposition useful? Will it help your listeners in some way? This category relates to all levels in Maslow's hierarchy. Listeners must be able to see how your suggestions can be put to use. They want to know that your proposal will help them gain sexual gratification, avoid physical danger, be accepted, achieve admiration, or acquire their dream. How-to books in all fields have gained wide and ongoing acceptance because of their practicality. Strive to make your proposition clearly and directly address the audience's questions, "So what?" "So what can *I* do about it?" "So what does it have to do with me? Does it have economic value? Does it involve ownership? Will it make my work easier?"

Notice how one speaker appealed to listeners' sense of the practical:

To be alive is not merely to exist. All people exist; but few really live. A living man is one imbued with a spiritual vitality channeled towards the really meaningful aspects of life. Thus it seems fitting to make a humble plea that you might never forget one who not merely existed; but lived.[19]

Pleasure.   Given a choice, a person will pursue a course of action that results in pleasure, happiness, or enjoyment. Pleasure, too, can relate to any of the major needs in the hierarchy. If you can relate your proposition to anything that will give your listeners pleasure, you are more likely to gain acceptance. Pleasure also comes from that which is considered playful. Listeners may respond favorably if your suggestion offers a new experience, activity, or adventure.

In a strong speech that attacked a popular magazine, notice the way one speaker made an appeal to pleasure in the final paragraphs of his speech:

You may be ridiculed. You may grow weary. You may find there are more needs to meet than you could care for in a thousand lifetimes. But it will be an adventure. No one can tell where it will take you. But I can tell you one thing, you won't be bored. You will find meaning, freedom, and joy.[20]

Knowledge.   People generally do not like to waste their time. Thus, if they must give time to listening to a speech, they want to learn something new—to expand their knowledge. This, too, refers to all levels of Maslow's hierarchy. Does your proposition offer a new perspective? If not, can you find facts, examples, or statistics that are new to the audience? Or, if the audience accepts your proposal, will it cause them to learn more or develop in some new way?

Another former president included an appeal to knowledge in one of his speeches: "The American people are wise," he said, "wiser than our opponents think. They know who pays for every campaign promise. They are not afraid of the truth. We will tell them the truth."[21]

You will note in the above discussion that many of these needs overlap. You need not limit your appeals to a single category. The broader the appeal, the more likely a favorable reaction will occur. Although the above list includes some of the traditional motives for action, speakers should not limit themselves to these. Listeners may also respond if they feel they will gain a sense of justice, increased responsibility, effective workmanship, better security, broader recognition, or more freedom. To understand audience motives is to help understand how people will be aroused, moved to action, or made to understand.

TRY THIS 7

Using the common motivational appeals discussed, which appeals would be *most* appropriate if you were trying to get members of the audience to:

1. Go to a new movie
2. Purchase a study guide for a course (or exam)
3. Attend more sports events

4. Read a new book
5. Run for a campus office
6. Open a savings account
7. Enjoy leisure more
8. Take up a new hobby
9. Eat more nutritious foods
10. Accept a blind date.

PERSONAL CONSIDERATIONS

Have you ever responded to another person by saying this person is really intelligent, really trustworthy, really reliable, or really competent? When you respond in this way, you are responding to that person's personal credibility. A person with high credibility is considered intelligent, trustworthy, reliable, and competent. They are people sometimes referred to as people of good will. If you know a person like this, do you turn to him or her for guidance? Of course. A speaker's credibility—the sum of these personal considerations—is a powerful communication factor, perhaps even more powerful than either logical or emotional considerations.[22]

How, then, do personal considerations fit into the Toulmin model? First, they add strength to the data. If listeners believe in you, as speaker, they are more likely to believe in the data you present to them. Second, personal considerations add force to the warrants. That is, listeners are more likely to see your data as relevant and significant to them—undermining their reluctance to accept your claim—because you say it is. Finally, they are less likely to qualify the results. Again, your credibility will add a degree of certainty to the claim. These effects (using "PC" for personality considerations) might be diagrammed as follows:

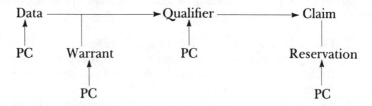

Thus, personal considerations have an all-encompassing effect on the communication.

The focus here, then, is on the perception of a speaker's character—*how* he or she is viewed by audience members. *Ethos* can be defined as the character of the speaker in the eyes of the audience. It should be clear that no two audience members are likely to view him or her in exactly the same way. It should also be clear that how a speaker is viewed may bear little or no resemblance to how he or she *really is.* There is often some discrepancy between one's personal self—the

111

way one is in private—and one's public self—or the way one projects oneself to others. Thus, we are dealing here with an image—the image or character of the speaker in the listeners' mind.

When speakers come before an audience, some audience members have already formed an impression of them. That is, they have prior knowledge of them. This is often true of keynote, graduation, or special occasion speakers who have been asked to speak because of their reputation. This prior impression is sometimes referred to as *extrinsic ethos* because it is credibility established external (actually prior) to this speech occasion. Sometimes we are not aware of the extrinsic ethos but are informed of it by the introducer or in a program notation. It is still extrinsic to the speech occasion since the speakers bring it with them.

TRY THIS 8

Write a short biographical sketch of yourself, building up your extrinsic ethos on a subject of your own choosing. Include as many items as possible, to raise your image in the eyes of an audience on this particular subject. (If there is no topic on which you have expertise, make one up and use hypothetical credentials to build your credibility in the biographical sketch.)

This exercise will familiarize you with the kind of items that make up extrinsic ethos. These items can become an important factor in determining audience attitudes toward you before you begin speaking.

Beginning speakers have little extrinsic ethos. They must earn ethos within the speech occasion. When speakers create their impression (or character) during a speech, we call this *intrinsic ethos,* or earned credibility. When we meet people for the first time, they must earn our respect and confidence. The same is true for a speaker we hear and see for the first time. Respect and confidence is built through competent handling of both the situation and the materials of the speech.

1. Listeners respond positively to speakers who reveal a solid knowledge base. This means speakers must appear qualified, informed, and authoritative. They should have fresh, clear, and specific supporting material.

2. Listeners respond positively to speakers who appear trustworthy. Nobody likes to be treated cruelly or in a hostile or unpleasant manner. It is the kind, safe, friendly, and pleasant person we come to trust. If people appear earnest and sincere, we are more likely to believe them or act on what they say.

3. Listeners also respond positively to speakers who appear bold and forceful. To be poised, dynamic, and assertive are characteristics that will help speakers cause persuasion to occur. If they can exhibit a sense of humor as well, they are still more likely to be successful.

These are characteristics that can be projected during the speech.[23] We are not talking about creating an appearance—a semblance of competence; we are talking about speakers' showing that they are genuine, honest, and sincere. To create an appearance of credibility without it truly being so is unethical. There are definite and specific ways for speakers to reveal competence, trustworthiness, and dynamism during a speech. For speakers who are relatively unknown, the following suggestions should prove helpful.

Speakers reveal *competence* when they come across as well-informed people who have done their homework. They are able to quote the experts, use the special vocabulary of experts (without being verbal show-offs), and list the important facts. If they are also well organized, they appear more competent. If they have done extensive research, they should refer to their research efforts and mention any other personal involvement they have had with the topic. Why the topic is even important for them might be one question they could answer.

Speakers reveal *trustworthiness* when their audiences feel they are being treated fairly and squarely. Are the speakers willing to be open with the audience and let it know some personal details of their lives that the audience would not otherwise come to know (without revealing intimate details, of course)? Does the audience feel respected by the speakers? Do the speakers appreciate the current beliefs and values of audience members? Do the speakers seem to want audience members to trust them? Does the audience feel the speakers are being objective on the topic or closed-minded and subjective? Have the speakers told the audience of any personal actions they have taken in the past that support their current beliefs and orientation? Do audience members feel that speakers' orientations are compatible with their own? As an audience, members trust themselves; can the speakers show that their orientation is consistent with that of the audience, so that the members trust their judgment? Does their nonverbal communication appear positive? Are they calm, firm, purposeful, honest? Do they appear to be of good character? These are questions that can be asked of all speakers.

Speakers reveal *dynamism* when an audience gains an impression of activity, when audience members feel the speaker is enthusiastic and energetic. Speakers should tell the audience what they will do or are doing as a consequence of their orientation to the topic. Speakers' messages should reveal complete ego involvement with the topic. When speakers feel hate, they should demonstrate hate. Speakers should be fluent. Hesitancies in speaking, such as "uh" or "er," can weaken dynamism. When a speaker slouches or leans on a lectern, dynamism is also weakened. Speakers who cannot project their voice to the back of the room also negatively affect their power and forcefulness. Dynamic speakers are both intellectually and physically powerful.

But power need not be viewed in terms of force; audiences also appreciate composure or calmness. Although extroversion is preferred over introversion, what is most appreciated is behavior that is relevant to the ideas being communicated. Sometimes it is force, sometimes calmness. Whatever the emotion revealed, it should be delivered in the spirit of sociability: dynamism within the context of good fellowship, friendliness, or camaraderie.[24]

Dynamism may also relate to speakers' purposes. Speakers who rely on one clear, powerful purpose are more dynamic than those who approach a topic from several different perspectives at once. This is similar to the strength that can be derived from speakers who take clear, unambiguous stands on issues.

Dynamism can also result from strong evidence. Speakers must choose facts, quotations, and examples that are reliable, honest, and typical. Is the evidence useful to the audience? If not, do not use it. Evidence should be justified with respect to the audience. Audiences need to know who the authority is and why this authority should be respected. Sources of facts and statistics must be identified and their objective worth demonstrated.

It should be clear that personal considerations have to do with appeals that derive from speakers themselves: their credibility. Audience members will respond to a speaker's personal appeal based upon whether they feel the speaker is competent, trustworthy, and dynamic.

TRY THIS 9

Using the specific proposition for your next speech, list the many ways you will use to build intrinsic ethos through *competence, trustworthiness,* and *dynamism.* Be as specific as you can in each instance. What do you plan to do?

SUMMARY

The logical, emotional, and personal considerations discussed in this chapter add up to identification. If we, as speakers, can get the audience to identify with our ideas, they are more likely to accept our claim. No part of a speech stands alone. A speech gains support because of the total impression it makes, but it should also be clear that the total impression can be destroyed through improper structuring, a poorly chosen piece of data, an unsatisfactory emotional appeal supporting wrong warrants, or lack of concern over personal appeals. Audiences are sensitive to such weaknesses—perhaps even more sensitive than they are to speech strengths.

All speeches require support—usually more support than we have at our fingertips. We will have to rely on data beyond what we ourselves possess. We are going to have to do some work—some investigation. How else can we discover the substance necessary to be impressive or convincing? How else can we gather sufficient data?

In this chapter we have discussed the structure of argument as well as different kinds of logical, emotional, and personal support. Their purpose is to guide listeners smoothly and efficiently to the conclusion you want them to reach. Getting them there requires careful thought and preparation.

Emotional considerations are important because a speech is seldom devoid of emotion. Although emotion may flow from the language and delivery, the speaker can also gain identification by appealing to audience needs—those aspects that motivate them to act and give substance to warrants. There are many motive appeals that speakers can use to influence listeners.

Listeners are also influenced by the credibility of speakers. Thus, speakers must think about the kind of image they have (extrinsic ethos) and the one they want to project (intrinsic ethos). Concerns over competence, trustworthiness, and dynamism will help them control, to the extent they can, the image listeners form of them.

The effect of the speech is a total impression: a fusion of elements. Although we often judge a book by its cover, we know that such judgments are weak and often wrong. The effect of the speech—what is between the covers of the book—is what is going to make the lasting impression; thus, efforts to control logical, emotional, and personal aspects are critical parts of speech preparation.

Enthusiasm and the desire to succeed evolve from having something to say. That fundamental motivation, which is the driving force for all other features of the public communication process, begins when one has found appropriate material. Material can be related to a logical, emotional, or personal framework. We must be conscious of each one of these.

Now that we are familiar with the types of material we will be looking for, the next step is to investigate methods for finding it. Where do we go? What do we look for? In the next chapter, "Locating Sources," we will discuss procedures that will help make library research fast and efficient.

NOTES

[1]Speakers can increase their credibility early in a speech. See Robert D. Brooks and Thomas M. Scheidel, "Speech as Process: A Case Study," *Speech Monographs,* 35 (March 1968): 1–7. Numerous studies have demonstrated that high source credibility enhances persuasion. For the major studies, see Kenneth Andersen and Theodore Clevenger, "A Summary of Experimental Research in Ethos," *Speech Monographs,* 30 (June 1963): 59–78. See also James C. McCroskey and Thomas J. Young, "Ethos and Credibility: The Construct and Its Measurement After Three Decades," *Central States Speech Journal,* 32 (Spring 1981): 24–34.

[2]For additional information on argument, see Douglas Ehninger, "Argument as Method: Its Nature, Its Limitations, and Its Uses," *Speech Monographs,* 37 (June 1970): 101–110.

[3]Stephen Toulmin, *The Uses of Argument* (New York: Cambridge University Press, 1964), Chapter 3, "The Layout of Arguments." By permission of Cambridge University Press.

[4]For additional information, see James McCroskey, "A Summary of Experimental Research on the Effects of Evidence in Persuasive Communication," *Quarterly Journal of Speech,* 55 (April 1969): 169–176; Frank S. Murray, "Judgment of Evidence," *American Journal of Psychology,* 81 (September 1968): 319–33; Robert P. Newman and Dale R. Newman, *Evidence* (Boston: Houghton Mifflin, 1969); T. B. Harte, "The Effects of Evidence in Persuasive Communication," *Central States Speech Journal,* 27 (1976): 42–46.

[5]For more information on attention, see Michael I. Posner and Stephen J. Boies, "Components of Attention," *Psychological Review,* 78 (September 1971): 391–408.

[6]Dean C. Barnlund and Franklyn S. Haiman, *The Dynamics of Discussion* (Boston: Houghton-Mifflin, 1960), pp. 110–112.

[7]*Family Weekly,* March 18, 1979, pp. 4–6.

[8]Original source: *Toledo Blade* (November 7, 1975).

[9]See Stephen K. Campbell, *Flaws and Fallacies in Statistical Thinking* (Englewood Cliffs, N.J.: Prentice-Hall, 1974). Also see Darrel Huff, *How to Lie With Statistics* (New York: W. W. Norton and Co., 1954).

[10]*Family Weekly,* March 18, 1979, p. 6.

[11]For another approach to evidence, see Douglas Ehninger, *Influence, Belief, and Argument: An Introduction to Responsible Persuasion* (Glenview, Ill.: Scott, Foresman, 1974), Chapter 5, "The Foundation of Argument: Evidence," pp. 51–66.

[12]Speakers are advised to use logical arguments, but should recognize that logic by itself may not be sufficient. Arguments are sometimes evaluated on the basis of what listeners want to believe. See William J. McGuire, "A Syllogistic Analysis of Cognitive Relationships," in Carl I. Hovland and Milton J. Rosenberg, eds., *Attitude Organization and Change* (New Haven, Conn.: Yale University Press, 1960), pp. 65–111.

[13]Speakers are more effective if their proposition is related to the audience's feelings. See Milton J. Rosenberg, "An Analysis of Affective-Cognitive Consistency," in Carl Hovland and Milton J. Rosenberg, eds., *Attitude Organization and Change* (New Haven: Yale University Press, 1960), pp. 15–64. Other studies are reviewed in Chester A. Insko, *Theories of Attitude Change* (New York: Appleton-Century-Crofts, 1967).

[14]Abraham H. Maslow, "A Dynamic Theory of Human Motivation," *Psychological Review,* 50 (1943): 370–396.

[15]Data from pp. 35–47, 51–57 in *Motivation and Personality,* 2nd Ed. by Abraham Maslow. By permission of Harper & Row, Publishers, Inc.

[16]Milton Friedman, "The Future of Capitalism," in *Contemporary American Speeches: A Sourcebook of Speech Forms and Principles,* 4th ed., Wil A. Linkugel, R. R. Allen, and Richard L. Johannesen, eds. (Dubuque, Iowa: Kendall/Hunt Publishing Company, 1978), p. 262.

[17]Jenkin Lloyd Jones, " 'Let's Bring Back Dad': A Solid Value System," in *Contemporary American Speeches,* p. 263.

[18]Jimmy Carter, "Fireside Chat: Unity on U.S. Goals," in *Contemporary American Speeches,* p. 348.

[19]Elizabeth Langer, "An Instrument of Revelation," in *Contemporary American Speeches,* p. 370.

[20]William M. Pinson, "The Playboy Philosophy–Con," in *Contemporary American Speeches,* p. 207.

[21]Gerald R. Ford, "Republican National Convention Acceptance Speech," in *Contemporary American Speeches,* p. 356.

[22]See Kenneth E. Andersen and Theodore Clevenger, Jr., "A Summary of Experimental Research in Ethos," *Speech Monographs* 30 (1963): 59–78. Aspects of credibility are summarized in Michael Burgoon, *Approaching Speech/Communication* (New York: Holt, Rinehart & Winston, 1974). See also McCroskey and Young, "Ethos and Credibility," p. 24–34.

[23]It is clear from one study that this can be accomplished early in the speech. See Robert D. Brooks and Thomas M. Scheidel, "Speech as Process: A Case Study," *Speech Monographs,* 35 (1968): 1–7.

[24]The conclusion from most of the studies of McCroskey et al. was that there were five dimensions of credibility: competence, character, sociability, extroversion, and composure. See McCroskey and Young, "Ethos and Credibility," p. 27.

six

LOCATING SOURCES

Library Usage

Now that we are familiar with the variety of material we can select as substance for our speech, we are faced with the problem of locating sources for that material. We must have the information that is found in books, magazines, or documents. If we were truly expert in the area on which we chose to speak, finding material would not pose a great problem. We would simply pursue our quest inwardly, depending on ourselves as the primary source. If you were to speak on what it means to be a student today or on local student hangouts, you might have ample material at hand. It is interesting, though, that the more expert one becomes in any field, the more one realizes how much he or she does *not* know. Even an expert seldom depends solely on himself or herself. Faced with the problem of locating sources, a student must (rather quickly in most cases) make use of all available resources. This generally means he or she must either go to the library or find experts willing to share their knowledge.

The library is not the only available source of material. Students should not overlook resident experts on campus—professors and staff members—or experts residing in the community. An interview with an expert will certainly count as an important source, perhaps even stronger than library sources because:

1. Audiences find it easy to identify with other people
2. It indicates you are willing to do extra work to get the information you need
3. Since the expert is probably a local authority, the information shared is likely to relate to the immediate community and is therefore likely to hold everyone's attention well

---

TRY THIS 1

Suggest campus or community experts whom you could interview on any of the following topics:

1. Studying habits of students
2. Junk foods and tooth decay
3. The quality of campus cafeteria food
4. Dieting
5. Abortion
6. Planned parenthood
7. Community support of organized religion
8. The decline of campus rules and regulations for students
9. Available sources of fun for students
10. Exercising and available exercise programs
11. Health spas
12. Roller skating for fun and exercise
13. What professors do in their spare time
14. Strikes by public employees?
15. The local bookstore rip-off

Students who intend to carry out interviews should plan their questions carefully. Interviewers should not waste the expert's time but should try to use the available time efficiently to get as much information as possible. If the interview is carefully preplanned, the interviewers are less likely to think of additional lines of questioning after the interview is over. It is difficult—and sometimes impossible—to make a second contact.

CONSIDER THIS

In my profession as an attorney, I've interviewed hundreds of people for positions—from lawyers to secretaries and other positions. In my business of operating a videotaped interview service for major law firms throughout the country, I've interviewed thousands of law students. Two things stand out from interviews: most knew nothing about the interview process, and most had a yearning to learn more about it, but didn't know where to start.

SOURCE H. Anthony Medley, *Sweaty Palms: The Neglected Art of Being Interviewed* (Belmont, Calif.: Lifetime Learning Publications, 1978), p. xii.

Before conducting an interview the interviewer should learn as much as possible about the topic to be discussed. This helps the interviewer to ask intelligent and pointed questions and helps guarantee that interesting areas or points will not be overlooked. Often, too, questions can be grouped so that the interviewer does not have to jump back and forth between the subjects covered—going to a new subject or idea and then going back to one already covered. Organization is important. Finally, the interviewer should know the questions that are going to be asked so that he or she will not have to read them. Practice in asking the questions helps the interviewer appear fluent and articulate as well as confident and poised.[1] However, flexibility should also be retained so that the interviewer can pick up on interesting sidelines or tangents that might add color or interest to the final speech.

TRY THIS 2

Plan an interview with one of your teachers. Quickly list five to ten questions that you might ask to determine the reasons for his or her approach to teaching. Or interview the teacher on any of the following:

Philosophy of education
Recreational pursuits
Hobbies
Educational background
Future goals and aspirations

Students can also find reserves of information in still other places. City and county offices often have stocks of information, depending on the topic. The local federal building may also be of help, for it houses numerous offices designed to dispense information and look after citizen welfare. Hospitals and clinics may have files of information. The local historical society may be able to offer assistance. Clubs and associations often retain stores of information on local events and happenings. The sources can be endless for students who are active and eager pursuants.

When it comes right down to it, however, the library probably offers the most information in the most readily accessible form. As a supplement to the previously mentioned sources, it is ideal. There is no greater repository for the variety and depth of material to be found there. Our main overriding suggestion would be to start early—give yourself plenty of time.

FIND A SPECIFIC PURPOSE

The assumption is that you now have your speech topic. You may not have it narrowed or know precisely what you want to say about it, but you have the topic. That is the first step.[2] (If you have your topic and specific purpose, you might want to skip this section and move on to "The Library: First Stop—Card Catalog." If, at this point, you do *not* have a topic, any of the following procedures are recommended:

1. Search your own experience and background for areas of interest. Many of the things you have seen, heard, or done would also interest others. Pursue yourself as a first source for ideas before pursuing outside sources.
2. Pick up a daily newspaper or weekly news magazine and read it. Does anything there catch your eye?
3. Go to the library and skim through a variety of magazines and journals. Does anything intrigue you?
4. Talk to roommates, friends, other students, or teachers about possible topics. The only problem is that you may find these sources recommending very commonplace topics—topics that have been spoken on so often that many people are tired of hearing about them.
5. In your library, find the *Reader's Guide to Periodical Literature.* It will be discussed in detail later in this chapter. Sit down with a copy of the latest issue and fan through the topics—subject headings. Do any of these merit further and closer consideration?
6. As a last resort, pick up several copies of *Reader's Digest.* Look at the titles of the articles on the front cover. Do any of these subjects look interesting?

TRY THIS 3

On a sheet of paper, write down a half dozen topics that you might like to speak on.

After generating these topics, order them by placing a 1 before the topic that you find most interesting or desirable, a 2 before the second-most interesting or desirable, and so on.

Consider the first or the first and second topics for a minute:

1. How much do you already know on the topic(s)?
2. What will be your primary sources of information on the topic(s)?
3. How much library work do you think will be required?

On the topic that you labeled as Number One, how much information do you think your audience already has on the topic? Are they well informed? Will you be able to push their knowledge base further? That is, will you be able to give them information they probably do not already have?

You do not get up to speak just to hear yourself talk; you speak for a reason. In public communication, we call this a purpose. A purpose grows out of the nature of the assignment, particular occasion (or situation), topic, material or information, or the speaker's intent.

You may already have a purpose. You should. It helps in the selection of material for a speech because it serves as an overall guide, helping you decide which material is the *most* informative, persuasive, convincing, or entertaining. A well-defined purpose, for example, can cut your preparation time by limiting what you need to read to the most appropriate material. You will not need to read everything on the topic. We suspect however, that in the back of your mind you do have a fairly specific idea of what you want to do. We will now try to enlarge and clarify that idea, formulating a specific purpose.

The specific purpose serves as a summary statement of what you want from your audience as a result of your speech. The process of moving from a topic to a specific purpose involves focusing—the methodological process of arriving at a focus with consideration of the audience being paramount. You might decide to inform, persuade, or entertain—these are general purposes or goals. The specific purpose is more detailed or narrow than that. Take the topic of marriage and family. One speaker phrased a specific purpose based on this topic as follows: "To explain to the class the three essential requirements for having a good family life." The speaker has stated exactly what she hopes to achieve with her topic. From the general topic of friendship, another speaker chose to discuss the importance of building strong friendships. He phrased his specific purpose to read, "To motivate the audience to establish strong friendships." His purpose, then, clearly stated the response he wanted from his audience. He could have phrased his topic as the first speaker did: "To explain three essential requirements for establishing strong friendships," or he might have taken a different tack and phrased it, "To prove that good friendships bring happiness." Any number of specific purposes can be drawn from a topic. It is important that you find a clear statement that supports a *single* purpose.

Notice something else about the purposes phrased above. They all use what are called "infinitive phrases"; that is, they depend on the infinitive form of the verb: to explain, to motivate, or to prove. Others might be: to show, to indicate, to convince, or to have. The *general* purpose (informative or persuasive) determines the verb to be used in its infinitive form at the beginning of the specific purpose statement:

Informative	*Persuasive*
To explain	To prove
To indicate	To convince
To show	To motivate
To increase the understanding of the audience	To have the audience believe or act

The infinitive part of the phrase indicates the intent of the speaker. The rest of the phrase contains the thesis statement.

Notice, too, how the speakers have narrowed the topic as they sought their specific purpose. From the general topic of marriage and family, the first speaker focused on *family,* then narrowed it further to concentrate on explaining only three requirements for having a good family life. She could have selected the other half of that topic as well:

Topic area: Marriage
Narrowed topic: Need for marriage
Possible specific purposes:

"Values of marriage" *(Incomplete: direction unclear)*

"Criteria for determining the need for marriage" *(Better, but still lacks specifics)*

"To explain to the class the three major criteria to determine whether you should get married" *(This is a strong speech purpose.)*

"To indicate to the class how backgrounds, interests, and life goals can bear on a marriage decision" *(This is a further development of the speech purpose above; it is more complete and more specific.)*

A speaker might select the topic area of *work.* This could be developed as an informative speech designed to explain or indicate—as above—or the speaker might choose to take a more persuasive direction:

Topic area: Work
Narrowed topic: People who do not work
Possible specific purposes:

"To convince the class that something should be done about people who do not work." *(This purpose lacks direction.)*

"To prove to the class that work should be made available to all those who are capable." *(Better, but still lacks specificity.)*

"To prove to the class that because a working society is a healthy society, the federal government should initiate a program whereby all eligible people would be given work commensurate with their ability." *(This is a more complete statement of this specific purpose.)*

Although intents are often separated according to the general purpose of informing or persuading, many speeches include both informative and persuasive elements. Some people contend that all speech is persuasive. An example of a speech designed to explain (an informative purpose) that might have persuasive overtones would be one that tried to show that there are no more heroes in our society. The speaker might successfully prove that there are none. Most persuasive speeches, too, must have an informative base. To prove that research dollars should be aimed at the development of a gonorrhea vaccine would necessarily mean the speaker would have to prove that the disease needs a vaccine. Or the speaker might need to answer such questions as: How serious is gonorrhea? How fast does it spread? Who does it affect? How much would it cost to develop a vaccine? (Development of such a vaccine has been frustrated because the disease does not produce lasting immunity, the bacteria of gonorrhea do not invade the bloodstream, and vaccines made from the whole gonococcus have uniformly failed.)

The process of discovering your specific purpose, as indicated earlier, is an important one. It should not be neglected or eliminated. The time it takes to find a clear and definite specific purpose may result in obtaining a clear and definite speech. Be sure to write it out; seeing it written will help you decide if you like the way it is worded. If you are not satisfied with it, change the wording. Do not hold to a first idea just because it was first. At this point in the process nothing is sacred!

Write the specific purpose as a complete thought expressing a single idea. It should be a complete sentence, not a fragment, a phrase, or even a question. It should be a simple sentence, "To explain to the class the importance of having the latest fashion in clothes," and not a compound or complex one in which two distinct ideas are offered. The speech purpose "To explain to the class the three major forms of leisure activity and to prove that human beings waste their talent and ability" includes two ideas, either of which could be used for a speech—but both ideas should probably not be used in one speech. The three major forms of leisure activity, however, could be incorporated as a natural and essential part of a speech designed to prove that human beings waste their talent and ability. Be certain, too, that the sentence includes (1) a general purpose, (2) the specific audience for which the speech is intended, and (3) the narrowed topic.

TRY THIS 4

Develop a specific purpose for each of the following topics:

1. Materialism
2. Fads
3. Living together without being married
4. Drug abuse
5. Divorce

6. Stress
7. Loneliness
8. Honesty in government
9. Two-career marriages
10. Pollution taxes

Developing a specific purpose, however, is not the focal point of this chapter. The purpose of this chapter is to streamline your library work. If the point of going to the library is to find material for a speech, your trip to the library should supply you with that material as quickly and efficiently as possible. Nobody with a speech to prepare wants to waste time, and a library can be a major time-waster if you are not careful. Determining your specific purpose before you go to the library will help give direction to your library efforts. With this direction, you will be better able to use the library's resources. This chapter will first discuss the card catalog, then magazines, and finally newspapers. Sources for additional statistics will be mentioned briefly. Finally, government documents will be offered as another source of information when available. Now, specific purpose in hand, you're ready to begin.

THE LIBRARY: FIRST STOP—CARD CATALOG[3]

To make the process more meaningful and understandable, let's develop a topic (find sources on it) with a specific purpose. Let's try to find out all the sources that *could be* used to shed light on this topic. We may discover more sources than we would need for a five- to ten-minute speech, but having a topic will make the discovery process more concrete.

The topic is "prisons," and the specific purpose may be tentatively phrased, "To increase the understanding of my speech class about prison living conditions." With this specific purpose I will be able to hold attention—and I may also learn something. Prisons have always intrigued me. I have visited some; I have seen movies that use prisons as the focal setting; I often read stories about prisoners and escapes. At least I am not starting from point zero as I head for the library with my specific purpose.

The card catalog—the single most useful library resource—is my first stop. Since I know of no books or authors on the topic, I select the part of the catalog labeled *subject*. Removing the appropriate drawer, I find a table where I can browse through the cards. Over 250 separate cards list *prisons* as a topic. It looks as if I will have no trouble finding material.

My next goal is to find current material. There is a limit to how much I will be able to read, and for this topic I want to concentrate on current material. I have to be realistic about the available time for research and the amount of material I can use in a five- to ten-minute speech.

As I file through the cards, I take note of different words referring to my topic. I write many of them down so that I will have different ways of finding information on my specific purpose when I go to other sources. *Prisons* is a topic that can be located by using many different words:

crime and criminals	houses of correction
workhouses	contemporary correction
inmates of institutions	correctional institutions
imprisonment	discipline and punishment
prison discipline	treatment of offenders
penitentiaries	reformation
prison riots	penal jurisprudence
prisoners	reformation of criminals
prison sentences	prison psychology
reformatories	punishment

In addition to the numerous cross-references noted above, I also find bibliographic guides that I can use to find even more information. If I were to start reading right now, I could easily read through this year and the next and still not read all that has been written on this topic! What a wealth of material!

I decide to go to the area where most books on prisons are housed and quickly browse through a number of books to locate those pertaining to my specific purpose. As I do this I realize my specific purpose that focused on "prison living conditions" might be too broad and could be divided into several main headings. I therefore decide to focus on in-prison activities—discipline, order (or lack of it), and sex. What happens behind bars? That becomes my focal question at this point. I am still willing to change the focal question depending on the information I might read or find; it is too early to get frozen in on an approach or focus, especially since I am just beginning my research.

I pick out some books that look as if they might help me. I don't know for certain, but I have found several—some by experts; some by people who went behind bars just to write about it; some by the prisoners themselves. I am seeking a *variety* of viewpoints. I find one written by a state prison society, one written by the American Prison Association, one written by a chaplain. I find an anthology of material that offers different perspectives. I also note some written on other countries (I might use these for comparisons) and some written by men who served time in prison. I look at publication dates and try to maintain currency, limiting myself to books within the past five years or so for this speech. This is not always possible, but it does help eliminate some of the many available books. I check out seven books, planning to look at them in greater detail back in my study. No need to waste precious library time on that now.

If I had known an author or exact title, I could have gone directly to the source—the book itself. Although this might have speeded up the process somewhat, I would not have known how many books are available on the topic nor the breadth of the topic. I would not have picked up those convenient cross-references either. In most instances it is probably wise to use the subject index in addition to using the author or title indexes.

I begin to take careful notes. This may seem out of place at this point (you may not feel ready to take notes), but I have found through experience that I often make the mistake of not being careful enough in the early stages. I try to go too fast, scribbling a name, or date so illegibly that I cannot read it later. Or I forget to write down the publishing information: place of publication, name of publisher, and copyright date. This information is essential if I am going to footnote ideas or quotes from any books I find or if I include them in my final bibliography. It is important to note the date of publication, since it makes little sense to cite statistics on our prison system from a book published in 1947—especially if they were recited as if they were current. I also record call numbers because, for the little effort it requires, it saves heading back to the card catalog when I find I want to use a returned book just one more time (see Figure 6–1).

If you find that your topic is not listed under the subject headings in the card catalog, you can ask for assistance at the reference or periodicals desk. The librarian there will likely be able to help you. Also, most libraries have available a standard list of subject headings, which contain the exact subject headings used in the card catalog. Examining this list could save time and point out other useful headings pertaining to your subject.

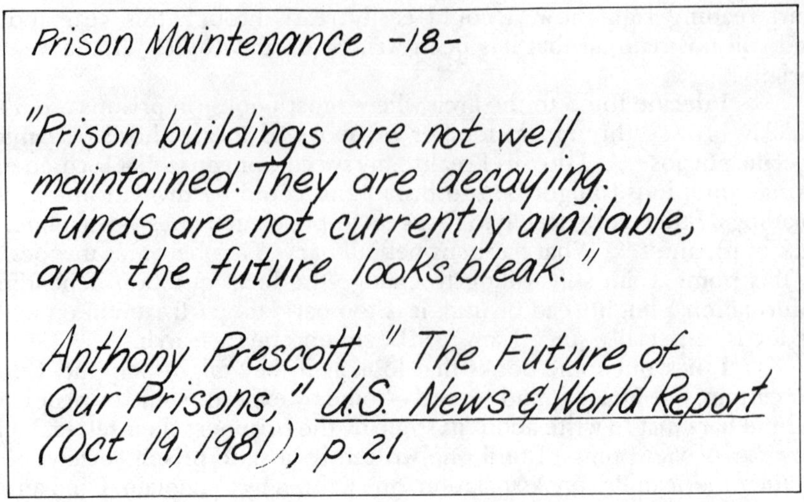
Prison Maintenance -18-

"Prison buildings are not well maintained. They are decaying. Funds are not currently available, and the future looks bleak."

Anthony Prescott, "The Future of Our Prisons," U.S. News & World Report (Oct 19, 1981), p. 21

Figure 6–1

One other point: If books listed in the card catalog are not on the shelf, do not panic. The circulation desk staff can tell you if the book is checked out. Sometimes these books can be called back in; thus, if you have started your research early enough, you will still have time to get the book before your speech. If it is not on the shelf and not checked out, the staff at the circulation desk should be notified. Before running to them, however, make sure you have checked the general area where the book belongs. The book can be missing for any one of several reasons.

1. Sometimes the book has been reshelved incorrectly, either accidentally or carelessly by people who have not taken time to pay attention to the order
2. Sometimes the book has been used and then laid down nearby because someone has not taken the time to reshelve it. Some libraries prefer that users not reshelve books, since there is a strong likelihood that they will do so incorrectly.
3. Sometimes the book is on a library truck waiting to be reshelved by library personnel. Check the surrounding area for loaded trucks.

TRY THIS 5

Take time to investigate the card catalog. See what is available there. Look at several cards and note how much information is on them. If you were missing bibliographic information, would you have to go back to the book to get it? Check out several topics from the listing below, checking each in the author, title, and subject catalogs:

1. Growing energy underwater
2. Growing food underwater
3. Synthetic fuel production
4. Immigration in the United States
5. The rise of two-income families
6. Leisure pursuits
7. The decrease (demise?) of quality production
8. Dating services
9. Sex and violence on television
10. Rights of the handicapped
11. Home-study courses as an alternative form of education
12. Slowing the rate of suicide

THE LIBRARY: SECOND STOP—
PERIODICALS

The second stop in my quest for information is the periodicals—the magazine and newspaper section of the library. *Time, Newsweek, Sports Illustrated, U.S. News & World Report, Playboy, TV Guide,* even *Modern Romances* are all periodicals. Newspapers are also periodicals. The more scholarly publications (often called journals) are also periodicals: *American Journal of Sociology, Harvard Business Review, Today's Education, Journal of Personality and Social Psychology,* and *Psychological Bulletin.* My research will take me to the magazines and newspapers probably not to the more scholarly publications. I will probably find enough information for a speech in the first two sources. If I were writing a paper, I might want to consult some of the scholarly publications—but not for a five- or ten-minute speech.

Magazines. I will likely spend most of the rest of my time in the periodical section of the library, for periodical literature is up-to-date (current), provides several different points of view of a topic, and has a tremendous variety of subject matter. However, there are some 11,500 periodicals published in the United States each year, and I have to locate those magazines that have articles that support my specific purpose. Fortunately, I can find out what articles have been written on my purpose by using periodical indexes—and there are a variety of these.

A periodical index lists by subject (and sometimes by author) the articles that have appeared in hundreds or even thousands of magazines. This eliminates the need to look through the contents or index of separate magazines. A few magazines are indexed at the end of a year; most (unless they fall in the category of scholarly publications) are not.

For my specific purpose, "Prison living conditions," I begin by looking in *Readers' Guide to Periodical Literature* because my topic is likely to be covered in general interest magazines. The *Readers' Guide* indexes articles appearing in nearly two hundred general interest magazines.

Again we see the importance of having a well-defined specific purpose before beginning the investigation. *Readers' Guide* is only one of many periodical indexes. They cover such specific disciplines as art, education, literature, music, and the social and natural sciences. With a specific purpose in mind, you can go to the exact index you need. If you do not know the index, a reference librarian can help.[4] Some of the common ones (alphabetically) are:

Applied Science and Technology Index
Art Index
Business Periodicals Index
Humanities Index
Public Affairs Information Service Bulletin
Social Sciences Index

If you do not know how to use an index, most periodical indexes contain in the preface precise directions for their use, as well as sample entries, lists of abbreviations employed, and a list of the magazines indexed. If you have trouble using an index, the problem can often be solved by going back and reading the preface.

In looking up *Prisons* in *Readers' Guide,* I am again baffled by the numerous categories. Do I want to change my focus to prison psychology, recreation, or reform? Do I want to focus on prisoner education, employment, furloughs, legal status, medical care, reading, recreation, rehabilitation, or treatment? I could change the focus, or I could continue trying to find out what prison life is really like. The trouble is that prison life is too broad. I could focus on order, discipline and sex, or on rehabilitation and treatment—since these latter two areas appear to be closely linked. I decide to retain my specific purpose as previously designed.

With the information at hand I can go directly to the magazine articles. A little time spent at this point might help me know if this is the area that interests me. Copying down *all* the information the index provides on an article will simplify locating the article and preparing footnotes or a bibliography.

Notice that at the end of a major subject heading, *Readers' Guide* lists *See also* and then provides other subject headings. For prisoners, the *See also* in the issue I am using includes:

convict labor	prisons
escapes	social work with delinquents
parole	and criminals
political prisoners	women prisoners

Any one of these topics could be developed into a speech. The ideas never seem to cease once you get into a subject area.

The various subheadings have not been particularly useful with the specific purpose involving prison living conditions, since it is a big topic with many different sources. Sometimes one can simply use the various subheadings provided to get all the needed references. It could be, too, that the major heading has fewer sources than one of the subheadings; a shift in topic focus could then be made.

After writing down (1) the name of the journal, (2) volume number or date of the issue, and (3) page numbers for every article I wanted to read, I go to the shelves to find the material. If a journal is not on the shelves, I check a copy of the Serials List at the reference desk to make certain the library has it. Most libraries subscribe to a wide range of popular, general interest magazines, but which ones they take often depends on the size of the library and its financial resources. Some libraries even keep a second copy on hand to provide a duplicate source when uncaring people have ripped articles out of the first sources.

When an article is extremely relevant and full of information, I make a copy of it to read later. When feasible, I take notes at first reading—making sure that I include complete footnote or bibliographic information. The information given in most indexes is incomplete. For example, indexes seldom list the first name of the writer or writers. I also make certain that next to each note I list the page number from which that particular note was taken. In this way, I try to make certain I never have to go back to an already used source. If I do, however, I have all the information to assure that the second trip will be shorter than the first— at least that's the plan!

Although *Readers' Guide* provide's many usable articles, I also check other indexes as well. I know, for example, that *Social Sciences Index* would be another useful source because of the nature of my specific purpose. One month's issue yielded more than ten articles on the topic of *prisons* and referred me to four other subject categories. The last hard-bound volume listed more articles and subject headings than *Readers' Guide.* This will not always be the case; *prisons* and *prisoner treatment* are social issues.

For my topic I also check *Psychological Abstracts.* Noting the topic *prisoners,* in the "Brief Subject Index," I record the fifteen numbers there and trace the numbers back to find several relevant articles. My goal is to discover some interesting facts, examples, or opinions that most of my audience will *not* already know. I want to make my speech different. After all, the specific purpose that includes life within the prisons has been used many times before. I want my treatment to be unique.

TRY THIS 6

Take a single topic and note how many citations can be found in the various indexes. Go to each index individually—especially those you have never used before.

Can you think of a topic for which all the indexes might supply worthwhile information? Can you think of topics that might be appropriate for each of the indexes separately?

Consider some of the following *common* speech topics and try to determine which indexes might be the most appropriate sources of information about them:

Capital punishment	Marijuana
Abortion	Smoking
Drugs	Euthanasia
Women's rights	Discrimination
Nuclear energy	Space exploration
Big business	Four-day workweek

Newspapers. Newspapers are a useful guide because they provide interesting local information on social, economic, and governmental activities. Many cover the national and international scene as well. One problem with using newspapers is that so few are indexed. To use the local paper, I simply began to keep my eyes open for related stories. I read the paper daily and found several interesting anecdotes and examples that will give my speech some local flavor.

I do not want to stop here, however. In quest of all possible information on my topic, I also consult the *New York Times Index* and the *Washington Post Index.* The *New York Times Index,* the index to the best-known and most used newspaper, presents a condensed, classified history of the world as it is recorded day by day. The *Index* consists of abstracts of the news and editorial matter entered under appropriate headings. The headings and their subdivisions, if any, are arranged alphabetically—the entries below them chronologically. With the precise reference—date, page, and column—to the item being summarized, I could tell at a glance if I wanted to see a microfilm of the whole story.

Newsbank service provides a subject index and reprints of articles in 160 newspapers throughout the United States. Also, *Editorials on File* provides several valuable newspaper editorials from major U.S. newspapers.

There are several other newspapers that I could also have consulted:

Christian Science Monitor Index
National Observer Index (1969–1976)
The Times Index (British)
Wall Street Journal Index

But time was creeping up on me, and I could see that I was accumulating a great deal of information as it was. Now I needed some statistics to indicate both the seriousness and the pervasiveness of the problems I planned to mention.

TRY THIS 7

Locate all the newspaper indexes available in your library. Find out if your local newspaper is indexed. Try using each newspaper index to locate information on a topic of your choice.

1. How are the indexes different?
2. How are they the same?

3. If you wanted to read an article indexed in one of them, how would you go about getting it?
4. How many different newspapers does your library house?
5. If you wanted to read a local newspaper daily, could you do it at the library?

FINDING STATISTICS

By singling out statistics for special consideration and treatment, I do not want to suggest a special preference or indicate any imbalance. The only reason it receives a section to itself is to familiarize you with certain library sources of primarily statistical information. There is no question that many of the statistics you need will come from the articles you read. But what if they do not? Is there a source for some general, broad-based statistics that will show the breadth, depth, or long-range nature of the problem?

Perhaps the best single source for such information is *Statistical Abstract of the United States,* published annually since 1878. It is *the* standard summary of statistics on the social, political, and economic organization of the United States. Not only does it summarize numerical data, but it also serves as a guide to more detailed data or statistics presented in a different arrangement. It guides by providing an introduction to each section, by offering source notes for each table, and by supplying an appendix, "Guide to Sources of Statistics and Guide to State Statistical Abstracts." The statistics presented are primarily national, although some state and regional data are presented. The index is most valuable as a guide to the various subjects covered. Going to the index of *Statistical Abstract,* on my topic I find the following:

> Prisons and prisoners
>> Average sentence and time served
>> Characteristics of prisoners
>> Characteristics of state prisons
>> Offenses and arrests, by type and race
>> Prisoners executed
>> Prisoners under sentence
>> Selective Service Act violations

Numerical data and other miscellaneous facts are also readily available in *World Almanac* and *Information Please Almanac.* If you are looking for information on subjects such as associations and societies, astronomy and calendars, awards, climate, economics and finance, education, energy, history, maps, nations, states and cities, news events, population and individuals, religions, sports records, and weights and measures, these are the sources to consult. And since the facts and data included on these topics may differ between these two almanacs, you might consult both.

Other statistical sources include *American Statistics Index* (an index to recent governmental statistics—to be discussed later), *Historical Statistics of the United States, Colonial Times to 1970*, and *Statistics Sources,* a subject bibliography of statistics sources.

GOVERNMENT DOCUMENTS[5]

Students are often reluctant to look into government documents. Even the name sounds overwhelming, complicated, or foreboding—too much red tape involved —yet government documents include information on almost any conceivable topic that touches the public in any way. And this information is available.

United States government documents, in both quantity and diversity, exceed those of any other governmental or commercial publishers. These documents come in sizes from the smallest pamphlet (even a single sheet) to large multivolume sets. They constitute an immense source of information that should not be overlooked.

One way to find this material is through the *Monthly Catalog of United States Government Publications.* Published monthly, as the title indicates, this catalog cites most publications put out by the United States government. Each citation provides full bibliographical information, including the Superintendent of Documents call number, pagination, series title (when appropriate), date of publication, and subject headings, as well as author and title. In one monthly issue I find another useful document on prisoner management and control. One looks up material under author, title, or subject indexes. With the number provided, one then looks under entries for that year. A citation is offered and if the document looks useful, it can then be secured. Libraries that are depositories will often have copies of the documents, although few libraries have every item available.

The *Index to U.S. Government Periodicals* provides access to the articles contained in one of the most comprehensive sources of information—the periodicals produced by more than one hundred agencies of the United States government. Each citation gives full bibliographical data about the article: author, title of article, periodical title, volume, pagination, and date. With the Superintendent of Documents classification number, the publication can be located. One annual volume (as opposed to monthly volumes) provides me with more than ten recent articles on prisoner rehabilitation and seven more on living conditions. This appears to be one of my best sources, and many of the publications I wanted were housed in my library.

CIS Index (a publication of the Congressional Information Service) indexes all publications of Congress except the *Congressional Record:* hearings, reports, documents, executive documents, public laws, and special publications. Under prisons, twenty-four more documents are listed. Many are not directly related, but one, "Sexual assaults, prevention and treatment," looks promising.

Two things are becoming clear as I continue using indexes and accumulating citations: (1) indexes are easy to use, and (2) they are all organized in essentially the same way. If you learn to use one, you will have learned to use most of them. Also, they are very fast and easy to use—a real timesaver. Instructions on their use are generally provided in an introductory section.

There are many other government reference documents, but these are the essential ones. Before closing this section, however, one source quickly passed over in the section on statistics, the *American Statistics Index,* should be re-emphasized. It is a commercial publication—the Congressional Information Service once again. I look under prisons, and it refers me, instead, to *correctional institutions.* There, I find—in one volume—forty-six references to the statistical data published by all branches and agencies of the federal government. This is a two-part issue consisting of an *Index* volume and an *Abstract* volume. Materials are indexed in the former under subject, name, category title, and agency report number. The citations in the *Index* lead one to the appropriate location in the *Abstract* volume. The abstract of the material gives me enough information about the content of the publication—plus full bibliographical information—to enable me to determine whether it contains any data I desire. It provides cost of maintenance figures and also refers me to the *Statistical Abstract of United States* for social, political, and economic data from past years, from which I can discover overall trends.

CONSIDER THIS

When I was younger it used to be thought a great compliment to say about someone, "He's a well-informed man." This meant that he was sort of a scholarly specialist in, say, medieval English, but a man able to say something of pith and moment about practically anything that was likely to come up at a dinner table or in a bar.

To be a well-informed man these days is almost unavoidable, and also it is a bit of a curse. I often wonder, is it worth the trouble?

For we are in the midst of what the Xerox people, in an adroit and widely publicized advertisement, call "The Information Crisis." The ad informs us that 72 billion new bits and pieces of information reach our shores each year.

"Consider," said the ad, "75 per cent of all the information available to mankind has been developed within the last two decades. Millions of pieces of information are created daily. And the total amount is doubling every 10 years. . . .

"The problem is, as with any crisis, one of management. With fuel, it's a question of making proper use of too little. With information, it's making proper use of too much."

That ad certainly speaks to me, as it probably does to you. I live in a sea of information. Too often, I feel I cannot cope with it. If Xerox with its copying devices, its lasers, and its electronic printers can help me cope with it, all the better. But the marines are landing almost too late, in my case.

SOURCE: Charles McCabe, "Drowning in a Flood of Information," *The Blade* (Toledo, Ohio), November 20, 1978, p. 17. Reprinted by permission of Chronicle Features, San Francisco.

HOW MUCH IS ENOUGH?

"How much is enough?" is a difficult question to answer. There is no doubt that you have *not* exhausted all possible sources of information. On most topics the number of sources available is almost endless. But there must be a stopping place. A time must come when you can rest assured that the key information has been found. The problem at this point is that we have not stopped to sift through much of what we have found; we have not tried to organize the material. We cannot tell, therefore, whether we have clear and distinct main points that are all solidly and thoroughly treated.

"How much is enough?" can also be viewed with respect to how much of the data is actually used in a speech (see Figure 6–2)—the center dot—as compared with how much data you have gathered for research—the circle around the center dot—and still further compared with the total data available—the huge outer circle. Although the answer to the question is relative, one can see from the figure that a speaker is likely to gather at least five to ten times as much material as is actually used in the speech, probably much more.

At this point—and this is the only way a reasonable answer to the question can be offered—the answer rests on the answers to several other questions:

1. What is your topic?
2. How much does your audience already know about it?
3. How long is your speech?

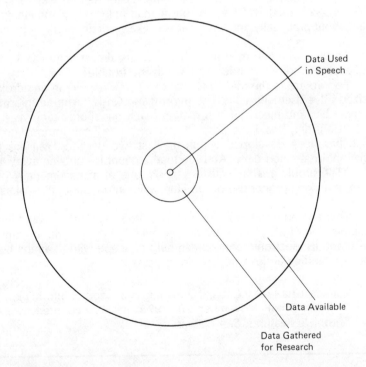

Figure 6–2

Even as each of these questions is considered in detail, rest assured that the answer still will not be clear. There is really no way to know for sure.

Topic.   The choice of the topic itself may narrow or limit the search for information. The more limited the topic, the more limited the available sources. Also, a very new topic may have little information available, whereas a very popular (older?) topic may have an overwhelming amount written about it. One student doing research for a speech on "Different Styles of Leadership" found that much of the information on the topic was written at the time of the last war when much government research money was available for research on leadership. The older material was overwhelming compared with what is available now.

One must choose a topic on which information can be found. It would be good, too, if the speaker could offer some new insights, alternatives, or approaches on the topic as well. If the members of your audience are similar in age and experience to yourself, then use yourself as a guide:

1. Is your information new?
2. Is your information interesting?
3. Would your speech hold your own attention?

You should also be concerned about *why* the speech is being given. Is it meant to be informative or to entertain? A speech to persuade may require your going to different lengths, too, depending on whether it is designed to present a new policy or to change a belief. These are not necessarily criteria that affect the length of a speech, but they can have an effect. You must have enough information to do what you intend to do successfully.

Audience Knowledge.   The more the audience knows, the more you must strive to go beyond that level of knowledge. Why simply discuss that with which they are already familiar? Again, if they and you are of similar age and experience, what you know of a topic will probably be just about what they know of it— although one should be cautious in using this as a measure.

There are several ways to find out how much they know. The first and simplest way is to ask several people. Ask some leading questions or some key, probing questions to find their knowledge base. The second way is to hand out a short questionnaire prior to the speech. The third way is to give them some informative and interesting reading material on the topic and tell them to read it before the speech. This will allow you to assume that your audience has a certain (perhaps basic) level of information. Teachers often use this technique: "Please read Chapter 6 before the next class so that we can discuss it." Of course, you also run into the same problem teachers have: Will they read your information before your speech?

Length of Speech.   The longer the speech, the more depth you should plan to provide. This does not mean you need to cover a larger number of major ideas. It should mean you can cover fewer main ideas with greater depth and analysis. This will be dealt with in greater detail in the next chapter.

The problem with the above comment about the relationship of length and depth is that it appears you can be superficial, given a short time limit. Many speakers have discovered that the *shorter* the speech is to be, the more research they must to do so as to make every second of that shorter effort count.

The key that I have discovered that governs the answer to the question, "How much is enough?" is: How much *feels* comfortable? Confidence grows from feeling comfortable with one's material. I want to know, as I get up to speak before an audience, that I have:

1. Found the major sources
2. Read the important authors
3. Discovered the key issues
4. Secured in my mind a wealth of additional facts, examples, and opinions, so that I can intelligently answer any question a hearer might ask me or adapt to any circumstance that could occur while I am speaking. I make certain that I have plenty of available stock in my storehouse of knowledge—my reserves.

When I go home from an excursion at the library, I want to feel good. I cannot be happy with myself or with my material if I know that a large number of stones have been left unturned. If I have, indeed, pursued the kind of quest outlined in this brief chapter: (1) consulted the card catalog, (2) examined magazine indexes, (3) pursued newspaper indexes, (4) found relevant statistics, and (5) surveyed available government documents, I can feel that I have accomplished my mission; I can feel comfortable drawing out the appropriate supporting material outlined in the preceding chapter and organizing this wealth of information as is to be discussed in the next chapter.

SUMMARY

Most people who go to the library want to find information fast. True, libraries have become social places, places to relax (or sleep), even places to eat, but when the goal is information, efficiency is a must. Thus, efficient use of library resources served as the primary focus of this chapter.

Library work need not be painful. The pain can be reduced or eliminated if one knows how to use the card catalog, indexes to magazines and newspapers, sources for statistical information, and government documents. As a necessary part of speech preparation, such work can be rewarding and exciting. If you need other motivation, think of the side benefits of the effort:

1. You are broadening your knowledge.
2. You are becoming an informed and knowledgeable person.
3. You are gaining depth on a specific topic in a specific area—becoming an expert.

Library research can be a worthwhile experience. To think of it as painful is to begin with the wrong attitude; your attitude can help shape the experience.

In the next chapter, the process of organizing all the material we have accumulated will be discussed. Once we get information, we must sift through it and organize it efficiently and effectively.

NOTES

[1]See Charles J. Stewart and William B. Cash, Jr., *Interviewing: Principles and Practices* (Dubuque, Iowa: Wm. C. Brown, 1974), especially pp. 92–94. Also see Charles J. Stewart and William B. Cash, Jr., *Interviewing: Principles and Practices*, 3rd ed. (Dubuque, Iowa: Wm. C. Brown, 1982), Chapter 4, "Questions and Their Uses," pp. 75–102; John Brady, *The Craft of Interviewing* (New York: Vintage Books (A Division of Random House), 1971); Anthony Medley, *Sweaty Palms: The Neglected Art of Being Interviewed* (Belmont, Calif.: Lifetime Learning Publications, 1978); Robert L. Genua, *The Employer's Guide to Interviewing: Strategy and Tactics for Picking a Winner* (Englewood Cliffs, N.J.: Prentice-Hall, 1979); and Melvin W. Donaho and John L. Meyer, *How to Get the Job You Want: A Guide to Résumés, Interviews, and Job-Hunting Strategy* (Englewood Cliffs, N.J.: Prentice-Hall, 1976); William H. Banaka, *Training in Depth Interviewing* (New York: Harper & Row, 1971); and Ken Metzler, *Creative Interviewing: The Writer's Guide to Gathering Information by Asking Questions* (Englewood Cliffs, N.J.: Prentice-Hall 1977).

[2]See Zebulon V. Hooker, *An Index of Ideas for Writers and Speakers* (Chicago: Scott, Foresman, 1965). Also see William M. Pinson, Jr., *Resource Guide to Current Social Issues* (Waco, Texas: World Books, 1968).

[3]Some information in this section is based on information found in *Library Research Skills: A Self-Paced Approach*, 2nd ed. (A Bowling Green State University Reference Department publication, 1979). Used with the permission of Mr. Tim Jewell, Head, Reference Department. Also see William L. Rivers, *Finding Facts* (Englewood Cliffs, N.J.: Prentice-Hall, 1975); Robert B. Downs and Clara D. Keller, *How to Do Library Research*, 2nd ed. (Urbana: University of Illinois Press, 1975); and Margaret G. Cook, *The New Library Key*, 3rd ed. (New York: H. W. Wilson Company, 1975).

[4]Also see Eugene P. Sheehy, *Guide to Reference Books* (Chicago: American Library Association, 1976); Louis Shores, *Basic Reference Sources* (Chicago: American Library Association, 1967); and Carl White et al., eds., *Sources of Information in the Social Sciences* (Chicago: American Library Association, 1973).

[5]Some information in this section is based on information found in *A Bibliographic Guide to U.S. and Ohio Documents*. Compiled by Melville Spence (Bowling Green State University Libraries, 1979), Bibliographic Series No. 74. Used with the permission of Melville Spence.

seven

ORGANIZING THE MATERIAL

Arrangement and Outlines

Between the end of the last chapter and the beginning of this one, there is an implied and as yet unstated assumption operating—that you have read much of the material you have discovered. Somewhere here a large, or at least comprehensive, knowledge base is assumed. The speaker must try to draw back the camera for a wide-angle picture of the subject. In drawing back, he or she must recognize that certain features will still be left out, certain features will be prominent and clear, and others will recede into the background and become a blur. But the wide-angle perspective is important as you begin to make some early decisions about organizing what you have found. Later, while still organizing, you will want to zoom in and magnify particular areas or characteristics of the larger picture. Those decisions are no less important than the ones facing you now, but you will need the big, overall picture to begin.

CONSIDER THIS

The communicator always fights against odds to capture and hold the interest of the audience, to lead it through his process of thought, and to reach the end with both parties' information and ideas as similar as possible. Any breakdown along the way that severs the link between them may make all the effort useless. In the old movie bedroom farces, something was always happening to interrupt the seduction. It might be a ringing phone, an intrusive neighbor, a pet, a child, food burning, or whatever the writer could imagine. In the communication process, every flaw that interrupts the process of communion between the communicator and the audience can just as effectively frustrate the result.

SOURCE: Philip Lesly, *How We Discommunicate* (New York: AMACOM, a division of American Management Associations, 1979), p. 104.

In this chapter, outlining techniques will be examined. The focus will be on the body of the speech, and the three processes that occur in developing the body of the speech will be explained: (1) finding main heads, (2) ordering them, and (3) supporting them. The chapter ends with a discussion of the introduction, conclusion, transitions and internal summaries, and includes a sample persuasive outline for your consideration.

OUTLINING

The goal of this chapter is to help you organize and outline your speech easily and effectively. At this point in our speech development, we have a large body of information available. We know the goal of our speech. We just have to get there in some organized, systematic way. To prepare an outline is to prepare a system: a group of interacting items that together form a unified whole. An outline is a condensed treatment of a particular subject in which the principal features or different parts are indicated. Thus, for a speech the outline should be a short, complete-sentence condensation of the whole speech. Putting an outline of the speech together early allows the speaker to examine the overall organization and development of the material. Is it strong? Is it logical? Will it do what I intend it to do? Although the answers to these questions are important, the questions cannot be answered until the overall system is laid out before us. Even then, to be realistic, some of our answers will have to be guesses since we can never know for certain how an audience is going to respond.

THE BODY OF THE SPEECH

One would think that in organizing a speech, one would begin at the beginning or, as you have undoubtedly heard someone say, "Let's begin at the top." The beginning of a speech—the top—is the introduction, not the body. But as you answer the next question you will see that in speech preparation beginning at the top is *not* natural: How can you begin working on the introduction—the beginning—when you do not know for sure what the body of the speech will look like? The introduction is designed to introduce what follows, and what follows has not yet been determined. By waiting to prepare the introduction until after you have the body of the speech, you will be able to:

1. Select the *best* material from the available pool, recognizing what the "best" looks like
2. Provide material that flows smoothly into and relates directly to the body, since the body will have been established
3. Save valuable time by not having to revise material in the introduction that turns out to be irrelevant or unnecessary

The body of the speech is the main, central, or principal part. It is the part that must carry out the intent of the speaker. The essential information, or content, of the speech is conveyed in the body. It is usually preceded by an introduction and followed by a conclusion.

Three processes are used in developing the body of the speech: (1) finding main heads, (2) ordering them, and (3) supporting them. Each will be discussed in order, for this is the natural process of development most speakers use.

Finding Main Heads

The main heads of the speech are like the hinged ribs of an umbrella over which fabric is stretched. They provide the structure of the speech. If an umbrella rib becomes bent or broken, the entire shape of the umbrella is changed. If you think of the specific purpose as the central pole of the umbrella, the ribs are second in importance, just as the main heads of a speech are second in importance to the purpose. To make certain that the shape of the speech will function accurately —that it will do what we want it to do—we must select and phrase our main heads with great care. If the speech purpose has been written carefully, the main heads may already be clear. For example, what would be the main heads for a speech developing the specific purpose, "To explain to the class how the bicycle can yield overall fuel savings for society, savings on fuel to the individual, and savings because of bicycle costs." The main points of the speech would be:

I. Returning to the bicycle could generate an enormous reduction in gasoline consumption.
II. The individual would save the cost of the fuel needed to drive a car, a saving that could be significant.
III. Bicycle prices are low compared with car prices or the cost of using public transportation on a regular basis.

TRY THIS 1

For the following specific purposes, write appropriate main heads:
- To show the class how working for big business can offer opportunities for self-motivation, self-reliance, and adventure
- To explain to the class that the key to appreciating good music lies in understanding rhythm, melody, and harmony

- To indicate to the class that the primary reasons why high-school graduates are unprepared for the world of credit and money management are because they lack math skills needed to understand financial dealings and because they lack awareness of their rights as consumers
- To show the class how American industry is conserving energy through recovering waste heat, using more efficient lighting, motors, and electrical devices, and improving maintenance of burners in boilers

---

With some specific purposes, however, the main heads are simply suggested, not overtly stated. In these cases, the actual main heads chosen could vary. A speaker who chose the specific purpose, "To indicate to the class how beer is manufactured," might deal with just one of the processes or might focus on the adjuncts used to give beer its color and flavor since this is where the essential differences between beers occur. He or she could, on the other hand, treat each of the major processes in beer manufacturing:

I. The materials used include malted barley, hops, water, yeast, and adjuncts.
II. The materials are first crushed, then mashed.
III. The mashed material (or wort) is boiled in a copper tank or kettle, then cooled.
IV. Fermentation begins when the yeast is added (or pitched) to the wort.
V. Kegging, bottling, or canning follows fermentation.

The speaker might even choose to combine steps I and II or III and IV.

If the main heads are not readily clear from the purpose statement, perhaps the purpose has not been stated as clearly or specifically as it could be. For example, a specific purpose such as "To speak to the class on running," is so broad that no main heads can be determined. Does the speaker want to talk on "America's obsession with running," "How to run properly," or "The power and joy that can result from running"? Perhaps the speaker should rephrase the purpose before selecting the main heads, for example, "To explain to the class the changes that occur in a runner's state of mind as he continues a life of running." Although this may still cause some confusion, the confusion is largely dispelled when the main heads are listed:

I. Runners often begin in a search for fitness.
II. Running can cause one to become calmer and less anxious.
III. Running allows one to concentrate more easily and for longer periods.
IV. Finally, running allows one to gain control of his or her life—a sense of quiet power.

In looking back over these three examples of main heads (the bicycle, beer, and running), several points of similarity can be detected. These points of similarity should help you in constructing your main heads. Notice, for example, that all main heads are:

1. Phrased as *complete sentences*—none are phrases or fragments
2. *Simple sentences* that are specific and to the point
3. *Vivid,* producing a strong, clear impression
4. *Parallel* in structure, with the same sentence parts occurring in corresponding positions

As you find your main heads you may also find that your topic yields too many of them. A music major, for example, might want to talk on the specific purpose, "To explain to nonmusic majors the musical instruments of an orchestra." The standard number of musical instruments in an orchestra is twenty-six, although the number may vary in accordance with musical requirements and the conductor's preferences. To speak on twenty-six main heads would be time consuming and boring. This music major knew, however, that all orchestra instruments, with the exception of the new electronic ones, can be classified into three groups; thus, her main heads were these:

I. Wind instruments create sound vibrations when air is blown into or across them.
II. Percussion instruments produce sound when struck in some manner.
III. Stringed instruments produce sound when a stretched string is set to vibrating.

This speaker realized that each main head had to be developed in some detail, and that it would be impossible for her to develop twenty-six of them. More than five main heads is impractical.[1] The speaker's goal is to help the audience *retain* the information given in the speech. Thus, the speaker has to limit the number of main heads by proper limitation of the specific purpose or by grouping main heads together under a single heading.

TRY THIS 2

The following is a general topic: skateboarding. Using this general topic, three specific speech purposes have been developed. Make up three main heads that might be used to develop each purpose *if* they were accurate:

SPEECH PURPOSE: "To explain the history of skateboarding"

I. _____

II. _____

III. _____

SPEECH PURPOSE: "To show how proper skateboarding is accomplished."

I. _____

II. _____

III. _____

SPEECH PURPOSE: "To indicate the features one looks for when purchasing a skateboard."

I. _____

II. _____

III. _____

Notice that for the topic *skateboarding,* any sport could be substituted: racquetball, paddleball, handball, roller skating, and so forth.

Ordering Main Heads

"May I take your order, please" is the first response you get when you drive up to the intercom of any drive-in restaurant. When that request is made, what is your response? Do you give the person your order in the proper order? Do you list the hamburgers, the french fries, the drinks, and then the desserts at a hamburger place? Have you ever tried to juggle the sequence of items? Do you order one hamburger to begin with, and then keep adding one or two more hamburgers throughout the rest of the order? Probably not. It would be too confusing. You would have little to gain—especially if you are hungry! The person taking the order has the various items listed in a logical sequence on the pad. Why? Because most orders are given in this sequence, and it is easier to listen and respond to the order if it follows this pattern. The items are also more easily remembered if they are in sequence. By the same token, if you want your audience to remember what you say, arrange your main heads in a logical sequence.[2]

Four basic speech patterns are followed most often when ordering main heads. They are *topic order, time order, space order,* and *problem-solution order.* These organization patterns will meet most of your needs for speeches of an informative or persuasive kind. Later, when we examine persuasive speaking, other variations of these will be considered.

Topic Order. This is one of the most common organizational patterns. In this pattern each main head develops part of the specific purpose. In an outline developing the specific purpose, for example, "To explain to Overeaters Anomynous members how getting thin requires eating at specific hours, and making eating a pure experience (not associated with other events)," notice that there will be two main heads (or topics):

I. Getting thin requires eating at specified times.
II. Getting thin requires making eating a pure experience.

Both main heads develop part of the specific purpose. The speaker has used the topic order form of organization.

The main heads may follow some logical order. They may, for example, go from what is considered least important to most important, or from specific to general. The main point here is that the *speaker* decides the order of the topics. It is not a function of the topic. For example, using the specific purpose, "To show concerned citizens how alcoholics can be recovered," the speaker can decide to:

1. Follow a step-by-step procedure showing how alcoholics are detoxified
2. Take a typical recovered alcoholic back through the process
3. Indicate the various organizations that help and how they can be contacted
4. Develop in detail the physiological and psychological changes in the alcoholic that must be reversed
5. Prove that interpersonal relationships (a possessive mother, domineering father, or spouse who keeps the mate dependent) directly affect the alcoholic
6. Show that the drinker must be motivated to want treatment
7. Describe the use of drugs (Antabuse, disulfiram, and Temposil [citrated calcium carbimide]) that can help alcoholics recover. The possible approaches to this specific purpose are almost endless—especially as you consider how they might be combined. The point is, however, that the approach to be used is chosen by the speaker as he or she considers the audience for which the speech is intended. The rationale for ordering a speech is found in the listeners.

Also, the topic order can be used in either informative or persuasive speeches. A speaker talking to the relatives of an alcoholic might try to get those relatives to look at their own behavior and to examine their relationships with the alcoholic—that is, get them to take action (as in No. 5 above). The speaker could use mother, father, and spouse as main heads (topics), further explaining and developing each in the speech.

A topical outline usually includes the main heads phrased as parts of the topic, as definitions, as causes, or as reasons. The example cited on the topic of getting thin illustrates the use of a topical order with the main heads developed from *parts* of the purpose. The previous example concerning the various instruments of an orchestra illustrates the use of main heads as *definitions*.

If a speaker wanted to develop the purpose, "To help the audience understand how the weather can have a negative effect on one's mood," he or she might choose a topic order based on *causes*:

I. The weather can aggravate a medical condition (heart condition, allergies, etc.)
II. Changes in the weather can cause stressful effects.
III. The weather can cause adverse reactions in people taking drugs or medication.

A previous example concerning the cost savings of a bicycle reflects a topic order based on *reasons*. Although this was an informative speech, a topic order based on reasons most often is used in persuasive speeches. For example, a speaker might wish to pursue the following specific purpose, "To prove to the class that grades motivate students." (Doesn't sound like a typical student position!) The main points would be the reasons why the speaker feels grades are valuable. It is sometimes useful to add a *because* following the purpose statement; this also helps to make certain that all main heads are parallel.

  I. (because) Grades are important rewards for work.
 II. (because) Grades serve as a measure for students to determine their own success (or lack of it).
III. (because) Grades are an accurate reflection of the competitiveness that exists in our society.

A topic order based on reasons works for persuasive speeches that attempt to prove that an idea, event, or thing is good or bad, right or wrong, important or unimportant, beneficial or detrimental, and so on. The form is as follows, with the speaker inserting whatever idea, event, or thing that is appropriate:

Specific purpose: "To convince the audience that _____ _____ is justified"
    (because)
      I. _____ can help society.
     II. _____ can help each one of us personally.
    III. _____ can contribute to our future.

The topic may be education, sports, self-improvement, physical fitness, or any other that you consider worthwhile. If a speaker wants to convince an audience that a movie is *worth* (the value) seeing, it can be framed in a similar manner with the "because" statements indicating the topics: action, acting, realism, photography.

Time Order. This pattern is especially useful in informative speeches. It should be used when the main heads follow a chronological (time) sequence. When it is important to the content that audience members see a sequence in the ideas or events, this organizational pattern should be used. For example, a speaker would use this pattern if he or she wanted to show:

• How to do something (play a sport)
• How to make something (build a piece of furniture)
• How something happened (passage of a law; re-creation of an accident)
• How something works (a high-quality stereo or word processor)

The sequence of ideas or events is important. If a speaker sought to develop a specific purpose such as, "To explain how to overcome procrastination," he or she might develop the purpose as follows:

I. Know the event about which you procrastinate.

II. Identify the emotional consequences you experience while procrastinating.

III. Discover the behaviors you engage in when you procrastinate.

IV. Objectively view your problem and dispute your irrational beliefs to effect changes in your behavior.

TRY THIS 3

For the following specific purposes, suggest some hypothetical time-ordered main heads:

A. To explain how to play tennis.

B. To explain how to plant a plant.

C. To explain the process of how a bill or resolution was passed in a particular state.

D. To explain how a musical instrument works.

E. To explain how one gets ready to do one's homework.

Space Order.   Like time order, space order is used primarily in informative speeches. It should be used when the main points reveal or indicate a spatial relationship. When an instructor explains the various parts of an outline—introduction, body, conclusion, transitions—he or she might use space order to organize the presentation, just as a music instructor might use a similar order to explain the parts of a musical instrument or a banker to show what the various numbers on a check mean.

When a speaker wants to explain an event, place, thing, or person in terms of its parts, space order is appropriate. The audience will remember the speaker's description best if he or she proceeds logically. That is, if the speaker is emphasizing the arrangement or function of the parts, he or she should move from top to bottom, left to right, outside to inside—or in any constant direction that will allow listeners to follow the presentation. For example, a speaker who chose to describe the make-up of a grain of wheat because, she noted, "wheat provides 80 percent of the food calories produced in the world," used space order (outside to inside), in the major part of her speech:

I. The grain or kernel of wheat is covered by a thin shell—the pericarp.

II. The next several layers—the bran coat—are generally reddish brown in color.

III. Inside the bran coat is the main storage organ of food (the main nutrients), called the endosperm and consisting of starch and protein (gluten).

Another speaker, talking to a group of freshmen on campus, used space order to describe the campus library:

I. The main use areas of the library are on the first floor: circulation, reference, and food.

II. The areas where you will get most of the books you will need are on the next two floors.

III. The fourth floor, at the top of the library, contains the specialized collections and rare books.

Problem-solution order.   This organization scheme is most appropriate for the persuasive speech. It is more specific than the other types because the pattern itself dictates the order of the main heads. It is effective because it follows the way people generally think. For example, if we (as an audience) were going to accept or act on the solution to a problem, we would first need to know:

I. What is the problem
   A. Does it require a change in belief?
   B. Does it require a change in behavior?
   C. Does it require both?
II. What is the solution?
   A. Is it reasonable?
   B. Is it practicable?
   C. Will it solve the problem?
III. Is *this* solution the best way to solve the problem?
   A. Has it worked before?
   B. Has it worked in other places?
   C. Are there better ways?

For example, a speaker with the specific purpose, "To convince the audience that the individual should take a hand in the decision as to whether he or she will have surgery," might follow the problem-solution format as follows:

I. Nearly one out of every ten Americans will be advised to have surgery this year; a significant part of this surgery is inappropriate.

II. Patients should challenge doctors until they are sure that the operation in question is appropriate.

III. When patients rather than doctors make the choices, there will be less deformity, discomfort, disability, and risk of fatal complications because of inappropriate surgery.

Another possible order would be a problem-causes-solution order. Using this order, the speaker would develop the problem itself, then the causes for its occurrence, and then the solution. This order is often appropriate when an audience lacks familiarity with the problem. A teacher might use this format, for example, in the classroom as he or she sought to change an already established classroom procedure:

I. (Problem) There have been some mix-ups in the grading that is being done on the papers.

II. (Causes) The mix-ups have occurred because students are not being careful in how they label their papers.

III. (Solution) Please make certain you use your full name. Place it in the upper right-hand corner of the first page. Place the date below your name.

Checklist   As you write your main heads, use the following checklist to test them for effectiveness.

_____ I have phrased each main head as a complete sentence.

_____ I have tied each main head *directly* to the specific purpose.

_____ I have been both specific and concise in my statement of each main head.

_____ I have chosen two to five main heads—no more than five.

_____ I have used parallel construction in developing the main heads.

_____ I have related my main heads to my specific audience.

_____ I have followed one of the four basic speech patterns: topic order, time order, space order, or problem-solution order.

TRY THIS 4

Indicate which organizational pattern would be most appropriate for each of the following specific purposes: TO—topic order; TI—time order; S—space order; P—problem-solution order.

_____ "To convince an audience that nuclear power should be used"

_____ "To prove to my audience that political reform in this country would be beneficial"

_____ "To explain to the class the many uses of lasers"

_____ "To show the class that commercial TV has come more and more under the influence of advertisers"

_____ "To explain to my audience the meaning of the sexual revolution"

_____ "To explain to the class the various parts and functions of a communications satellite"

_____ "To motivate audience members to make changes in their life now that will add years to their life later"

Supporting Main Heads

We have been given the menu and have ordered, so we know what we are supposed to be served, but we have little food in front of us. The support for the main heads is the food—or substance—of the speech. The main heads, like bones, provide the structure, but without the flesh we really have no food before us.

In Chapter 5 we considered the various elements of support that would be needed: facts, examples, illustrations, opinions, statistics, and personal experience. In Chapter 6 we considered the sources for material. Now we must sort through the material to select that which is most significant, relevant, and interesting:

> *Significant*—likely to have influence on or affect the audience
>
> *Relevant*—likely to relate directly to the specific audience for whom it is intended
>
> *Interesting*—likely to engage the audience's attention

This is not to suggest that the process of selecting material has not been going on while the materials were being amassed. The criteria for screening should be at work *throughout* the preparation process—beginning as one sorts through one's own experience and background. At this stage of the process the final—or near final (change can occur up to the moment of delivery)—selection occurs.

To select your material, first write down the main heads that you intend to support. Leave plenty of space between them. As you read through your material, look at your evidence cards, or examine your notes, try to find material that is appropriate to each of them. Just write the material down, make a brief notation, or try to capture the essence of the piece of evidence; you do not need to order it at this point. But do note where it came from so that you can quickly recover the full context and substance of the piece when needed. For a specific purpose that reads, "To convince the audience that marriage for women is not necessarily ideal," one speaker laid out her three main heads as follows:

> I. Marriage is not the ideal state for every woman.
> II. The single life provides many benefits.
> III. Women should be allowed to develop their full potential.

As she read the material again and sorted through her notes, she ended up with comments under main head I that read like this:

> Some women want to be career women and do not have the time to give to a marriage.
>
> One out of three marriages ends in divorce.
>
> Many women are unhappy with their marriages: one authority has stated that only one out of ten marriages is happy.
>
> Two-career families are on the rise.
>
> My own parents stayed together only until their children were raised.
>
> Sixty-two percent of divorces are initiated by women.
>
> Conflicts in careers create tension and marital discord.
>
> The number of divorces has doubled in the last decade.

She did the same for her other two main heads as she worked on the first one rather than going back over all the material for each main head.

Her ideas now needed to be organized. Some were more important than others. Some were subordinate, or really occupied a lower class or rank. This needed to be shown. Using the following numbers and letters, these relationships could be indicated:

   I. Main head
      A. A major subdivision
         1. A minor subdivision
         2. A second minor subdivision parallel with No. 1
      B. A second major subdivision parallel with *A*
  II. A second main head
      A. A major subdivision
      B. A second major division of equal worth, parallel with *A*
         1. A minor subdivision
         2. A second minor subdivision
            a. Further subdivision
            b. A further subdivision parallel with *a*

This is an outline for two main heads. Rarely will the breakdown of points go further than the small letters. If needed, however, Arabic numerals in brackets should be used: (1), (2), and (3). It is important to note that if an *A* is used, a *B* must also be used, and if a *1* is used, a *2* must also be used, but a *C* or *3* need not necessarily be used. The purpose of an outline is to show divisions in an area. If an area cannot be divided, it should be part of the category directly above it in the outline—that is, the category to which it is directly subordinate. This avoids outlines where only one subdivision, minor subdivision, or further subdivision is listed. Although this is a formal rule in standard outlining procedure, it is not always followed.

Using the format outlined above, the speaker organized her material under the main head, "Marriage is not the ideal state for every woman," as follows:

      A. Many marriages end in divorce.
         1. One out of three marriages ends in divorce.
         2. The total number of divorces in the United States alone has reached 10 million.
         3. The number of divorces has doubled in the last decade.
         4. My own parents stayed together only until their children were raised: They lived together—unhappily—for fifteen years.
      B. Many women are unhappy with marriage.
         1. An authority on marital relations has surmised that only one out of ten marriages is happy.
         2. Sixty-two percent of the divorces are initiated by women—which suggests that they are more unhappy than the men.

3. Some women want to be career women and do not have the time to give to a marriage.
   a. Two-career marriages are on the rise; by 1990, 75 percent of all women will hold jobs.
   b. Conflicts in careers between spouses create tension and marital discord.

Notice that the speaker has used a variety of supporting material: statistics, personal experience, expert opinion, and personal opinion. One does not need to use all the material collected; it is far better to have much more material than is actually needed. Then one can pick and choose the best.

Also, remember as you pick and choose that you may want to use some especially strong material in either the introduction or the conclusion. If you find some attention-arresting material, label it and put it aside for a moment. Plan ahead.

In the outline the speaker has begun to construct, she has used complete sentences. This helps her see the logic of the material. Sometimes the subdivisions beginning with Arabic numerals (1, 2, and 3) can be developed with phrases. Also, each of her subdivisions contains just a single idea. Do you see what could happen if a subpoint contained two ideas, and you went on with further development of that point? How would you know which point was being developed? In addition, none of her heads overlaps another; each is separate and distinct. The main head (*I*) is an assertion; the major subheads (*A* and *B*) are also assertions in this outline. An assertion is simply a positive or forceful statement. It gains support from the evidence that follows it. Strong assertions lend vigor and aggressiveness to an outline (and speech)—as long as they are supported with correspondingly strong evidence.

When a speech is fully outlined, go back and check two major points:

1. Coordination—all headings indicated by the same designation (*I, II, III,* or *A, B, C,* or *1, 2, 3,* etc.) within the same grouping, should be approximately equal or parallel in their rank, quality, or significance.
2. Subordination—all minor headings should directly support or relate to the next major head.

To use parallel headings under a topic order illustrates coordination. It also indicates that you, as speaker, consider the headings to be equal in value. Through custom, we have come to consider things similar in structure or size as being equal in value. When phrased similarly, the headings make equal claims on our attention. In addition, when a new heading is mentioned, the structure calls attention to this fact: "Here is a new heading." If the heading were: "Using off-peak buying to get more for your money," coordinate points beneath that heading might be:

A. Time your clothing purchases.
B. Telephone very late or early.

C. Look for last year's models.

D. Travel during off-season.

Notice that each begins with the same form of a verb, each point is parallel, and *all* support the main head concerning off–peak buying.

Subordination is also important. A subordinate point occupies a lower rank. In the above example, all points are subordinate to the main heading regarding off-peak buying. Consider the following, too, as an example of subordination:

I. Mental institutions are inadequate.
A. They suffer from a lack of funds.
B. They have experienced a lack of regulation.
C. They reveal a lack of planning and foresight.
D. Most of those admitted are repeaters.

Check the final point, *D* in this outline. Notice that it is *not* coordinate with *A, B,* and *C;* it is also *not* subordinate to *I* in the same way *A, B,* and *C* are; therefore, it should either be placed elsewhere or eliminated from the outline altogether.

TRY THIS 5

In each of the following examples, suggest *one* coordinate idea and *one* subordinate idea:

Example: Good shoes are necessary for tennis.
Subordinate point: They must be comfortable.
Coordinate point: A good racquet also helps.

1. An appreciation of music is important.
Subordinate point:
Coordinate point:

2. Outlining is an essential process in the development of a speech.
Subordinate point:
Coordinate point:

3. Food at this institution could be improved.
Subordinate point:
Coordinate point:

THE INTRODUCTION

Now that you know what you want to say in the body of speech, you are ready to assemble material in a form that will put your audience in the proper frame of mind to listen to it. If first impressions are as important as people say they are, then the introduction is the audience's first impression of your speech—and maybe of you. It has to (1) get their attention, (2) establish rapport or good will between you and them, and (3) lead them into the main content of the speech. Rapport is the establishment of a relationship characterized by harmony and attraction. These are the three minimal expectations of an introduction. Each is important.

Attention. Getting and holding the audience's attention must be one of our foremost goals; if we do not have their attention there is little reason for us to talk. We must think about holding attention not only at the beginning of the speech but throughout the entire effort; however, if you do not gain the audience's attention in the beginning, you are unlikely to win it later. The audience members' minds will have already wandered. Your job, then, is to turn their thoughts toward you and your topic as quickly as possible. There are *many* different techniques for doing this; here are some of them:

1. Tell a story.
2. Use a startling statistic.
3. Open with a question.
4. Cite an example or illustration.
5. Use an anecdote or a personal reference.
6. Create suspense.
7. Be humorous.
8. Compliment the audience
9. Refer to the situation or occasion.
10. Cite a quotation or an important opinion.

Rapport. Many of these same techniques will also help you to gain rapport with the audience—especially if your opening has either involved them in some way or touched their lives. Your job is to make them feel good about listening to you. You can increase the chances that this will occur by keeping these admonitions in mind during your planning:

1. Show how your topic relates to them.
2. Tell how you will help them in some way—that is, not only is the topic related to them but there is something in it for them.
3. Explain what you have in common with them. The more similarities they can see, the more you will be accepted as "one of the bunch."
4. Tell something of a personal nature about yourself that only you could know. You might mention your fear of public speaking, your reasons for being interested in the topic, or some of the values you hold that have caused you to take the orientation you have. However, this is *not* a time for personal confessions or for you to reveal intimate details of your life.
5. Tell the audience how much you respect them for their current beliefs and values.

6. Convince them of your objectivity. Indicate that you are aware of the alternative approaches or positions, but that you have thoughtfully rejected them.

7. Give a short account of your previous commitments. Show them that your prior actions support your current stand or approach. Consistency is often considered a virtue, and your prior actions may speak louder than your words.

What you do not tell them verbally may, in part, be revealed to them nonverbally. Maintain eye contact. Be calm. Strive to be firm and purposeful, reveal honest emotional expressions, and use an appropriate tone of voice. You do not want to be perceived as a threat—someone who may tell them what they do not want to hear, make them do what they do not want to do, or make them feel uncomfortable—at least at the outset. Keep avoidance of threat as your goal as you establish rapport and good will.

Content. You must also get the audience to focus on the goal and substance of the speech. This should be done with ease and naturalness. If you have been successful in gaining attention and in establishing rapport, you do not want to lose what you have gained by clumsiness and lack of planning. Sometimes the technique used to gain attention can be tied to the content with a transition. A speaker might use a personal experience and then say, "With that in mind, I want to look at how this topic touches all our lives in three different areas. . . ." By stating the three areas he is going to treat in the speech, he is using *initial partition* —that is, he has shown what he intends to cover initially (at the beginning), before beginning to cover them. Telling your audience what you plan to cover is especially useful and important in informative speeches. A persuasive-speech situation may be somewhat different: Whether or not you want to use initial partition depends on the nature of the proposition as well as audience attitudes and knowledge. Sometimes in persuasive speaking it is better to move directly into the heart (or body) of the speech after gaining attention and establishing rapport.[3]

Two guidelines will help you prepare an introduction. They are intended only as guidelines; you should add your own creative, unique touch and adapt the introduction to your own specific needs.

1. Outline or *write it out.* To feel the flow of the introduction, it is better to see it outlined or written out. There is nothing wrong with outlining it, although some introductions do not easily lend themselves to outline form. Outlining or writing it out, too, will give you more confidence at the outset of the speech. If you do not like what you have outlined or written, begin again. There is nothing wrong with outlining or writing several introductions to the same speech, and then choosing the one you like best.

2. *Begin strong.* This does not mean that you should put your strongest sentence at the beginning; doing so may cause the audience to miss it. People need some time to adjust or become oriented. To begin strong is to capitalize on first impresssions. This is why we suggested

saving one of your strong pieces of evidence for this spot. To begin strong is to show that you have confidence, that you are in control, and that you know what you want from your audience. To begin strong:

- Do not apologize. An apology plants an unnecessary seed of suspicion, doubt, or possible failure in the minds of audience members.
- Try to get right to the point. Avoid rambling, wordy, or boring introductions.
- Avoid using unnecessarily controversial material, excessive dogmatism, offensive remarks, and unsavory humor. If the audience perceives antagonism, they may discount anything you have to say.
- Make certain all your introductory material directly applies to your subject, audience, and occasion—and that they see the connection. If they think it does not relate, it doesn't!

TRY THIS 6

Write out two introductions for each of the following specific purposes. Then compare them and select the best one for each special purpose.

1. To prove to this class that public speaking is an important course to have in the curriculum
2. To explain to this class how many students tend to waste their time in college

---

THE CONCLUSION

The conclusion is your last opportunity to make the impression you want on your audience. Research has shown that what the audience members hear last—that is, what is most recent in their minds—*does* have an effect.[4] The speaker must try to capitalize on this recency effect by making certain that the main points have indeed hit home. A well-planned succinct conclusion can make a lasting impression. Although it is unlikely to save a poor or mediocre speech, any speech will be enhanced by a strong, dynamic conclusion. A speaker who has worked hard on the body will not want to see this effort wasted by a weak, ineffective conclusion.

The conclusion should serve three purposes, although the first two may be combined: (1) it should summarize the speech, (2) it should leave the audience with the overall purpose, and (3) it should make an impression. These are minimums; it can do more.

Summarizing. Perhaps the easiest conclusion to use is the summary.[5] The speaker who is talking on the subject of *weather* might say, "Thus you can see how

155

the weather can aggravate a medical condition, how changes in the weather can cause stressful effects, and how the weather can cause reactions in people taking drugs and medication." The speaker is simply repeating his main heads. Although appropriate and easy, this is not enough. Also, it certainly does nothing to excite or arouse the audience—although it should be clear that this excitement or arousal does not always have to be part of a conclusion. The problem is that most speech conclusions do not offer a unique or interesting twist. Consider another conclusion for the speech on weather:

> Every one of us is affected by the weather; we talk about it every day. But the more we know about it and its effects, the more we will understand behavior—our own behavior and that of other people. Since weather can aggravate a medical condition, bring on stressful effects, or cause reactions in people taking drugs—even aspirin or alcohol—you can see how your moods—how you feel right now—may be determined by what the weather was yesterday or the day before. Thus, a weather forecast doesn't just predict the weather, it also predicts *your* health, *your* energy, and even *your* job performance. Don't blame yourself or your friends; blame it on the weather!

Because a summary is often not enough, you may want to supplement your summary to heighten the impact of the conclusion. We will discuss some of the ways to heighten its impact under the heading, "Being impressive" which follows.

Stating the purpose. If the audience members leave after your speech not knowing what you talked about, it is probably *your* fault, not theirs. But if only one member out of a possible thirty or forty missed your point, it was probably *not* your fault. It is not necessary to state the purpose of the speech in so many words. Did the speaker above state that he was trying to help the audience understand how the weather can foul their mood? No—at least not precisely. But it was clear from the conclusion.

As stated before, the purpose can be part of the summary, but sometimes it is not. The audience should know what you were driving at—why you were speaking—whether or not it is part of the summary. Make certain the audience gets the kernel of truth in some form. Too many speakers assume that their point is obvious. It is better to assume that if the purpose is not conveyed, they will not get it at all.

Being impressive. Just as in the introduction of the speech, there are many ways a speaker can be impressive in the conclusion. Whether the speech is informative or persuasive, most of these techniques will work. As a speaker, you must select the appropriate one, or combination of several, that will heighten the emotional impact, arouse the audience to active belief, action, or concern, and cause the message to be inscribed in their mind in indelible ink.

A conclusion can accomplish these aims if is is not left to chance. Some speakers say, "Oh, I don't have to worry about the conclusion, I'll just say whatever occurs to me at the moment." Such conclusions usually fail because they are long-winded, unplanned nonsense. Unlike the well driller, who stops when he hits water, such speakers do not know when to stop boring. The best conclusions are carefully planned and depend for their effectiveness on one or more specific techniques.

The first is a direct appeal to the audience. This can be a logical appeal when you describe exactly what you want them to do or accept or understand. For example:

> Now that you have heard how much surgery is inappropriate and can cause serious or fatal results, don't you think its time that we—the ones who get operated on—stand up for our rights?

An appeal used in an informative speech might be phrased:

> See how important it is for us to understand this little grain of wheat [speaker holds one up]. We eat it every day of our lives, and yet we never give it a second thought.

CONSIDER THIS

A rallying cry. Something that touches listeners, something they can remember, a combination of words that crystallizes the subject. Words people can empathize with and feel a part of, words that make them part of the group and not alone, convince them that they *can* win, and will.

You should consider this technique as a way to give your ideas greater horsepower, the power of uniqueness and memorability, extra power because it is so seldom used in the meeting situation.

SOURCE: Frank Snell, *How to Win the Meeting*, p. 158. Copyright 1979 E. P. Dutton, Inc. (Hawthorn Books)

The direct appeal can be emotional as well, as when the speaker directly plays on the emotions of the audience:

> Do you care about *your* education? You want it to be worth something after you have invested all this time, energy, and money? And when you get older and marry and have kids—do you want *their* education to be worth something too? Grades are not only an integral part of our educational system, but they help maintain the integrity of the system as a whole. Stick up for grades. They make a difference in your life, and they will make a difference in your children's lives too.

A second technique that can be used in a conclusion is a challenge to the audience. Two of the above examples also include a challenge: "Stand up for our rights" and "Stick up for grades." The other example includes an implied challenge, "Give it a second thought." Other challenges might be "Do it," "Try it," "See it," "Be concerned about it," "Think about it," or "Believe it."

A third technique is to use a final example, illustration, or personal note. These forms of evidence have high interest value. To use them at the end of the speech should make certain you have audience attention as you close. For example:

> You might wonder why we should try to understand the plight of those who come from a broken home. Who cares? I can tell you it matters—it can affect a friendship, a work relationship, even a marriage. They sometimes see life through a different pair of eyes than those who come from normal families. I know, because I come from a broken home myself. Just to know that often helps us to better understand another person.

Finally, speakers can use a humorous or light approach. Caution should be advised here, since many people have trouble using humor. The humor that works best arises naturally from the situation; it is neither forced nor contrived. If it is appropriate to the material, no matter where it appears in the speech, most audience members will appreciate it. Humor makes the audience feel good about you, and when they feel good about you, they are more likely to accept or adopt your message.

A young woman talking on the importance of being polite ended by saying, "Remember, nothing is ever lost by being polite—except, perhaps, your seat in the lecture hall." Also, the woman who spoke on the advantages of staying single said, "I'd like to end with a special request to all the single men in the audience. You will help us out a great deal if you will just: Stay single!"

TRY THIS 7

Try your hand at writing some short conclusions based on the following specific purposes:

1. "To prove to the class that textbooks are *unnecessary* in performance classes"
2. "To convince the audience that no classes should be offered on Fridays"
3. "To explain to my class the relevance of competent outlining skills to other college courses"

TRANSITIONS AND INTERNAL SUMMARIES

Transitions are the glue holding the speech together. They provide the even flow of ideas. They not only link main heads together, but they also allow the audience to see how the various parts of the speech relate to each other. Thus, a transition is a signal or signpost that tells the audience: "The speaker is moving from one part of the speech to another." If the headings of an outline are the bricks in a foundation, the transitions are the mortar. They are more necessary in speaking than in writing because speech is a one-time event: because listeners cannot go back as they can in reading, they must be carefully led.[6] Internal summaries serve the same purpose; however, they also summarize the points just covered within the speech.

Too often transitions and internal summaries go unplanned—left for the last minute or inserted when the speech is delivered. In general, this does not work. A transition that is not part of the outline seldom gets used. When transitions are *not* used the speech appears rough or staccato. With many sharp edges, the audience loses the train of thought or the relationship of the points, and there is no unity or coherence to the speech—it does not hold together well.

There are many different kinds of transitions. Which kind works best depends on the subject matter, the speaker, and the audience; however, if there is a question about whether or not one should be used, it is better to insert it than to leave it out.

The easiest and shortest transitions are simply single words that indicate you are moving to another idea: *next, now, further, also, similarly, likewise, furthermore, so, therefore, consequently, thus, certainly, yet, still, nevertheless, besides, first, second, third, finally,* and *lastly* are all useful, especially when used in combination with transitional phrases. The problem with single words is that they are short and can be easily missed by listeners; if missed, they of course have not served the intended purpose. Listeners are left on one side of the river while the speaker has crossed to the other side—the bridge across has been missed.

Transitional phrases do not differ greatly from transitional words. They are simply longer and more likely to be heard. The following list is far from complete and is not in any particular order, but it should serve as a guide. Pick and choose those phrases that serve your purposes best. Use as your guide the phrases that sound or feel the best; you must be comfortable with them.

TRANSITIONAL PHRASES

In the first place	Parallel with that
The first step	Comparable with that
The first matter we should discuss	In the same category
In connection with this	More important
Together with this	Next in importance
It follows, then	Add to this
With respect to this	In addition to
Concerning this	Best of all
Related to this	As a result
For example	Because of this
An illustration of this	For this reason
A case in point would be	This is to be explained by
To summarize	The reason is
We have traced	On the other hand
As we have seen	At the same time
Up to this point	Not only . . . but

Insert transitional phrases between and after the following ideas so that the ideas are (1) tied together and then (2) summarized before another point is made:

1. a. The immediate family has most relevance to an individual.
   b. Close friends are important as well.
2. a. State fairs offer adults a chance to be entertained and to see various displays.
   b. State fairs offer children rides, sideshows, and games of chance.
3. a. Gifted students should not be accelerated and isolated.
   b. Gifted students should be allowed to help tutor poor students.

Now, go back and provide an initial partition before each group of two statements. If you had to suggest a third point for each series of two, could you do it?

THE OUTLINE

Now the various parts are to be fused together into a single outline. The following is a student outline that is persuasive in nature. We have incorporated transitions into the outline so that you can see how they should be inserted. The content is on the left; comments about the content are on the right. The outline has been prepared for a 7- to 9-minute speech.

CONTENT

Specific purpose: To persuade the audience that marriage for single women is not necessarily ideal.

Introduction: When I told my father I was coming to Learnland College, he told me that girls were supposed to get married. Most people feel that a girl should get married to lead a fulfilling life. It's the old stereotype we all believe: "They get married and live happily ever after." But I want to point out that marriage has failed many women and is not necessarily ideal.

COMMENTS

Place the purpose at the top of the outline to provide direction—a goal. Make certain all points of the speech relate to it.

To write out the introduction will help you gain confidence at the outset of the speech. It may be outlined as well. Remember that it should (1) get attention (note the personal reference), (2) establish rapport or gain good will (note how it involves the audience), and (3) lead into the content of the speech (notice the final statement that reveals the purpose).

(*Transition:* I not only want to show why it is not an ideal state for every woman, but I also want to point out that there are many benefits to the single life, and that women should be allowed to develop their full potential.)

This initial partition serves as a bridge between the introduction and the body. The speaker tells the listeners what the three major parts of the speech will be. Transitions need to be written out or they probably will *not* be included in the final speech.

Body

I. Marriage is not the ideal state for every woman.

The speaker begins with an assertion as main head *I.*

    A. Many marriages end in divorce.

First subhead, subordinate to *I,* is also an assertion.

        1. One in three marriages ends in divorce.

This point is subordinate to *A* and includes a statistic as evidence.

        2. The total number of divorces in the United States alone has reached ten million.

This subhead is also subordinate to A and is coordinate with "1." It also includes a statistic.

        3. The number of divorces has doubled in the last decade.

This subhead is subordinate to *A* and is coordinate with *1* and *2.* It is also a statistic.

        4. My own parents stayed together only until the children were raised; they lived together —unhappily—for fifteen years.

This subhead is subordinate to *A,* and coordinate with *1, 2,* and *3.* It is a personal experience. Too many statistics used consecutively can be boring.

(*Transition:* The number and possibility of divorces is one problem; unhappiness is another.)

This transition ties *A* to *B.* It is useful because there were four points under *A;* considerable development.

    B. Many women are unhappy with marriage.

This second subhead is subordinate to *I* and coordinate with *A.* Note that it is parallel with *A.*

1. One authority on marital relations surmises that only one out of ten marriages is happy.	This first subhead is based on expert opinion. It is subordinate to *B*, not *A*. It is coordinate with the points that follow: *2, 3,* and *4—not* with *1–4* above.
2. Sixty-two percent of divorces are initiated by women—which suggests that they are more unhappy than men.	Subhead 2 is a statistic. Although we may question the inference the speaker draws here, this use of statistics makes them more interesting to the listeners.
3. Some women want to be career women and do not have the time to give to a marriage.	Subhead *3* is subordinate to *B* and is coordinate with *1* and *2*. It gains support from *a* and *b* below—both subordinate points.
a. Two-career marriages are on the rise; by 1990, 75 percent of all women will hold jobs.	This is a statistic. It will gain strength when the speaker cites its source during the speech.
b. Career conflicts between spouses create tension and marital discord.	This could be based on personal experience or an informal survey, or it could be simply an illustration.
(*Transition:* Not only should we look at the negative side of marriage but we should also look at the positive side of staying single.)	This transition serves as a bridge between main heads *I* and *II*. Notice how these transitions are easier to write when the mainheads are parallel: coordinate.
II. The single life provides many benefits.	Main head *II* is coordinate with *I*. Note that it is part of a topical order.
A. The single woman has more independence.	Subhead *A* is subordinate to *II*. It is an assertion.

(*Transition:* Along with independence, education is also important.)

Note that a transition can occur *wherever* the speaker thinks there is a need.

    B. She has a better opportunity to further her education.

Subhead *B* is coordinate with *A.* It is, however, a personal observation, supported by specific cases in the two categories that follow.

        1. She is free of family problems.

Two cases will also be used here as illustrations in the actual speech.

        2. She is free of family financial problems.

(*Transition:* In addition to independence and education, a woman also may be concerned about a career.)

Again, the coordination between *A, B,* and the following *C* helps make the transition easy to write.

    C. She is likely to have better career opportunities.

Subhead *C* is coordinate with *A* and *B.* It is an assertion supported by *1* and *2.*

        1. Women in the higher grades of white-collar occupations are typically unmarried.

This is based on expert authority. It will improve when the qualifications of the expert and the source are given.

        2. *The Report of the President's Commission on the Status of Women* indicates the advancement of single women is noticeably greater than that of married women.

Here, the source of the expert opinion is cited. Note that this subhead is coordinate with *1* and subordinate to *C.*

(*Transition:* We've looked at marriage and compared it with the single state. Now let's look at the woman herself.)

All transitions are important; those between main heads especially so. Note the continuation of the topical order— from the wide view to the more specific —the woman herself.

III. Women would be able to develop their full potential.

    A. This would benefit society because their skills would be utilized for the benefit of all.

    B. They would be able to do what they wanted; their lives would be more fulfilling and complete.

    C. There would be fewer unhappy housewives, divorces, disturbed children, and broken homes.

Conclusion: Because marriage is not an ideal state, because the single life has many benefits, and especially because a woman has more opportunity to develop her full potential, you can see that picturing marriage as a utopia for women is wrong. Marriage for single women is not necessarily ideal so look at the single woman for what she is—just as total a woman as any married woman.

Main head *III* is coordinate with *I* and *II*. It is subordinate only to the speech purpose.

This is an assertion that will be supported by several personal examples and an illustration.

This is simply an assertion.

The speaker has tried to tie her final comments back to her statements under main head *I*. This assertion would depend on evidence throughout the speech for support.

Note, first, that the speaker did *not* include a transition between the body and the conclusion. Her first concluding statement serves as a transition.

Notice that her conclusion (1) summarized the speech (note the three main points), (2) left the audience with the overall purpose (marriage is neither an ideal state nor a utopia), and (3) tried to make an impression with her last comment: The single woman is just as total a woman as any married woman.

BIBLIOGRAPHY

Encyclopaedia Britannica, 1970 ed., "Marriage." Also 1979 *Britannica Book of the Year,* "Marriage and Divorce Statistics," p. 301.

Narramore, Clyde, *A Woman's World.* Grand Rapids, Mich., 1963, p. 65.

"Report of the President's Commission on the Status of Women," *American Women,* 1963, p. 33.

"Two Incomes: No Sure Hedge Against Inflation," *U.S. News & World Report,* July 9, 1981, p. 45.

SUMMARY

The process of organizing a speech is important. Some people do not prepare an outline; they have a method of preparation that works for them. Other speakers can prepare an entire speech in their head. Most of us, however, are not so lucky. We must proceed through the steps discussed in this chapter, at first drawing back from the subject to get the big picture and then zooming in to pick up some of the variety of details.

The chapter began with a discussion of outlining. Outlining involves finding the main heads for the body of the speech, ordering them, and then supporting them. Useful organization patterns are topic order, time order, space order, and problem-solution order. As the outline develops, the speaker should check the numbered and lettered statements in the outline against the following points:

1. Statement contains only one idea.
2. Coordinate statements have a common relationship.
3. Subordinate statements support the general statement.
4. No statement overlaps another item.
5. Outline follows some natural sequence.
6. Each statement reveals the importance that the symbol used to designate it indicates (*I*—a main head; *A*—a major subhead, etc.)

Following the development of the body, the speaker can turn his or her attention to the introduction, conclusion, and transitions. All of these should be written out in full for the following reasons:

1. It is easier to judge their effectiveness when one can see them.
2. Changes and adjustments are more easily made when working with something concrete.
3. There is more assurance that each will be well planned, and not left to chance or accident.

Our speech now has structure. It has taken on a specific shape or form. Our next goal will be to consider the language we intend to use to clothe our ideas. We want to stretch the fabric over the umbrella ribs, or adorn the flesh with clothes. Language—word choices—will be considered in the next chapter.

NOTES

[1]See George A. Miller, "The Magical Number Seven, Plus or Minus Two: Some Limits on Our Capacity for Processing Information," in Richard C. Anderson and David P. Ausubel, eds., *Readings in the Psychology of Cognition* (New York: Holt, Rinehart & Winston, 1965), pp. 242–267.

[2]Messages are better comprehended and more persuasive if they are well organized. See Raymond G. Smith, "Effects of Speech Organization upon Attitudes of College Students," *Speech Monographs*, 18 (1951): 292–301; Ernest Thompson, "Some Effects of Message Structure on Listeners' Comprehension," *Speech Monographs*, 39 (1967): 51–57; Harry Sharp, Jr., and Thomas McClung,

"Effect of Organization on the Speaker's Ethos," *Speech Monographs,* 33 (1966): 182–183; James C. McCroskey and R. Samuel Mehrley, "The Effects of Disorganization and Nonfluency on Attitude Change and Source Credibility," *Speech Monographs,* 36 (1969): 13–21; Arlee Johnson, "A Preliminary Investigation of the Relationship Between Message Organization and Listener Comprehension," *Central States Speech Journal,* 21 (Summer 1970): 194–207; James F. Vickrey, Jr., "An Experimental Investigation of the Effect of 'Previews' and 'Reviews' on Retention of Orally Presented Information," *Southern Speech Journal,* 36 (Spring 1971): 209–219; and Christopher Spicer and Ronald E. Bassett, "The Effect of Organization on Learning from an Informative Message," *Southern Speech Journal,* 41 (Spring 1976): 290–299.

[3]It should be noted that speaker credibility and message effectiveness are enhanced if arguments likely to gain listener acceptance are presented first. See Percy Tannenbaum, "Mediated Generalization of Attitude Change via the Principle of Congruity," *Journal of Personality and Social Psychology,* 3 (1966): 493–500; and James C. McCroskey and Samual V. O. Prichard, "Selective Exposure and Lyndon B. Johnson's January 1966 State of the Union Address," *Journal of Broadcasting,* 11 (1967): 331–337.

[4]Research indicates that ideas are better recalled by listeners if they are placed at the beginning *or* at the end of a presentation. More than ten related studies are summarized by Gary Cronkhite in *Persuasion: Speech and Behavioral Change* (Indianapolis: Bobbs-Merrill, 1969), pp. 195–196. Also see Ralph L. Rosnow, "Whatever Happened to the 'Law of Primacy'?" *Journal of Communication,* 16 (March 1966): 10–31.

[5]See John E. Baird, Jr., "The Effects of Speech Summaries Upon Audience Comprehension of Expository Speeches of Varying Quality and Complexity," *Central States Speech Journal,* 25 (Summer 1974): 119–127.

[6]Messages are better comprehended and accepted if transitions are used. See Ernest Thompson, "Some Effects of Message Structure on Listeners' Comprehension," *Speech Monographs,* 34 (1967): 51–57; D. L. Thistlethwaite, H. DeHaan, and J. Kamenetsky, "The Effect of 'Directive' and 'Non-Directive' Communication Procedures on Attitudes," *Journal of Abnormal and Social Psychology,* 51 (1955): 107–118.

eight

CHOOSING THE LANGUAGE

Word Selection

It has been said that style makes the person. *Style* can mean many different things. In a speech situation, a speaker's style is conveyed, in part, through movement and gestures, personal appearance, and the use and management of language. In this chapter the focus is on the language. It is the words that give the speech refinement. When you hear a person speak, your first impression is based, in part, on the quality of the style. With respect to the language, quality of style depends on the words the speaker chooses, how they work together, and how the speaker makes those words work throughout the speech.[1]

Looking at the choice and use of words from a practical standpoint, we must strive to capitalize on the effort we have already invested in this speech. If, indeed, we have laid a solid foundation and built a strong and impressive structure, we must not suddenly decide to relax or to hold back or to consider the job finished. We must be concerned about how the structure looks. After all, our final goal is to get our audience to understand our meaning, believe us, want to accept our ideas and recommendations, and remember our message.[2] All this is more likely to occur when we polish and refine our ideas through the use of effective language. Our language can influence the way our audience receives and perceives our public communication. It is an important link in the chain of events called speech preparation.

This chapter begins with a brief consideration of the nature of language —how it works and some of the major concerns we should have. The focus will then turn to language choices—specifically, the need for clarity, simplicity, accuracy, appropriateness, and dynamism. Finally, six different ways we can improve our language will be mentioned.

The point of this chapter is that language makes a difference. If language is inappropriate, it can cause a complete breakdown in the communication process. If it is appropriate and properly reinforced by the speaker's physical and vocal delivery, the desired meanings and feelings can be evoked in the audience. But effort and planning is required to make language work effectively. It cannot be left to chance. Perhaps surprisingly, speaking effectively is not as natural as breathing.

THE NATURE OF LANGUAGE

To increase your language effectiveness, you will need an understanding of the basics. In this section we will briefly discuss how words (1) are symbolic, (2) are static, (3) have many uses, (4) are perceived differently by different people, and (5) have both denotative and connotative meanings. The summary of this section offers the conclusion, discussed briefly in an earlier chapter, that (6) meanings are in people.

Words are Symbolic

Our ability to understand and use symbols is perhaps the feature that most distinguishes us from all other living creatures. It is so much a part of us that we take it for granted. It is automatic. It is part of every facet of life, whether we see, hear, touch, think, or even dream. Our entire waking time—and some of our sleeping time—is affected by our production, receipt, or interpretation of symbols. We are not speaking of language alone—for words are symbols because they represent objects, ideas, concepts, or feelings. We are speaking of all our perceptions, judgments, feelings, and behaviors. They are all affected by our responses to symbols—things that have communicative value.

In the next chapter we will discuss nonverbal symbols such as facial expressions, eye contact, posture, movement, and gestures. There is another

HAGAR THE HORRIBLE by Dik Browne. © King Features Syndicate, Inc., 1978

class of nonverbal symbols called paralanguage—our ability to use our voice to convey sincerity, pleasantness, or animation.[3] In addition, our appearance, including the way we dress and groom ourselves, and those items with which we choose to surround ourselves can be classified as object language—or object symbols. Also, one must recognize that the verbal and nonverbal operate together, mutually reinforcing and enhancing, or undermining and detracting from, the message. This is all part of our symbolic world.

But what is the point of all this? Why is a view of language as symbolic so important? First, it is important because symbols are the basis for all communication. Because of our limitations as human beings, we cannot make contact with all of reality. We do, however, respond to fragments of it. As we respond, we interpret, apply labels to, and categorize what we perceive. Our categories are the basis for our thinking as well as for our use of language. We organize the world into categories. For us, these categories become reality—*our* reality. After all, what other reality could we have, considering our limitations? For example, we encounter "teachers" early in our educational career. After experiencing one (or several), we form impressions of how "teachers" are supposed to act and how we are supposed to respond to them. This category of "teacher" can help determine our attitude toward formal education, learning, and even knowledge. This indicates how categories are often interlocking. As we talk to others about teachers or education, it is the shape or content of this category that provides the base—our reality—that provides us the information and insights we share. We can call this reality, then, *symbolic reality*—since it is based on our personal category system. It helps us determine what we select to perceive as well as how to interpret and classify what we perceive. Language is the primary medium used to produce perceptions, judgments, and knowledge. Our language, too, will be affected by our whole process of perceiving, just as our perceiving will be affected by our language. The point is that as we depend on language, we must realize we are depending on representations of reality—symbols—and not reality itself. What is "real" for one person is not necessarily what is "real" for another. No two of us have the same world.[4] Thus, language has meaning only in terms of the associations established by the people using (or responding to) that language.

What determines the associations that people have for words? *All* the experiences we have had. Our education (or miseducation) from parents or teachers. All the sermons and lectures we have heard from other significant people. The movies, radio programs, television shows we have experienced. The books, magazines, newspapers, and comic strips we have read, and the conversations we have had with friends and associates. It is these associations that help form the images that are an important part of the view of communication as *transaction*.

CONSIDER THIS

We'd like to say a word for the campaign being waged by Bill Gold, a *Washington Post* columnist, to help save the English language.

We are cheering Bill on because we see an explosive increase in the number of writers and speakers who can't be bothered about meanings of words, singulars and plurals of nouns, tenses and moods of verbs, the right places to put punctuation, or ways to arrange sentences to show what goes with what. . . .

Sloppy writers regard all this as a narrow concern of scholars, whereas, as a matter of fact, regard for good English is central to accurate communication. . . .

"Just because some people have corrupted various words and usages," the columnist retorts, "there is no need for careful writers and speakers to be guilty of the same transgressions. Slovenly usage poses the danger that language will become a collection of vague grunts, y'knows and other whatchamacallits."

SOURCE: Marvin Stone, "Due Dismay About Our Language," *U.S. News & World Report,* April 23, 1979, p. 102. Copyright 1979, U.S. News & World Report, Inc.

Two things appear obvious: (1) When you choose to select words to phrase your ideas, you are selecting from your own category system, and (2) when you speak to others, you are attempting to communicate with their category systems: not only with their physical and psychological environment or their feelings at the moment but also with their memories of all the relevant associations they have or are able to make. For your listeners, not only will their experiences be different but also their memories of their experiences will differ.

TRY THIS 1

Briefly write down the *first* association you have for each of the following words:

disease	school	art
teacher	travel	love
magazine	drink	book
church	sport	play
bully	tree	pet

- Is this association likely to be different from that of other people?
- Would this association likely be different for you if you were to make the association at some later time?
- Is it easy to write down a single association? Or did you have to pick from several to write down just the one?
- Do you know what caused you to make the association you did?

Our view of language as symbolic is also important because it causes us to realize that when we select a word there is no guarantee that the word we select represents reality. The word is not the thing—only a representation of it—*our* representation of it. Thus, in a speech, if we tell our audience that " 'pets' are an unnecessary nuisance," does this accurately reflect what we mean? The question is not, "Do the words fit the facts?" The question is, "Do the words communicate to the audience what the speaker intends?" In answering, we must try to be as objective as possible.

Words are Static

One time I was told that whenever you go to work for people, their first impressions of you will stick for as long as you are there—that there is little you can do to change those first impressions. Words also have that effect. They are used to represent objects, ideas, concepts, and feelings in the real world, but the real world is changing—just as an employee changes. Our meanings for words, however, often do not make the corresponding adjustments to the real world—they are static. Although word meanings change, *our* meanings for words often do not. Thus, our concern must be to try to represent the world *as it is*—not *as it was.* We must be active and accurate perceivers of the dynamic nature of life if our word symbols are to be effective.

One way we have of increasing the chances that our perceptions will more accurately represent the world *as it is* would be cross–checking. The more people we talk with, the more reading we do, the more sources we consult, the more likely we will get to the truth. Truth is elusive, but the only way we have to approach it is through pursuit—active inquiry. We must be willing to pose and answer questions.

Words Have Many Uses

In his newspaper column, "Strictly Personal," Sydney Harris wrote "If you know only 3,000 of the most frequent words in the English language out of a running sample of 100,000 words, you have an understanding of 95 percent of all the words."[5] Considering the number of things in the world we use words to describe, you can see that we do not have one word for each thing or occurrence. Instead, a limited number are used to represent a large number of things. Much misunderstanding occurs because of this. We use the same words to represent many things, forgetting that just because we use a word in one way does not mean that our listeners will interpret and understand it in that way.

Examples of words that have many meanings are numerous. What, for example, is your meaning for the following words:

date	drip	diet
fairy	dog	dig
bar	wasp	bear
tip	sex	young
sap	crash	prank
pin	joint	pan
high	hack	hit

All have at least two obvious meanings—and numerous other meanings when you consider the perceptions, memories, and experiences people have had with these words. That is, these words take on many additional shades, colors, hues, or textures because of people's associations. Fan through a dictionary and you will notice a considerable number of words with ten or more meanings—some have twenty-five or more.

Our concern, as speakers, is to be careful when we use words that have many meanings. If we strive to use words that people can directly translate, we will be clear. If we must choose words with a variety of meanings, then we should define them for our listeners—to indicate *our* use or *our* context.

TRY THIS 2

Can you give more than one meaning for each of the following words or word pairs?

bounty	go down
end	honor
family	light
get off	order
heart	regular
pick up	state
weak	turn
part	yield

Can you state a third or fourth meaning for each of them? Can you use them in sentences that reflect each of these different meanings? Do you see how an audience member might become confused if the exact meaning or context were not defined within a speech?

Words are Perceived Differently

We perceive things and events selectively. We perceive less than one one-hundredth of what goes on around us at any time—and we choose what we will see, hear, touch, taste or smell—most of the time. We can choose to step out of the smoke of a barbecue grill; we may not be able to step gracefully or quickly out of the smoke of our burning house. In most instances, however, we choose. Thus, if we see an object or event, we see in it exactly what we choose to see. What you get from a movie is based on your previous contacts and experiences, as discussed before. You have not seen or heard all there was to see and hear, just what you could gain based on your personal limitations. But if someone mentions the name of the movie to you—the one that you saw—those specific feelings, thoughts, or impressions will be called up or aroused. You will remember what you perceived (or what you remember of what you perceived). The same is true of any word that is used. A word, like the name of the movie, will arouse only a limited picture of what was—or what is. That is why stereotypes are so powerful; a word arouses a quick mental, but partial, picture.

When you present ideas to others, in the same way, you only give them a partial picture. You have selected what to say—or the picture you want to paint.

Even those speakers who go on and on giving every minute detail of an experience cannot give us a complete picture. That cannot be done given *any* amount of time.

What bearing does all this have on public communication? For the speaker, once again, this fact (selective perception) should underline the need for selecting with care words to be used to describe objects and events. A speaker can qualify his or her statements and observations with phrases such as, "As *I* saw it" or "From *my* vantage point" or "According to what *I* heard" or "This is, of course, just *my* point of view."

For listeners, this fact has broader implications. Listeners, in order to fully understand the speaker, must wrestle with the following factors:

1. They must realize that what speakers leave out can be as important, if not more important, than what they include. Speakers select and choose to make their point or their case.
2. They must understand that what speakers say reflects not just the thing or event being described but also the speaker's prejudices, biases, and past experiences—his or her entire belief and value structure.
3. They must appreciate the fact that speakers cannot describe (nor often, fully understand) what they have no labels for. A speaker's vocabulary places limits on how he or she is able to describe reality.

Listeners will almost always benefit if they simply remind themselves that they are not getting the whole story. There is *always* more. The image they construct in a transaction is *always* a partial one.

Words have Denotative and Connotative Meanings

This feature of the words of our language further complicates accurate communication. A word that has a denotative meaning refers fairly accurately or directly to the object it represents. Since language is symbolic, it is always representing something. The more accurate or direct this representation is, the more denotative the meaning of the word. Do you remember the first books you used as you began to read? In some of them, there would be an object and then one word on the page—for example, a ball, and then the word "ball." This is highly denotative for a child—especially if the object described is new to him or her. Take the word *zebra.* Most children have not seen a zebra, but even if they have, a zebra does not look like any other animal, and most zebras look alike; thus, *zebra* would be a highly denotative word. Most listeners agree on denotative meanings.

Connotative meanings are a problem because of their subjective nature. Speakers who use words that have highly connotative meanings can run into serious problems because of the abstractness of the words. People have their own personal definitions for such words; often they attach emotional overtones to them as well; sometimes their feelings for such words are also ambiguous—so ambiguous, in fact, that "words cannot express how I feel." Define *love* or *sexuality.* Sometimes a prejudice or a bias is so strong that it colors our thinking and arouses intense feelings: The words *liar, cheater, robber,* or *swindler* might, for some, cause such reactions.

For communicators the key word is *awareness.* If we are aware that words may have a broad range of meanings for people, that they may stir up unwanted prejudices and biases or may simply create confusion because of their abstractness or diffuseness, we are less likely to take communication for granted. The first step toward change in any endeavor is awareness.

TRY THIS 3

Select from the following list those words you feel are more denotative than connotative. Check each of these words:

_____ freedom		_____ fire hydrant	
_____ chair		_____ democracy	
_____ automobile		_____ gift	
_____ hope		_____ fence	
_____ strive		_____ liberation	
_____ censorship		_____ radio	
_____ motivation		_____ typewriter	
_____ faith		_____ fork	

Can you see how it is helpful if audience members hear denotative words rather than connotative ones? What must speakers do when they choose to use highly connotative words?

The Meanings of Words are in People

When speaking to a group of listeners, you do not convey meaning—that is, meaning is not in the words you express nor in the message as a whole. As a speaker, meaning lies in your head—in the many associations that are aroused or evoked (brought forth) when you conceive ideas. That is your meaning. Listeners also have such a set of associations. Speakers use words as triggers to stimulate the appropriate associations in their listeners. Their goal is to cause the audience to come up with similar associations. Words, then, must be carefully controlled to create this occurrence—especially when one considers their symbolic nature, how many uses words have, how differently they are often perceived, and their denotative and connotative meanings.

Because no two people have exactly the same experiences, no word can evoke exactly the same associations for two people. The speaker's goal must be to select words that trigger close associations—that is, words that approach the ideal of identical meaning. To have *communication,* a reasonably common set of words must be used—and to have *understanding,* a reasonably common set of associations must be attached to those words by both speaker and listener.

LANGUAGE CHOICES

Knowing the nature of language and recognizing how language relates to reality is helpful as we strive to make our language choices as effective as we can. But some specific guidelines are also useful to help us make specific choices among words. When faced with a choice of which words to use, we should strive for words that are (1) clear, (2) simple, (3) accurate, (4) appropriate, and (5) dynamic. If we use these guidelines, our language will become more effective.

Words Should be Clear

Clarity is achieved when the words the speaker uses are immediately meaningful to the listeners—that is, when there is a close correspondence between the speaker's meaning and the meaning evoked in the minds of audience members. If we, as speakers, can arouse specific and definite meanings, we have a good chance of being understood. We must strive to use words free from ambiguity and confusion.

CONSIDER THIS

Every time he speaks to someone the conventions of society demand that he automatically adjust his language, moment by moment, according to his relationship with those to whom he is speaking. This demand involves two independent aspects of the relationship: the difference in formal status between speaker and listener and the degree of intimacy and familiarity that they enjoy.

SOURCE: David S. Thomson, *Language* (New York: Time–Life Books, 1975), p. 124. Courtesy Time-Life Books Inc. Human Behavior, *Language* © 1975 Time Inc.

Some speakers feel they can speak off the top of their heads and automatically attain this clarity. No doubt some can. But in speaking off the top of our heads we tend to ramble, take shortcuts, or make improper assumptions about the audience's knowledge and understanding. We are not as precise or specific as we would be if we had given more time to the planning of our language.

Clarity can be attained if we practice the following three rules.

1. We should have a clear picture in our mind of precisely what we want to say. We should refrain from opening our mouths until our minds are fully in gear.
2. We must be able to clarify and elaborate on what we want to say. Redundancy—saying the same thing again, in different words—helps.
3. We should be receptive to the feedback we get and use it to further guide our communication efforts.

Words Should be Simple

Some people have an idea that public communication is formal, and because of its formality, big words should be used. This is far from the truth. It is the short, simple word that gains understanding. In informal conversation, we use short, simple words. Public communication is simply extended conversation. Our goal is still to share ideas, information, and feelings, and we do this best if we adopt a natural, easy manner. A large, stilted, or formal vocabulary can create confusion, can sometimes cause distance between speaker and audience, and tends to distract from the message. Such vocabulary may be appropriate for some occasions; not for most. For example, a student arguing for more balance between practical and theoretical courses in speech might say:

> In our pedagogical scheme, practical, application–oriented courses should be accompanied by a comprehensive speech curriculum that also includes substantive theoretical courses.

This needless use of large words (pedagogical, comprehensive, and substantive) does little to aid communication. The student could make the same point by saying:
> We need a broad–based series of course offerings that offers us both practical and theoretical choices.

William Strunk and E. B. White, in their short book, *The Elements of Style,* say it best when they state, "Do not be tempted by a twenty–dollar word when there is a ten–center handy, ready, and able."[6] This does not mean one must be dull or childish—using words appropriate for an elementary–level listener. If one truly understands "The Nature of Language," then one can see that words are often vague and complicated. The choice of a simple word can avoid an unnecessary communication breakdown.

How does one attain simplicity? Begin with these three guidelines:

1. Use your ear as a guide. Be sensitive to the words you use.
2. Consider your own vocabulary and background. Do your words feel comfortable and natural? Do they reflect your normal conversation?
3. Take note of your audience's knowledge and background. Do not talk down to them; strive to approach them at their level of sophistication.

An alternative to simplicity is a concept called *refinement.* To refine one's language is to improve it by introducing subtleties or distinctions. To refine one's language means avoiding pomposity, confusion, and ostentatiousness. Refinement can whet interest in listeners in ways that simplicity cannot. Simplicity can be a barren leveler of language. Refinement can make it a surging elevator. Why, for example, simply say "the complexity of government" when you can refine this language to convey an image of "the complex web of government" or "the tentacles of the government octopus"? "Motivated by a new day," could be refined to "motivated by the challenges that a mere twenty–four hours offered . . ." Refining can increase exactness and specificity. It need not increase the length or wordiness.

CONSIDER THIS

It's odd how words that are so different in their psychological dynamics can come to mean much the same thing in ordinary language. I am thinking here of the two words "vanity" and "conceit," which most people use interchangeably, though they are worlds apart.

Except that they are both concerned about the self, they differ in almost every respect. While most people are vain, to some degree, few people are truly conceited. A conceited person is insufferable; a vain one may be merely annoying, or pathetic, or even amusing. The crucial difference between the two, of course, is that conceit thinks too well of itself, while vanity wants others to think well of itself. Vanity is an all–too–human emotion; conceit is pridefully Satanic; it is the sin that made the Prince of Angels fall.

It is conceit that does the real damage, not vanity. A Napoleon happens to be both, but whereas his vanities were ridiculous, his conceit led a continent to disaster. A merely vain man will reflect, or reflect on, the opinions of others; a conceited one is impervious to public opinion, private correction, or the pangs of conscience.

We should really learn to distinguish better between the two, not only for psychological accuracy, but in order to detect and identify the really dangerous characters in our lives—those who listen to only one voice, and it is always their own.

SOURCE: From STRICTLY PERSONAL by Sydney J. Harris. © 1979 Field Enterprises, Inc. Courtesy of Field Newspaper Syndicate.

Words Should be Accurate

We must try to select words that convey what we mean. We must try to fill as many gaps as we can, so the meanings stirred up in the listeners' minds come close to those in our own. Most of the time we do not say what we mean because we do not give our listeners enough information. Because we already know the subject it is easy for us to visualize what we are talking about. We sometimes forget that the listeners lack our experience. When we refer to an object or event we must let the listeners know which object or event is being discussed and provide enough details so that they can also think about it. For example, if you were describing lack of driver safety or responsibility and witnessed a car run a stop sign and hit a child, you could just say that a driver hit a child. But that would convey none of the drama of the moment nor provide an impression in your listeners' minds about what had happened. The incident could be described with more detail and specificity:

> A fellow in his early twenties was traveling west on Liberty Street at about fifty miles an hour (in town) when he came to the stop sign at Seventh Street. Instead of slowing down, he put his foot on the accelerator even harder—just as a little girl of about seven crossed the intersection on her new two–wheeler. He hit the girl; she was thrown for nearly thirty feet

into the trunk of a big maple tree. She was killed upon impact—and her new bike looked like spaghetti—all crumpled, twisted, and mashed.

TRY THIS 4

Tell a short story about any one of the following topics, providing as much specificity and detail as you can:

1. An accident you witnessed
2. A book you have recently read
3. A movie you saw
4. The way you helped someone else
5. A trip you recently took
6. A vivid experience you recently had

Besides omitting details, we are sometimes inaccurate because we use words unfamiliar to our audience. When we become immersed in a subject, we begin to pick up the accompanying vocabulary. We know the words and we become so comfortable using them that we forget our audience has not had the same experience. Thus, our symbols have no meaning for them.

We can attain accuracy if we remember these rules:

1. Keep the number of examples used few enough so that we can give fairly complete details: names, places, dates, and other facts.
2. Select specific and concrete words that by their nature are accurate and clear.
3. Avoid uncommon words or technical language with which members of our audience may not be familiar.

Words Should be Appropriate

Words should be designed for a *specific* audience, not for just any listeners, but for the listeners who are to hear the speech. If the audience were to change the words would undoubtedly need to be changed. They would have to be adapted to different needs, interests, knowledge, and attitudes. In Chapter 4, "Analyzing the Audience: Idea Adaptation," we talked about the need to find out as much as possible about the audience. It is on this information that language selection must be based. Here, too, we must remember that needs, interests, knowledge, and attitudes change—they are not static. Thus, your language must reveal similar flexibility and adaptability; it must be designed not just to correspond with your audience but also to correspond with your own growth and development, with changes in your purpose, or with differences that occur in the situation.

CONSIDER THIS

His "house" was not a "home." He might "have" a bath, but he would never "take" one. At nature's irresistible summons, he would use the "lavatory" or the "loo," but certainly not a "toilet." This was the proper–speaking English gentleman, as anatomized by Nancy Mitford in a 1955 article in Encounter magazine that popularized the terms "U" and "non–U"—for upper- and non–upper–class speech. Mitford had borrowed the concept from philologist Alan S. C. Ross, who maintained that language was the last remaining distinction between the upper class and "the others." But since then, according to an irreverent new Debrett's Peerage tome called "U and Non–U Revisited," even that slender demarcation has gone muzzy.

Nowadays, say the English cultural arbiters who contributed to the book, one can barely tell a nabob from a navvy by words alone. Thanks largely to mass education and television, most Britons speak an egalitarian patois, compounded of cockney slang, corporate jargon and crass Americanism. Such slang phrases as "drop dead" or "big deal" can be heard at the best Belgravia dinner parties.

SOURCE: David Gelman, "Talk of the Town," *Newsweek,* April 30, 1979, p. 84. Copyright 1979, by Newsweek, Inc. All Rights Reserved. Reprinted by Permission.

Appropriate word choice has another side as well. Sometimes speakers strive to make their language appropriate to their audience when they should not! That is, what they perceive as appropriate is not. A middle–aged person speaking to a group of teen–agers should not imitate the speech patterns of teen–agers in an attempt to be appropriate. Trying to use their language would make this person look ridiculous. It would be wiser to preface the use of teen–ager terms with, "what you call _____" or avoid such usage altogether. The same situation can occur when a white person speaks to a black audience. Just as the black handshake is used to promote a feeling of unity or singleness of purpose, so is some of the black language. A white speaker using black English sounds artificial and forced. It is better to use such references sparingly and most carefully; inappropriate or incorrect usage is quickly picked up by listeners and can seriously affect speaker credibility. Appropriate language enhances the trust bond between the speaker and the audience.

Here are some simple rules to follow in order to make certain your words are appropriate:

1. Base your choice of words on the audience analysis you performed. Always choose words that relate directly to the audience.
2. Select material that has audience appeal. Your choice of language will be easier if your facts, examples, illustrations, opinions, statistics, and personal experiences already relate.
3. Avoid questionable words—that is, words you are not sure the audience would understand. Select another word rather than take a chance on confusion or misunderstanding.

4. Use personal pronouns such as *you, us, we,* and *our.* These give the audience a verbal clue to your interest in them.
5. Use audience questions. These create the impression of direct audience contact and of direct conversation. They generate a sense of personal involvement.

Words Should be Dynamic

Words should be vivid and impressive.[7] They should enhance the content through emphasis and imagery. Your words are the attire with which you clothe your thoughts. Although you do not want them to come across in tuxedo and tails for a family picnic, you also do not want the audience to lose the essence of your ideas because of the language. In other words, you want strength with minimal distraction. This section focuses on (1) some of the ways in which speakers can gain strength from their choices of words, and (2) some of the major distractions they should try to avoid.

Strength. Language that is clear, simple, accurate, and appropriate will be understood. But if you want to hold the audience's attention, if you want to maintain their interest, and if you want to create a lasting impression, then your language must also be vivid and impressive. It should arouse images in the listeners' minds. Have you ever tried to describe to someone the beauty of a sunset? The aching muscles you experienced after jogging some distance or after a long bicycle ride? The unbelievable Polynesian food you ate at an exotic restaurant? The thumping, driving, all–possessive beat of rock music at some local lounge? Words are used to create such images—to draw upon the imaginations of listeners. Along with visual aids, physical delivery, and voice, we—as speakers—can cause our listeners not only to relive old experiences but also to create new ones through their imagination.

How do we gain such strength? What means do we have for accomplishing this? We will consider several ways, but first we must realize that strength of words comes from strength of thought. None of the following techniques will work if you do not *first* have a strong mental picture of what it is you want to communicate. The more vividly you can see this in your mind's eye, the more likely you will be able to state your ideas strongly. Some useful techniques for indicating strength are using figures of speech, evaluative language, and active language, and getting other support from language.

Of the numerous *figures of speech,* the most common are metaphor, simile, antithesis, personification, and hyperbole. A *metaphor* provides a comparison between two unlike things: "We must not allow ourselves to become an island of selfishness from lack of concern."[8] A *simile* is similar to a metaphor because it also compares two unlike things, but it announces that a comparison is being made with the words *like* or *as:* "He had a mind like a steel trap." An *antithesis* places two opposing ideas side by side: "Our success is not an end; our success is but the beginning." *Personification* attributes human characteristics to inanimate objects: "Such laws lack the warmth and compassion that are supposed to characterize our society." Finally, *hyperbole* is simply exaggeration or overstatement: "Her power controls and manipulates the very strings that govern our lives." Several other sources develop figures of speech in some detail.[9] The treatment here is brief for several reasons: (1) it is unlikely that figures of speech will be a prominent part of your early speeches, (2) the use of figures of speech requires both practice and experience, and (3) the goal of speaking should be a free, spontaneous style that comes naturally, with the words largely determined at the moment of utterance. Because figures of speech must often be planned, they lend themselves to a formal, manuscript style of presentation, not an informal conversational style.

TRY THIS 5

Can you think of a metaphor, simile, antithesis, personification, and hyperbole to accompany each of the following experiences? Be creative. Make them up for as many of these experiences as you can:

Drinking   A date
Summer vacation   Studying
Being lazy   Eating too much
Working too hard   Wasting time

Evaluative language also can reveal strength. It is sometimes referred to as "loaded" language because it introduces an evaluation into a description. The kind of evaluation the speaker uses can determine how the audience reacts. Is it severe? Is it mild? Is it unimportant? No matter what the thing, idea, or event being evaluated, by naming it you will evoke a response. The intensity of the response will be determined by the label you choose, as in the examples below.

- Something costs less: It is cheap, inexpensive, low–priced, a good buy, a real steal.
- Someone cheated: He bent the rules, deceived, defrauded, swindled, hoodwinked.
- Someone was murdered: He was butchered, killed, assassinated, eliminated, neutralized.
- Something is unimportant: It is insignificant, unessential, trivial, petty, namby–pamby, measly.

The point to remember is that when you name it, you evaluate it. Whether the name is favorable, neutral, or unfavorable, it is evaluative. Thus, as speaker or listener, you must judge whether labels are correctly used—that is, do they meet the conditions under which those labels are normally applied? Should they be used in the present instance? Do they satisfy the purposes the speaker intends? Is the speaker correct or right in using them in this way?

As speakers we do label ideas, objects, and events. As we do so, we must make judgments about appropriateness—ethical judgments that are sometimes difficult to make. Evaluative labeling can be devious, but awareness will guide us both in making certain our use of such labels is accurate and can be supported by the facts, and in evaluating their use by others.

Active language is often achieved by word choice and sentence construction. A sentence that depicts someone doing something is much stronger than one that describes a state of being: "A sense of calm was experienced" is not as strong as "we lay down on the beach to rest—calm because we knew we had been successful." Words can be active and strong instead of passive and weak:

Passive	*Active*
walk	stagger, stumble, limp, stroll, tramp, march
sit	plop, perch, straddle, slouch
beautiful	radiant, striking, knockout, graceful, stunning, devastating
strength	brute force, powerful, virile, robust, stout, vigorous

When these words depict a person doing something to someone or something, they take on further strength. For example:

The student staggered into the fourth bar that evening.
The teacher straddled the chair in front of the class.
She possessed a radiant gracefulness as she walked before us.
In one stout hand he picked up the chair and brutally broke it over his opponent's blistered back.

Nouns can be active. Note the strength of the words *activist* and *radical* —or *deviant!* Sometimes it is wise to select the unusual, unique, word just to capture strength from what the audience perceives as new. It captures attention because it has shock value, causes surprise, or creates a striking image. Care must be taken, however, to avoid confusion. Words should not distract listeners from the essential message.

Adjectives and adverbs can also be active. "He was a vicious arguer," illustrates the use of a strong adjective. "She moved swiftly to the heart of the issue" illustrates the use of a strong adverb. Words add the force that causes the message to have impact. Appropriate, powerful words will drive the point home and make it memorable.

TRY THIS 6

For each of the following words, substitute dynamic (stronger) words that say essentially the same thing:

slept	clear
drove	good
quiet	exciting

handsome	scared
late	extrovert
active	different
healthy	first
dumb	talkative
shy	ill
poor	muscular

Can you see the advantages of these dynamic words in a public speech? What limitations are placed on you, as a speaker, regarding the selection of dynamic words?

In sentence structure, select sentences cast in the active voice rather than in the passive voice. Make certain you have a *noun* doing something: "He fights fiercely and relentlessly." In the passive voice this sentence does not have the same strength: "The fierce and relentless fighting was done by him."

Dynamism occurs because of active words and sentences. This is not to make a case for unnecessary or irrelevant hyperbole; but when you can be more specific or more exact in description by using a word that fits the idea, object, or event being described with more precision, use it. To use a technically inappropriate word just for its shock value is unethical.

Other *supports from language* that will add strength to the message are *repetition, refrain,* and *parallelism.* They must be used with discretion and are designed to drive home a point. To repeat a point once adds emphasis: "People are basically lazy. People *are* basically lazy." In the second statement, a slightly different vocal emphasis can be given to add emphasis—the italicized word indicates the change that could occur in this sentence.

A refrain is a sentence or phrase that occurs at regular intervals in a passage or speech: "We know that many things we do every day could become habit forming. *But we don't make habits of them.* We may go without a shower and let our facial hair grow. *But we don't make habits of them.* We may go without a meal and take an afternoon nap. *But we don't make habits of them*"

Parallelism occurs when exactly the same sentence structure is used repeatedly: "Do you know what it means to have someone tell you *when* you can shower? Do you know what it means to have someone tell you *when* you can exercise? Do you know what it means to have someone tell you *when* you have to go to bed?"

CONSIDER THIS

Those who reject the importance of speaking style are free to follow their own inclinations largely because of one man who knew that how you say it can make all the difference. The free world was saved because Winston Churchill said, "I have nothing to offer but blood, toil, tears, and sweat"—not "It's going to be a tough fight but if we accept sacrifices we can win"; "We shall fight on the beaches, we shall fight on the landing ground. . . . We shall never surrender!'' —not ''We'll fight wherever they show up, and we can beat 'em''; ''This was their finest hour. . . . Never have so many owed so much to so few'' —not ''Boy, did they do a job! We sure owe those guys a lot!''

SOURCE: Philip Lesly, *How We Discommunicate* (New York: AMACOM, a division of American Management Associations, 1979), p. 91.

Strength can also be gained by selecting striking facts, meaningful quotations, impressive epigrams, sharp descriptions, graphic illustrations, or words and thoughts that add surprise and suspense or create climax or conflict.

Much of the strength in language results from speakers' willingness to stamp their own personal imprint on the speech. Not enough can be said for speakers' originality and uniqueness—what they can bring to the speech effort just because they are who they are. Authors or instructors can make suggestions, the suggestions will be read or heard and understood, but the final choices are left to the speakers.

TRY THIS 7

Think of the first *strength* you might use to bring three of the following ideas to life. That is, if you were speaking on three of the following topics, how would you, through strength of language, gain a dynamic presentation?

1. Inflation
2. Prayer in the public schools
3. Professional sports
4. Noise pollution
5. Reading other people's nonverbal communication
6. Keeping fit
7. Chemical warfare
8. Dreams

Distractions. In striving for strength, however, speakers must be careful to avoid certain weaknesses that can result from choosing words that distract. Some distracting elements have already been mentioned; in this secion we will discuss several more. As you read these, realize that this is by no means a complete catalog. Avoiding these will help prevent some communication problems but not *all*. Even after removing all the distractions you can from your speech, you must realize that some are likely to persist. We all have some poor language habits that are deeply ingrained and not easily eliminated. If we can eliminate the major problems, however, we can work on the more persistent, difficult problems over a period of time. In reading about the following distractions, note that in certain situations they may be appropriate. Once again, the speaker must make the distinction as to when something is appropriate and when it is not. We will discuss verbal clutter, jargon, big words, triteness, slang, and empty words.

Verbal clutter is verbal interference. It is like static on the radio, picture distortion on television, or a scratch or nick on a phonograph record. You know what it is when you hear it—especially if a speaker overuses it. It is the *uh's* or *um's,* the *well, ah* or *okay* and the *you know* used as filler material. We use them when we are looking for an idea, when we are very nervous, or when we are tense. Although they are natural occurrences, they are also distracting and thus can crowd out meaning. If you become aware of your own use of these interferences, you can begin to work on eliminating them. A tape recorder will help you identify problem areas. Practice in speaking without using verbal clutter will help eliminate it.

Jargon is simply the use of technical language. Every field and every subject has its own jargon—from plumbing to electrical engineering, from prison to hospital, from baseball to backgammon, from rock music to poetry, from flying to sailing, and from social psychology to computer science. Terminology that is clear to the specialists in one field or area is not necessarily clear to the expert in another. Thus, verbal symbols selected from any one field may need defining. If there is a question of whether or not a word needs defining, it is better not to take a chance. Define it.

Big words can be distracting if used inappropriately. Why needlessly exhibit your vocabulary? What do you gain? Some speakers think that they gain greater credibility and prestige, that others will look at them as "people who know." The trouble is that too often the speakers lose because they avoided using a short, hard–hitting word that would have resulted in greater accuracy, precision, and impressiveness.

Triteness refers to words and phrases that have been overused and overworked. People hear the phrases used by others and they pick them up because the phrases are easy to use and require no thinking. Here are some examples of trite phrases:

> In conclusion, I would just like to say . . .
> Last, but not least . . .
> It's the principle of the thing.
> It gives me great pleasure . . .
> Tell it like it is.

CONSIDER THIS

Insensitivity allows the continued use of phrases that started as inspired images but are now so hackneyed neither the user nor the audience has any image in mind when they are used: "fishing in troubled waters," "run of the mill," "toe the line," "go to bat for," "have no axe to grind," "stand behind you four–square," "take up the cudgels for" (who uses "four–square" or "cudgel" in any other form today?), "upset the apple cart," and countless others.

SOURCE: Philip Lesly, *How We Discommunicate* (New York: AMACOM, a division of American Management Associations, 1979), p. 100.

Many phrases are made popular by television shows and are quickly absorbed by listeners to become part of their vocabularies or repertoire. Because of the faddishness (and vacuity!) of these phrases and their immediate overuse, they quickly become shopworn and are best avoided.

TRY THIS 8

The following list includes some trite phrases that have been in vogue. Can you add five or more phrases to update the list?

laid back	in the public interest
the bottom line	no problem
off the wall	ballpark figure
out of the closet	have a nice day
it's the pits	in the time frame of
I could care less	maintain yourself
and I mean that	you've got to be kidding

Are there both advantages *and* disadvantages to using such phrases in speeches? Are there times (certain audiences/special occasions) when the use of such phrases might be helpful or supportive?

Slang is closely related to trite words and phrases and should be avoided for the same reason. Slang is often viewed as harsh, coarse, or vulgar language. Using slang tends to lower the status of the user. Just as in using trite words, using slang is easy. It takes effort to avoid these habitual dependencies, but the result can be a fresher, more dynamic language. Language free from slang helps to clarify ideas, makes ideas vivid, and raises the speaker's image in the eyes of the audience. Obscene language might also be included in this category.[10]

Finally, *empty words* are those that have *no* meaning. We live in a world of superlatives: Everything is bigger, better than excellent, fantastic, or super. Consider the labels placed on packages as one example: How much bigger is a box marked "super king size" than one marked "king size" or "super size"? Where does "family size" or "giant size" fit in? How outstanding is something when a person calls everything *super*? Considering the effect that advertising has on us, the confusion is not surprising. But one must remember that we are all affected. Thus, to use these same words to describe an idea, object, or event simply has little or no meaning. Our senses have already been anesthetized. The words have been rendered impotent by excess. A user of such words may not be given the same attention, or consideration that he or she would have had different word choices been made.

We select the words we choose to use. The same principle applies to word choice as to selection of a speech topic. Why make the speech situation more difficult than it need be? Why choose a topic that may not relate to our audience and then try to make it fit? Why select words that may distract if we can choose others that do not have the same potential? To enhance our ideas, we must choose words and phrases that add interest and attractiveness—that clothe our ideas in attire that will appeal to our audience.

IMPROVING OUR LANGUAGE USE

Because our language habits have been with us for so long, they are hard to change. But the rapidity with which we pick up a trite phrase, an advertising slogan, or a television star's latest verbal mannerism proves that change can and does occur. We simply must control the change so that it operates in the direction of improvement. Rules and formulas offer no recourse; however, the following guidelines will be helpful. All require some dedication and commitment to the process of improvement; all will work over a period of time.

1. Monitor your use of language. This, after all, was how you established your initial vocabulary; the only difference is that your father and mother did the monitoring (and coaxing)—not you. Now you must be the one to note the clarity, simplicity, accuracy, and appropriateness of your words, and the dynamism in your language. When you notice problems, make the appropriate adjustments. Work at improvement all the time.

2. Be aware of how others use language. We discussed skillful listening in Chapter 3, "Listening to Others: Learning, Discovering, and Developing." Apply the principles of effective listening as you listen for the five categories—clarity, simplicity, accuracy, appropriateness, dynamism—in other people's use of language.

Listen with the goal of discovering new words and new uses for words you already know. Note the context in which the words are used and overall impact of the words used.[11] Make language part of that minuscule sector of what goes on around you that you attempt to oberve.

3. Use a good dictionary. Getting into the habit of using a dictionary is like calling on a friend in time of need.[12] It's like a child growing up with an encyclopedia in the home. Every question can be attacked or at least approached; the child forms a dependency. Using a dictionary can be habit-forming—but it's a healthy habit.

A book of synonyms can also be useful. Using the dictionary and book of synonyms, you will gain the following advantages:

1. You can find the meaning of new words you hear or read.
2. You will learn how to pronounce words correctly.

3. You can discover alternative words to those you are accustomed to using, and thus greatly increase your word power and vocabulary.

Try to remember your discoveries. There are two keys to remembering: (1) Write down any word or expression that interests you and (2) use the new word or expression in conversation. As you use it, often you will notice how it becomes more comfortable, natural, and available when needed.

TRY THIS 9

Using a book of synonyms, find alternatives for the following words:

good	opposition	feeling
relevant	pleasure	great
excellent	speech	imagination
useless	thought	perfection
absurd	attention	power
agreement	belief	right
cooperation	certainty	success
hope	communication	truth
important	failure	ambition

What help does a book of synonyms provide for a public speaker? Have you ever found yourself addicted to a certain word? When did you tend to overuse it? Did you depend on it too much?

---

4. Read broadly. Public communication is closely linked to both reading and writing. Improvement in one may not guarantee improvement in the others (although it is likely); there is a strong likelihood, however, that vocabulary used in one will show up in the others.

Extensive reading will not only add to your vocabulary but will also suggest new ways of phrasing ideas. In addition, it adds vicarious experiences to your memory bank. Those speakers who are most enjoyable to listen to are those who have vast memory banks.

CONSIDER THIS

Before I start to dictate, I prepare for writing just as I did before. I do the required reading, digest the material, and think about it; I then jot down an outline of a page or so, listing in order the major points I want to make. Then, instead of composing a legible draft on the typewriter, I begin talking into the machine as if I were lecturing to a small group of students.

As a primarily auditory person, when I speak, I appear to be following the dictates of an inner voice—that is, I don't see any words in front of me, but I hear what I am about to say and find myself virtually transcribing the sounds of the words with my tongue. Often I proceed as quickly as if I were talking to a class, though at other times I will slow down—or even swear to myself.

SOURCE: Howard Gardner, "On Becoming a Dictator," *Psychology Today,* December 1980, p. 14. Copyright © 1980 Ziff-Davis Publishing Company.

---

5. Write carefully. Careful writing helps greatly because in the writing and revising process we develop better ways of expressing our ideas. One writer, for example, found that writing out ideas in longhand proved far better than typing because the longhand process provided more time to search for the word or phrase that best promoted clarity or conveyed a desired impression. The writer converted from a quicker means of writing to a slower method that improved the style.

6. Increase your speaking opportunities. This may not be a favorite way to improve, but it helps in learning to use language. By speaking more, the speaker learns those words and phrases that are most effective in accomplishing the purpose, building an idea, making an impression. Practice may not make perfect—but it goes a long way toward increasing one's effectiveness.

7. Become more aware of words.[13] We tend to see what we want to see; thus if we focus on words, we will discover a whole new area that is generally overlooked. How do people use symbols to influence others? What part do symbols play in communication breakdowns? In misunderstandings? In accidents?

SUMMARY

The use of language is not a skill that is separate and distinct from other processes mentioned in this book. The study of language must also include the study of an audience, the use of the voice and body, and the various purposes to which language is put (informing or persuading, for example). It is a highly interrelated subject and must be examined in the whole public communication context.

In this chapter we have focused on language as a separate and distinct entity, although at times we have tried to indicate its interrelated aspects. In the first part of the chapter we briefly discussed the nature of language.

Let me review the major concerns that grow out of the section, "The Nature of Language."

1. Reality—what is considered real—differs for different people.
2. When we speak, we depend on our concept of reality to try to communicate with the listeners' concepts of reality.
3. When we select words, there is no guarantee that the words do, indeed, represent reality.

4. As communicators, we must try to represent the world as it is, allowing our words to change to represent a changing reality.
5. Since words have many meanings, we must try to limit these meanings either by the choice of another word or by defining the words we use.
6. We must acknowledge that our view is limited—a partial picture—and that the view of others represents just part of the whole as well.
7. Because words have both denotative and connotative meanings, we must be aware of the words we use and exercise caution and care—especially when the words we use have abstract or intangible meanings.
8. Meaning resides in people's heads, not in the words. Words serve as triggers causing people to ascribe meanings (associations) to the words they hear.

The second section, on language choices, provided guidelines for the use of words. The language we use will be more effective if our words are clear, simple, accurate, appropriate, and dynamic. Dynamism in language results when we capitalize on strengths and diminish weaknesses or distractions.

In the final section we examine seven ways to improve our language use. We recognize that such changes do not occur easily and require a great deal of commitment; but change *is* possible if we begin to monitor our use of language, beware of the language used by others, use a dictionary, read broadly and write carefully, increase our speaking opportunities, and become aware of the use and misuse of words.

Think of public communication as extended conversation. It is not a highly formal and distinct enterprise in most cases. We must capitalize on the positive aspects of conversation—the way we converse—such as our ease of language use, the natural and comfortable vocabulary, and the fluency or flow of language that generally takes place in conversation. We must also try to increase our ease in using our body, developing natural and comfortable mannerisms, gestures, and movements. We will discuss nonverbal communication in the next chapter. Remember, however, that the verbal and nonverbal operate together and cannot really be separated in a public communication presentation; it is their combined impact that should interest us. It is their combined impact that influences the images we form of others as well as the images they form of us.

NOTES

[1]For two general sources on language, see Peter Farb, *Word Play, What Happens When People Talk* (New York: Knopf, 1974), and S. I. Hayakawa, *Language in Thought and Action,* 3rd ed., (New York: Harcourt Brace Jovanovich, 1972).

[2]See G. Wayne Shamo and John R. Bittner, "Recall as a Function of Language Style," *Southern Speech Communication Journal,* 38 (Winter 1972): 181–187.

[3]See Gerard Nierenberg and Henry Calero, *Meta–Talk: Guide to Hidden Meanings in Conversations* (New York: Simon & Schuster, 1973).

[4]Research studies have demonstrated that persons from different backgrounds and different age groups have different labels for the same concepts. See Charles F. Vick and Roy V. Wood, "Similarity of Past Experience and the Communication of Meaning," *Speech Monographs,* 36 (1969):

159–162; Roy V. Wood, Joanne S. Yamanchi, and James J. Bradac, "The Communication of Meaning Across Cultures," *Journal of Communication,* 21 (1971): 160–169.

[5]From STRICTLY PERSONAL by Sydney J. Harris. © 1979 Field Enterprises, Inc. Courtesy of Field Newspaper Syndicate.

[6]William Strunk, Jr. and E. B. White, *The Elements of Style,* 3rd ed. (New York: Macmillan, 1979), p. 76. Copyright © 1979, Macmillan Publishing Co., Inc.

[7]For additional information on expressive language see Robert E. Pittenger and Henry Lee Smith, Jr., "A Basis for Some Contributions of Linguistics to Psychiatry," *Psychiatry,* 20 (1957): 61–78; and Norman A. McQuown, "Linguistic Transcription and Specification of Psychiatric Interview Material," *Psychiatry,* 20 (1957): 79–86; William J. McEwen and Bradley S. Greenberg, "The Effects of Message Intensity of Receiver Evaluations of Source, Message and Topic," *Journal of Communication,* 20 (December 1970): 340–350.

[8]See John Bowers and Michael M. Osborne, "Attitudinal Effects of Selected Types of Concluding Metaphors in Persuasive Speeches," *Speech Monographs,* 33 (1966), 147–155.

[9]See Jane Blankenship, *A Sense of Style: An Introduction to Style for the Public Speaker* (Belmont, Calif.: Dickenson Publishing Co., Inc., 1968), pp. 65–77; Michael M. Osborn and Douglas Ehninger, "The Metaphor in Public Address," *Speech Monographs* (August 1962), 223–234; Jane Blandenship, "A Linguistic Analysis of Oral and Written Style," *Quarterly Journal of Speech,* 48 (December 1962), 29; Stephen Ullmann, *Language and Style* (New York: Barnes & Noble, Inc., 1964).

[10]See Anthony Mulac, "Effects of Obscene Language Upon Three Dimensions of Listener Attitude," *Communication Monographs,* 43 (November 1976), 300–307. Research suggests that intense language such as this hampers message effectiveness and speaker credibility. See John Waite Bowers, "Language Intensity, Social Introversion, and Attitude Change," *Speech Monographs,* 30 (November 1963), 345–352; Michael Burgoon and Lyle B. King, "The Mediation of Resistance to Persuasion Strategies by Language Variables and Active-Passive Participation," *Human Communication Research,* 1 (Fall 1974), 30–41; and Michael Burgoon, Stephen B. Jones, and Diane Stewart, "Toward a Message-Centered Theory of Persuasion: Three Empirical Investigations of Language Intensity," *Human Communication Research,* 1 (Spring 1975), 240–256.

[11]Methods of analysis are discussed in Frederick Williams, "Analysis of Verbal Behavior," and Mervin D. Lynch, "Stylistic Analysis," in Philip Emmert and William D. Brooks, eds., *Methods of Research in Communication* (New York: Houghton Mifflin, 1970). Some other alternatives are discussed in Gerald R. Miller and Henry E. Nicholson, *Communication Inquiry: A Perspective on a Process* (Reading, Mass.: Addison-Wesley, 1976).

[12]See Felicia Lamport, "Dictionaries: Our Language Right or Wrong," *Harper's,* September 1959, p. 49.

[13]See James J. Bradac, Catherine W. Konsky, and Robert A. Davies, "Two Studies of the Effects of Linguistic Diversity Upon Judgments of Communicator Attributes and Message Effectiveness," *Communication Monographs,* 43 (March 1976): 70–79.

Nine

USING THE BODY

Nonverbal Communication

What is communicated to your audience by your body, face, or voice can give them more information about you than you may realize—or want. Perhaps the most important part of your communication that they receive through the nonverbal channel has to do with your attitude toward (1) them, (2) your verbal message, and (3) yourself. Researchers generally agree that more social meaning is carried through the nonverbal channels than through the verbal channels.[1] If the information the audience receives from the verbal and nonverbal channels conflicts, it will probably believe the nonverbal. This does not mean that speakers' nonverbal cues are more valid than the verbal, because nonverbal cues can also lie about speakers' attitudes. It does, however, underscore the importance of understanding nonverbal communication as it relates to public communication.

This chapter will first discuss the nature of nonverbal communication, offering a basic but broad understanding of it. With this foundation, it will be easier to comprehend the comments and suggestions made in the second section on nonverbal choices. In that section the physical components of nonverbal communication are divided into two major categories: body and face. Vocal elements (paralanguage) are discussed in a third and separate part. During nonverbal communication, of course, these separate parts are fused into one; mutually reinforcing and enhancing or perhaps distracting from and undermining the essential message. They are separated here for the purposes of discussion and explanation. A brief final section on improvement is included for those who wish to enlarge and expand their current repertoire of behaviors.

THE NATURE OF NONVERBAL COMMUNICATION

In Chapter 2, "Understanding The Process: Basic Principles," an axiom of communication that stated "We cannot not communicate" was discussed, and the underlying reasons for this axiom were presented. Here, it is examined in greater detail. Nonverbal communication is the primary reason for the existence and support of this axiom. Although only certain aspects of nonverbal communication will be examined here, keep in mind the potential impact of all nonverbal communication. *Every* possible aspect of a communication situation that has communicative value and that is not part of the speaker's verbal message *is* part of the nonverbal message. The speaker does not have total control over the nonverbal message, but with an understanding of it, he or she may be able to compensate for its potential negative aspects. More on that later.

In this section, six aspects of the nature of nonverbal communication will be discussed: (1) its sheer wealth, (2) the effect of minor cues, (3) its complexity, (4) its low awareness level, (5) how it is affected by differing interpretations, and (6) the complex relationship between verbal and nonverbal symbols. The treatment is brief. Whole courses are built on nonverbal communication and many books are available on the topic.[2] The reference point throughout this discussion will be public communication. Consider each of these aspects an awareness that could be prefaced with the words, "We should notice ... "

The Sheer Wealth of Nonverbal Cues

I have said above that *everything* that has communicative value, other than the actual verbal message, can be classified as nonverbal communication. But I have not provided any classification system to illustrate the point. Before I offer a list of potential categories, consider a few items in this realm that could influence your audience if you were the speaker:

1. Body movement (kinesics)
2. Use of space (proxemics)
   a. Distance from the audience
   b. Distance from the lectern
3. Use of voice (vocalics or paralanguage)
4. Use of objects (artifacts)
   a. Appearance
   b. Use of notes, manuscript, or other aids
5. Use of touch (tactilics)
   a. Touching another person
   b. Touching of lectern
   c. Displaying something that must be touched to be appreciated (furs, gems, etc.)

6. Odor (aromatics)
7. Use of time (chronemics)
   a. How long it takes you to get to the lectern
   b. How soon you begin speaking
   c. How fast you talk
   d. How long you continue speaking
   e. How rapidly (or slowly) you return to your seat
8. Your physical characteristics—body type (Are you underweight, overweight, or just right?)[3]
9. Your use of visual aids (graphics)—configuration of writing and printing
10. Environmental factors
    a. Size of room
    b. Temperature of the room
    c. Time of day
    d. Weather
    e. Comfort of the seating
    f. Arrangement of the room

TRY THIS 1

Next time you are in a lecture hall or listening to a sermon, jot down one or two characteristics of the particular situation and note how it conforms to or fulfills each of the following characteristics:

1. body movement	6. odor
2. space	7. time
3. voice	8. physical characteristics
4. objects	9. graphics
5. touch	10. environment

What control do you have, as a speaker, over such nonverbal cues? Do you think control over these cues is important?

The items outlined are *not* a complete listing, but from this list you can begin to see the breadth of this area. Again, do not think of these elements as separate and distinct. Think of them as interacting. As you think of various combinations, you begin to realize the problems researchers have had in trying to determine what different nonverbal cues mean. One cannot examine a particular nonverbal cue apart from another one or without looking at the whole context. If you consider the sheer number of nonverbal cues, you will begin to understand why the interaction of cues must be the focus—no single cue taken separately. We must look at each public communication situation for what it is, a separate, unique experience that can in no way be re-created in all of its aspects.

There is no catalog of nonverbal cues with various meanings attached, such as nodding means yes, stamping the foot denotes anger, turning thumbs down signals disapproval, opening the eyes wide indicates surprise. At times even such seemingly obvious cues may mean something else. Then, too, consider the length of the list that would be generated if one were to capture all the directions, commands, and feelings that can be conveyed nonverbally. Who would want to read such a catalog?

Even Minor Cues Elicit Distinct Meanings

A minor cue is one that we might use unconsciously or consciously with little thought or concern. For example, in walking to the lectern we might shake our head and throw our eyes to the ceiling, probably not realizing that some audience members will notice. We also may not realize how some might interpret these actions:

1. The speaker does not want to talk to us.
2. The speaker is unprepared.
3. The speaker is looking toward heaven for possible help or assistance.
4. The speaker is scared.

None of these impressions are particularly positive or helpful. Anything that may give a possible negative impression should be avoided. We must be at war with distraction!

CONSIDER THIS

A basic tenet of law holds that a person cannot be convicted purely on circumstantial evidence. Yet the people we meet every day immediately judge us on the circumstantial evidence of our clothing and appearance. They determine how to behave toward us, whether or not to trust us and how they think we will behave toward them almost entirely on how we are dressed and appear to them. The first impression we make on others is of crucial importance in our success in dealing with our fellow human being, whether it be in the business, social, or even the religious world. We, in turn, form instantaneous opinions of those we meet, based on their appearance, which influence the way we will behave toward them. One of the main reasons we instantly judge people is that we are survivors in a harsh, cruel world. We must immediately decide if this particular person will be either beneficial or harmful to our future, family, or finances.

SOURCE: William Thourlby, *You Are What You Wear: The Key to Business Success* (New York: New American Library [A Signet Book], 1978), p. 22. Copyright, 1978, William Thourlby. Reprinted with permission of Andrews and McNeel, Inc. All rights reserved.

What minor cues do speakers sometimes give? Unfortunately, a list of such cues could be *very* long, since different speakers give different cues and have different mannerisms. The cues themselves vary. When does a minor cue become a major one? The distinction we are making has to do with purpose. When a nonverbal cue is clear, planned, and purposeful, we will consider it as major. When it is unclear, unplanned, or lacks purpose, we will consider it as minor. The distinction is not as important as the distraction. Often we are distracted when a speaker displays any of these mannerisms:

Looks at the clock

Fumbles at or plays with his or her notes

Mispronounces words

Scratches or picks at his or her body

Chews gum or eats (sucks on) candy

Adjusts eyeglasses

Pushes hair off face, or constantly pats it down

Looks over the heads of the audience members

Loses place in speech

Adjusts clothing

Looks unnatural or ill at ease (fidgets or twitches)

If it is a simple error or fumble, it is better to move on as if it did not happen. The sooner a speaker forgets such instances, the sooner the audience will too. We must realize that we are *not* perfect, and we need not look or act as if we were perfect! It is better to come across human, and your message is more likely to be accepted if you appear human and not perfect.

If the error or fumble is highly conspicuous—such as dropping your notes on the floor or stumbling (or falling) on the way to the lectern—either ignore it or, still better, try to find humor in the situation. For example:

(after dropping your notes) "Until this very moment, I thought I was perfect," or "It is times like these that keep a person humble," or "Until now, I had never done anything wrong. Now you are all witnesses to my first mistake."

(after stumbling or falling) "God gave most people a left *and* a right foot, but by the time he got to me He had run out of right feet," or "I was always told to make my entrance dramatic. This time, I just got carried away!"

Again, caution is needed; however, you should realize that the audience feels embarrassed *for* you, and a good laugh or giggle—stimulated *by* you, with *you* as the focal point—allows everyone to overcome the embarrassment, get the nervousness out of their systems, and move on with the activities. It is a tension reliever.

As speaker, you are on display. Every twitch of eyebrow or wrinkle of the nose can be perceived and will probably be interpreted. To avoid sending out inadvertent cues, you must exercise control. Of course, you cannot control every cue. But as your awareness that even minor cues elicit distinct meanings increases, you can achieve greater control over those cues that *are* under your control and gain greater assurance that the impression you want to convey is being conveyed.

TRY THIS 2

At your next opportunity to hear a public speaker, take special note of the speaker's minor cues. List an aspect of the communication situation that falls into each of the following categories and could be considered a minor cue:

body movement	facial expression
voice	environment

Think of ways that you, as the speaker, would have controlled these minor cues. Could you have kept them from distracting the audience?

The Complexity of our Inference Process

When you are an audience member viewing a public speaker, you may look at a nonverbal cue, such as the speaker's taking a deep breath while approaching the lectern, and interpret that cue as an indication that the speaker is feeling a little nervous or queasy—but you might dismiss it with the thought, "Most speakers experience such feelings." Then you may see the speaker grasp the edge of the lectern for support, and this, combined with the first cue, may cause you to think, "He's really nervous!" But as the speaker begins, he speaks powerfully, clearly, and with no hesitancy whatsoever. Suddenly you realize that his speaking counters the other cues: He probably took a breath of air to strengthen his courage, and he grasped the lectern as an act of firmness and control. But look at the inference process (the process of drawing these conclusions) that occurred before you reached the final conclusion. All this inferring likely took but a fraction of a second.

As we examine any event, our minds draw from the multiplicity of available cues those that have meaning for us. We snythesize them or pull them together in our minds, then make sense of them—or attach meanings to them. But the exact process determining which cues are actually seen and combined and what meanings and associations are attributed to them is unique to every individual. No two people see exactly the same thing.

It is, indeed, the complexity of the process that makes control of it so difficult. As a speaker, how can you possibly predict the cues that will be seen or combined by your listeners? It is impossible. As a speaker, how do you know to what the audience will attend? It is impossible to predict. But that need not frustrate you. While researchers attempt to move us closer and closer to prediction and control, the complexity of the event reinforces the fact that human beings are involved, and they are complex and are not totally predictable. But even while total prediction and control are not possible, a great deal of control *is* possible and *is* available to the speaker. We will discuss how it can be achieved in the section on nonverbal choices. Just realize for the present that total control is never possible.

CONSIDER THIS

Jackie Onassis might be able to get away with going through life with a whisper, but for the ordinary working woman, a little-girl voice is the kiss of death.

Speech, like everything else in the male-dominated worlds of business and politics, is judged by male standards. Because men and women have been raised to speak differently, women often have problems speaking with as much authority as their male colleagues.

"I've had some brilliant young women MBAs who couldn't get placed," Dorothy Sarnoff, the internationally famous speech consultant and author of *Speech Can Change Your Life,* says. "They were financial experts and Phi Beta Kappas, but they just didn't come across with a sound of authority."

Women, linguists have recently discovered, do talk differently than men. They frequently express statements as questions, and they speak in italics and hedge when it comes to stating a definite opinion. These tendencies are not necessarily bad, and some experts say that they allow for more sensitive, humane interactions. But in the business world, it's still necessary to adapt to the way people with power do things.

Fortunately for the woman on her way up, experts have turned their attention to improving women's speech. It's mostly a matter of changing habits, they say.

The upglide (ending a sentence like a question) is a serious problem. "If you answer with an upglide, I say, 'Well, aren't you sure?' If you're an executive, you better not go around with an upglide,"Miss Sarnoff said.

"The tentative sound is an enemy because it makes people sound unsure of themselves. Lack of smooth phrasing is also an enemy. And nasal resonance is the most irritating thing of all."

It's all part of image—as important, the experts say, as your dressed-for-success suits, your perfect haircut, and your briefcase.

"The minute we begin to speak," says Sandy Linver, author of *Speak Easy: How To Talk Your Way to the Top,*" our spoken image becomes dominant and overrides our visual image and all our other images based on job, age, sex, color, class, and nationality.

"Our spoken image consists of much more than the words we say. It's how we say the words, the sound of our voice, the way we use our body as we speak—all of which determine how effectively we convey our message."

And how does one go about changing? Practice, practice, practice.

The books are a help, but even the most diligent student will probably make faster progress by attending a class or private lessons.

Practice speaking in public whenever you get the chance. "Get up and deliver a paper. Don't wait until you're perfect," Miss Sarnoff advises.

"Women are not going to get anywhere until they get on their feet and speak."

SOURCE: Beverly Stephen, "Women Execs Need Sound of Authority." Reprinted by Permission of Tribune Company Syndicate, Inc.

The Low Awareness Level at Which Nonverbal Communication Operates

There would be, very likely, more potential control of nonverbal cues if all responses to them were obvious and overt. If a listener knew which cue caused a particular impression, that cue could then be controlled. But when a listener perceives and processes a nonverbal cue, it may be done with little awareness that the cue was even taken in. The listener often has little awareness of responding to the cue and, further, of allowing it to influence his or her behavior. For example, a listener who is responding to subtle cues of nervousness or even embarrassment given off by the speaker, might not know why he or she feels uncomfortable. It is not unusual for audience members to "feel for the speaker." Or, for another example, have you ever heard someone say, "I don't know what it is about that person, but I just don't trust him"?

Another area where low awareness level plays a major part is in response to the voice. Ofttimes, a speaker can convey subtle shades of meaning with the voice alone. Then it becomes not *what* the speaker said, but *how* he or she said it. Consider, for example, sarcasm. Speakers who want to deliver cutting remarks or bitter comments may depend entirely on *tone* of voice—a tone that not only may be conveyed subtly but also may be perceived at a low awareness level.

Because of the low awareness level at which nonverbal communication operates, it is difficult to teach. It is often thought of as "second nature." Probably easier to teach is the reception and interpretation of cues. For example, what kind of cue do you use when you are trying to make a quick evaluation of a speaker's trustworthiness or credibility? In such situations rapid reception and interpretation of cues occurs. Evaluation of nonverbal communication can play a part in making such judgments.

Differing Interpretations by Different People

The problem with attributing meaning to nonverbal cues is often that the meanings given are more a function of who is doing the attributing than what is actually being communicated or analyzed. A catalog of meanings, then, is a reflection as much of the cataloger as of what is being cataloged. People from different cultures or from different regions of the country will give slightly different meanings to different cues. If you pick up various books on nonverbal communication, you will find different interpretations given to the same nonverbal cues.[4] Considering the various contexts in which communication occurs, this is not surprising.

199

The point of this is simply that we are all unique. Just as we bring a variety of different associations to words that we hear, we bring the same variety of associations to the nonverbal cues that we see. What is a correct interpretation by one person is not necessarily a correct interpretation by another. Thus, if you plan to use a nonverbal cue to gain a particular effect, you could fail to achieve the effect you want—at least by the cue you controlled.

CONSIDER THIS

Our heritage and our culture have caused most Americans to assume not only that our language is universal but that the gestures we use are understood by everyone. We do not realize that waving goodbye is the way to summon a Filipino to one's side, or that in Italy and some Latin-American countries, curling the fingers in a beckoning motion is a pantomime of farewell.

Those private citizens who sent packages to our troops occupying Germany after World War II and marked them GIFT to escape duty payments did not bother to find out that *Gift* means poison in German. Moreover, we like to think of ourselves as friendly, yet we prefer to be at least 3 feet or an arm's length away from others. Latins and Middle Easterners like to come closer and touch, which makes Americans uncomfortable.

Our linguistic and cultural myopia and the casualness with which we take cognizance—when we do—of the developed tastes, mannerisms, mores and languages of other countries, are losing us friends, business and respect in the world.

SOURCE: J. William Fulbright, "My Turn: We're Tongue-Tie," *Newsweek,* July 30, 1979, p. 15. Copyright 1979, by Newsweek, Inc. All rights reserved. Reprinted by Permission.

Because different people interpret the same cues differently, you should probably not waste your time trying to control specific nonverbal cues. It is wiser to gear your approach to the overall mood or feeling you want to convey, then let your nonverbal cues naturally and comfortably reinforce that mood or feeling. The whole impression is more important than any of the individual parts—unless they detract from that impression.

TRY THIS 3

Have you ever differed with someone over the interpretation of an event? Have you ever found one aspect positive when someone else found it negative? Or did you give it one meaning while someone else gave it another? The next time, try to discover *why* these differing interpretations occurred.

1. Did the other person see the situation in the same way?
2. Did the other person see cues or aspects you missed? Or did you see things the other person missed?
3. Did the other person focus on just one aspect while you focused on the whole impression? Or vice versa?
4. Did the other person have different associations connected with the cues perceived?

Do you see why getting audience members to understand just your meaning is so difficult? Do you have ways as a speaker, to make this process easier or more successful?

The Complex Relationship Between Verbal and Nonverbal Symbols

Although we have said this before, it deserves emphasis in this context. Nonverbal communication in public communication cannot be adequately studied without considering the verbal. Verbal and nonverbal operate together. A speaker does not—in fact, cannot—use one to the exclusion of the other. But the exact relationship between the two is determined by the speaker and listener in concert—acting together. The speaker provides the verbal and nonverbal symbols; the listener in this specific context perceives the set of symbols and draws interpretations (attributes meaning) based on the set (how the elements interact for him or her).

This interrelationship increases the complexity of the whole process. No one can tell a speaker exactly *how* to convey a specific feeling through words and actions so that a listener will *feel* the feeling desired. True, suggestions can be made; however, since speakers have their own ways to say things and feel things, the best guide is personal comfort and ease.

Our nonverbal communication is often a natural part of us. If someone asked you, how do *you* express joy or sincerity or discontent, you may not be able to explain. It's similar to the story of the centipede that had no problem walking until asked to explain how—then, having to stop and analyze the process, it fell all over itself. Our nonverbal communication is part of our personal style, acquired through years of learning. It is often quite inflexible and quite beyond our control. That is precisely why, as a speaker, you should strive for the big picture —what feeling or mood are you trying to express or convey? It is likely that the appropriate nonverbal expression will naturally follow. To analyze it may cause you to fall all over yourself: to become awkward, ill at ease, unsure of yourself.

NONVERBAL CHOICES

The point of discussing nonverbal choices certainly is not to cause you to become awkward and self-conscious. Effective nonverbal communication—just as effective words—does not call attention to itself; rather, it serves as a vehicle to stimulate meaning. If used correctly, it stimulates the correct meaning. If used incorrectly, it detracts. The purpose of this section, is simply to increase your sensitivity to some of the available nonverbal choices.

No matter what nonverbal choices are made, the choices should be sincerely motivated; if they are planned, or if they are performed out of a sense of need ("I was told to gesture more!"), listeners may detect insincerity. Also, nonverbal choices should not be overused. As in almost everything else, moderation should be your guide. Variety is invaluable: With ample variety, no one choice is unlikely to be overworked. The nonverbal choices must also be appropriate for the situation. They must be based on speaker responses to the occasion. A larger auditorium, for example, would call for larger, more expansive gestures and movements, whereas a smaller room might well require more control.

The major choices, or nonverbal channels, discussed in this section are (1) body, (2) face, and (3) voice. These are by no means all the channels that could be considered, but they are the major ones over which speakers have some degree of control.[5] Speakers who learn to use each of these well are likely that to feel comfortable with other nonverbal choices they face.

Body

Body is usually the first of the nonverbal channels to be noticed. It can be divided into four parts: (1) appearance, (2) movement, (3) posture, and (4) gesture.

Appearance. Appearance is how a speaker looks—his or her general appearance—as well as how a speaker dresses. Attractive people generally make better persuaders—that is, people like to listen to an attractive person more than to an unattractive one.[6] But people who base their judgments about the credibility of a speaker on his or her general appearance—matters that are not within the control of the speaker—are making decisions based on irrational and irrelevant factors. Attractive people can be dishonest, ill-informed, or stupid!

Concern for one's dress and grooming is different from general appearance because the speaker has control over these features; thus, they communicate something. As a speaker, one must try to dress appropriately—that is, so that one

does not distract from the message. Listeners judge whether or not something is communicated and if what is communicated is relevant either to the message or to the speaker's credibility.

One's appearance can be manipulated, but how much should a speaker manipulate his or her appearance for the sake of an impression? Self-respect may be at issue here. Listeners, on the other hand, should be aware that a speaker's attire and grooming can be misleading. There is not necessarily a relationship between appearance and competence or trustworthiness. The speaker must decide what image he or she wants to project just as a listener must try to decide what image the speaker is trying to project.

TRY THIS 4

On several different occasions, after hearing several different speakers, make notes about how the appearance of each speaker communicated a message. Write down what each speaker's appearance revealed to you.

Type of Dress	How It is Worn
Informal	Neat and trim
Formal	Sloppy and disheveled
Uniformed	Dirty
Other	Other

How important do you think appearance is to the success of a speaker? If you were to speak before a group of your peers (other students), then before parents, and lastly before teachers and administrators, would you alter your style of dress between appearances? How would you dress if you were asked to come back to your old high school and give a speech before the graduating seniors?

Movement.   Movement (kinesics) includes both facial movements and bodily movements, but because of the importance of the face, it will be discussed in a separate section. Our control over our movements is crucial because our listeners will be very sensitive to movements.[7] We are often unaware of the messages that movements can stir up. That is, we take our motions for granted. Listeners who hear our verbal message look to our body (and face) for nonverbal reinforcement or lack of reinforcement. Movement, then, has the potential of stirring up meaning. If a speaker is disturbed, listeners will look to the speaker's body to see *how* disturbed he or she is. If a speaker verbally indicates wild enthusiasm but fails to reinforce it with bodily action, the listener must decide which message to believe.

Movement can also stimulate attention. People are attracted to motions. If you are reading a book in a lounge or study area and something suddenly moves, you look up—distracted by the movement. You are in a lecture hall and the lecturer is speaking; if someone enters, you look up—again, distracted by movement. Driving through a town lit up with neon lights, you see the steadily glowing signs, but those you notice most are the flickering neon ones—you are attracted by movement. Thumbing through a magazine, you are most likely to notice the advertisements depicting action. Movement attracts attention.

Because movement attracts attention, we, as speakers, must take care that our movement reinforces and enhances our message and does not distract from it. Awkward, inappropriate, and distracting movements can and do occur, and audience attention can be as easily drawn to these as to graceful, appropriate, and helpful movements.

Movement should be comfortable and natural. Its effect on the listener should be subliminal—not overt or obvious. When listeners notice a speaker's movement, they are being distracted from the verbal message. The speaker's purpose then suffers. Thus, movement should not call attention to itself.

Meaningful movement of the body usually occurs when the speaker moves from one idea to another. It is often accompanied by a transition. It can be as obvious as "moving to the next idea, then . . ." or as subtle and quick as some of the one-word transitions mentioned in the last chapter: *thus, so, next,* or *further.* Movement to either side of the lectern (or to the center) usually signals a change from one point to another in the message. Movement can also be used to make an idea more emphatic: The speaker moves closer to the audience. For example, the speaker says, "But, *we* can't afford to make such mistakes, can we?" and leans closer to the audience to make the point sharp and definite.

Posture.   Posture is the position or bearing of the body as a whole. Sit down and watch the way people carry themselves as they walk. Especially notice their posture. Notice how you can often tell the importance of their mission (or at least how important it is to them) by the way they carry themselves. Those who feel their mission is important will stand or move erect. Their posture could be characterized as bold, aggressive, even forceful. They look important by the way they hold themselves.

To reveal to your audience a sense of importance, you must hold yourself erect and alert. To allow your shoulders to slump or to appear the least bit slovenly will be a key nonverbal cue suggesting lack of concern, lack of caring, or lack of importance.[8]

TRY THIS 5

Stand up and then let your shoulders slouch. Relax your upper torso completely. Feel good?

Now draw your shoulders back (slowly)—chest out a bit, stomach in—but not too much. Does your attitude or feeling change correspondingly?

Does the erect posture cause you to feel more alert? More poised and in command? Ready to respond or react?

Can you capture these same feelings when your shoulders are slumped forward?

Do you think your posture has an effect on how you deliver a speech? It is likely to influence the audience?

Posture is important not only during actual presentation, but also as you move to and from the lectern. Remember, the key is what feels comfortable for you. The drill sergeant stance can be as distracting as the slouch. It can also be as inhibiting, for it is difficult to move other parts of the body when using either of these extremes. Be comfortable—but alert and ready to respond.

Gestures.   In gestures, the arms or hands are the means of expression. Gestures are probably that part of bodily movement most inhibited by the public speaking situation. A person who can use gestures lavishly in normal one-to-one conversation sometimes freezes or becomes inhibited in front of an audience.

Speakers use gestures (1) as emblems, (2) as illustrators, or (3) as regulators. When speakers use a gesture to indicate something that we associate with that gesture, they are using it as an *emblem.* An emblem is a "nonverbal word." The index and forefinger raised to signify victory, the index and thumb forming a circle to indicate *okay,* the hitchhiker's raised thumb are all common examples of emblems. When speakers use gestures along with the oral message—to accompany and complement it—they are using them as *illustrators.* For example, a speaker might indicate the approximate length or height of something: "That animal probably came up to here on me [indicating where] when it was on all fours." Gestures used as *regulators* serve to encourage or discourage the participation of others. If you observe a speaker handling a question-and-answer period following a speech, you may witness a heavy use of regulators as he or she controls the flow of questions. The speaker may have to control who asks the next question while restraining others from jumping in before their turn.

One rule of thumb regarding gestures is: Don't plan your gestures, but plan to gesture. Again, as in all bodily movement, planned nonverbal behaviors may appear counterfeit. Unless they are natural, gestures may look artificial and awkward. The suggestion offered at the end of this chapter for increasing their naturalness is to practice and use them first in informal conversation.

Face

Facial expression is one of the most revealing nonverbal cues. As listeners, we read signs of the speaker's attitude toward us, toward the topic, and toward himself or herself from the face alone.[9] The face is one of the most important sources for revealing the speaker's sincerity; from it listeners can often tell whether a speaker likes them or not. A warm, pleasant attitude is easily conveyed—and easily faked. Listeners can tell whether the speaker is enthusiastic or deeply concerned about the topic from facial cues. They can also read the speaker's personal attitudes and feelings: Is he or she self-confident? The face can convey a wide range of emotions: confidence or doubt, courage or fear, happiness or sadness, surprise or expectation, love or hate. That is why facial expressions are sometimes referred to as affect (feeling) displays.

TRY THIS 6

Reveal as many of the following emotions as you can, using just your face. Have a friend or roommate guess the emotion you are trying to portray.

contentment	sorrow	love
indifference	joy	anger
frustration	shyness	loneliness
hope	fear	warmth

How many of these emotions are likely to be revealed in public speaking situations? Do you feel comfortable expressing them in front of an audience? Can you see why being able to express them clearly can be an asset to a public speaker?

Facial expression is very important in revealing emotion. Without it, a speaker loses a significant part of the strength of a communicative effort. The animation will be missing—animation meaning the spirit, support, vigor, zest, or action that is designed to bring a speech to life. A speaker who reveals little or no facial expression often lacks other aspects of nonverbal behavior such as bodily movement and vocal variety. Lack of animation may be read by listeners as apathy or boredom.

If a speaker is indeed bored with a topic, he or she should change the topic rather than to try to fake interest or animation. A listener who suspects or detects a false display of emotion will be distracted by it and will pay little attention to the ideas of the speech. If one's lack of animation results from inhibitions, the necessary freedom can be obtained by putting oneself into the proper psychological climate—commonly referred to as "psyching oneself up."

Eye contact. Eye contact is a very important part of facial expression.[10] A speaker who refrains from looking at his or her listeners eye-to-eye can elicit various reactions:

1. "The speaker doesn't care about us."
2. "The speaker is lying."
3. "The speaker is unsure of his or her ideas."
4. "The speaker lacks confidence."
5. "The speaker is scared."

All these reactions, of course, are detrimental and must be avoided. Eye contact will be given additional attention in the next chapter when effective delivery is discussed.

Voice

When discussing the nonverbal aspects of the voice, we are referring not to the words themselves but to *how* the words are said; it is sometimes called *paralanguage.*[11] The way a word is said has a direct relationship to the word itself—just as when a child calls another child a name. If the name is derogatory and is said meanly, it is more offensive than if the name is complimentary or perhaps a fabrication (a nonsense term) said in the same way. Even a perfectly innocent word can be used derogatorily. One person says "Oh, foot!" instead of swearing or cursing and gets the same satisfaction and emotional release that others obtain when using *hell* or *damn* or other common terms. Fulfillment comes from how a word is said, not from the words themselves.

Variations in the physical characteristics of the voice (rate, pitch, loudness, articulation, and quality) produce differences in the way listeners perceive the emotional states of the speaker, but these perceptions are not necessarily accurate and do not affect their understanding of the message or their willingness to change their opinion. Thus, if a speaker wishes to convey a mood or feeling —an emotional state—a change in the voice characteristics can be successful.[12]

Our voice serves to punctuate our speech. Notice, for example, how you tend to raise your voice slightly at the end of a question. Notice how you often pause briefly at the end of a sentence or idea. You may hurry your pace and raise your voice slightly for a sentence deserving of an exclamation point.

TRY THIS 7

Vocally punctuate the following sentences:

> "He made me go."
> "Were you the one who told that story?"
> "I can't believe that!"
> "So I finished my term there. But I began again almost immediately . . ."
> "Now you really can't expect us to do that, can you?"
> "You should have seen her face!"
> "There's only one way to relax. Believe me, it isn't by doing more work."
> "I got the prize."

In speaking, it is important to pay particular attention to *how* the words are said. Even if you, as speaker, do not, you can be certain your listeners will. Take the time to allow your voice to provide the subtle shades of meaning you intend.

The voice can affect the meaning of a message. For example, see how many different ways can you say "Sally was the one." Say it four times, each time emphasizing a different word. Notice that when you place emphasis on the word *Sally,* you seem to indicate it was *her* and no one else. When you place emphasis on the *was,* it is as if you are declaring that you were correct all along. With the emphasis on *the,* it seems she was the only one—ever! When I say that, I feel like putting up my index finger (an emblem) to reinforce the thought—she was *the* one! When the emphasis is on *one,* it sounds as if Sally is to blame or at fault— as if you had finally found out who it was. Imagine the complex relationship of voice and word (vocal emphasis and phrases) as the sentences become more complex. That is what happens when we speak. The way a sentence is said is often far more important than what is said.

Voice can also affect our impression of a speaker as a person.[13] Unfortunately, we stereotype people by their voice type. We do not attribute as much authority to a high, nasal, whiny, or weak voice as we do to a low, clear, strong one. People often have little or no control over their voice quality—it was given to them in much the same way as was their body shape or type. And yet, our impressions of them are still related to these features. The problem is that such judgments of people can be highly inaccurate. A person of strong courage and enthusiasm may, indeed, have a weak, thin voice, just as a deeply commited, passionate person may have a monotonous voice. And a voice that reveals genuine sincerity and enthusiasm may hide a person who is unprincipled, deceitful, and dishonest. The voice can serve as both a map and a mask.

Vocal variety is a key to holding attention.[14] We have already seen how movement grasps our attention. Voice movement or change has a similar effect. Although we want to avoid monotony, we must be careful not to introduce variety in the voice just for the sake of holding attention. Changes should be clearly tied to the message we want to get across. Otherwise they may well distract by calling attention to themselves. There are a number of vocal characteristics that can be changed: (1) rate and pause, (2) pitch and inflection, (3) loudness or volume, (4) articulation and pronunciation, and, finally, (5) quality. These are all elements over which we, as spearkers, have some control.

Rate and Pause.   Rate and pause can be separated since both can serve different purposes and have different effects. They are linked because we can vary rate by interjecting more pauses or by decreasing the number or length of pauses. Pause affects rate as does the duration of sound—the time it takes to utter a sound. Rate is simply how fast we choose to speak.

Rate can affect how well the audience is able to comprehend the message. A speaker who speaks too fast may not be understood; one who speaks too slow may create boredom—put the audience to sleep. Variation in rate is the key. Although 125 to 150 words per minute is considered a satisfactory rate of speaking, a speaker must plan to adjust speaking rate to the size of a room, the use of a microphone (and how sensitive it is), audience reactions, the environment or speech occasion, and the material being presented.

It is amazing how a change of rate can affect the feeling or tone being conveyed. For example, if you wanted to emphasize an important concept or idea in a speech, one way to do it is to slow down: You would change the rate at which you speak each word and perhaps emphasize each word separately. If you wanted to reveal excitement or surprise, you could speed up the rate. A somber, gloomy mood can be conveyed by a slower rate.

Rate can also affect how much is said in a given amount of time. In the Ford-Carter Presidential debates, each candidate was allotted an equal amount of time to deliver his ideas. But Carter was able to say much more because he speaks considerably faster. When researchers discovered this, the Equal Time and Fairness Doctrine to which broadcasters subscribe was questioned.

A pause provides emphasis. It can also indicate a transition between ideas. If you ask the audience to think about the answer to a question, you might pause and allow time for a mental response. Parenthetical expressions and other asides are often set off by a pause. A storyteller will sometimes pause just before the punch line or moral to the story is given. If pauses are misplaced, they can be distracting. If the pause signals a mental blank rather than an effective, well-timed break, it can disrupt the flow of ideas. If pauses are filled with unnecessary verbalizations, such as *uh, er, like, you know, okay,* and *right,* they can also cause distraction. Such vocalized pauses should be eliminated to the greatest extent possible. Instead, the speaker should simply insert a silent pause in their place —no noise, just a break or hesitation.

CONSIDER THIS

We speak in deep chest tones to signal strength, dependability, firmness, solidity. The Victorian father resonated from the chest to come up with an authoritarian voice. The father of today tries raising his voice to produce the same metamessage, but just increasing the volume doesn't do it. Instead, it signals spontaneity and lack of control. Resonance signals something more deliberate. The watchful child can read both messages and figure out which father means business.

Father may use deep tones to signal strength and dependability, but a low resonance isn't confined to him alone. When Mother speaks in a low register we know that she means what she's saying.

A woman with a low voice, low in register and pitch, sounds self-assured and we're inclined to trust her. Some women use the low register to come on sexually. Julie London, the singer, does a commercial for television in a low, husky register, and it literally oozes sex.

SOURCE: Julius and Barbara Fast, *Talking Between the Lines: How We Mean More Than We Say* (New York: Viking Press, 1979), pp. 22–23. Copyright © 1979 by Julius and Barbara Fast. Reprinted by permission of Viking Penguin Inc.

Pitch and Inflection.   Like rate and pause, pitch and inflection are also directly related to each other. A speaker's pitch is determined by his or her vocal key. Key is determined by the vibration of the vocal folds. Slow vibrations (like the vibration of the strings if a bass violin) produce a low key, whereas faster vibrations create a higher key. Thus, pitch can be defined as the difference in the relative vibration frequency of the human voice. These differences contribute to the total meaning of speech. As we use various pitch levels, we make use of inflection. Inflection involves changes or variances in pitch. Thus, as our voice slides into different keys to add emphasis, to ask a question, to make a point, or to gain attention, we are using inflection. A person whose speech makes no use of variances in pitch—whose voice has no inflection—we call monotonous. Monotony is simply sameness in tone or sound.

Not only is monotony in a speaker's voice a powerful sedative for listeners, it also robs the words and phrases of their meaning. A monotonous voice that is a result of many years of conditioning, is not easily changed. Working with a tape recorder, observing and imitating others who are expressive, and using the advice and suggestions of those who would help can bring changes over a period of time.

Loudness, or Volume.   Loudness, or volume, is an obvious vocal characteristic. It is obvious because when it is missing it is the first to be noticed. When it is overbearing it can cause physical discomfort. We must find for ourselves a comfortable volume that satisfies all listeners and suits the situation and topic. Once again, it is not the volume itself that holds attention—it is the changes in volume. Listen to a piece of music played by an orchestra and notice the many changes in volume that occur throughout the piece (called crescendos and diminuendos). Imagine how the piece would sound without these changes. A speech needs the same variety for many of the same reasons. This saves the speech from becoming dull and tedious.

Advertisements on both radio and television are broadcast at a higher volume level that regular programming. If you have ever listened to an easy-listening station of FM radio, notice the jolt that can occur when an advertisement comes on. It gets attention by the surprise of its higher volume, among other things.

One very effective means of emphasis is for a speaker to suddenly drop the vocal volume to a softer level. Notice what effect can be gained in the following passage by reading all the italicized (parallel) portions in a softer volume than the other parts:

> They have now begun an all-out effort to halt crime. They have, for example, made the penalties more severe. *It hasn't mattered.* They have used scare tactics on those populations most likely to follow a life of crime. *It hasn't mattered.* They have begun elaborate educational programs that can be adopted and used in the elementary and secondary schools. *It hasn't mattered.*

It adds an air of frustration to the passage—like, "What else can they do?" Reading or reciting it at the same volume level gives a different meaning.

CONSIDER THIS

If he [your boss] entered your office, planted both fists in the middle of your desk and demanded sharply, "What *are* you doing?" you would certainly feel some apprehension and wonder what had gone wrong to force him from his comfort zone.

If, however, he leaned over your desk, put clenched fists on your papers and shouted in your face, *"What are you doing?"* you would know that you were in trouble and had better find out what you could do to get things back to normal once more. He would have your complete attention until the problem was solved. Yet in each case the same words were used. Only the tone of voice and body language were different. When this happens to you, you interpret the changes very carefully. But when you are talking to someone you are not nearly as careful.

SOURCE: Jard DeVille, *Nice Guys Finish First: How to Get People to Do What You Want . . . and Thank You for It* (New York: William Morrow, 1979), pp. 86–87.

Articulation and pronunciation.   Articulation and pronunciation can affect the clarity of the sounds we produce just as much as our loudness, pitch, or rate. They, too, are related in that both can result in clarity or confusion, and both depend, in part, on how we use our organs of speech. Articulation, however, has to do with distinctness, pronunciation with correctness. One can articulate a word distinctly and still pronounce it incorrectly. The word "et cetera," for example, is sometimes said "ec-cetera." It is clear—articulate—but wrong because the correct pronunciation is "et'-set-ə-rə."

Most articulation problems result from laziness. We blur our enunciation because we are too lazy to establish the correct placement of the lips, tongue, or jaw—our articulators. Instead of *going to,* we say *gunna,* dropping the *t* much as we do in *want to* when we say *wanna.* We do much the same when we say *I dunno* for *I don't know.* We take shortcuts. We also make substitutions. For example, we substitute a *d* for a *t* when we say *wader* (actually, *wah-der*) for *water.* We substitute *d* for *th* in such words as *these* and *those* in phrases such as *dese guys* and *dose ladies.* We are lazy. We drop the *ing* ending on words when we say *winnin* for *winning* or *goin* for *going.* The errors are numerous. Many can be corrected if we simply monitor our use of language, change sloppiness to neatness, and counter laziness with purposeful and meaningful activity.

The best means one can use for gaining correctness in pronunciation is to listen to educated speakers in your region. Pronunciation changes from one geographical region to another. Another guide is a dictionary. Correct pronunciation is important because a mispronounced word calls attention to itself and quickly distracts a listener from the message. The mispronounced word becomes a message by itself. If you have a question—a shadow of doubt—about how a word is pronounced, ask someone else to say the word. If you still feel uncertain about it, perhaps you can find another word to use in its place.

Quality.   The voice characteristic of quality is not as easily changed as the others. It is the one distinction that often enables us to tell one singer from another. We may describe a singer's voice as mellow, harsh, squeaky, sharp, low, high, rich, or smooth—but those singers whose voices are not distinctive often do not last long in the field of popular music. Although vocal quality is largely an inborn characteristic, it can change throughout our lives. Tenseness or nervousness can also cause subtle changes—as when a voice becomes thin or strident because of taut throat muscles. Anger can produce a harsh or aspirate (breathy) quality. When a speaker becomes nostalgic, his or her voice can become hushed and intimate—a mere whisper. As a speaker becomes involved in the message, his or her vocal quality can reflect the emotions and sentiments expressed.

TRY THIS 8

Write a brief analysis of a speaker's strengths and weaknesses in the area of *vocal variety:*

1. Rate and pause
2. Pitch and inflection

3. Loudness or volume
4. Articulation and pronunciation
5. Quality

If you were asked to help this speaker improve, what suggestions could you make to help change weaknesses to strengths? Did you find that some weaknesses were more obvious and important than others? Did the speaker's strengths tend to mask his or her weaknesses? Could they?

IMPROVING OUR NONVERBAL COMMUNICATION

Many of the suggestions made at the close of the last chapter on verbal communication can also be used to improve our nonverbal communication. For example, improvement is likely to result if we (1) monitor our use of nonverbal communication, (2) be aware of its use by others, (3) increase our speaking opportunities, and (4) become more aware of nonverbal communication in the world by reading about it and, perhaps, pursuing our study of it in somewhat more depth than is possible through casual observation. Here are several other ways to improve:

1. Enlist the aid of friends who can give you an honest appraisal of your strengths and weaknesses. Have your nonverbal communication evaluated by others. Have it examined not only in public communication situations but also in informal conversations as well as in small group discussions.
2. Ask your speech instructor to provide you with an analysis of your nonverbal strengths and weaknesses. Perhaps you could arrange a conference with him or her to discuss areas that need further work.
3. Practice. Strive to perfect your bodily movements and vocal variety. When in informal settings, begin to add to your repertoire of movements and gestures. Seek to add vigor and enthusiasm to *everyday* conversations. Curb your weak and inefficient mannerisms. As you improve in informal, casual settings, changes will carry over to the public setting—given enough opportunities to speak in public.

CONSIDER THIS

Even total strangers can hold awesome power over our lives in giving or taking away opportunity, sometimes without you ever being aware the opportunity was within your grasp. Have you ever met someone you didn't know when you were unshaven, wearing a T-shirt and cut-offs, drinking beer, and acting up, only to find he was the brother of the company's president?

We may verbalize it differently (like "we must learn to 'drive defensively'") but in reality we are constantly learning to anticipate the actions and reactions of others. As you learn to understand why this knowledge can work for you, how it works, and when to use it for yourself, your family, and your future, you will begin to control your life.

You are beginning, probably for the first time, to intellectualize your decision-making, instead of letting your subconscious, subjective, and emotional feelings about someone—"I don't think I like him"; "He's not one of us"; "I feel funny about him" —direct your decisions. Once you learn the why and how of any decision you make and understand you are being judged by the effects of such decisions, you will move onto a new plateau of power.

SOURCE: William Thourlby, "You Are What You Wear: Keeping A Sincere Upper Lip," *The Blade* (Toledo, Ohio), April 19, 1979. Copyright 1979. Universal Press Syndicate. Reprinted with permission. All rights reserved.

SUMMARY

This chapter has focused on the nature of nonverbal communication and on making nonverbal choices; it has also suggested some methods for improvement. Since it is likely that your audience will gain more social meaning from your nonverbal communication than from your verbal communication, the time spent on making your nonverbal impression more positive, effective, and efficient will surely bring rich rewards. But remember, too, the verbal and nonverbal operate in harmony with each other. They are directly related.

The broad and basic understandings were established first. It is important to understand, for example, the sheer wealth of nonverbal cues, the effect of minor cues, the complex nature of nonverbal communication, the low awareness level at which it operates, how it is affected by differing interpretations, and, finally, the relationship between the verbal and nonverbal channels. Such analysis should make you more aware of the breadth, depth, and complexity of this area of study. Nonverbal communication is by no means a simple, clear-cut discipline.

Although it would be impossible to discuss all the nonverbal cues that trigger meaning in the minds of listeners, those most relevant to the public communication situation—body, face, and voice—were considered. Any division is really designed for discussion only, since all cues combine for a general effect and are usually not perceived separately and distinctly. Appearance, movement, posture, and gesture were discussed under the topic of body movement. Under facial expression, the importance of facial expression as well as the importance of eye contact were examined. Under vocal expression the characteristics of rate and pause, pitch and inflection, loudness or volume, articulation and pronunciation, and quality were discussed.

A significant factor in your success with nonverbal choices will be your ability to *adapt*. The importance of adaptability has been mentioned throughout the chapter with respect to specific items; here it is emphasized. Success results when one has adapted nonverbal behaviors to oneself, one's message, one's audience, and one's situation (including the occasion and environment). These are the four basic factors found in every public communication situation. Their effect differs, just as your adjustment to them must differ.

Although little could be added to the methods mentioned at the close of the last chapter on improving verbal communication, it was suggested that you enlist the aid of friends and the aid of your speech instructor. It was also suggested that you begin at once to build your repertoire of nonverbal communication behaviors. *Do not wait* for public communication opportunities. To increase your repertoire within the confines of informal conversation gives you (1) a more protected environment in which to practice, (2) more opportunities to practice, and (3) more variety in the emotions and experiences to illustrate or reinforce nonverbally. Improvement here will likely carry over into your public communication experiences—although no guarantees can be made.

Nonverbal and verbal behavior are part of the presentation of the message. Since we have examined the specific elements of each, in the next chapter they will be put into the actual presentational context: the delivery of the message. Delivery, then, becomes the synthesis, or drawing together, of all the elements into a coherent, unified, and effective whole. It is the result of all our efforts thus far.

NOTES

[1]See John A. Starkweather, "Content-Free Speech as a Source of Information about the Speaker," *Journal of Abnormal and Social Psychology,* 52 (May 1956): 394–402. Starkweather suggests that those exposed to both verbal and vocal cues rely more heavily on the vocal cues to judge the personality of the speaker. Also see Ray L. Birdwhistell, *Kinesics and Context: Essays on Body Motion Communication* (Philadelphia: University of Pennsylvania Press, 1970), pp. 157–158. Birdwhistell suggests that in two-person conversations the verbal elements carry less than 35 percent of the social meaning.

[2]Textbooks on nonverbal communication include Shirley Weitz, *Nonverbal Communication: Readings with Commentary,* 2nd ed. (New York Oxford University Press, 1979); Abné Eisenberg and Ralph Smith, Jr., *Nonverbal Communication* (Indianapolis: Bobbs-Merrill, 1971); Randall P. Harrison, *Beyond Words: An Introduction to Nonverbal Communication* (Englewood Cliffs, N.J.: Prentice-Hall, 1974); Mark L. Knapp, *Nonverbal Communication in Human Interaction,* 2nd ed. (New York: Holt, Rinehart & Winston, 1978); Mark L. Knapp, *Essentials of Nonverbal Communication* (New York: Holt, Rinehart and (Winston, 1980); Dale Leathers, *Nonverbal Communication Systems* (Boston: Allyn & Bacon, 1976); and Albert Mehrabian, *Silent Messages: Implicit Communication of Emotions and Attitudes,* 2nd ed. (Belmont, Calif.: Wadsworth, 1981). Also see nontextbook sources such as Flora Davis, *Inside Intuition* (New York: New American Library [A Signet Book], 1973); and Julius Fast, *Body Language* (New York: Pocket Books, 1971).

[3]If you are underweight, some listeners may see you as detached from them, serious, cautious, sensitive, shy, and anxious. If you are overweight, you may be viewed as tolerant, affectionate, generous, relaxed, and sluggish. If you are just the right weight, you might be viewed as dominant, cheerful, optimistic, enthusiastic, efficient, compettitve, and independent. See Abné M. Eisenberg, *Job Talk: Communicating Effectively On the Job* (New York: Macmillan, 1979), p. 21.

[4]See, for example, R. Dale Guthrie, *Body Hot Spots* (New York: Pocket Books, 1977); Gerard I. Nierenberg and Henry H. Calero, *How to Read a Person Like a Book* (New York: Pocket Books, 1973); and Gerard I. Niernberg and Henry H. Calero, *Meta-Talk: Guide to Hidden Meanings in Conversation* (New York: Pocket Books, 1975).

[5]Also see Paul Ekman and Wallace V. Friesen, "The Repertoire of Nonverbal Behavior: Categories, Origins, Usage, and Coding," *Semiotica,* 1 (1969): 49–98.

[6]See Judson Mills and Elliot Aronson, "Opinion Change as a Function of the Communicator's Attractiveness and Desire to Influence," *Journal of Personality and Social Psychology*, 1 (1965): 73–77; R. N. Widgery and B. Webster, "The Effects of Physical Attractiveness Upon Perceived Initial Credibility," *Michigan Speech Journal*, 4 (1969): 9–15.

[7]See Paul Ekman and Wallce Friesen, "Head and Body Cues in the Judgment of Emotion: A Reformulation," *Perceptual and Motor Skills*, 24 (1967): 711–724.

[8]See Albert Mehrabian, "Orientation Behavior and Nonverbal Attitude in Communication." *Journal of Communication*, 17 (1967): 324–332; and Albert Mehrabian, "Relationship of Attitude to Seated Posture, Orientation, and Distance," *Journal of Personality and Social Psychology*, 10 (1968): 26–30.

[9]See Paul Ekman and Wallace Friesen, "Nonverbal Leakage and Clues to Deception," *Psychiatry*, 32 (1969): 88–106.

[10]See Michael Argyle and J. Dean, "Eye Contact, Distance, and Affiliation," *Sociometry*, 28 (1965): 289–304.

[11]See John A. Starkweather, "Vocal Communication of Personality and Human Feelings," *Journal of Communication*, 11 (1961): 69; and W. Barnett Pearce and Forrest Conklin, "Nonverbal Vocalic Communication and Perceptions of a Speaker," *Speech Monographs*, 38 (August 1971): 235–241. Also see George L. Trager's "Paralanguage: A First Approximation," *Studies in Linguistics*, 13 (1958): 1–12; and "The Typology of Paralanguage," *Anthropological Linguistics*, 3 (1961): 17–21. For a thorough review of paralanguage see Ernest Kramer, "Judgment of Personal Characteristics and Emotions from Nonverbal Properties," *Psychological Bulletin*, 60 (1963): 408–420.

[12]See Joel R. Davitz, ed., *The Communication of Emotional Meaning* (New York: McGraw-Hill, 1964).

[13]See D. S. Ellis, "Speech and Social Status in America," *Social Forces*, 45 (1967): 431–451; and W. Wilke and J. Snyder, "Attitudes Toward American Dialects," *Journal of Social Psychology*, 14 (1941): 349–362.

[14]See Mark L. Knapp, *Nonverbal Communication in Human Interaction*, p. 349.

ten

FOCUSING YOUR ENERGY

Delivery

Even if you have spent the time preparing your speech that previous chapters have indicated is necessary, your well-prepared speech can lose its effectiveness if it is poorly delivered. Speakers who deliver their message in a disinterested, monotonous, or stone-faced manner are likely to extinguish whatever enthusiasm an audience might have had for the message. Through their delivery alone they doom a well-prepared speech to ineffectiveness. Even a mediocre speech can be effective if delivered in an impressive or striking manner. Delivery cannot be ignored if you intend to improve your public communication ability. The "message" is an all-encompassing aspect that includes who delivers it as well as how it is delivered. When we talk of delivery, we are talking about the process of communicating with the audience.

One of the predominant interfering variables to effective delivery is, of course, anxiety. Everyone experiences anxiety. All the surveys indicate that it is the paramount concern of students and professionals alike. One of the main reasons why people take speech courses is to overcome anxiety. Delivery is the first cue to which listeners are exposed, and this fact alone makes it important. It is also the most obvious aspect of a performance, and if weak, it can destroy an entire effort. But above all, it is that aspect that causes the most anxiety, nervousness, and even fear. Despite that, delivery must not become *the* paramount concern in public communication. If it is thought of in this way, it becomes magnified and emphasized out of all appropriate proportion. One goal of this chapter will be to try to encourage a proper perspective.

The overriding theme of this chapter is that the most important part of the speech communication effort must be the intended message the speaker wishes to impart. Delivery is simply the vehicle used for conveying verbal and nonverbal symbols (words and bodily and vocal cues) to the audience. Delivery should not become a message; it should not be noticed at all. It is the means the speaker uses to reinforce, underscore, or emphasize the essential message.

Because delivery should always be secondary in importance to the essential and intended messages does not mean that it always is second in importance. We have all experienced situations where the speaker's delivery caused us to be distracted from his or her message. It called attention to itself. Ideally, the speaker will be so excited by the importance, significance, relevance, or interest value of his or her ideas that the delivery necessary to communicate those ideas to the audience will follow *naturally*. Delivery will be a natural outgrowth of the ideas. If this were always the case, there would be no need for a chapter on delivery. All that would be needed would be guidelines for finding ideas that would stimulate the dynamic enterprise.

Since we seldom live the ideal, however, not only do we have chapters on delivery but we also directly address the problems we commonly face when standing before an audience. If you are, indeed, fired up about what you want to say, you may wish to skip the material in the next two chapters. In such a case, you have probably already solved the major delivery problems:

1. You have no major problem with anxiety and nervousness; your enthusiasm will submerge it.
2. You are motivated to engage in thorough preparation and practice because you have exciting ideas to share.
3. You know the style of presentation you wish to use: It will be that most appropriate for your information and most comfortable and natural for you.
4. You are able to impress your message on the minds of your listeners through your own credibility and self-assurance. A person who is sincere, serious, and stimulated as a result of good ideas makes a positive and memorable impression on the audience.
5. You have no difficulty in remembering information or having enough experiences and examples in reserve to allow flexibility and adaptability. You will not only be knowledgeable because of having good ideas but also you will have plenty of material left over that you will not use in the speech itself.

These five topic areas will be discussed in the two chapters on delivery: (1) anxiety, (2) preparation and practice, (3) styles of presentation, (4) building credibility, and (5) memory. The first two topics will be examined in this chapter and the last three in the next one. Remember as you read these two chapters that these topics are closely related, and such a division is arbitrary—based solely on decisions concerning space: not subject matter.

Effective delivery, although essentially a physical process, also draws together both the emotional and intellectual. Nonverbal cues reflect the speaker's emotions while words convey his or her intellect. These are not clear-cut divisions, however, but they underscore the importance of delivery as a synthesized process—a drawing together of important elements.

ANXIETY[1]

To worry about something over which you have no control is a waste of your precious time and energy. Blaming someone else for your troubles or taking all the blame on your own shoulders also decreases your energy. This section on anxiety will help you focus your energy *positively*. [2] All the energy that goes into worry, fear, apprehension, concern, and misgiving can and should be rechanneled—refocused to make it work for you. Admittedly some uneasiness is healthy and helpful, but do not fear: all that could be said about refocusing this excessive level of energy could not rid you of it altogether. Some anxiety will persist; some nervousness is normal.[3] Knowing that will help. It will aid you in delivering your speech. More about that extra, leftover amount of energy later.

CONSIDER THIS

In her early years on the stage, Helen Hayes would experience a severe case of the jitters before every opening night performance—so severe at times that it would impair her hearing.

The actress made her first big hit on Broadway in 1926 in Barrie's "What Every Woman Knows." Shortly before the curtain rose, her nervousness flared up and her hearing suddenly failed her. Despite this, she played her role to perfection.

When the final curtain came down, however, and she could hear only faint applause, she was convinced that her performance had been a disaster. With tears welling in her eyes, she hastened to her dressing room to pour out her anguish to her mother.

"I was a failure!" she sobbed.

"What are you talking about?" said her mother sharply. "You received an ovation!"

Source: E. E. Edgar, "Tales That Are Told: Stage Fright," *The Blade* (Toledo, Ohio), September 19, 1978.

There are ten ways to focus your energy more positively: (1) set goals, (2) accept givens, (3) focus on a better world, (4) don't plan too grandly, (5) confront the task, (6) focus on the here and now, (7) take time off, (8) confide your feelings, (9) engage in self-analysis, and (10) reward yourself. Each of these will be considered briefly. Some may be things you already do. The point is to get going—and to get at the task in a reasonable and responsible manner. This system, or series of guides, counters both procrastination—not getting started at all—and the shotgun effect of panic when you start to expend energy in all directions with no control, focus, or purpose.

Set goals

Every speech assignment comes with a deadline. You will know rather precisely when the assignment is due. Thus, you know how much time you have to prepare and what is expected of you. Setting goals entails making lists, establishing aims, arranging things to do, even preparing a checklist for yourself. A broad checklist of items might look like this.

_____ I have analyzed the audience.
_____ I have found appropriate material.
_____ I have organized my material.
_____ I have chosen appropriate language.
_____ I have considered the nonverbal elements of my presentation.
_____ I have practiced my performance.

Of course each of the items listed above could be the heading for a large number of subpoints. But the purpose of setting goals, whether broad or specific, is to organize your time efficiently: to move from a starting point (getting the assignment) to an ending point (the presentation) by using a systematic approach. You just do not have time to get nervous, and any nervousness that is experienced is channeled into useful, productive effort. This is what is done with extra, leftover amounts of energy.

CONSIDER THIS

Select, say, the first five goals from your list and establish a program to achieve them; this will probably entail a detailed series of stages with deadlines and well-thought-out behavioral, emotional, or practical strategies for their attainment. You may find this is easier to do if you were working with somebody else, that is, that you could share your goals and levels of attainment as you were progressing through your self-directed program. If this would be useful, deliberately try to seek some support from a trusted work colleague, friend, or family member.

SOURCE: From the book, *The Stress Check,* by Gary L. Cooper. © 1981 by Prentice-Hall, Inc. Published by Prentice-Hall, Inc., Englewood Cliffs, New Jersey 07632.

TRY THIS 1

Think realistically about your next effort. Make a simple list of the things you must do before the speech is due. List all the items on a separate piece of paper. Now, go back and number these items in hierarchical order. Use this list as you face your next speech assignment.

Accept the Givens

There are certain aspects of the communication situation you undoubtedly did not choose, whether it was the general purpose of the speech, the length of the speech, the audience for the speech, or the date the speech is to be given. These are the givens. Since they are dictated and established, accept them. It is, once again, foolish to feel tense about things over which you have no control. True, it is the uncontrollable and the unpredictable that make us most nervous, but we must shift this concern. Instead, we must focus on our options. We must focus on those areas where we have some degree of control.

CONSIDER THIS

Everyone begins as a beginner. The fact that others are "better" than you are is irrelevant. You, too, will be better the second time than you were the first.

You may notice that the people who do things are not necessarily the ones with the most ability. Those who "make it" are the ones who decide to use what ability they have and the ones who conquered fear. You can be your own heroine by deciding to do the same.

Psychologists call our advice "reaction formation." Musically, it's the "whenever I feel afraid, I hold my head erect and whistle a happy tune so no one will suspect I'm afraid" strategy.

We call it being brave and faking it.

If there were a magic formula to release a flow of brilliant, clear and fitting language for each occasion, especially the difficult early ones, we would reveal it to you. The fact is we all learn by doing. Maybe it will be easy and your improvement will be rapid. Or you may adapt slowly, through failure and error.

SOURCE: From Janet Stone and Jane Bachner, *Speaking Up: A Book for Every Woman Who Wants to Speak Effectively* (New York: McGraw-Hill Book Company, 1977), pp. 37–38.

In a speech assignment, what are your options? Often, though not always, your options will include choice of topic, selection of specific purpose, kind and nature of supporting material, organization and approach in the speech, and creativity—the uniqueness of the effect. If, indeed, these are your options—even if you have a few more or a few less—focus on them. Realize that the more options you have, the more choices you must make. The more options, however, the more likely you can stamp your own seal of uniqueness—your personality—on the effort.

The exciting thing about a speech assignment is that despite certain givens, it is a highly creative activity. Your words become you; that is, they open the door that allows your audience to see who you are. When you accept the givens and do not allow them to become restricting harnesses, you can allow your creative energy to flow: to make this activity the most meaningful and effective representation possible.

Focus on a Better World

When you turn on a television news program or pick up a newspaper, you will notice how the news media often focus on all the bad things in the world. Since news is a big part of our lives, it is easy to let its preoccupation become your own. We let the bad things in the world get to us and we become depressed. It would be easy to write down all the bad things about having to give a speech—but why? This would only aggravate the problem, like rubbing salt in a wound. It will better serve your purpose to believe that the flow of our entire human culture is positive —that there is a good reason for this assignment and for the task that lies ahead. Begin to think optimistically rather than pessimistically, positively rather than negatively.

Begin now to believe in what you are doing or in what you have to do. Believe, for example, that you have something to say, that what you have to say can make a difference in your life or in the lives of your audience members, and that the people listening to you will really care. The audience is your friend. There is an exciting prospect here for improvement and change. If you do not believe that, you will find it difficult to get anyone in your audience to believe it.

Too often in a classroom setting students believe that the situation is artificial. They believe the other students are forced to be present and do not really want to hear speeches, that they have no choice. Or they believe that this is just an assignment—something done merely to get a grade or pass a course. Neither impression is healthy. Despite their motivation for being present, other students are human beings and can be moved to think, believe, or act. Here is an opportunity to influence them. A good speech can cause audience members to say, "I never thought of it in that way," or "Maybe I have been thinking of that in the wrong way all this time," or "I really think something *can* be done about that," or "I am going to take part; it sounds like a good idea!"

TRY THIS 2

To show that you can focus on a better world, and to shift your focus from the negative to the positive, think of all the benefits that can accrue from a speech assignment. You might list such things as learning how to organize, learning more about a topic, gaining experience, and so on. List as many benefits as you can think of—for *you* personally—on a piece of paper. There are many challenges in giving speeches. Meeting these challenges will help you to become a well-rounded, interesting, and more responsible person.

Don't Plan Too Grandly

Control your optimism; don't get carried away. Do not bite off more than you can chew. Be realistic. If you ask your audience for a little change or a little action, you are likely to get it. Ask for the world, and they will consider you unreasonable. They cannot deliver, so why ask? The way to reach any goal is by taking one step at a time. If you can get your audience to complete a small step, you will feel a sense of accomplishment—a success experience. Since you are unlikely to get an audience to do very much, try to get them to do a little! Instead of tackling the whole problem of "cheating" in our society, just try to get the audience to understand cheating on examinations. Instead of reforming education, speak on specific changes that could occur on your campus or at your institution.

CONSIDER THIS

Relief from stress and the beginning of wisdom come when we stop denying the basic uncertainty of life and our lack of control over many of its outcomes. Then we can step back and contemplate both our remarkable possibilities and our awesome limitations, without emphasizing one side of the picture at the expense of the other. We can keep both limitations and possibilities in full view as we make important choices and commitments. Living this way may demand a sometimes painful shedding of illusions, a great deal of maturity, creative risk taking, and the elimination of many comforting excuses and rationalizations. The rewards of this approach, however, can be very substantial. They may include the deep pleasure of self-acceptance and a certain invulnerability to the nagging self-doubts and chronic tension of stressful living.

SOURCE: Robert L. Woolfolk and Frank C. Richardson, *Stress, Sanity, and Survival* (New York: New American Library, 1978), p. 84. Copyright © 1978 by Robert L. Woolfolk and Frank C. Richardson. Reprinted by permission of Soverign Books, a Simon & Schuster division of Gulf & Western Corporation.

Confront the Task

There are always things in this world that we prefer to do rather than doing other things, and we often do the easiest or most liked tasks first—hoping, of course, that the others will disappear, become inappropriate, or be taken care of by someone else. The tasks we dislike remain to nag at us, annoy us, and create fear and tension that tend to build on themselves; thus, fear causes greater fear, tension causes strain and nervousness. You can spend more time and energy worrying about giving a speech than it would take to prepare an effective speech. Also, the worry will interfere with your concentration and thus serve as a constant drain.

The best way to alleviate mounting fear and nervousness is through ventilation: Let it out through action and problem-solving. It is too easy to let thoughts and feelings like the following work away at you:

> I'll fail.
> I'll look stupid.
> I'm unattractive.
> I'm not sure.
> They might not like me.
> Something bad will probably happen.
> I know I'm going to feel awful.[4]

Attack the cause directly. Get at the task. The best way to learn is by doing it. And the sooner the better. Confronting the task at once has several benefits:

1. You realize it is not as difficult as you had expected.
2. You have time to hone and perfect the product.
3. You provide time for the material to sink in and make a lasting impression on your mind. You have time to learn the material.
4. You can allow time for picking up examples, facts, and statistics that can be added. As you continue your reading, certain ideas fall into place and can be used to fill out the speech.

The longer you have the information, the more comfortable and at ease you will feel with it. It becomes more and more a natural and logical extension of yourself—your thoughts and feelings as well as, perhaps, your beliefs, values, and needs.

CONSIDER THIS

Giving a lecture is like running a race. I am never sure how well I will do. I always have a slight feeling of dread, the nagging worry that this one will be a disaster. So I approach every talk as I would a race.

I fast. I warm up. I get myself psyched. When I get up to speak I want to be lean and hungry and have every fiber of my body at the ready.

I eat lightly that day and not at all during the three or four hours before the lecture. If I am the after-dinner speaker, my meal goes untouched. Food and drink slow my synapses ever so slightly. I seem to be on a one-second delay. I lose the quickness of mind I need once the speech gets under way.

Another essential in this preparation is an hour's run. Coleridge once said that you will never fail in a talk after a 10-mile walk. I know what he meant. This warmup run reaches beyond the second wind of my body to the third wind of my mind.

After a half hour or so I begin to see the theme of my talk and the direction it will go. Then this outline fills in with examples and experiences that suddenly surface in my consciousness. "In any man's head," writes William Gibson, "the voices of the past are infinite, the undigested odds and ends of his lifetime, a bedlam of sights and sounds and touches of the world since his first breath."

Gibson is right. The place where I find that treasury is running on the roads. And then I use it for my talk.

You would think I could give the same talk each time. I would like to, especially well. But it is impossible. Memorizing never works.

I had a high school teacher who told me, "You can't think and remember at the same time." If I try to duplicate a past triumph I am reduced to the "D" in public speaking I earned in school.

So I speak without a prepared text. I need no notes, no cue cards, no aids when I am on stage. The run has filled my stream of consciousness with all the odds and ends, sights and sounds relevant to my theme. I am now so filled with my subject I just have to get it out.

Sometimes as I enter the hall before the talk a person will come up to me and say "I'm very interested in hearing what you are going to say." And I will reply quite honestly, "So am I." When things go well that is just the case. I am as interested in what I am going to say as I hope the audience is. In fact, my interest assures theirs.

The beginning is always difficult. On one occasion my mind went completely blank and the memory of that feeling of panic still haunts me. I am also a person known only to runners. Most of my listeners have no idea who I am or what I do. All they see is a nervous, scrawny-looking 60-year-old who is about to use up some valuable time.

I have a defense against this. First I admit I am nervous. This gets their sympathy. Then I suggest that I should have brought my American Express card. That gets the first laugh. Then I suggest that jogging is boring. That gets the second laugh. From then on it is the audience lifting me and me lifting the audience.

There are times when so many new and interesting ideas fill my head I mentally hang the talk on a peg about 15 feet in the air off to my left and promise to come back later. Then I pursue some interesting anecdote or incident to its conclusion.

The audience is a partner in this enterprise. A great deal depends upon them. Give me salesmen any time. They are listeners by profession. They also have a disdain for facts and an appreciation of rhetoric.

Technical people are a different breed. When I say something to a group of technicians, it just lies out there and they look at it for quite a while.

Now I am able to size up the audience and know how to give and talk. Again, it is like a race. I run differently over hills and against the wind; there are some talks that are just like that.

Every once in a while things fall into place. I have caught the absolute attention of the crowd. My timing has become professional. Every illustration I use is new and exciting. I feel virtuoso. I am willing to go on and on—and the audience wants me to.

In the end I am never sure what I have said. All I can recall is the enthusiasm and the exhilaration. I know for 40 minutes or so these people and I have entered each other's minds and hearts.

Then comes the applause, surely one of the most moving things any creature can do for another. And then in this every-once-in-a-while experience, that strange and wonderful and spontaneous union of performer and audience, a standing ovation.

For that there can be only one fitting reaction. The clenched fists over the head indicating that we are all winners.

SOURCE: Dr. George Sheehan, "Working Out: Getting Psyched Up For A Talk," *The Blade* (Toledo, Ohio), November 8, 1979, p. 7. Material is from "Dr. Sheehan On Fitness."

Focus on the Here-and-Now

We tend to be rear-view-mirror gazers. We look at the past and become preoccupied with it when our energy should be and needs to be expended now—in the present. Ask yourself what it is about what you are doing right now that makes you feel good, that satisfies you, that pleases you. Look for that ingredient.

Distraction from the here and now occurs easily. When you catch yourself looking back and seeing other failures—or others' failures—or when you start taking the blame for things that have happened in the past, distraction begins. You are wasting precious energy. Do not worry about speeches in the past that have not worked out successfully. Do not worry about other speakers who have failed miserably in their efforts. Stop thinking about the past; turn your attention to your immediate needs.

The same preoccupation can occur as you anticipate the future. You cannot predict it. When you try to anticipate the future, you are not paying attention to that which needs attention now—the "now" that needs attention. Some future planning is necessary as we attempt to gear our material to audience wants, needs, and interests, but any preoccupation with anticipated failure or a negative reaction in the future can gnaw away at us and siphon off energy into distractions. Because of the unique combination of elements that occurs when a speech is given—including the whims and fancies of all audience members (including the instructor)—it is impossible to accurately predict exactly how a message will come accross. Since this is true, it is wise not to waste precious energy in constant worry.

Take Time Off

If you have followed the first step—setting goals—you should be able to take time off occasionally as you move systematically toward your goal. Sometimes the thinking motor needs to be shut off for a while—or its attention moved to something else—if it is to operate well while focused on *this* project. If you have procrastinated, you may not have the time available!

If you are good at setting goals, set small, attainable ones for yourself. For example, you might decide to get support for the first main head of a speech, then take a short break before writing the transition and moving into the second main head. To write a paper or a chapter, I work by segments. When a section is complete, the completion is reinforced and rewarded by walking around, getting a cup of coffee, some peanuts, or a fresh piece of fruit. The return to work is then refreshing; a new sense of vigor sets in. Neither all work nor all play should be the order of the day.

Confide your Feelings

We all have moments when we become frustrated, annoyed, disappointed, and scared. You have an exam. A paper is due. Too much is coming at you at one time. A speech must be prepared. Then, too, teachers often seem to think that their class is the only one you are taking. One way to cope with these pressures is to confide your feelings to others. When you have expressed them, you often feel an amazing release of frustration. You have, in a sense, relieved yourself of a terrible burden.

When you confide your feelings, worries, and wants, it is not suggested that you release your innermost secrets nor that you tell all. You must be selective. When you feel under stress because of a forthcoming speech, you can relieve some of this tension by telling someone else.

Release of these feelings can also prevent sickness. People who keep everything inside over a long period of time can become mentally ill or even physically sick. They can get upset stomachs and headaches—or still more serious ailments. If they lose sleep as well, the problem is compounded. If you worry a lot, talk your worries out a lot.

It is common knowledge that many entertainers get physically upset—even sick before a performance. Nervousness causes a variety of responses in people. To become sick to your stomach is not unusual. Talking to others not only allows you new insights, but they may also suggest other ways to cope.

Engage in Self-Analysis

Stop and analyze why you are so upset. What are you really afraid of? If what you are afraid of *really* happened, would it be the end of the world? It is amazing what our imagination does with fears; they become magnified and more intense as we retain them. Try to refocus your attention. Ask, once again, what are you doing that you feel *really* good about? Even call in friends and have them tell you what you do well. Sometimes we cannot see the forest for the trees, and friends can provide a more objective, clearer view. They can call attention to our good, beneficial, useful, or worthwhile qualities if asked. What is more, they would probably like to!

In your self-analysis keep reminding yourself that *you* are not the target of conflict. *You* are not responsible for the world. *You* did not create the problem. Sometimes it helps to get outside yourself and look at yourself as another person, a higher self. Put yourself in a different perspective; do not get trapped inside what you understand in your mind. Transcend your mind and look into the things you do not understand. Everything does not need to make sense, and by experiencing *only* what you understand, you limit your world.

Many of the benefits of speechmaking have already been outlined: broadening of your horizons, organizing material, researching ideas, presenting ideas before audiences, developing self-confidence and poise, and so on. Any one of these can be a basis for active and eager involvement. What is it you want from life? It is likely that portions of the speechmaking process or the process as a whole will offer benefits.

CONSIDER THIS

Have you any idea what fear was rated No. 1 in a recent survey among adults?

Speaking before a group.

That's right, the anxiety of standing before an audience beat out fear of death, fear of failing, fear of heights, and fear of alienation. (Come to think of it, they all mean the same thing.)

It occurred to me that this year a virtual army of amateur speakers will, for the first time, take to the podiums to conduct club meetings, volunteer seminars, and instructional classes.

How do the professionals handle it?

- Demand a podium capable of supporting a dead body (yours) up to 187 pounds. Throw yourself over it, being sure to hook your arm over the microphone so you won't slip away.
- Adhere to the old wive's tale, "Feed a cold crowd, starve a speaker." It cuts down on spitting up.
- Insist on a table near the restroom. For some unexplained reason, speakers have a kidney wish.
- Never read a speech. Use note cards which serve a double purpose. You can rearrange them to fit your audience, and in the event the person who introduces you uses the jokes on your first eight cards, use the sharp cutting edges on your wrists.

Believe me, I know what you are going through. A couple of years ago, my son brought home a mimeographed memo from school announcing that the principal was having 12 parents in at a time to "engage in dialogue about the future of the school."

At the beginning of the meeting, he announced that before the session was over he wanted to hear from everyone. If they didn't volunteer, he'd call on them.

One by one, I watched them get it over with. Questions on what the administration was doing to raise standards of education . . . could he please interpret the test scores in relation to those given the previous year . . . did he feel that schools were becoming isolated or were they addressing themselves to alternatives, such as technical or vocational classes.

As a professional speaker, I waited until he called upon me. Then I casually poked myself in the eye with a green felt-tipped pen and stood up to reveal the back of my dress which was superbonded to my body.

I opened my mouth to discover my tongue had dried up, causing my lip to shrink.

I cleared my throat, folded my arms over my chest (the green ink would never wash out), and asked, "Yes, do the nuns really shave their heads?"

SOURCE: From AT WIT'S END by Erma Bombeck. Copyright 1979 Field Enterprises, Inc. Courtesy of Field Newspaper Syndicate.

Reward Yourself

Nobody else can judge how important something is for you. When you accomplish something you find difficult, find a way to reward yourself for success. You need not wait for total success; even just getting through a speech experience may merit some reward.

Other people are unlikely to appreciate how important or difficult something is for you, thus, oftentimes they cannot appropriately reward your achievement. *You* do it. Give yourself a gift, a little time off for good behavior. Tell a friend. Boasting or claiming credit for a job well done is an energizing activity so long as it does not become bragging.

Another personal experience will reinforce the point. As a writer, I seldom write one chapter directly after another with no break in between. I reward myself with the freedom to turn my attention to other matters for several days —I catch up on correspondence, read, pay bills, or whatever. Then, once again, I return to writing refreshed. It is a necessary break—a cleansing of the soul.

TRY THIS 3

Of the ten items mentioned, check those you feel you already do:

_____ 1. Set goals   _____ 6. Focus on the here and now
_____ 2. Accept givens   _____ 7. Take time off
_____ 3. Focus on a better world
_____ 8. Confide your feelings
_____ 4. Don't plan too grandly
_____ 9. Engage in self–analysis
_____ 5. Confront the task   _____ 10. Reward yourself

Do the items you did not check appear to be things you can reasonably accomplish? Which are likely to be easiest? Which will be hardest? Can you see how each of these activities relates to the process of putting a speech together?

PREPARATION AND PRACTICE

The key to decreasing anxiety is preparation. The fully prepared person is less likely to experience the intense anxiety felt by those who are unprepared. In this section, a series of activities will be discussed that will help guarantee a feeling of complete preparedness. Guarantee? The activities relate to delivery, not content. Because they are comprehensive (perhaps more than you will need), a guarantee is in order. But no two speakers are likely to prepare for a speech in the same way. The more experience you have in speechmaking, the more likely you will find a method that is comfortable for you. Comfort, ease, and thoroughness are goals.

The assumption throughout this section is that you have prepared *all* your written material: You have collected the supporting material, organized it, and selected appropriate words to express those ideas that are most important or that must be clear. Not every thought in the speech needs to be couched in words before you practice; however, those thoughts you want to present with particular clarity or strength or vividness should be. Be careful to limit the number of ideas you phrase and the extent of the phrasing. The more memorizing you must do, the more problems you are likely to encounter. There will be more on memory work later.

Before beginning delivery preparation, try to have a fairly clear picture in your mind of where you will be giving the speech. If need be, visit the place. If you can actually practice there, do so. At the very least, form a vivid impression of the place. An impression of the audience will help as well. How many persons will be there? How will they be seated?

No matter which style of presentation (see the chapter that follows on manuscript, memorized, extemporaneous, and impromptu styles) you plan to use, the end product should be the same: an effective delivery should not be noticed. You want your essential message to be first, foremost, and always in the minds of audience members.

Also, you want your message to appear to be part of you. You want it to flow from you as an extension of your personality—your thoughts and feelings. After all, your message not only reflects your thoughts and feelings but a great deal of your time and energy as well.

You have re-created the situation as closely as possible, and you know what your goal is—a conversational style that is not noticed. Now, begin to go over the material. Try to use the same material (manuscript, outline, or notes) in practice as you will use in the final presentation. You can condense what you use as you continue by eliminating words or by finding key words or expressions. Try not to simply repeat words. Vividly and clearly strive to see and feel the meanings associated with the words. Understanding the ideas is different from learning a series of words (more on this in a moment).

During the final stages of practice you will find that your recollection of specific language will give way to the recall of ideas. You will know when this happens because one or all of the following are likely to occur as a direct result:

1. New ideas will come to mind.
2. Additional details and illustrations will occur.
3. A new way to state an idea will be suggested.

When you have a strong, organized speech, that organized whole controls the various parts and will suggest new and unanticipated items.

Another goal of practice is to bring freshness and spontaneity to your language. Because you have repeatedly worked with the words and ideas, you can easily become bored with them. As you rehearse, pretend it is for the first time; re-create the words and ideas with enthusiasm and energy.

Concentrate on the meanings and ideas, as mentioned above, not on the words. Basic ideas will be stamped on your memory if you can link main heads and subheads or see how certain statements are linked to the specific purpose. Once the structure of the speech as a whole can be recollected, you can begin talking the speech through without outline or notes, unless, of course, you are going to deliver it from memory or from a manuscript. Your goal here is to achieve full responsiveness to the *meaning* of what you are saying and to attain a true sense of communication with your audience. The more you become absorbed in the meaning of what your are communicating, the less you will be concerned about anything else.

TRY THIS 4

Can you think of a time when you have been so completely immersed in something that you have not noticed other things going on around you? Were you reading? Listening to music? Working on a project? Following a hobby? Recall a *vivid* impression of such an experience right now.

This is the kind of concentration and focus that is desired in speech communication. The focal point is the message and the desire to have that message be the one the audience ends with. The concentration and focus on the message is so complete that the various aspects of delivery are effectively blocked out. They become secondary to the message.

What type of rehearsal works best? Ideally, a rehearsal would be held in the same room or place where the speech is to be delivered. As styles, methods, and approaches that do not resemble the final outcome are included, the rehearsal can become less and less meaningful. For example, if you know you will be standing with limited notes before a class, it is probably not wise to simply go over your outline in your mind while lying on your bed; more rigorous rehearsal is needed. Some speakers, find that using a variety of rehearsal methods works best. They practice the speech orally while standing up. They read the speech. They also listen to it via tape recorder. When circumstances allow, they also may try to see a video tape of their rehearsal. The more stimuli they can use, the more the ideas are likely to be impressed on their mind. Some speakers record their speech on a cassette, and then listen to it wherever and whenever they can: eating a meal, dressing in the morning, traveling in a car, going to sleep at night. A practice session before going to bed allows the subconscious to work with the ideas while you sleep.

How long should you practice? There is no one answer to this question. It varies not only from speaker to speaker, but also from speech to speech:

1. The complexity of the ideas will affect practice time. Obviously, the more difficult the ideas, the longer it will take to commit them to memory.
2. How exact must you be? A high degree of exactness will require more rehearsal time. Less rehearsal time is needed for a casual and informal presentation.
3. The length of the presentation is likely to affect how long you need to practice. It is generally thought that the shorter the presentation, the *more* practice time required. The longer the speech, the less practice time. Longer speeches, in general, do not require the exactness or conciseness that shorter speeches do.
4. How successful are you at remembering ideas? Some people remember better than others. If you have a weak memory, you will probably need more rehearsal time—more time to secure the ideas in your mind.
5. How long does it take you to become comfortable, fluent, and at ease with the ideas? Because the ideas should appear as a natural extension of yourself, you must gauge your rehearsal time with your own command of the information. This is not just remembering, it is also achieving comfort and ease. The more familiar you are with the material at the outset, or the more it comes from your own experience, the less practice time you will require.

The sooner you get all your material assembled, the sooner practice can begin. It is to your advantage to allow yourself plenty of time. Confidence grows as you practice your delivery.

TRY THIS 5

Check each item in the following list that directly characterizes your speech or your own personal needs.

_____ The ideas are complex.

_____ It will be necessary to be exact.

_____ The presentation is short (under eight minutes).

_____ I have difficulty remembering ideas.

_____ The ideas of the speech, in general, are new to me.

A checkmark simply indicates that a certain aspect of the speech situation is going to require more time and energy. For each check you will probably need to increase your rehearsal time.

Practice needs to be conducted in the best possible framework. To make the best use of practice time, first strive for a positive mental attitude. Success often results when the speaker assumes a successful attitude: "I can do it." "I will do it." "I want to do it." "I will succeed." Second, strive for strength of conviction: This is an extension of the positive mental attitude as it relates to the material. "I believe in what I am doing." "I believe in my ideas." "I think they are significant for my audience." Finally, develop enthusiasm and dynamism. Tell yourself: "I want to do this," "What I am doing is important," and "I want to present my ideas with all the energy and interest I can muster." Just as the final presentation relies on the proper state of mind, so does practice. This mind set can be an important variable throughout the entire speech preparation process. It can, indeed, be the key factor that causes us to summon up *whatever* energy is needed to meet the demands placed on us!

SUMMARY

This chapter suggests ways to focus your energy. In the first part of the chapter, ten ways to focus your energy positively were presented. These methods offer a realistic, logical means of channeling your energies. When your energy goes into worry, fear, apprehension, concern, and misgiving, it is not working for you. It is, instead, eroding your powers of concentration and effectiveness.

If you begin your speech efforts by setting goals, accepting givens, focusing on a better world, planning realistically, confronting the task, focusing on the here and now, taking time off, confiding your feelings, engaging in self-analysis, and rewarding yourself, you will be approaching your task in a reasonable and responsible manner. These positive behaviors will also help you remove some of the anxiety commonly and naturally associated with the public communication situation or experience.

In preparing and practicing a speech, you should visit the place where you will give the speech. Also, keep in mind the goal of not allowing your delivery to be noticed. Allow your message to appear to be part of you. Do not to simply repeat words during practice; instead, try to add freshness and spontaneity to each practice session by concentrating on meanings and ideas. Comments on the type of rehearsal and the length of time needed to practice were also added. The need for a positive mental attitude was the final comment on making preparation and practice useful and beneficial.

In the next chapter various styles of presentation will be discussed, and the kind of relationship the speaker should try to establish with the audience will be mentioned. As you consider delivery aspects of communication, try to see all elements working smoothly together—complementing and reinforcing each other.

NOTES

[1]Ideas in this section on "Anxiety" were adapted from John E. Jones, "How to Maintain Personal Energy," in John E. Jones and J. William Pfeiffer, *The 1979 Annual Handbook for Group Facilitators* (LaJolla, Calif.: University Associates, 1979), pp. 113–116. Used with permission.

[2]See James C. McCroskey and Virginia P. Richmond, "The Effects of Communication Apprehension on the Perception of Peers," *Western Speech Journal,* 40 (Winter 1976): 14–21. An excellent bibliography on communication apprehension appears in H. Thomas Hurt, Michael D. Scott, and James C. McCroskey, *Communication in the Classroom* (Reading, Mass.: Addison–Wesley Publishing Co., 1978), pp. 156–162.

[3]See Keith Jensen, "Self-Reported Speech Anxiety and Selected Demographic Variables," *Central States Speech Journal,* 27 (Summer 1976): 102–108.

[4]See Wayne W. Dyer, *Pulling Your Own Strings* (New York: Avon Books, 1979), p. 32. See his chapter on "Operating from Strength," pp. 27–51.

eleven

STYLES OF PRESENTATION

Delivery

A style of presentation is simply the way the speech is to be delivered to the audience. The style of presentation you use for a given speech may be part of a class assignment; your instructor may tell you to use an extemporaneous style. The style could also be dictated by the occasion. The speech might be part of a formal event in which the selection of the words is very important—in which case a manuscript or memorized style of presentation is given. In this chapter, various styles will be discussed, then some of the aspects of a speaker's relationship with his or her audience will be mentioned. The chapter closes with a discussion of memory and how it relates to effective delivery.

Although there can be variations and combinations of delivery styles, the most common include memorized, manuscript, impromptu, and extemporaneous. Each will be discussed and some specific requirements mentioned. Since each style has its strengths and weaknesses, these will be outlined. In this way, speakers given a choice of which style to use will have a better basis for selecting the most appropriate one. In addition, ways to build credibility will be discussed. Credibility will be examined as a function of a speaker–audience relationship. A final section on memory and its relationship to effective delivery will conclude the chapter.

MEMORIZED DELIVERY

Memorizing the prepared language in full was, perhaps, the earliest speechmaking style. It was favored by the ancients. When a manuscript is committed to memory, the speaker can polish the wording of ideas and look at the audience while delivering the speech. To memorize a speech one must go over and over it, much as an actor might do to learn lines for a theater production.

A memorized form of delivery has still other benefits. It gives the speaker freedom to move in front of the audience. He or she need not be tied to a manuscript or lectern. It allows the speaker to concentrate on the delivery of the ideas. Since the words and ideas have already been selected, the speaker's primary job is to bring them to life. It also can make a positive impression on the audience as its members hear a fluent set of ideas that appear to flow naturally and spontaneously from the speaker.

One problem with a memorized delivery is that it often sounds memorized. Few people can successfully master the technique. When a speech sounds memorized, it has a negative effect on the audience. To memorize a speech so well that it sounds natural and spontaneous requires a great deal of time and energy, and yet a natural spontaneity is the final goal. It is best for beginning speakers to avoid this style in their early efforts.

The other major problem with memorizing is that in mastering the wording, the speaker learns a specific word order. Any mistake then requires that he or she backtrack (or skip ahead) to recall the specific word order. The focus is on the words—not *any* words—*the* words. When this becomes the focus, three facts become readily apparent to the audience:

1. The speaker has not really mastered the content—just the words. (The ideas appear to be secondary in importance!)
2. The speaker can provide no additonal insight into the topic. (He or she is committed to this set of words only, with no flexibility!)
3. The speaker has allowed for no specific audience adaptation at the time of the presentation. (Some of the excitement of the moment is lost!)

It takes time to memorize a speech to the point where it sounds spontaneous, and most beginning speakers find it difficult. That is why beginning speakers should avoid this style. But if you are faced with the situation of having to give a memorized speech, the following suggestions are offered:

1. Rehearse orally. Learn the sequence of ideas and practice expressing those ideas until they become fluent. Go over and over the material.
2. Record the speech on tape and listen to playbacks of it.
3. Strive to grasp the material as a whole, rather than working on individual sections or points. To learn a speech as a whole takes advantage of the internal logical and sequential properties of the lines; it also minimizes omissions of material in performance.

4. Give the material your complete attention. Isolate yourself from music, radio, television, or roommate interference. Only after you have given it your full concentration can you add elements of additional noise and distraction to more nearly approximate the actual speaking situation.
5. Use many short practice sessions rather than a few long sessions.
6. Make certain you have a thorough knowledge of the subject. This base of information assures a large number of associations.

The ideas above will help you in the practice sessions that precede the final delivery of the memorized speech. Such practice is directed toward several goals, which serve as guidelines for the audience-centered presentation of the actual speech:

1. Strive to concentrate on the ideas so that you do not sound like you are simply repeating words—words that are not tied together in useful and meaningful ways.
2. Strive to maintain the appearance of spontaneity and flexibility of thought characteristic of conversation. Avoid appearing stilted, formal, rigid, and inflexible.
3. Strive to maintain a relaxed conversational pace. Many speakers who memorize their material hurry their words. They lose naturalness.

Remember, memorization takes time. Speakers who memorize must develop confidence so that they do not lose their place in a speech. They must also *feel* comfortable and in control of the situation, and to do so they must plan to spend great amounts of time with the manuscript. It is the only way full memorization can occur, and it is the only way to ensure that a memorized speech will not sound memorized.

TRY THIS 1

Presentation of a memorized speech requires a good memory. Start trying to remember things better. You can do this in two principal ways:

1. Use mnemonic devices. Examples of such devices are the system used by some to remember the lines on the music staff—E, G, B, D, and F: *Every Good Boy Does Fine*—an acronym used to remember the names of the five Great Lakes by remembering *homes*—*H*uron, *O*ntario, *M*ichigan, *E*rie, and *S*uperior. How about remembering the four voices of a quartet by picturing a quartet being stabbed? *Stab* gives you the initial letters: *s*oprano, *t*enor, *a*lto, and *b*ass. You will remember new information best if you can associate it with what you already know.

2. Practice linking ideas together. This will strengthen your memory because one item will lead to the next one. A speech is just a sequence of thoughts, but you must be able to picture the thoughts in your mind. Try to make the pictures ridiculous. In this way they will be more easily remembered:

a. Substitute an ordinary picture with one that will be more easily remembered. Instead of trying to rememeber the name on a book, put the name on the side of the Goodyear blimp.
b. Blow things out of proportion. Try to visualize things larger than life. Instead of a teacher, try to see a giant. A clover could become a giant tree.
c. Exaggerate things. Instead of seeing just one thing, see millions of the item.
d. Finally, get action into your mental pictures. Action is also easy to remember. Instead of seeing things standing still, see them flying or hitting something.

The point in all of this is that your memory needs exercise. The more exercise it gets, the more likely it will work when you call on it.[1]

MANUSCRIPT DELIVERY

In manuscript delivery the speech is written out in full and then read aloud. As in the memorized style, the wording can be carefully planned. To prepare for using this style, the speaker should proceed in much the same way as he or she would if trying to memorize the speech. The speech must be well rehearsed if the delivery is to sound spontaneous and natural and if the speaker is not to be tied to the manuscript.

Presidents, heads of state, and other dignitaries use the manuscript style to avoid mistakes that might result from the wrong choice of words or improper sentence construction. This is also the form of delivery used by network newscasters who read the manuscript from a teleprompter. The better the newscaster is at reading, the better he or she is received by the viewers. Other benefits of the manuscript style include:

1. Availability of the words. If a speaker forgets material, the words are readily accessible.
2. Advantage of prior preparation. A speaker can carefully prepare the exact wording of each idea.
3. Possibility of last–minute preparation. Speakers can couch their ideas in clear, appropriate langauge, even just prior to a performance.

The problem with this style of delivery is that the written words become a crutch. Speakers begin to like having the whole speech written out in front of them. Even when they know the material well, they often become dependent on the manuscript. Audiences, on the other hand, do not like listening to someone read, and a speaker who reads is often boring and uninteresting. The speech lacks energy and stimulation. It lacks that natural spontaneity referred to above. Often, too, because the speech is written out, it lacks audience adaptation and the flexibility that usually accompanies a free and natural delivery. Unless the delivery of a manuscript is a special assignment, this style of presentation should be avoided.

CONSIDER THIS

Once a year somebody asks you to make a speech—your church, garden club, civic club, professional organization.

And once a year you are scared stiff—because you feel inadequate. Right?

Well, hang in there, friends. Help is on the way. Here comes a speech communication consultant from Forest Hills, N.Y., John P. Monaghan, former speech teacher, college debate coach, actor, and network television writer.

Mr. Monaghan, in Philadelphia to conduct speaking workshops, talks about what he says is the most important thing for inexperienced speakers to remember:

"Know exactly what you want to do—how the audience will be different when you finish. The biggest mistake speakers make is not clearly defining their purpose."

Some other tips from Mr. Monaghan:

• Try to determine in advance what most likely will ring a bell with an audience. It's always a guess, but it's a good idea to ask yourself: "Will this example prove my point to this audience?"

• Write out your opening and closing remarks and "learn them cold." When you do that, everything else falls into place more easily. Some speakers plan the end of the talk first, because "if you don't know what the end is, how will you get there?"

• Don't write out the whole speech and read it, because this turns off an audience. Use the fewest notes possible. If you can't remember the structure, how do you expect the audience to remember? An outline containing a few key words is preferred by many speakers.

• Don't worry that you will make a fool of yourself. Audiences are malleable and friendly. They won't laugh at you. They'll do anything you ask. "In my lifetime I've not seen three hostile audiences."

• Stay away from humor until you are more experienced as a speaker.

• Never apologize to an audience. Don't begin your talk by saying: "I don't know why they asked me to do this, but . . ." This is a game played by people who are afraid of not being accepted.

• If you make a grammatical error, forget it and keep plowing ahead. "Almost nobody notices when you make an error. If you go back and correct it, everybody notices."

Mr. Monaghan says that speakers should keep in mind two factors—what he calls the "COIK" and "WIIFM" factors.

COIK stands for "clear only if known" and, Mr. Monaghan says, it is important that people delivering technical messages understand that the technical vocabulary must be changed into everyday words—if the audience is made up of nontechnical people.

WIIFM means "What's in it for me?" The good speaker, Mr. Monaghan says, puts himself in the audience and asks about his own speech: "What's in it for me?

What will I learn from the speech—how to transplant peonies, get a promotion, save more money?''

Well, what about it, you once–a–year speakers? Are you still a little nervous?

If you are, don't think there is anything wrong with you. Even the best and most experienced speakers, Mr. Monaghan says, fight butterflies before they begin to talk–not because they're uncertain what they are going to say, but because they are uncertain how the audience will react.

SOURCE: Darrell Sifford, ''Expert's Plan Captures Speaker's Butterflies,'' Knight News Service, *The Blade* (Toledo, Ohio), December 18, 1977.

The best suggestion for preparing a manuscript speech is to prepare it as if you were going to give an extemporaneous speech. This can be accomplished in two different ways. One way is to write the speech as if you are speaking orally. If this is difficult, use the second way. Prepare an outline or notes and practice with them. As you give the final speech in practice, record the effort and type the manuscript from the tape. From the tape, you can polish the wording as necessary. The purpose in both methods of preparation is to ensure an oral style of delivery rather than a written style.

Once a manuscript is prepared, practicing with that manuscript is necessary. The goal in practice is to become so familiar with the material that you do not have to give the manuscript your full attention as you present the speech. You must be so familiar with it that you can maintain eye contact with the audience while reading. This may require three or more run–throughs at this stage. As you are presenting the information, your eye contact with the audience will serve as a guide to tell you when and if you need to change the speech from what is written. Unless there are restrictions regarding the degree you are allowed to deviate from the written manuscript, feel free to adapt and change to meet changing circumstances. Remember as a guiding principle that audiences do not like to be read to; thus, the more you can make the manuscript speech appear to be extemporaneous, the easier it will be to maintain audience attention and interest—which is your goal.

In preparing a manuscript speech, you should strive for clarity, vividness, emphasis, and appropriateness of language. Remember that the reason for using a manuscript is is to make certain the language is exact. If concern for exactness is not a problem, perhaps the speaker should consider the values inherent in the extemporaneous style.

When it comes to putting the words on the paper you plan to use before the audience, remember the goal is to have a clear, readable product. Type the manuscript double or triple space. It will be easier to read, too, if you can use a pica–sized typewriter. Some persons find capitalizing all words to be useful, just as the news comes from a wire service. If there are words that are difficult to pronounce, spell them in a way that will help you know them when you come to them. Hyphenate and accent them as necessary. Sometimes it is useful to underline them in red in the manuscript. Then, when you see them coming, you can mentally prepare for them.

Also, it is useful to highlight or underline places in the manuscript that need emphasis. Use special marks to indicate pauses (//) or places where you need to speed up (——►) or slow down (////). Do not allow a sentence to be carried over between two manuscript pages; in reading such a sentence unintended pauses can occur.

Pages should be numbered clearly, then if the manuscript is dropped, it can easily be put back into order. Numbers also help you double–check before beginning to see that all pages are in order. When you finish the pages as you read, pull them to one side. Never lift them up from the lectern or turn them over —this creates unnecessary distraction. Material should never be placed on the back of a manuscript page. It is always wise to make a last-minute check to be certain you will have a lectern on which to place the manuscript.

TRY THIS 2

Practice reading aloud. It is the very best way to become proficient in front of an audience. Those who are skillful at it are generally good oral readers. You, too, can develop skill if you practice the following procedures.

1. Read parts of your homework assignments out loud. Take a few moments and read passages from this book out loud. Read the passages again and again until it becomes comfortable and easy.

2. Pick an editorial from your newspaper and read it aloud. Pretend you have written it and it is your viewpoint. Make it sound as if you really care about it.

3. Take a speech or portions of a speech written in *Vital Speeches of the Day* (a periodical available at your library), and use this speech for practicing manuscript delivery.

Learning how to deliver a manuscript effectively is an important skill, useful in special circumstances. When needed, it is useful to have already polished it—to be prepared.

IMPROMPTU DELIVERY

When speaking is done on the spur of the moment, it is known as *impromptu* speaking. No previous, specific preparation is involved. An instructor might give students several ideas to choose from, allow several moments for them to collect their thoughts, and then have each of them speak on one of the topics. This is impromptu speaking.

The reason for the generally poor quality of impromptu speaking is simply the surprise factor. It is as if speakers in such situations find themselves in deep water. Losing their head, they thrash around wildly looking for any idea that can be clutched in desperation, hoping it will save them. Because of the wild, uncontrolled nervousness, the delivery is halting and staccato, the remarks become inane and irrelevant, and the material is repetitious and disjointed.

Good impromptu speaking is rare. This is simply because impromptu speaking, in general, lacks specific preparation. Anyone can get up and speak on just about anything; however, the results are just about what one would expect —a great deal of hot air reflecting little prior planning or thinking. And we already have enough hot air! But when impromptu speaking is good, it can be very, very good. It can, for example, capture the emotions and passion of the speaker at the moment; reflect the years of experience, plus background information that is personal and vivid for the speaker; and provide an immediate, real, direct, and spontaneous experience that builds on present feelings and thoughts.

Impromptu speaking is not recommended for formal speech assignments. Most people—especially inexperienced speakers—cannot handle this style well. Too, it would be foolhardy to leave formal preparation to chance. That is like throwing out all the previous chapters in this book and depending on your own glibness and informality to pull you through. Most audiences expect speeches to reveal depth and substance that results from prior thinking and planning. Most speakers need prior thinking and planning in order to offer depth and substance, and to establish their own credibility.

On some occasions impromptu speaking is not only appropriate but is expected. The question is, of course, "How can one *plan* for an impromptu situation?" There *are* things a speaker can do.

Anticipate the Situation

What are the chances you might be called on to speak? Might you be given an award, presentation, or recognition? Have you been away? Taken a trip? Received an award or special recognition elsewhere? Have you recently acquired new information or a new perspective? A new job or promotion? Do you have a special skill, talent, or ability? Knowing you *may* be called on, plan a few remarks. Organize some thoughts, some ideas, some relevant observations.

Listen Carefully

Follow what is being discussed or what is being said by others. If there is a chance you will have to speak, what others before you have said may either provide you with material or suggest some relevant information or experience. If you think you may be called on for a reaction, brief notes may help you respond well. To be able to state any of the following with clarity and directness will indicate strength and may be an effective approach:

"I think the previous speaker has overlooked an important point."
"I feel that this argument tends to be a weak one."
"I believe the speaker is correct as far as he went. What he failed to say was . . ."
"There seems to be some inconsistency here."
"Let me just add a couple of additional examples that may help clarify the situation."

The most effective communicator with small groups that I've known was a woman with none of the traits one might expect from a master persuader. She was not young or beautiful; in fact, she had such an unassuming appearance that she was often overlooked in a group. She didn't arouse confidence, awe, affection, or even respect on first meeting. She hadn't taken courses in forensics and public speaking, and her voice was not unusual.

What she did have was mastery in sensing her audiences and attuning herself to them. A few moments after she joined a group she seemed to have a mental picture of its makeup, its mood, its inclinations, its interests, and its doubts. Then she became the person who could treat that audience effectively. She would be disarmingly casual or calmly assured. She would exhibit her interest in the concerns of her listeners with a sincerity that could not be doubted. She used charm to beguile others into listening, but not to the point where it focused attention on her.

Source: Phillip Lesly, *How We Discommunicate* (New York: AMACOM, a division of American Management Associations, 1979), pp. 155–156.

Control Yourself

Relax. Breathe regularly. Remember that fear builds on itself. If you can squarely face the situation at hand, appropriate material is more likely to occur to you. Is there a question to answer? An issue that needs resolving? If you can have the question restated, you will gain a couple of moments to collect your thoughts.

If you can lead off with a strong central idea and then support it with some specific examples, you can conclude by restating the opening idea and briefly summarizing your major points. This is, in essence, the quick and easy organizational scheme of telling them what you are going to tell them, telling them, and then telling them what you told them.

If, indeed, you have nothing to say, everyone will appreciate your contribution most if you simply and graciously admit it and add nothing. Too many speakers with nothing to say use up a great deal of human time and energy saying it. Sometimes you even have to listen a long time to find it out! The best approach is to say, "I'm sorry, but I don't have anything to say [or add] to what has already been offered." If you have been listening closely and have something to say on a related point, this might be the place to offer it (as part of a gracious retreat): "... but I do have a comment on such–and–such a point ..." (then *use* your notes).

Organize your Thoughts

As we have already suggested, your ability to quickly and efficiently gather your thoughts together will help you control your emotions. Also, as noted previously, the least that can be expected of an impromptu speaker is that he or she frame a simple, sensible sentence and support it with an example or two. You might consider using any of the ready–made outlining principles such as "past, present, and future," "who, what, when, where," or "principle–demonstration." Anything else will be considered a positive addition.

Remember that most of the material for impromptu speaking comes from personal experience. Bring your full background to bear on the situation: your education, reading, conversing, observing, experiencing, thinking, traveling, and questioning. The greater your experience, the more likely you will have grist for the impromptu mill. Develop a knack for swiftly arranging your remarks, and remember to keep the conclusion short and to the point. Summarize, restate your thesis in the conclusion, and sit down. The three B's are pertinent here: Be brief, be to the point, and be seated—and then you won't be the fourth B: boring.

Be Positive

Much of your success in public communication is dependent on your having the proper mental framework. A negative attitude drains off important energy, whereas a positive one channels it in the right direction. This is not to suggest that a positive attitude guarantees positive results; nothing can do that. But it does provide a sense of mission and responsibility; it energizes the spirit.

Try to put everything into the proper perspective. The audience recognizes that this is an impromptu situation. Nobody expects a polished production. Audience expectations are not the same as they would be in the situation where the speaker has had time to prepare. If you are asked to speak impromptu, remember that others *want* your firsthand observations or reactions. It is a compliment to your ability. Display of speaking skill is not as important here as an honest, immediate observation.

TRY THIS 3

Practice giving impromptu speeches informally as you converse with other people. Try to keep a two–minute time limit, athough, since the situation if informal, this time limit is also flexible. As you listen to others speak, try to find a key idea to which you can react. Think in advance about your goal. Is your overall point of view on the matter to inform others, or will your point of view be to persuade them? Begin your "speech" by making an opening statement that sets the tone for the message to follow. Once this is accomplished, use appropriate supporting materials for amplification. Think about the possibility of using explanations, illustrations, comparisons, and even hypothetical examples. Let your personal experiences and examples help to add fluency to your delivery. Close your mini-speech with a restatement of your opening position: "Thus, you can see why I feel. . . ," or "That is why it is important for us to. . . ." Remember in each case, as you practice, to use the guideline: Keep It Simple and Straightforward (the *K.I.S.S.* formula!)

EXTEMPORANEOUS DELIVERY

The ideal style of delivery is the one that allows the speaker to prepare and practice thoroughly, but allows the exact wording of the speech to be determined at the moment of utterance. It is the extemporaneous style. This style is discussed last because it includes a little of each of the others. But a speaker who gives an extemporaneous speech once and then repeats the speech the same way from then on falls into the same traps as if he or she had memorized it. The advantages of extemporaneous speaking are strong:

1. A speaker can prepare thoroughly, then look free and natural in performance.
2. A speaker can adapt to the situation or to the audience readily and spontaneously.[2]
3. A speaker is free to move in front of the audience as needed. All that would constrain him or her would be the note cards.

You will have the best opportunity to take advantage of this style if you prepare an outline at least a day in advance of a short speech (up to five minutes in length), or two to three days in advance of a longer speech. You may also want to convert the key parts of the outline to note cards. Read through your outline several times to become familiar with the structure and flow of ideas. Check the time when you begin to speak. Using your notes as necessary—so that you do not miss *key* ideas—give the speech. Do not stop. Complete it. Check the time again when you finish to see how long the speech took. Now go back and look at your outline and analyze your effort: Were *key* ideas omitted? Were some ideas discussed for too long or too short a time? Did all the ideas receive proper and appropriate clarification and support? Did you "feel" the presence of your future audience?

Although it is seldom that a speaker must give a speech using *no* notes or outline, it is wise to begin working toward a goal of *not* using them. Especially with beginning speakers, the tendency is to use them like a manuscript—as a crutch. We put too many ideas onto a note card, then we use it too much. Notes should by key ideas or key words and phrases designed to trigger your memory. The fewer the better. They should also be written large enough to be seen from a distance. Short speeches should require but a single 3 by 5 note card whereas a ten-minute speech might require two or three. In addition to a key word or phrase, you might wish to write out a brief quotation or an important statistic. Brevity is important. Write on one side of the cards only; you should never have to turn a card over for more information. This is distracting to the audience. (See Figure 11–1.)

As you continue practicing, use your notes just as you will in the final speech itself. Refer to them *only* when necessary. Be sure to say the speech differently each time, using the ideas to trigger the words. Then, when delivering the speech, you will have many different options for phrasing the ideas; you will not be frozen into a single word order or word choice, as often occurs in memorization. The purpose or goal here is to give yourself a variety of options.

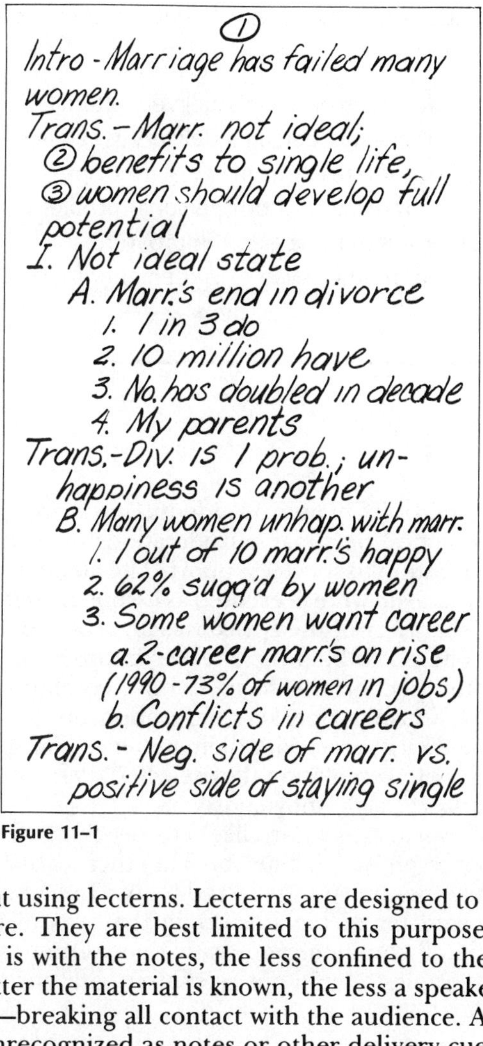
①
Intro - Marriage has failed many women.
Trans.-Marr. not ideal;
② benefits to single life,
③ women should develop full potential
I. Not ideal state
A. Marr.'s end in divorce
1. 1 in 3 do
2. 10 million have
3. No. has doubled in decade
4. My parents
Trans.-Div. is 1 prob.; unhappiness is another
B. Many women unhap. with marr.
1. 1 out of 10 marr.'s happy
2. 62% sugg'd by women
3. Some women want career
a. 2-career marr.'s on rise (1990-73% of women in jobs)
b. Conflicts in careers
Trans.- Neg. side of marr. vs. positive side of staying single

Figure 11–1

A note about using lecterns. Lecterns are designed to hold the speaker's notes—nothing more. They are best limited to this purpose alone. The more familiar the speaker is with the notes, the less confined to the lectern he or she will be. Also, the better the material is known, the less a speaker will have to look down at the lectern—breaking all contact with the audience. A lectern should be just as subtle and unrecognized as notes or other delivery cues. It is a prop—an aid for the speaker. It can easily become a distraction—a barrier between speaker and audience.

TRY THIS 4

Do a short informal study of styles of presentation. Using your teachers as subjects for this experiment (as well as ministers or priests or rabbis, television personalities, visitors to your campus, and politicians), try to find three people who use different delivery styles (memorized, manuscript, impromptu, or extemporaneous).

For each of the three examples of styles (three people—three styles), answer the following questions:

1. What are this person's delivery strengths?
2. What are this person's delivery weaknesses?
   a. Do they result from the style of presentation used?
   b. Do they result from personal problems the speaker has?
3. How might this person improve his or her delivery style?
4. Given another style of presentation, would this person have been more effective?

BUILDING CREDIBILITY

Toward the end of Chapter 5, "Identifying Appropriate Material: Speech Support," a section on personal considerations offered ideas on speaker credibility and its contribution to speech support. The elements of competence, trustworthiness, and dynamism were presented as essential elements of credibility. The focus was on the character of the speaker as an aspect of speech support, and suggestions were offered to help the speaker improve his or her image.

In this section the focus is on credibility as it arises from a speaker–audience relationship. Speakers have opportunities to improve their ethos as a result of *how* they interact with their audience. Part of this, certainly, would result from the style of presentation they selected. Part would result, too, from *how* they handled whatever style they chose.

As a speaker, you are likely to get the audience to understand, believe, or act *if* they accept *you* as a person.[3] In other words, audience acceptance of your ideas often hinges on your own credibility.[4] In persuasion literature, this is called *ethos:* the character of the speaker in the eyes of the audience.[5] Credibility is important in all communication situations. Often, we sell our ideas only to the extent we are able to build our credibility with our audience. Ideas do not stand alone.

CONSIDER THIS

The word "halo" is associated with saints by most people. But not by psychologists. Psychologists are well aware that what we call the halo effect has nothing to do with goodness or godliness, but with first impressions. And unfortuantely, first impressions are not always good impressions.

The halo effect can be negative or positive. Whichever it is, it radiates out in all directions from the initial effect or impression. At its best, it helps make people think we are even better than we are.

You can use the halo effect to help you succeed in business or almost anything you set your mind to. It is a key factor in the make–or–break moments of your life—in first encounters; in job interviews, business lunches, and sales presentations; the first time the boss invites you home to dinner. All are crucial moments when the halo effect can determine success or failure.

There are many techniques for building credibility. Some will work in one situation and not in another. These techniques vary, just as your ability to use them is likely to vary, from one situation to another. But some techniques can be listed. They all must be used in an honest, forthright, and sincere manner.

The first way to build credibility as a speaker–audience function, is to help your audience members feel important. Make them feel they are an important part of your message or the potential results of your message. Include them in your presentation by using pronouns such as *we, us,* and *our.* "This is our problem, and with determination we can solve it together."

Treating your audience courteously is another way to build credibility. It helps them know what you think of them. Be on time. Keep your speech within the appropriate time limits and, generally, be brief and to the point. Dress appropriately. Express gratitude for courtesies that have been extended to you.

Remind yourself that your audience members are important. If you truly believe this, your attitude will get across. Treat them as special; reveal acceptance, approval, and appreciation. Neither try to dominate them nor to jam your ideas down their throats. Consider them as equals—people who will rationally weigh your ideas and come to decisions regarding them.

Also, notice audience members individually. Pay attention to them. Put them in the spotlight by looking at them (individually) eye–to–eye when you speak.

Talk with your audience. Do not try to control, manipulate, or dominate them. Share your ideas with them. Try to maintain an attitude of sharing ideas. Too many speakers talk *at* their audience. The audience must feel they are a part. Extended conversation makes them feel included; formal delivery styles often alienate them. This helps you build credibility as a result of staying on their level and not dominating them.

Be enthusiastic. Enthusiasm is catching—just as its opposite—indifference—is! Sell yourself on your ideas and on your message first. Allow your leftover, extra energy to be used in movement, gestures, and other constructive, positive activity. Activity indicates enthusiasm—as long as it does not distract. Audiences like enthusiasm and are more likely to credit you with positive credibility if you can show it.

Act confidently. If you reveal confidence, your audience will respond to you as if you possess confidence, and their response will help you believe that you have confidence. Make your movements strong and decisive. Command the situation by acting as if you know what you are doing, know what you want, and know how you are going to get what you want. Well–defined, controlled movement is important. It works as a self–fulfilling prophecy: confidence breeds confidence.

247

- We like people who know what they want and act as if they expect to get it.
- We like people who hold up their head, look others in the eye, and move as if they have somewhere to go and mean to get there and act as if they have something to say and mean to say it.
- We like people who believe in themselves and act as if they believe in themselves.[6]

Let your voice reveal strength. Do not allow your tone of voice to indicate hopelessness or lack of courage. It should reflect a tone of boldness and self-assurance—expressive control. Do not mutter or babble. Also, eliminate such mannerisms as "uh" or "you know" and other vocalized pauses.

CONSIDER THIS

Boredom has always been the eighth deadly sin, a malady none of us wants to come down with. But, sometimes, just trying too hard not to be a bore can make you the worst one of all. What's a bore to do?

The following tips should prevent you from becoming a bore:

- Don't slouch or hang your head. This kind of bad body language conveys the idea that you have nothing interesting to say.
- Don't bite your lips, twist your fingers, or toss your hair out of your face. These are nervous mannerisms which distract from your appearance and annoy others.
- Don't apologize for an opinion. If you constantly say, "Well, maybe I'm wrong, but I think . . ." you dilute the effectiveness of what you are going to say.
- Make eye contact with the person to whom you are talking. Look at the person, hold the gaze until there is some response.
- Do not smile, joke, or laugh just out of nervousness. This habit is self-defeating and seems like an apology for existing.
- Do not qualify every statement with "just" and "really," i.e., "I'm really not in the mood . . ." Women have been conned into believing that unqualified statements are rude when they are, in fact, reassuring.
- Don't be overly dramatic. If you are too flamboyant, it is a strain on the listener.
- Don't hedge on statements by ending them with ". . . wasn't that right?" or ". . . don't you agree?"
- Don't evade responsibility for your actions by using vague syntax. If you did it, use the pronoun "I."

SOURCE: From Janet Stone and Jane Bachner, *Speaking Up: A Book for Every Woman Who Wants to Speak Effectively* (New York: McGraw-Hill Book Company, 1977).

Since it may be difficult to think about all the factors that go into effective delivery, it might be wise to concentrate on the following five qualities or criteria of communication. Concentrating on these qualities will keep your mind on our content—the message—and not allow us to become sidetracked by aspects of delivery:

1. Effectiveness—striving to achieve the intended purpose.
2. Efficiency—striving to achieve the greatest effectiveness with the least amount of cost. Some speech situations require a high level of investment in cost and energy; others do not. Efficiency means considering the effectiveness–to–cost ratio.
3. Comprehensibility—striving to achieve clarity of information as well as a clear understanding of feelings, meanings, intentions, and consequences.
4. Validity—striving to achieve believability in the message. What creates believability?
   a. A message that conforms to what receivers know and believe
   b. A message congruent with the receiver's conceptual-evaluative system—how he or she evaluates ideas
   c. A speaker the receivers can support or believe in
5. Utility—striving to achieve a message that is useful for both communicator and audience.[7]

"Nothing succeeds like success." The momentum that resulted in any prior success you have had is likely to result in momentum that leads to further success. To apply the processes described previously to get success requires motion. The motion comes from *you.* It may even come from what you *do* with your successes. These successes may well be small events as well as major triumphs. It may mean applying just one of the recommended techniques. It may be simply realizing that you hold the key to success in your head. You do because it all starts right there.

Everyone has had some successes in his or her life. We must begin to capitalize on those successes. Bring them to the forefront of your mind when worry or fear sets in. Operate from one success to another. Capture the urge, the need to move forward, that you get from capitalizing on successes. Get excited. Let that excitement fill your being. Feel it. Experience it. Feed on it. As you allow success—or your memory of success—to seep into the fibers of your being, it will create the momentum to find further successes to feed on.

TRY THIS 5

What successes have you had that you can remember? Anything. Stop and file through your memory bank until you can come up with *five* successes. They do not have to relate to anything we have been discussing. Think of the good feelings associated with these experiences. Write down a key word or phrase that will help you to remember each of the experiences quickly.

Use these successes and the feelings associated with them as a beginning point. Feed on them. Success feels good. Public speaking assignments offer more opportunities to achieve success. As you experience each new success, allow it to motivate new action.

MEMORY

Strong, effective delivery requires a good memory. But there are two applications of the word *memory* to delivery: (1) our ability to remember our ideas, and (2) our ability to draw from our storehouse of knowledge for additional resources and supporting materials. We must depend on our memory for delivery effectiveness. But our concern over a loss of memory can result in worry and fear. What happens when we "draw a blank"?

We are less likely to draw a blank, as mentioned previously, if we avoid word–by–word memorization. But it still can happen. The major problem is not losing our place; the problem is allowing such a slip to become more of a problem than it deserves to be. "How embarrassing," we think, and yet drawing a blank happens. It is a very common human process. We are not perfect nor do we have perfect memories. People do not, cannot, and should not expect to be perfect; therefore, the problem is just not that important. Being able to put the situation into proper perspective can help reduce any anxiety associated with a memory lapse. If it happens, it should be handled directly and without embarrassment.

The best way to handle the problem of drawing a blank is to pause briefly and try to catch the lost word or phrase. Since the loss of memory is obvious to the audience (but so what?), it is better just to pause. If the pause becomes excessive, then simple, direct honesty with the audience is the best advice. There really is no comfortable, easy method for regaining composure; the best advice is to avoid a style of presentation that relies on the memory of exact wording.

Unless word–by–word memorization is required, it is better to strive for memorization of major ideas and allow the exact words to be dictated by those ideas at the time of delivery. The following procedures can help you learn your major ideas:

1. Narrow the focus of the message to a few key, or essential, ideas.
2. Identify and concentrate on the natural and logical relationships between these key ideas.
3. Transcribe these major ideas on a single index card, and practice delivering your speech with this single card.

The second application of the word *memory* is far more important because it is the memory most speakers depend on: the storehouse of ideas. As mentioned in previous chapters, there is no substitute in public communication for vast experience. The more experience people have, the more examples and illustrations they will have available to use. Their repertoire is larger. The purpose behind using memory as a storehouse of ideas is to have the flexibility to adapt to changing factors in the speech situation. If speakers feel they need to provide more depth, or if their attitude toward the topic shifts in any way, this additional reserve of information will help them adapt. If speakers' feedback tells them the audience does not understand, another example may be deemed necessary. If it tells them the audience is bored, they may need to add more interesting or more intense information. Speakers may also feel the message requires greater clarification through the presentation of a more specific or sharpened example. Also, the situation might change. If something unexpected occurs, speakers with a repertoire of unused ideas will have more confidence and security in dealing with the new situation. The reserve base increases the depth of the foundation on which speakers stand.

The best way to build a storehouse of ideas beyond what you plan to present involves several processes:

1. Early preparation. The earlier preparation is completed, the more time speakers will have to find additional supporting ideas and experiences. That unified whole—the speech—will cause other events and observations to fall into place. Once our mind is oriented in a specific direction, selective perception follows as we sift through our life experiences for further related material.

2. Thorough reading and analysis. We must go beyond minimal expectations. We should not mistake floors for ceilings. When assignments are made, minimal expectations (floors) are often taken as restrictions (ceilings). To extend our efforts beyond the minimums adds both depth and breadth.

3. Observation. Once the speech is prepared, do not consider it set in cement. Go to other places or sources where you will be likely to find relevant information. Explore. Discover. Ask questions. Push your horizons. Be aware of everything in all that you do—even when you are not working on a specific speech!

TRY THIS 6

Make a personal commitment right now to expand your own personal horizons on your next speech assignment. Start building your storehouse of information on the topic now. Check the following items that you can do *right now:*

_____ Read more.

_____ Take nothing for granted.

_____ Do more; experience more.

_____ Ask more questions.

_____ See more; look for hidden meanings.

_____ Make more friends; expand your circle of friends.

_____ Write down new ideas.

_____ Immerse yourself in a variety of new activities.

_____ Become committed to something.
_____ Take on new hobbies.
_____ Push your imagination.

There is little doubt that your next speech will benefit because of this commitment. So would all your speech efforts if such a commitment continued.

SUMMARY

The discussion of delivery was covered in two chapters because of length, not because of subject matter. The reader should remember that the material in these chapters is logically connected and should be considered together as a whole. Material on anxiety, from the last chapter, obviously relates to various styles of presentation just as solid preparation and practice, also a topic covered in the last chapter, can make a difference in effectiveness no matter which style is selected, and it can make a difference in how successfully speakers are able to build a close relationship with an audience.

In the first section of this chapter, "Styles of Presentation," the memorized, manuscript, impromptu, and extemporaneous styles were mentioned. Under the preferred style—extemporaneous delivery—further *specific* ideas that will aid in effective delivery were offered.

The eight ideas that will help speakers build credibility with their audience include: (1) helping audience members feel important, (2) treating audiences with courtesy, (3) remembering that audience members are important, (4) noticing audience members individually, (5) talking *with* audiences, (6) being enthusiastic, (7) showing confidence, and (8) letting the voice reveal strength. These are likely to result if a speaker can concentrate on the five qualities or criteria of communication: (1) effectiveness, (2) efficiency, (3) comprehensibility, (4) validity, and (5) utility. Success in any one of these can provide enough energy and drive to move you toward another success.

Finally, the two types of memory were discussed: the rote memorization of ideas and memory as a storehouse of ideas, examples, and illustrations on which to draw in unanticipated situations. A full storehouse gives a speaker flexibility and adaptability at the time of the actual presentation. The need to focus on ideas, and not words, was discussed. Also discussed were the best ways to build a storehouse of ideas: (1) early preparation, (2) thorough reading and analysis, and (3) observation.

Delivery is essential. Words must be moved from speakers to listeners and delivery is the vehicle. But delivery is not the most essential aspect of a communication situation. If a message does not deserve communication, delivery should not be used to convey it. A speaker must first have an essential message.

Although delivery is a key element in any kind of communication situation, it can be especially important in informative speaking. When seeking understanding, one aspect of the communication situation that can bring the message alive is delivery. We should neither underestimate its importance nor overly exaggerate our emphasis on it. Balance is necessary in both preparing and presenting the message.

NOTES

[1]See Harry Lorayne and Jerry Lucas, *The Memory Book* (New York: Ballantine Books, 1974), Chapter 2, "In the First Place: Association," pp. 5–13, and Chapter 3, "The Link," pp. 14–19. Also see Kenneth L. Higbee, *Your Memory: How It Works and How to Improve It* (Englewood Cliffs, N.J.: Prentice-Hall, 1977), Chapter 3, "Principles of Memory Improvement," pp. 37–54, and Chapters 5–10 on Mnemonics, pp. 71–169.

[2]Both audience comprehension and satisfaction are enhanced when speakers attend to audience feedback. See H. J. Leavitt and R. A. H. Mueller, "Some Effects of Feedback on Communication," *Human Relations,* 4 (1951): 401–410.

[3]See Catha Maslow, Kathryn Yoselson, and Harvey London, "Persuasiveness of Confidence Expressed via Language and Body Language," *British Journal of Social and Clinical Psychology,* 10 (September 1971): 234–240.

[4]Don A. Schweitzer, "The Effect of Presentation on Source Evaluation," *Quarterly Journal of Speech,* 56 (February 1970): 33–39.

[5]For one of the best synthesizing studies on ethos see Kenneth Andersen and Theodore Clevenger, Jr., "A Summary of Experimental Research in Ethos," *Speech Monographs,* 30 (June 1963): 59–78. Also see James C. McCroskey and Thomas J. Young, "Ethos and Credibility: The Construct and Its Measurement After Three Decades," *Central States Speech Journal,* 32 (Spring 1981): 24–34.

[6]Although good delivery may not be solely responsible for enhancing a speaker's effectiveness, unfavorable aspects can affect audience comprehension, source credibility, or the persuasive impact. See Kenneth C. Beighley, "An Experimental Study of the Effect of Four Speech Variables on Listener Comprehension," *Speech Monographs,* 19 (November 1952): 249–258; Gerald R. Miller and Murray A. Hewgill, "The Effect of Variations in Nonfluency on Audience Ratings of Source Credibility," *Quarterly Journal of Speech,* 50 (February 1964): 36–44; Kenneth K. Sereno and Gary J. Hawkins, "The Effects of Variations in Speakers' Nonfluency Upon Audience Ratings of Attitude Toward the Speech Topic and Speakers' Credibility," *Speech Monographs,* 34 (March 1967): 58–64; and James C. McCroskey and R. Samuel Mehrley, "The Effects of Disorganization and Nonfluency on Attitude Change and Source Credibility," *Speech Monographs,* 36 (March 1969): 13–21.

[7]Stephen W. Littlejohn, *Theories of Human Communication* (Columbus, Ohio: C. E. Merrill, 1978), pp. 51–52.

twelve

SEEKING UNDERSTANDING

Informative Speeches

All communication has both an informative and a persuasive dimension, and one cannot communicate without using both.[1] The distinction between speeches to inform and speeches to persuade rests on the speaker's purpose. In an informative speech the purpose is generally to increase or secure understanding, whereas in a persuasive speech the purpose is to secure a change of commitment in either belief or action. We do not deny that an informative speech may change beliefs or that a persuasive speech may enhance understanding. Information certainly helps to shape attitudes and influence conduct.

Despite the overlapping dimensions, there are times when the speaker's primary goal or purpose is to explain an idea, concept, or thing clearly. As you, whether a student, a member of a business organization, or an informed citizen, become more knowledgeable in an area of specialization or gain a position of increased responsibility, you will be called upon to convey to others some of the information you have acquired. As a person going to college or as one with a college degree, you will be considered more informed than others with no college background and thus looked to for advice and comment. As a student you will be giving reports and discussing relevant topics; as a person in business you will have to convey complex data to others; as an artist or musician, you may have to explain innovative patterns, trends, or methodologies; as an educator, you will be called on to explain and clarify ideas as well as to motivate others to learn. Such procedures will require an ability to provide information and to increase the understanding of audience members on significant issues.

CONSIDER THIS

We like to hear what makes us feel comfortable and self-assured. Yet this is exactly what we have no need of hearing; only those who disturb us can improve us. We become strong by chewing and digesting verbal roughage; the chocolate creams of compliments merely make us fat and lazy.

Source: From *STRICTLY PERSONAL* by Sydney J. Harris. © 1979 Field Enterprises, Inc. Courtesy of Field Newspaper Syndicate.

This chapter is designed to provide greater insight into the process of informative speaking. Four aspects of informative discourse will be considered: (1) various kinds of informative speeches, and (2) ways speakers have to increase the understanding or learning of their audiences. One of these ways, because of its importance, will be singled out and discussed in the section (3) on visual aids. Finally, an important part of speech situations, that of (4) answering questions, will be discussed. Bear in mind throughout the chapter that as speakers our goals are to get listeners to become more receptive to our information, to help them understand it and retain it.

INFORMATIVE SPEECHES

Several different kinds of informative speeches may not always clearly separate; they often can overlap. The three kinds we will discuss are (1) explanations and directions, (2) reports and lectures, and (3) descriptions.

Explanations and Directions

Much of our communication includes explanation and directions. We see explanation and directions used by teachers, preachers, doctors, lawyers, businesspeople, and salespeople—all professions and vocations depend on this form of communication, because it is often necessary to tell others how to do something, how to make something, and how something works. Informally, we use explanation and directions to give others instructions: (1) what assignments were given in a class, (2) how to figure out a math problem, or (3) how to use a calculator. In sharing ideas with others we explain past experiences, we explain how we perceive things occurring now, and often we explain how we perceive the future.

If your desire is to explain a concept, idea, or process, your goal is to get the audience to understand that concept, idea, or process. If the audience can remember the concept, idea, or process, and even apply it on their own, you have achieved success. The more complicated the concept, idea, or process, the more care you must take in the explanation.

Informative speeches that involve explanation or giving directions are often thought of as the easiest kind of speech to give. However, because many speakers think such speeches are easy, they do not give them the necessary time or thought. To give an informative speech the speaker must first select a topic that is narrowed and focused and that is not common knowledge. People are knowledgeable about many things: sports, hobbies, games, and recreational activities. The opportunities are endless, the pursuits are many. If they have not engaged in the particular activity, they have undoubtedly read or heard about it. The speaker must find out the audience's knowledge base and then attempt to expand those frontiers by narrowing the topic, focusing on a specific area, and being precise and accurate.

Merely having competed in a sport, pursued a hobby, played a game, or engaged in a recreational activity does not give a speaker solid knowledge and experience—or not enough to share with others in a meaningful manner. What these speakers *can* share is a level of common knowledge that is neither exceptional nor unique. Greater depth and breadth is needed for an uncommon speech, as is careful planning.

TRY THIS 1

Brainstorm to discover areas where you have the sufficient breadth and depth to share with others. What are some topics on which you have already done extensive reading? What hobbies have you pursued over many years? Which sports activities do you know very well? What projects have you engaged in? What organizations have you been a part of? What games do you enjoy? In what occupations do you have enough expertise to share what you know with others? Write down as many as possible. Here are some areas to consider:

travels	organizations
hobbies	sports activities
projects	occupations and jobs
games	experiences

After speakers have gained added necessary depth—more than can be provided by mere exposure—they must organize their ideas in an effective manner. Again, speakers cannot simply assume that the steps in explaining the process or activity are natural and will follow once they begin to speak. Determining the best sequence for an explanation takes planning and forethought. The fewer the main points, for example, the more likely audience members will remember the points. But how can speakers follow this advice when the process they are explaining requires numerous steps? The key is grouping, as shown in the following example from a speech on ways to improve one's memory.

Set I, Steps	Set II, Organized

<table>
<tr><td>

1. Concentrate
2. Observe closely
3. Use all your senses
4. Get eye impressions
5. Repeat ideas at intervals
6. Repeat ideas a few minutes before they will be needed
7. Associate ideas with other facts

8. Place all the facts into relation with each other
9. Think over new facts from all angles
10. Ask questions about them
11. Get a logical order
</td><td>

I. Get a deep, lasting *impression.*
  A. Concentrate
  B. Observe closely
  C. Use all your senses
  D. Get eye impressions
II. *Repeat* the ideas
  A. Do this at intervals
  B. Do it just before it is needed
III. *Associate* the ideas
  A. Use them with facts you already know
  B. Place them into relation with other facts you know
  C. Think them over from all new angles
  D. Ask questions about them
  E. Try to gain a logical order or sequence of ideas
</td></tr>
</table>

The point of the above sets of information is simply that audiences would be more likely to remember Set II, "Organized," because this set has three major elements rather than eleven: impression, repetition, and association. Often, the discovery of such a supersystem of organization requires only a little additional thought. It can be reinforced or emphasized if the speaker also uses a visual aid (see the section on visual aids that follows). Speakers should try to limit their information so that they do not overwhelm the audience or cause information overload.

Finally, explanations often work better if the audience is involved. There are three levels of participation and each has advantages.

Level 1. Total participation, in which all members of the audience have materials or do the process. This results in excellent participation but requires strong control and the ability to regain the attention of the audience.

Level 2. Surrogate participation, in which a sample audience member(s) participates and the audience does so vicariously. This is a lower level of participation, but this level allows good control by the speaker.

Level 3. Visualization as participation, when the speaker alone supplies examples or does the process for all to see and understand. This is the level of participation and is the most difficult in terms of wording and delivery, but this level allows the greatest control by the speaker.

Audience participation of some kind will increase both interest and recall. It is a strong method of explaining, and it reinforces directions.

TRY THIS 2

Think of all the things you could *explain* to a class right now, if you were given an opportunity:

- How a machine (sewing machine, car engine) runs
- How a record or recording star is promoted
- How to can fruits and vegetables
- How to buy a car
- How to put make-up on or give a permanent
- How to play a game or sport
- How to prevent boredom
- How to select a book, movie, or greeting card

List some of your own possibilites. Place an asterisk by those you would feel most comfortable explaining. How much research would be necessary to feel completely comfortable with the topic?

Reports and Lectures

Few students will get through a college career without experiencing the lecture technique. It is the most widely used teaching method, the most strongly criticized one, and perhaps the most abused. The lecture technique is often the same technique the student uses when asked to report on a reading or assignment, the official uses to report the results of a fund-raising campaign, or the elected politician uses to explain the cost or potential benefit of a recent bill. In this section the lecturer is discussed, but please remember that ideas, comments, and suggestions apply to both lecturer and reporter.

The problem with reports and lectures is that because of many years of weak, ineffective models, we have come to believe that a lecture—by definition —must be:

1. Boring and uninteresting
2. Passive and uninvolving
3. Poorly organized and presented
4. Irrelevant, not current or accessible elsewhere
5. Aimed toward the masses and not toward the individual

PEANUTS by Charles W. Schulz. © 1979 United Features Syndicate, Inc.

And we do little to counter this impression. It is, once again, an example of the self-fulfilling prophecy at work. We believe it *is* so, thus, we do little in our preparation, in our attitude, or in our presentation, to change the impression. And—would you believe it?—the lecture or report is both ineffective and ineffectual. How could it turn out otherwise?

We must begin by checking our attitude. Does it need to be changed? There is no reason why a lecture cannot illustrate the application of facts and principles to practical situations or why factual data cannot be organized into new relationships that make learning more meaningful. Lectures and reports can be exciting, stimulating, challenging, involving, and rewarding, but this is not likely to occur if the speaker does not accept these possibilities:

1. Lectures and reports can produce desirable affective learnings (learnings that relate to the feelings and emotions).
2. Lecturers can communicate enthusiasm.
3. Lecturers do not need to rely solely on a textbook or syllabus.
4. Lecturers can challenge audience members to examine their own personal lives.
5. Lectures can be current and relevant to audience needs.
6. Lecturers can gear the length, complexity, and vocabulary of the lecture to the audience maturity level.
7. Lectures can include visual aids.
8. Lecturers can prepare well and present the message effectively.

The point is that there do not need to be significant and important differences between lectures and reports, and speeches. Poor preparation for a speech results in a weak presentation just as poor preparation for a lecture results in a weak effort—and for essentially the same causes: defective organization, lack of variety, poor voice control, and lack of enthusiasm. These are speaker or lecturer deficiencies. Just as training is necessary for effective speaking to occur, effective lecturing or reporting requires training; it is not a natural nor an easy skill. But little time is devoted to the organization, delivery, or evaluation of a lecture. Lecturing is most appropriate when a lecturer with special information wants to share a complex intellectual analysis, to synthesize or draw together ideas, to compare and contrast new concepts, principles, or ideas with those already known, or to unfold recent results, findings, or processes.

One key area of lecturing that can be improved is the degree of interaction that traditionally occurs between the lecturer and the audience. Lecturers and reporters can encourage listener participation. They can provide listeners with opportunities to interact with the material to be presented by doing the following:

1. Encourage greater informality. There is no reason that a lecturer or reporter must stay behind a lectern. Walking among the audience and establishing eye contact with the listeners will help. The greater informality that results from moving closer to or among the audience will provide valuable information for the lecturer. He or she can more easily gauge whether the listeners are following the logic of the speech and understanding the material, and whether they want to ask questions.

2. Incorporate questions or probes into the material. These tie the audience to the material with directness. Questions or probes that can be included are:
   a. "What meanings or applications can you see in your own life for this?"
   b. "Suppose you met a person who had never heard of this, how would you explain it?"
   c. "Take a second or two and think of all the ideas I have just mentioned that mean something to you."

3. Utilize the rhetorical question. Although similar to item 2, the rhetorical question requires no overt, outward response. It can be phrased in many different ways; here are some suggestions:
   a. "How many times have you . . .?"
   b. "Do you ever remember seeing . . .?"
   c. "When was the last time you . . .?"
   d. "Haven't you ever felt . . .?"
   e. "Now, what do you think about that?"
   f. "What would *you* do in similar circumstances?"
   When audience members have a chance to verbalize, even if only to themselves, it enhances their attentiveness and involvement. One researcher found that asking questions rather than presenting statements of fact not only improves learning, but also increases audience interest in learning about the topic.[2]

4. Provide further support and reinforcement. Outlines, fill-in-the-blank or short-answer questions, or other material related to the lecture that can be handed out can be used to increase involvement. Some such material can be presented with an overhead projector and transparencies; some can be provided on slides.

Lecturing is an unnatural act. The extended monologue—as a lecture has sometimes been called—requires extended attention to both audience and topic.

But the technique can be learned. Perhaps good lecturers are not as rare as good lecture listeners; both are necessary for a lecture to be effective.

TRY THIS 3

If you had to give a brief (fifteen minute) lecture on a topic, could you do it? How would you plan? What supporting materials would you prepare? Plan to give a ten- to fifteen-minute lecture on one aspect of public communication. You may choose any one of the following topics as your focus, but you need not limit yourself to these:

Effective listening
Adapting to a specific audience
Best places to get information for a speech
How to use the library
Organizing material for a speech
Selecting the most effective language
Nonverbal communication (kinesics, proxemics, chronemics . . .)
Alleviating anxiety associated with speechmaking
Techniques of delivery
Assertiveness in the speech situation

Descriptions

A descriptive speech is designed to provide a clear and vivid impression through accurate and informative material. Description is important in any speech because it is the material that makes an impression remembered by listeners. The descriptive speech focuses on a specific and concrete object, structure, place, or being. The point of the descriptive speech is to provide the audience with new information. For example, a speaker could focus on cholesterol as an object, the structure of DNA, the campus pond as a place, or another person or animal as a being.

To provide an accurate, vivid picture of what you are describing, you must offer listeners a way of mentally seeing your subject. Listeners need to be able to "see" the size, shape, and weight of the thing as well as its color and composition. The age, condition, and location can also be provided. The more specific the information, the more likely it is to leave a lasting impression. The ultimate test of descriptive information is that it should enable listeners to visualize. As a speaker, you should err on the side of too much information rather than not enough.

When giving a descriptive speech, the speaker must depend on a clear organizational scheme. Things must be clearly laid out, in a definite order, if the audience is to understand. Referring back to Chapter 7, "Organizing the Material," you can see that the spatial or topical orders are especially relevant. In the spatial order, you describe the object, structure, place, or being by moving sequentially from one part of it to another: left to right, top to bottom, outside to center. Using a topical order, the speaker could describe by using equal subdivisions of the subject. For example, a speaker could describe the manufacturing process of a product by covering the major steps: (1) raw material, (2) breakdown and development of raw material, (3) use of additives, and (4) packaging. These organization patterns help determine the arrangement of the various points of the speech.

Finally, a descriptive speech relies on the speaker's language for its effect. Words are used to create the vivid impression. The essential components of language discussed in Chapter 8, "Choosing the Language," in the section, "Language Choices"—clarity, simplicity, accuracy, appropriateness, and dynamism—are applicable and appropriate here. Words are your primary means of getting your audience to visualize your subject.

Several cautions are in order. Although effective language is essential, the speaker's language must not become poetic—so picturesque or florid that it becomes distracting. Your emphasis should not be on the beauty of the language, but on the informative purpose of the message. Language, like delivery, must serve as a vehicle, not as an object to be viewed or admired for its own sake. You must strive to gain clarity, simplicity, accuracy, appropriateness, and dynamism without sacrificing honest, sincere naturalness. If your language appears affected or artificial, the audience is likely to question or doubt your message—the very information you wish to share.

Honest, sincere naturalness results from language that occurs when you think of the idea. Again, you must rely on the storehouse of your memory. Remember, there are unlimited ways to say something. Do not limit yourself to just one. Strive to use different wordings to express yourself. Then, when in front of your audience, exhibit flexibility and spontaneity.

TRY THIS 4

Try to be descriptive as you talk with your friends or with your roommate. Your ability at description is likely to improve with such informal practice. Next time you are talking with anyone try to describe, with vividness, specificity, and accuracy, one of the following things that have occurred recently in your life. (If one of these situations has not happened to you, add your own example.)

An impressive movie you have seen recently
An accident you witnessed
A person who impressed you
A book you have read that excited you
A speech you heard recently that challenged you
An enjoyable dance or party you attended

A vivid and stirring trip you took
An event or occurrence that you have read about
An opportunity you had to be assertive, dramatic, or impressive
A recently completed assignment or project of which you are proud
Some impressive aspect of nature (a sunrise, clouds, trees) that you witnessed

While you are describing this thing or event, try to get your listener to see it in his or her mind's eye. Try to make it as impressive or moving as it was for you.

WAYS TO INCREASE UNDERSTANDING

Basically, the variety of ways we have available to increase understanding have already been mentioned throughout the preceding pages of this book. The informative speaker will depend on those techniques and will perfect and polish methods to make the informative speech highly rewarding and exciting. But several techniques can be especially important in an *informative* situation. In other words, these techniques contribute strongly to *this* speech purpose because of its unique nature.

The informative speech situation is a *learning* experience. The speaker's purpose is to increase audience learning; thus, the speaker, to be effective, must concentrate on those areas that result in more learning. Learning is most likely to occur when audience members are motivated to respond. This is the beginning point for learning. First, they must know there is something to be gained: "What's in it for me?" Second, they must know that the motivation—the reason for listening—will be fulfilled by the particular information they are going to hear: "How important is this to me?" Third, that information must be reinforced: "Give me the essential information at once," and "Show me once again how this can help me." To help meet the demands of learning that this pattern suggests, the following areas will be discussed: (1) focusing on principles, (2) organizing, (3) motivating, and (4) emphasizing.

Focusing on Principles

A principle is a unifying factor. Once you know the principle, the parts that come under the principle begin to fall into place and make sense. Learning becomes easier. If you understand the principle of the umbrella, then the need for the parts that raise, lower, and support the fabric make sense. If you understand the principle of the game, the various rules and procedures make more sense. However, if one goes through the rules and procedures before explaining the overall principle, the rules and procedures may have to be reviewed or re-explained once the principle is revealed.

In a speech, too, speakers may effect greater learning if they can depend on a few effective, clear, overriding principles rather than a whole bag of bits of information. Speakers who find that they must present a long series of steps, procedures, or details should plan to ditto, mimeograph, photocopy, or reproduce the material and distribute copies to the audience. Just as a long list of statistics or historical dates and anecdotes can be boring, so can *any* long list of data. For example, a speaker who wanted to speak on "Twelve Ways to Study Better," might more effectively develop three basic principles for studying: (1) attitude, (2) organization, and (3) environment.

We do not want to suggest that informative speeches should not contain details, but details should not appear as ends in themselves. Rather than asking an audience to concentrate on or learn details, these details should be used *only* to explain or amplify and enhance the main ideas, generalizations, and principles. If many details are necessary, to hand them out in written form will help the speaker make the main ideas clear.

Organizing

Closely associated with placing an emphasis on principles is the problem of organizing. The purpose of this brief section can be capsulized in one short statement: Effective organization increases learning.[3] It can affect both the comprehension and frustration of audience members. It can also affect your own credibility as speaker. Do not leave organization to chance. It not only makes a difference, but also it can be developed and enhanced by a concerned speaker. The reasons for effective organization are twofold: (1) Audience interpretation and evaluation of a message will be influenced by its organization, and (2) new or useful information will be learned more easily if the message is organized and the organizational pattern is revealed to the audience. Time spent outlining and structuring ideas is likely to make an important difference. Since the informative speech is designed to enhance learning, anything a speaker can do to enhance the structure will be to his or her advantage. To ignore organization is to ignore one of the fundamental precepts of education: Education is more efficient when learning is well organized.

Motivating

Appropriate material for a speech results from an analysis of audience needs. Once speakers know what audience members' wants or needs are, they can motivate them to respond.[4] The same principle applies to learning: People learn best when they are motivated to do so. Thus, the most effective informative speech is one that motivates listeners; it makes the listener *want* to learn.[5]

How can you make listeners want to learn? The key is to give them a reason or reasons for learning the ideas, skills, or information you present. Be specific.

- Tell them *how* it will affect their lives.
- Tell them *what* they can do with the material.
- Give them definite, practical, clear suggestions that they can consider and apply.

Do not assume that audience members will "get it," "understand it," "see it," or "apply it." Rather, tell audience members in no uncertain terms. You, as speaker, make the application. Be direct and specific if your purpose is to motivate them. The clearer the mental image you get them to construct, the more likely they will be able to see themselves as part of that mental image.

Emphasizing

In any speech you make, you will find that some points are more important than others; these points must be emphasized or stressed. The techniques for emphasizing important points were discussed in Chapter 4, "Analyzing the Audience: Idea Adaptation," in the section on "What We Do With the Information" from audience analysis (see page 81).

Emphasis need not be left to chance. It can be planned. The points needing emphasis can be carefully selected, and the type of emphasis can also be determined before the presentation. The only caution necessary is that, as in all things, emphasis can be overused. A speaker who is *always* saying "this is important" or is *always* repeating ideas is almost as bad as a speaker who is always shouting at you. The only reaction can be doubt, skepticism, or outright rejection. One simply is unwilling to accept everything a speaker says as important.

TRY THIS 5

Select a topic for a short informative speech in which you can emphasize the previous ways to increase understanding: focusing on principles, organizing, motivating, and emphasizing. Think of topics that can be narrowed to fit a short time limit. Some examples might be:

Establishing credit at a local bank (or getting a bank loan)

Casting your horoscope (signs and meanings of signs)

Interviewing for a job (factors that lead to success)

Organizing your time (principles of effective time management)

Discovering your strengths (how to engage in self-analysis)

Getting published (the ways one has to get his or her best ideas in print)

Traveling cheap (how to save money and see the world too)

Finding a mate (what to look for; what to avoid)

One can see that any of these topics could be turned into an enjoyable, worthwhile speech that would offer listeners many interesting facts and pointers. If the above topics do not appeal to you, discover one or two that do. As a matter of fact, a topic that might be considered would be:

Finding a topic for an informative speech (how to go about it)

VISUAL AIDS

If we had to include a fifth way to increase understanding, it would be "using visual aids." But this technique is so important that we wish to give it more consideration than a subsection merits. It is, perhaps, the most effective technique for adding clarity to an informative speech.[6] Why? It is a well-known educational principle that people learn better as the number of senses through which they receive data is increased.[7] In most cases, listeners *hear* information. It is the verbal channel—the words—that carries the essential message. They also get a nonverbal message; however, this is generally reinforcement and enhancement of the verbal message—if all goes well. Thus, for us to understand or learn, we must hear what the speaker says. But that verbal message can be directly reinforced through redundance—the provision of a *duplicate* (not just a reinforcing or enhancing) message.

Types

Visual aids help in amplifying—or expanding—the speech because they offer a new dimension. It is also true, as just pointed out, that people tend to learn more when the visual channel and the aural channel are combined. Some possible aids include:

The Object.   To show the object itself has strong, visual impact.

A Model.   Showing how a device or apparatus operates, or its basic design, may be effective. You might use a small model a large object (an engine) or a large model of a small object (bacteria).

Chalkboard.   Most drawings should be completed before the audience arrives, covered, then revealed only when appropriate. Chalk lines must be dark enough for all audience members to see.

Graphs.   To show relative sizes or amounts, graphs are effective. Line graphs can show two or more variable facts. Bar graphs can show the relationship of two sets of figures. Pie graphs can show percentages. Pictorial graphs can show relative amounts by the size or number of symbols represented.

Diagrams.   To show inner workings of objects or external aspects, diagrams are effective. They vary in complexity. Three-dimensional views often provide a great deal of information.

Charts.   To show the parts of an organization or the structure of a business, a chart is helpful.

Overhead projectors.   The advantage of the overhead projector is that a drawing can be drawn in front of an audience or it can be produced beforehand and then shown for all to see. It is convenient and easy to use.

Slides.   To add interest and promote understanding, slides can offer variety. For projecting an outline of the material or illustrations, slides can add color too.

Movies.   Although requiring more equipment than the other aids mentioned, movies provide the additional benefit of action.

Advantages.

"Saying" something in a second, more redundant, way is only one of many advantages. Visual aids also cause movement or change. When using a visual aid

266

the speaker must *do* something besides talk. Again, it is the change that holds audience attention. A visual aid can also help in several other ways:

1. It can clarify something the audience may find difficult to understand: a complex process, for example.
2. It can illustrate something that is impossible to see otherwise: the inside of a nuclear reactor might be an example.
3. It can compare facts, statistics and uses of things: expenditures of two corporations on environmental cleanup could be done this way.
4. It can show trends over a period of time: governmental expenditures on education from 1950 to 1980, for example. (The comparison of trends can also be illustrated.)

Using Visual Aids.

The choice of visual aids must be based on the speaker's own ability and knowledge, the demands of the information (the kind of material that needs amplification); the audience's needs (What will it take for them to understand the material?), and the situation itself (How large is the audience and the room?) This helps determine the kind, size, and use of the visual aid.

Whatever visual aids are chosen some basic principles govern their use. No matter what kind you plan to use, you will need to pay attention to the following cautions:

1. Rehearse with your visuals. Do not use your visuals for the first time at the actual presentation. Try to practice in conditions similar to those in which you will actually use them. Set a chart or graph in the front of the room and check if it can be seen from the back. Gauge how you plan to support or attach the visual aid. Will it work? Is there an electrical outlet close at hand? Chalk for the blackboard? Tape or tacks for a bulletin board? Plan and prepare.

2. Let your audience see your visual aid *only* when you are talking about it. If the audience can see it before you are ready to use it, it will distract. When you show it to the audience, be sure your words are related to it. When you finish talking about it, put it away at once.

3. Make certain the visual aid is large enough for all audience members to see. A snapshot is generally too small, as is anything reproduced on an index card. Check to see that a chart or graph is not too light or its lines not broad enough to be seen from the back of a room.

4. Make certain the visual aid is simple. A complex visual aid can counter the very purpose that one is trying to achieve by using it. It can cause confusion.
   a. Do not put too many details on the visual aid.
   b. Color-code the different parts for easy identification.
   c. Include only the basic elements that are necessary.

5. Talk to the audience and not to the visual aid. First, remember that a visual aid, no matter how effective, does not explain itself. It needs interpretation. Second, it is the audience, not the visual, that needs the interpretation; tell

Population of the United States
Total Number of Persons in Each
Census: 1790-1970
Number in Millions

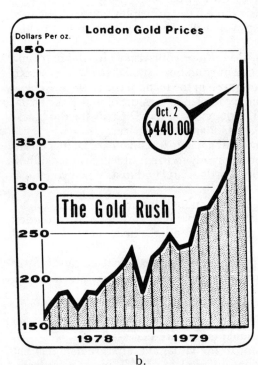

a.

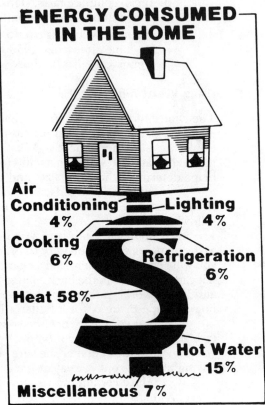

c.

b.

Figure 12–1 Various types of graphs: (a) bar graph (U.S. Government Printing Office: 1979); (b) line graph (Associated Press Wirephoto Chart); (c) pictograph (*The Blade,* Toledo, Ohio); (d) pictograph (U.S. News & World Report); and (e) pie graph (U.S. News & World Report).

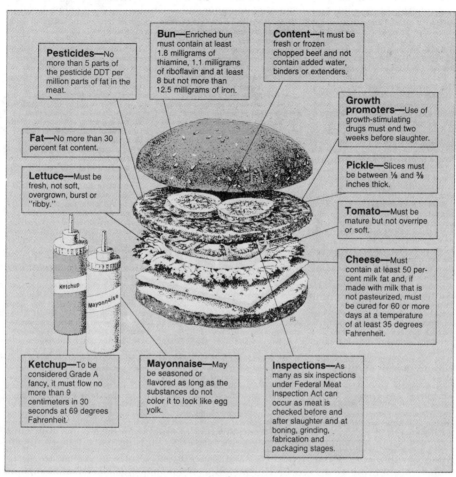

Pesticides—No more than 5 parts of the pesticide DDT per million parts of fat in the meat.

Bun—Enriched bun must contain at least 1.8 milligrams of thiamine, 1.1 milligrams of riboflavin and at least 8 but not more than 12.5 milligrams of iron.

Content—It must be fresh or frozen chopped beef and not contain added water, binders or extenders.

Growth promoters—Use of growth-stimulating drugs must end two weeks before slaughter.

Fat—No more than 30 percent fat content.

Pickle—Slices must be between ⅛ and ⅜ inches thick.

Lettuce—Must be fresh, not soft, overgrown, burst or "ribby."

Tomato—Must be mature but not overripe or soft.

Cheese—Must contain at least 50 percent milk fat and, if made with milk that is not pasteurized, must be cured for 60 or more days at a temperature of at least 35 degrees Fahrenheit.

Ketchup

Mayonnaise

Ketchup—To be considered Grade A fancy, it must flow no more than 9 centimeters in 30 seconds at 69 degrees Fahrenheit.

Mayonnaise—May be seasoned or flavored as long as the substances do not color it to look like egg yolk.

Inspections—As many as six inspections under Federal Meat Inspection Act can occur as meat is checked before and after slaughter and at boning, grinding, fabrication and packaging stages.

d.

Dividing Up the Military Dollar

Out of each dollar spent by the armed services in 1981, as planned in the President's budget—

Weapons purchases 21¢

Troops (pay, benefits) 23¢

Research, development 10¢

Retirement pay 10¢

Operations, maintenance 33¢

Construction 2¢

Other 1¢

USN&WR chart—Basic data: U.S. Office of Management and Budget

e.

FUNKY WINKERBEAN by Tom Batiuk. © 1978 Field Enterprises, Inc. Courtesy of Field Newspaper Syndicate, Inc.

the audience what to look for; how to interpret the lines, figures, symbols, or percentages; and what the various parts mean. Do not talk to the visual aid.

6. Consider the problems with passing visual aids around:

    a. People are distracted from you or your message.

    b. People are prompted to think about or react to the material they hold in their hands.

    c. You will not have control of all members of your audience.

If you plan to pass something around, try to make certain all audience members have the same picture or item. You might, for example, photo-duplicate a chart for each member of the audience instead of making a large one. An added advantage is that audience members will have something to take away with them.

    If a speech is complicated and many details must be communicated, a hand-out, which may be a ditto of the speech's outline, can help the audience follow along. Pamphlets and brochures are also valuable because the listeners have something to reinforce the message later at home.

    7. Use visual aids with discretion. Like everything else, too much of a good thing can have detrimental effects. You must decide when and where to use them. In a speech where numerous visual aids could be used, you must decide which are the most important points or the ideas that need the emphasis. Remember that visual aids are simply another form of emphasizing, and emphasis can be overused. When a speaker emphasizes everything, nothing stands out. Visual aids should never substitute for effective speaking.

    We have dwelt on suggestions for using visual aids effectively because visual aids also have the potential for creating strongly negative effects. A poorly prepared speaker may waste audience time by fumbling and searching. Ineptness may bore, exasperate, or even anger listeners. Care, concern, and thoroughness must be the guiding principles for using visual aids. Because visual aids can enhance a speech and can help a speaker achieve his or her purpose does not necessarily mean they will do so!

Select three topics on which you might be able to deliver a five- to seven-minute informative speech. Below each topic, explain a visual aid you could plan to use to accompany the speech.

Now, go back and rank the topics first, second, and third in order of feasibility. Determine this ranking by asking yourself which topic would be best for you, the audience, and the occasion. Also, determine which speech could be amplified by the strongest possible visual aid.

ANSWERING QUESTIONS

Answering questions is an intrinsic part of informative speaking. For an audience member to ask a question for more information or for clarification is a *realistic* outgrowth or extension of an informative situation. Thus, an informative speaker can expect to be asked questions following the speech. In certain cases, the speaker may encourage questions during the presentation, particularly if the group is small or when an informal atmosphere is being promoted or encouraged.[8] To encourage questions from a large group is asking for trouble—especially if there is no systematic way of handling them. When the group is large, questions can be submitted in written form, but even then the process of screening the questions can be burdensome.

In more formal situations, the speaker may want to cover the topic in the allotted time, and thus will discourage questions, unreasonable or otherwise, or other interruptions. Inexperienced speakers can get shaken in such a situation. If you have no experience in handling questions before a large audience, the best advice is to avoid encouraging them *during* the presentation. Handling them afterwards is less cumbersome. It is often easier to handle questions when the essential, planned message has been completed, when the speaker is freed of one responsibility and can turn his or her full attention to audience questions.

BEETLE BAILEY by Mort Walker. © King Features Syndicate, Inc., 1979.

Four considerations regarding the use or encouragement of questions during a speech should be mentioned here. They determine the proceudre you, as speaker, will use.

1. Audience size
2. Time restrictions
3. Material to be covered
4. Control

That last word, *control,* needs further explanation. Speakers must maintain control in any public communication situation. *Control* does not refer to authoritarian, dogmatic, or dictatorial power. It simply means looking strong and in command of the situation. It refers to the image—the credibility—that results from appearing to know what you are doing, to know what you want, and to know how to get what you want.

A real problem for many speakers seems to be a fear of not being able to answer every question that is asked. Ideally, a speaker would be so well prepared on a topic that he or she could answer any reasonable question. But anyone can be asked an unanswerable question, and few of us know everything there is to be known. The best approach is the direct, honest one. When you do not know an answer, admit it. Some people are prone to make up a pretentious answer to a question so that they will not be thought ignorant. Such a spurious response is often detected. Maintain your credibility with honesty rather than deceit. No human being is expected to know everything!

There are particular techniques for handling a question period following a public communication effort. Again, an informative speech situation, by its nature, encourages the asking of questions. We will assume that the audience is of a reasonable size—no more than fifty people. Providing that questions from the audience can be handled efficiently and effectively, then the following guidelines apply:

1. Know your material and your listeners. The more thoroughly you have researched your topic, the more likely you will feel yourself an expert and be able to discuss or converse about the topic. Remember, you will know more about the topic than most audience members.

2. Anticipate the situation. Is it likely to be a question-asking situation? Will a period be offered for direct audience feedback? To know in advance will help relieve unnecessary anxiety. Also, look at your subject matter. Anticipate those areas where questions are most likely. Ask yourself what questions you might raise.

3. Be honest, forthright, and direct in answering questions. You do not have to know all the answers, but at least listen to the questions and respond courteously to each one. Rather than alienate a listener, it is better to respond even to irrelevant questions. Also, some questions may require clarification; for other questions postponing the answer would be best.

4. Restate questions so that all audience members can hear them. Try not to carry on a dialog with a questioner while the rest of the audience members either strain to hear or begin to talk among themselves. Think of the entire

audience as you restate, clarify, and answer questions for the benefit of all—not just the questioner. Restating the question has the additional advantages of (1) checking to make sure you have understood the question, (2) giving you time to think about an answer, and (3) providing your mental processes with a stimulus in seeking an answer.

5. Maintain a proper attitude. Strive not to become overbearing or argumentative. Questioning may be discouraged if you appear too dogmatic or overbearing. On the other hand, if you appear pompous or dominant, the audience members may decide to give you a bad time. Good questions can be encouraged with the proper attitude.

Speakers, no matter what the context, must be ready for the unexpected. Questions from the audience, although they may be unexpected, tend to occur rather frequently; thus, it is better to be prepared for such occasions. This includes the proper mental set. Remember, the person asking the question, in most cases, has a sincere desire to know or to find out. That person must be treated with dignity, affection, and concern. To alienate or offend a listener may, indeed, alienate and offend the entire audience.

TRY THIS 7

For your next speech, plan to encourage questions from the audience following the speech. Generate participation from the audience by using any one or several of the following techniques:

1. Ask a general question in order to get a reaction.
2. Ask a specific person in the audience a short, clear question that requires more than a yes or no response.
3. Build questions into your speech that will stimulate audience thinking or encourage participation.

Once questions from the audience are asked, try to restate a question and redirect it to the questioner or to another audience member. If it is already clearly stated, simply try your hand at redirecting it.

SUMMARY

Informative speeches are an important part of public communication. Although the essentials for giving a speech—whether informative of persuasive—have been carefully detailed in preceding chapters, this chapter highlights aspects that are especially important to this form of communication.

The chapter began by discussing three different kinds of informative speeches. Informative speeches that involve explanation or giving directions are, perhaps, the easiest to give. Besides suggesting that the speaker should have thorough knowledge of the subject, it was also pointed out that the speaker should limit the main points to be covered. Slowness in the presentation of such a speech helps drive points home. Audience involvement also aids learning.

In the section on reports and lectures, the characteristics of the typical lecture were described. Some possible ways to try to change the preconception about lectures were outlined. Three ways a lecturer or reporter can encourage listener participation were offered. Lack of interaction with the audience is one of the key weaknesses of this type of presentation, but by encouraging greater informality, incorporating questions and probes, and providing further support and reinforcement, a speaker can reduce this problem.

Three major suggestions were made for giving descriptive speeches: First, the speaker must be concrete and specific. Second, the speaker must clearly organize his or her presentation. Third, the speaker must choose language that creates clear mental images—language that is clear, simple, accurate, appropriate, and dynamic.

The informative speech is a *learning* experience, thus, a speaker who chooses to use this form must be concerned about how people learn. People learn best (1) when their attention is focused on principles, (2) when they are presented information that is clearly organized, (3) when they are strongly and effectively motivated, and (4) when the main points are emphasized.

Another way to increase understanding is through the use of visual aids. Visual aids offer a second system—a visual system—for receiving information normally delivered orally. They also offer change and movement as well—both of which will grasp audience attention. Other advantages to using visual aids include clarifying complex ideas, illustrating things impossible to see otherwise, comparing facts and statistics, and showing changes in things or trends over time.

The main problem with visual aids comes from how they are used. Seven suggestions were provided for effective use: rehearsing, revealing visual aids only when they are talked about, making certain they are large enough, making certain they are simple, talking to the audience and not to the visual aid, recognizing the problems with passing visual aids around, and, finally, using them with discretion. Visual aids have the potential for creating negative effects, thus the speaker must be cautious in their use.

In the final section, answering questions, suggestions for encouraging questions from the audience were provided. Five guidelines for handling them were given: (1) know your material and your listeners, (2) anticipate the situation, (3) be honest, forthright, and direct, (4) restate questions for the whole audience, and (5) maintain a proper attitude. The key to handling questions effectively and efficiently lies in being prepared for the unexpected.

All communication has both an informative and persuasive dimension. As you study the chapter on persuasion, which follows, do not forget the material here. It is an important and relevant foundation. Even though your purpose may become persuasive, you are unlikely to shed the still necessary role of seeking understanding—the role of informative speeches.

NOTES

[1]David K. Berlo, *The Process of Communication* (New York: Holt, Rinehart & Winston, 1960), p. 9.

[2]D. E. Berlyne, "A Theory of Human Curiosity," *British Journal of Psychology,* 45 (1954): 180–181. Also see D. L. Thistlethwaite, *College Press and Changes in Study Plans of Talented Students* (Evanston, Ill. National Merit Scholarship Corp., 1960).

[3]See Ernest Thompson, "Some Effects of Message Structure on Listener Comprehension," *Speech Monographs,* 34 (March 1967): 51–57; Christopher Spicer and Ronald E. Bassett, "The Effect of Organization on Learning from an Informative Message," *Southern Speech Communication Journal,* 41 (Spring 1976): 290–299; David Katz, *Gestalt Psychology* (New York: Ronald Press, 1950).

[4]See Charles F. Vick and Roy V. Wood, "Similarity of Past Experience and the Communication of Meaning," *Speech Monographs,* 36 (June 1969): 159–162.

[5]See Charles R. Petrie, Jr. and Susan P. Carrel, "The Relationship of Motivation, Listening Capability, Initial Information, and Verbal Organizational Ability to Lecture Comprehension and Retention," *Communication Monographs,* 43 (August 1976): 187–194.

[6]For more information on the use of visual aids, see Edgar Dale, *Audio-Visual Methods in Teaching* (New York: Dryden Press, 1946); William J. Seiler, "The Effects of Visual Materials on Attitudes, Credibility, and Retention," *Speech Monographs,* 38 (November 1971): 331–334.

[7]Research shows that people taught by methods using both visual and oral channels have better recall immediately after the presentation and also after a period of time has elapsed. People who only *heard* the message had an immediate recall of 70 percent and recalled only 10 percent after three days. Those taught both visually *and* orally had an 85 percent recall immediately after and 65 percent after three days. See Robert Craig, *Kansas City Times,* April 19, 1967. Craig is chief of the United States Public Health Service Audio-Visual Facility. This research is reviewed in Wil Linkugel and David Berg's *A Time to Speak* (Belmont, Calif.: Wadsworth, 1970).

[8]See Alicia Fortinberry, "The Art of Piquing Art Questions," *Psychology Today* (April 1980), pp. 30–33. According to research by Caryl Marsh, a psychologist who is also curator of exhibitions and research at the National Archives, the number of "evaluative" questions visitors will ask a tour guide can be increased up to seven times by (1) paving the way for challenging questions, (2) having tour guides pose questions in their own presentations, and (3) pausing for at least six seconds after asking a question in order to give people time to mull it over. A paper on her work was presented at the 49th Annual Meeting of the Eastern Psychological Association in Washington, D.C.

thirteen

CHANGING ATTITUDES

Persuasive Speeches

Most of the communication you engage in and listen to everyday has an underlying—or obvious—persuasive intent. You want the persons with whom you are speaking to change their attitudes as a result of your communication. Perhaps the best examples we have of persuasive speakers are politicians, advertisers, and religious leaders.

In this chapter persuasive communication is discussed. The first section addresses your potential persuasive imapct. The second section differentiates the various persuasive propositions. The third section examines the process of influencing attitudes, and the fourth looks at several persuasive organizational patterns. The final section discusses persuasion and ethics.

YOUR POTENTIAL PERSUASIVE IMPACT

In our society there are several things that will affect a persuader's personal impact. They are discussed here to keep the whole persuasive process in proper perspective. The following sections will treat (1) the amount of information available, (2) potential persuasive elements, (3) the likely effect you, as one individual, can have, and (4) where persuasion actually takes place.

Amount of Information Available

In our society, we get information from many sources. Obvious sources are newsmagazines, newspapers, television, and radio. But we must not discount people as sources of information. When a speaker speaks to an audience, the amount of information the speaker can share is likely to be minimal compared with the tremendous amount the audience members are getting (or have gotten) from other sources. Just think about how you acquired the information you have. Much of it came from friends and from the groups to which you belong. Family members are invaluable as sources, as are teachers, ministers, rabbis, or priests. Then add to these sources all the news media to which you are exposed and on top of that place your own experiences—observing and responding to things that you see, do, or hear. The speaker can shape, narrow, or focus the information, but he or she cannot hope to provide the base that is otherwise available. A speaker seldom should assume a zero information base (no information) on the part of the audience. Rather, it is more appropriate to assume that the base of information that the audience possesses varies dramatically among its members in both breadth and depth.

Potential Persuasive Elements

People in our society are influenced (persuaded) by a wide variety of factors. More often than not, the persuasive factor is not a single element at all, but a combination. Think of how you are moved to change your attitudes about something. It is often a very complex process, perhaps difficult to explain. That is because the process does not always operate in a clear and distinct manner. It is subtle, often operating at a very low awareness level and requiring the compilation of a variety of inputs. We get information from so many varied sources.

There are many reasons why we change an attitude. Sometimes we change our attitude toward something because of what we have read or heard from a highly credible source; that is, we hear something new from someone we believe in. We might change our attitude, too, because we heard something from many different sources; we change because we hear this new piece of information over and over again. We might change our attitude, too, simply because something that was once remote has begun to touch our life directly. Changes in the environment, in our physical condition, in our capabilities, even in our friends may bring about changes in our attitude.

In considering reasons for changing our attitude, we must not overlook the role that we ourselves play as a persuasive factor. Two researchers suggest that when speakers find information and formulate their arguments in support of a position they want to advocate, they begin to develop strong attitudes toward the topic.[1] Thus, self-persuasion is likely to be a factor in attitude change.

Just as newsmagazines, newspapers, television, radio, and other people are sources of information, they are also potential persuasive sources. We are continually being affected—barraged—by sources bent on persuasion, whether they are advertisers, politicians, salespeople, teachers, or others. As you consider the total picture, think of how you—one persuasive speaker—fit in. What effect can *you*—as one individual—have when you consider how many potential persuasive elements exist?

Likely Effect You Can Have

Think, first, about the length of time you will be speaking before the class. Rather short when you consider it. Second, think about who you are with reference to your audience. Are you more experienced and knowledgeable than they? Are you older or younger? If you will be talking to people of approximately the same age and experience, how do you expect to stand out from them? To be considered a source worth listening or responding to? Third, consider your own personal power and ability to influence others. Are you generally effective as a persuader in everyday life? If, by virtue of your personality and inherent characteristics, you consider yourself shy, weak, or introverted, these same characteristics will probably affect *any* persuasive situation in which you find yourself. Numerous factors will affect the outcome of a persuasive situation and *you* can (1) know what many of these are, (2) control those under your control, and (3) predict the probable outcome.

You might also consider two other factors that will influence the effect you can have: (1) the audience's mind set, and (2) its skepticism. The first point relates to both the amount of information available and the potential persuasive elements available. Because we are always being persuaded, our senses become numbed—desensitized. Think, too, of the other speakers who have preceded you. Are the audience members ready for "just another speech"? You may have to rise above their mind sets—their expectations. If you "fit right in," you will simply match audience expectations—"just another speech."

Besides having their senses numbed by numerous previous efforts or exposure to similar activities, audience members also have a natural (and I think healthy) skepticism. They have learned to question, not to accept ideas on first hearing, and to attempt to come to decisions by themselves. This is, of course, not always the case. But our educational system encourages such a posture. Thus, you must also consider audience predispositions. Audience members are not as open, flexible, malleable, or persuadable as one might think. Remember, they have been exposed to shoddy persuasion in the past from salespeople who hard–sell a lousy product, advertisers who do more to mislead than to inform, politicians who speak from both sides of the mouth, and teachers who say one thing and then shift ground when they grade. Audience members have every reason to question and doubt—even to be cynical. How are they to know that *you* are different? You have some convincing to do.

The purpose here is not to be pessimistic, but to approach persuasive speaking realistically. Anything you do with others fits into a total framework; it is not an event or activity that stands alone in time with no ties to what has happened, what is happening, or what is going to happen. Even if you do not acknowledge or recognize these ties, the audience will make the associations in their own minds. These associations may well be more powerful and convincing than anything you can say or do. For example, you might talk on the benefits of donating your body to medical science. Can you imagine how that might affect an audience member who has just experienced the death of a loved one? Or how a person who has recently witnessed a fatal traffic accident would react? You cannot predict all the associations that can be made, but you *can* be responsible for the obvious ones.

Taking your own public speaking class as an example, and using your first persuasive proposition (or topic), list some considerations that must be heeded (or studied) in each of the following categories:

Amount of information (How much do your audience members know?)
Potential persuasive elements (What are the ways they are persuaded?)
Likely effect you can have (How much influence can you have on them?)

The purpose here is to alert you to the audience analysis that is necessary in the persuasive speaking situation. Audience analysis *is* important in persuasion.

Where Persuasion Takes Place

We often feel that speakers persuade audiences. This is not so. When persuasion takes place, audience members actually persuade themselves. We all hold basic beliefs about many things. When we hear a subject discussed, the topic stirs up associations—even conclusions and answers—on the issue. A speaker then tries to influence *our* associations.

Although speakers attempt to stir up appropriate associations, the kind of identifications that listeners make between their past knowledge and experiences and the speaker's topic cannot be fully or accurately predicted. The more accurately a speaker can identify the associations listeners will make, the more likely he or she can predict the kind of discussion of supporting materials needed. But the speakers do not do the persuading. Just as the meaning of any word lies in people's heads, people persuade themselves. A speaker simply provides a stimulus or cause for listeners to think or associate in certain ways. But if they do not do so, no persuasion occurs, and listeners go on acting or believing the way they did before the speaker appeared.

TYPES OF PERSUASIVE SPEAKING

Although a distinction is made between three basic types, or purposes, in persuasive speaking, it should be clear that some persuasive speeches include two or even all three of these types. The classification here is based on the kind of audience response the speaker is seeking.

Convincing.   If you want an audience to agree with you, your purpose is to *convince:*

- Grades are used by teachers to manipulate students.
- Grades are detrimental to student motivation.
- Lectures are too often boring, dull, and not worthwhile.
- Lectures are an ineffective means of educating students.

The speaker, in each of these cases, is trying to secure agreement with each of his or her points. Propositions of fact and value (to be discussed in the next section) lend themselves to speeches to convince. The first and last statements are propositions of fact (they can be proven true or false), whereas the second and third are propositions of value because they place emphasis on the value term: *detrimental* and *not worthwhile* respectively.

Actuating.   If speakers seek action from the audience on some matter, their purpose is to *actuate.* Sometimes audience members must be convinced first before they can be moved to action. This is where there is some overlap—actually reinforcement—between these types of persuasive speeches. Speeches to actuate are usually formulated around a proposition of policy:

- Grades should be (must be, ought to be, have to be) eliminated.
- Large lecture sections ought to be eliminated (or must be divided into smaller discussion sections).

The actuating part of these speeches might include having students sign a petition, speak out against the system, avoid courses in which lectures are a component, write letters to the president of the college or university, conduct discussions on the topic in other classes, and talk about the topic informally with others.

A speech to actuate could make a variety of requests or suggestions, depending on the topic. The speaker could, for example, ask audience members to:

—buy a particular brand of product,
—support a particular political candidate,
—do something in a new or different way (exercise, eat, read, study, or other),
—find out something (learn the facts, pursue a topic, or read a certain publication),
—attend a lecture, speech, concert, play, or event,
—support the school (run for office, attend sports activities, go to school-sponsored activities),
—get more experience (travel, see, and do more in life),
—donate to charity (give of your time and money to people in need),
—take a certain course.

Stimulating.   There are times when the audience already believes as you do. They feel the same way. What such an audience might need is reinforcement or rejuvenation—not convincing. Their feelings need to be heightened or sharpened or simply brought to the fore. A speech designed to do this is called a speech to *stimulate.* Examples are rather common:

- The Sunday sermon is often designed to stimulate.
- At a pep rally, a speaker wants to heighten present feelings.

- An after–dinner speaker often wishes to excite an audience on a topic it already supports.
- A commencement address attempts to reinforce common, accepted ideas and principles.

Although all three of these purposes—convincing, actuating, and stimulating—may be goals of a speaker, generally only one purpose will constitute the final goal. For example, though we may all agree that a particular procedure (such as physical exercise) will help us, we may not have all the facts. The speaker may begin by stimulating us, reinforcing this already present knowledge; then convince us of its importance by offering additional facts, and finally actuate us by providing a simple series of exercises we can do every day. Every proposition of policy has within it an implied proposition of fact and value. To say we all should do a simple series of exercises every day, implies, first, that such exercises exist (proposition of fact) and, second, that such exercises are both valuable and worthwhile (proposition of value). These two propositions are instrumental in getting the main purpose (a policy) accepted by the audience.

TRY THIS 2

Suggest two topics for persuasive speeches for each of the three types of persuasive speeches just discussed:

1. A speech *to convince.*
2. A speech *to actuate.*
3. A speech *to stimulate.*

Which of these topics would you prefer to speak on? Which of these topics would it be easiest to find material on? Which of these topics would your audience most like to hear a speech on?

PROPOSITIONS

The three basic types of propositions have already mentioned. They are:

1. Propositions of fact
2. Propositions of value
3. Propositions of policy

Since these are basic to persuasive speaking, they will be explained in more depth and detail at this point. Learning the distinctions between these three types will help you become clearer and more distinct in your persuasive speeches. You will find it easier to focus in on and to narrow topics.

Propositions of Fact

A proposition of fact alleges (suggests) the existence of something. A speaker using this kind of proposition tries to prove or disprove that this fact exists (that it is true or false). Some examples:

- Marijuana helps relieve certain medical problems.
- Horoscopes are self-fulfilling prophecies.
- Witches still exist in our society.
- Certain kinds of junk food contain the adult minimal daily requirements of vitamins.
- Television serves as an educational aid.
- The political process in the United States discounts the importance of the "little person."
- Jazz can be characterized by looking at its four major elements.

Each of these statements is (or can be) disputed on a factual level. That is, the proposition alleges existence or truth; it becomes *your* job as speaker to prove it. Whether the proposition refers to past, present, or future, your job is to amass the facts necessary to convince your audience one way or the other—that is, to convince them of the truth *or* falsity of the proposition. Strong factual evidence is important here.

Propositions of Definition. A proposition of definition is a form of factual proposition. A definition is a phrase that expresses the essential nature of a person, idea, or thing. A proposition of definition places the definition into a formal, persuasive mode: something offered to an audience for consideration or acceptance. The following are some examples of propositions of definition:

- Musical form can best be understood by examining its essential elements: repetition, variation, and contrast.
- The term *narcissism* is derived from Greek mythology and refers to a morbid condition in which a person is intensely interested in his or her own body.
- The thinnest glass fibers ever made are invisible except by microscope and were developed to protect the Columbia space shuttle from re-entry heat.

Notice that each proposition suggests that something is true, and each can be disputed on the factual level. It will be the speaker's job to prove the proposition with facts. The first develops the idea of musical form through *classification:* by setting out the boundaries of the word. The second develops the idea of narcissism through *etymology:* providing an account of the history of the word. The final proposition looks at the *function* of the fibers: explaining the use of these thin glass fibers as applied to the exterior of the space shuttle Columbia.

Propositions of Value

A proposition of value contains a value judgment as part of the proposition. A speaker using this kind of proposition maintains that something is good or bad, beneficial or detrimental, justified or unjustified, worthwhile or worthless, and so on. The proposition itself contains the value term. It is obvious and can be underlined if necessary, as in the following propositions:

- Education that is dictatorial or authoritarian is *detrimental.*
- Movies are a *rich* and *valuable* source of information.
- The violence in professional sports is *unjustified* and *detrimental.*
- The accumulation of garbage in our society is *unnecessary* and *wasteful.*
- Cheating is *bad.*
- Drinking alcoholic beverages is a *beneficial* way to relieve excessive nervous energy.

Just as in propositions of fact, propositions concerning values may treat ideas or events of the past, present, or future.

To support a proposition of value requires the use of opinion or testimony. The mistake many speakers make, however, is to depend most on their *own* opinion. This is usually insufficient. It is necessary to first use facts to prove the importance or existence of the issue, event, or thing. Opinions and testimony can then be used to support the value term. Legislators, doctors, lawyers, educators, and writers in the field must be used to buttress the speech. There is no harm in using your own opinions, but realize that your own opinions often do not reflect extensive background and experience on the topic, and thus you may have little credibility in the eyes of the audience. One experience is insufficient to establish credibility. Strong evidence is important here, but the speaker must add to factual evidence the use of opinions. These statements, however, should not lead you to assume that the *only* evidence possible with propositions of value is that of authority. It is usually the major form of evidence, but other forms may also be applicable.

Propositions of Policy

A proposition of policy proposes a course of action. A speaker who uses this type of proposition argues that something should or should not be done. Within the proposition of policy, one of the following terms must appear: should, ought to, have to, or must. A speaker might support any one of the following propositions of policy:

- Teachers should be more available to students.
- Sports at the college level ought to be abolished.
- The petroleum industry must be controlled by the federal government.

- Televised self-instruction, as an educational teaching form, has to be abolished.
- Students must strike in order to get better learning conditions.
- Assertiveness must be used to succeed in our society.

As previously suggested, propositions of fact, value, and policy often depend on each other. If, for example, you wanted to propose abolishing general education requirements (the language, math, science, or social science requirements that everyone must take), you might want to establish other propositions first:

What are the general education requirements? (proposition of fact)

Who must take general education requirements? (proposition of fact)

To what extent are general education requirements worthless, detrimental, or unjustified? (proposition of value)

General education requirements must be eliminated. (proposition of policy)

The above list by no means exhausts the possibilities of propositions that could be used to obtain the final outcome (abolishment), but it indicates how the various types might be interdependent and reinforcing.

To support a proposition of policy requires some of the same support suggested under propositions of fact and value. Facts and opinions are essential. But one of the strongest forms of support would be actual situations or examples where the policy has already been adopted and implemented. To show where the solution has been successful and the corresponding effects—positive feelings and attitudes—can be strong material.

TRY THIS 3

On each of the following general topics, prepare propositions of fact, value, and policy. Every topic can be approached from each of these vantage points. It should be clear, however, that some topics lend themselves better to one or another of the propositions. Follow the example provided.

Example:

Habits: *fact:* Everyone has habits.
value: Habits can be harmful.
policy: Negative habits should be eliminated.

| Habits | Fads | Pornography |
| Dieting | Loneliness | Procrastination |

INFLUENCING ATTITUDES

The whole purpose of persuasive speaking is to influence the attitudes of listeners. An attitude is a tendency or predisposition to behave in a certain way. Speakers can start, stop, change, or reinforce them. In doing so, they start, stop, change, or reinforce the psychological set of listeners so that they will act in a particular way—the way the speakers want—in certain circumstances. A speaker may try, for example, to get audience members to change their attitude toward impulse buying. Later, when an audience member is in a situation where she or he might be inclined to buy on impulse, the speaker's ideas might cause a change in behavior.

Speakers can determine audience attitudes in two ways. First, they can observe audience members and from their behavior can ascribe or attribute attitudes. A speaker might observe that students spend a great deal of time talking about and attending parties and suggest that students' attitudes toward partying are highly favorable. Attitudes toward alcohol, achieving success, finding adventure, or participating in sports could be discovered in the same manner. If a speaker is the same age as the audience members, observation might involve some self-analysis as well. Ask yourself, "What do I like? What do I do? How do I feel?"

A second way speakers have of discovering attitudes is to ask audience members what their attitudes are. Speakers can ask, for example:

> Do you support busing of public-school students?
> Do you feel that marijuana should be legalized?
> Should no-fault divorce be instituted?
> Do you think the parking situation on this campus needs attention?
> Are dormitory regulations too strict?
> Is cheating rampant on this campus?

Once attitudes are determined, a speaker can more precisely and accurately approach the audience. When you know where people stand on an issue, it is easier to persuade them. To change or reinforce those attitudes, a speaker can show listeners how the adoption of the attitude will help them structure their world. That is, the speaker should try to show how accepting the attitude is really a logical extension of what audience members already know or feel. People try to rationally structure the world they live in. Knowing this, a speaker might, for example, show

- How a deemphasis on grades will raise the *quality* of education. (This fits into the audience's picture or vision of a better world.)
- How better organization of one's time will result in *more time for oneself*. (This fits into the audience members' needs to be independent and to control their own world.)
- How more concern for one's eating habits will result in *better health and better feelings*. (This fits into the audience's vision of a better, healthier future.)

285

Attitudes are also formed as a result of rewards and punishments. That is, we will tend to feel a certain way if there is something in it for us, or another way if we think we might be hurt or punished. Thus, a speaker who can show an audience the benefits or handicaps of adopting certain attitudes can help cause persuasion to occur. For example:

- The free enterprise system will allow you to *set your own prices and make your own decisions.*
- Free speech allows *you* to say what *you please* about the government.
- A special fee collected from everyone for the use of this facility means that even if you do not use it, *you still pay for it.*
- Voting for this slate of officers will keep things the way they are; voting for that slate will bring about change and new opportunities.
- A pass–fail system of grading will allow *you* more freedom, more choices, and more variety with few of the restrictions of a graded system.

Attitudes are also formed because we want to defend our ego. When we feel there is something that will make us look good or bad, we change our attitude accordingly. The point is, we want to look good. An example is the college student who never thought much about clothes or cars until he became a businessman in an area where clothes and cars are important to image. He changed his attitude—valuing clothes and cars—because it became important to his image. A person who rebels against authority may change his or her attitude as a result of becoming an administrator who has control over others. If speakers can show audience members how their topic will, in some way, affect listeners' egos, there is a good possibility for persuasion to occur. For example:

- Personal hygiene will make you feel better about yourself.
- Learning to listen to others will win you more friends.
- Caring about the clothes you wear will raise your image in the eyes of others.
- Reading and experiencing will make you a more interesting person.
- If you begin to feel good about yourself, others are more likely to respond positively to you.

People want to appear strong and positive in the eyes of others. If their egos are threatened in any way, they will move quickly to remedy the situation.

But it is not just the attitude the audience has toward an issue that makes a difference. How the audience came by the attitude may also count. For example, if you have heard from a friend that a certain teacher never gives As, you might be inclined to believe it until the teacher herself persuaded you differently. An attitude like this is not held strongly and may be changed fairly easily. Attitudes are not so easily changed when a listener has been brought up to believe in their basic truth. Examples might include attitudes such as these:

Abortion is wrong.

Wearing seat belts is a farce (even dangerous).

Premarital sex is bad.

Republicans (or Democrats) have the answers.

Euthanasia (mercy killing) is wrong.

Some of these attitudes may have been learned early in family life or from peers and then reinforced over and over through rewards (praise) by family members or peers—or by example. The attitudes become rather firmly entrenched and are unlikely to be easily changed. Thus, *how* people learn to feel as they do becomes an important ingredient as well. It will give the speaker knowledge about (1) how strong the attitude is, (2) how likely the attitude can be changed, and perhaps (3) how change can or should be approached (if change is desired).

The last point is important. How a speaker approaches a group of listeners may depend on why the attitude is held. For example, people who are against alcohol would certainly be against allowing it on campus. It could be against their religion. People who do not eat meat would probably care little about tightening government standards on the handling of meat. Often, people who consider themselves vegetarians hold these views quite strongly. People who support public schools would probably support a raise in taxes if it were to help the schools. People brought up in an education–oriented climate are likely to hold these views firmly. In approaching an audience, it might be necessary to convince those opposed to your ideas by showing them your situation is different and stimulate those who already agree with you to become more active. But, it is also useful to note that views rooted deeply are not likely to be changed with ease. Persuasion is sometimes a slow (and painful?) process.

Plan a persuasive speech in which you will try to influence the attitudes of your audience in some direct and meaningful way. Write your proposition on a sheet of paper.

Now answer the following questions about this proposition.

1. Does any aspect of this proposition affect the way audience members structure the world they live in? If so, how?
2. Will acceptance or rejection of this proposition cause audience members to receive any rewards or punishments? Explain.
3. Does acceptance of this proposition help audience members defend their ego in any way? If so, how?

The extent to which your proposition does 1, 2, and/or 3 above is the extent to which it will intimately and directly affect and involve audience members.

PERSUASIVE ORGANIZATIONAL PATTERNS

The material in this section will emphasize some patterns of organization unique to the persuasive situation. These patterns are especially strong, then, because they lend themselves to situations where the speaker's intent is to change audience attitudes. The following patterns will be discussed: (1) inductive patterns, (2) deductive patterns, (3) causal patterns, and finally, (4) a special problem–solution order. Our assumption is that the basic components of organizing behavior have already been learned and are being used. The choice of which organizational pattern to use depends on the demands of the particular subject and audience. The ultimate choice of pattern is determined by insight into the subject–audience interaction.

The material here will be presented as it relates to the Toulmin model developed in Chapter 5. As you recall, Toulmin's model of reasoning emphasizes a logical relationship between the specific evidence one gathers for a speech effort (data) and the conclusions one draws from that evidence (claims).

Inductive Patterns

Speakers use induction when they move from the specific to the general. This might mean using specific data to build a case, then drawing it together with a general claim once the case is sufficiently supported. When the speaker feels an audience may be hostile to his or her ideas, this approach is often wise. To state the general conclusion first, without the evidence, may turn the audience off and not allow the case to be made—audience members may no longer be listening.

If one were to diagram the inductive speech, one might picture it as shown in Figure 13–1.

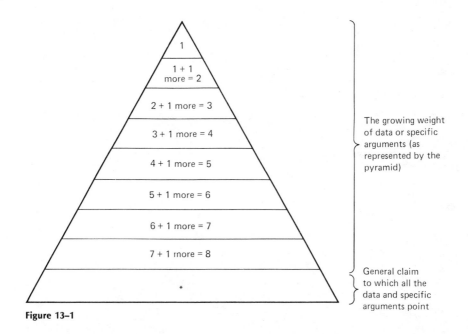

Figure 13-1

Again, the specific pieces of data and the specific arguments are provided first, and from these the speaker draws the claim.

Deductive Patterns

Deductive patterns are the reverse of inductive patterns. The speaker states the claim first and then follows it with specific data or arguments (or both) to support the claim. This is the more common pattern of the two. It provides the audience with a clearer picture of what is coming in the speech because the synthesizing comment, purpose, or claim is provided at the outset. This enables the audience to understand all that follows. However, a diagram of this (see Figure 13–2) would *not* be a simple reverse of the inductive diagram shown in Figure 13–1. That is, one would not simply stand that triangle on its apex to illustrate the deductive process.

Causal Patterns

A speaker using the causal pattern can move from the cause to the effect or from the effect to the cause. Cause to effect is more common. A speaker using this pattern might state specific behaviors, such as:

> We can boycott the dining hall,
> We can speak to the dieticians,
> We can speak out against the food we must eat.

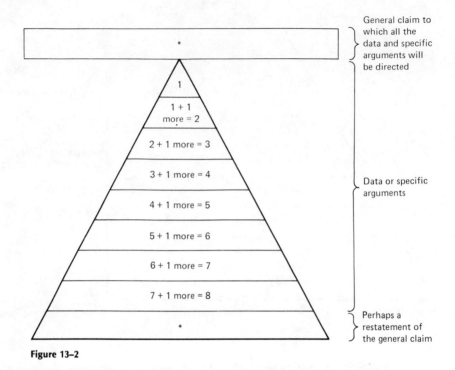

General claim to which all the data and specific arguments will be directed

Data or specific arguments

Perhaps a restatement of the general claim

Figure 13–2

From these, the speaker could state the claim:

—If we do all of this, we *can* be successful in getting our menus changed.

This is just one of the many examples of a cause–to–effect pattern. It moves from an analysis of present causes to the future effect. Using an effect-to-cause pattern, the speaker might begin with the claim:

The bill providing for deposits on bottles and cans did not pass.

The speaker would follow this claim with the specific data such as:

There was a strong campaign against it.
People did not believe it would do much to help clean up the environment.
People did not want to pay more money for returnable containers.
People do not want to be bothered.

In this case, the pattern of organization moves from a description of a present condition to an analysis of the causes which seem to have produced it.

A Problem–Solving Pattern

One popular and workable problem–solving pattern in persuasive speaking was developed by Professor Alan H. Monroe in *Principles and Types of Speech Communication*. He called his pattern the "motivated sequence."[2] It is useful for two principal reasons:

1. It provides a clear and definite pattern to follow for getting from the definition and analysis of a problem to its solution.
2. It follows the normal process of human reasoning—the way people normally think.

Although his full pattern—using five steps—is designed for a problem–solving speech, the pattern can be adapted to other speeches as well. Our concern here is with the problem–solving speech alone.

To utilize the full pattern in a problem–solving speech, one would use the five different steps as follows:

1. Attention—to call attention to the topic or situation.
2. Need—to explain the audience needs being addressed. How does this topic relate to the needs of my audience?
3. Satisfaction—How can the needs be satisfied? How will my topic or proposal solve the needs (problems) presented in step 2 above?
4. Visualization—Once the solution (satisfaction step) is implemented, what changes will result? How will things be improved and changed? (This is probably the most important step because of its power to persuade.)
5. Action—What kind of action by the audience is necessary to bring about this change? What is needed or required?

If this five–step sequence is committed to memory, it can serve as a handy, organizational tool for any problem–solving situation. Because all of the stages are important, let us examine each in detail.

The attention step. This is often thought of as the time when it is most important to gain the attention of the audience, but because the duration of focus of attention is short and because it comes in spurts, attention must be a concern of the speaker *throughout* the speech. The introduction cannot be thought of as the only time for gaining attention.

In the attention step the speaker should let the audience know about the topic itself. Why is he or she speaking on it? Why is it important? Why should they listen? The speaker must call attention to the topic and to the occasion, to make certain the attention of the audience is focused on the specifics of the speech and situation.

The need step. This step can draw from and capitalize on a successful attention step. Now that audience attention is focused on the topic, *why* does it require our attention and concern now? Involve the audience in this. The speaker must not only demonstrate the significance and magnitude of the problem but must show dramatically and forcefully how it touches the lives of audience members. The need creates a dissonance without which the audience would not be able to change. Without a dissonance—an unresolved feeling or discordant note —audience members would just continue along their way—or in their same old rut, from the speaker's viewpoint.

If you think of a need step in terms of Toulmin's *warrant,* you realize that it can serve to put the audience into the proper frame of mind to see the relationship between the data and the claim. People must be shown why the problem touches their own, personal lives. To prove that a significant need exists may require strong personal credibility. It may require appealing to audience desires, emotions, or motives. It may also require the use of logic—proving a need exists by using statistics, examples, and expert opinions.

To support the need step you should research the problem thoroughly to isolate the causes. Then phrase the need clearly and precisely. You will probably not be able to present all your findings, but because of the thorough research you did you will be able to speak confidently in an informed manner.

The satisfaction step.   This step relates directly to the need step because here the speaker must offer the claims that will satisfy the need established above. Because of having researched the problem and thereby commanding a thorough knowledge of it, the speaker is in a position to recommend a workable claim. A simple statement of the claim is necessary, but that is not all that is needed. The speaker must also address the various reservations audience members may have regarding the claim:

1. Does the claim treat the causes of the problem?
2. Will the claim be practical?
   a. Will it cost too much money?
   b. Will it take too much time?
   c. Will it create new or more difficult problems?
3. Will the claim be acceptable?

Be as specific as possible at this point, showing the audience directly and forthrightly how the adoption of *your* claim will satisfy their reservations: their objections and concerns.

TRY THIS 5

Apply Monroe's motivated sequence to some of the advertisements you see on commercial television. Does it fit? If so, how well? Why do you suppose it is followed by advertisers? In a commercial, what is the most important step in the motivated sequence? That is, which step is the one that is most likely to convince the audience?

On a separate piece of paper, jot down the major parts of a specific advertisement next to the major steps of the Motivated Sequence:

Attention

Need

Satisfaction

Visualization

Action

The purpose of this exercise is twofold: (1) to become familiar with the pattern, and (2) to find examples of the various steps of the sequence as they are used. It is hoped, too, that this exercise will impress upon you the value of the visualization step.

The visualization step.   This step may require the most time and attention in a problem–solving speech. In this step, you *demonstrate* how the claim you have outlined satisfies the need. This is the warrant in Toulmin's model, and if successful, in this step the speaker provides audience members with a clear relationship between the data and the claim that follows from the data: between the satisfaction step and the need.

The visualization step is precisely what it sounds like: You create a mental picture for audience members of how things will look or be if your solution is put into action. You can do this positively by showing the many benefits of adoption, or you can do it negatively by illustrating vividly the dire consequences that will occur if your solution is not adopted, or you can do both. This step, when completed successfully, should create a motive to change. Without this motive to change, the audience would simply go back to the original state, saying, "I'm glad *somebody* is going to do something about that problem." It puts audience members into the specific situation and has them actually doing what is being asked for or, at least, seeing what is being asked for being done by others.

It is important that audiences see what the results are likely to be. If you can cite examples where your solution has already been put into effect, this helps. If you can show the audience, even hypothetically, what things will look like once your solution is supported, this also helps. Think of this step as similar to that portion of advertisements where we see the product has done its job: people winning friends because of cleaner breath, people with whiter clothes or clearer floors because of using a product, people having more fun because they are part of a new generation. Television commercials do not have to create a mental picture; they can show us. But as speakers we must create clear, impressive mental images that make the need for our solution strong and memorable.

The action step.   In this final step the speaker calls for action or change. The speaker asks the audience to adopt his or her claim. The action step must be specific. It must tell the audience *how* to act. If you are not concrete and specific, the audience is unlikely to do anything. In general we (as audience members) do not act!

Answer the question, "What do you want the individuals in your audience to do?" You cannot have them sign petitions unless you either *have* the petitions for them to sign or tell them where they can go to sign them. You cannot have them vote unless they know where and how to register and where and how to vote.

You cannot have them contribute money unless they know who to give it to and where and when this person will be available. You cannot ask them to read an article or book unless they know the author and title and where it can be found. You should even give them the cost and availability of useful pieces of information. What stores have it? What is the library call number? Answer all questions, and be as specific as you can.

TRY THIS 6

For the following propositions, think of information that could be used to illustrate each of the steps in Monroe's motivated sequence:

We must stop eating junk food.
    Attention:
    Need:
    Satisfaction:
    Visualization:
    Action:

Prostitution should be legalized.
    Attention:
    Need:
    Satisfaction:
    Visualization:
    Action:

PERSUASION AND ETHICS

If all speakers considered the feelings of audience members, adapted their message to the audience's frame of reference, and worked toward mutual understanding and mutual benefit, a section on persuasion and ethics would be unnecessary.[3] Obviously, they do not. No matter what profession, what level, or where, unethical persuasion occurs. Ethics are simply the principles of conduct governing speakers and listeners. It is my intent here to be blunt and to the point.

Speakers should be truthful.   Lying is unethical. Attempt to present your audience with the truth as best you understand it. That is all that you or audience members can expect. Truthfulness also means presenting the facts without exaggeration or distortion. Many people regard exaggeration to be the same as lying.

Speakers should be informed. When people choose to speak on a particular topic, they must prepare themselves as thoroughly as they can. Only in this way can audiences discover the information necessary to make reasoned choices.

Speakers should keep audience interests in mind. If audience members are to listen to a speech, or if they are asked to change their attitudes or behavior, it should be for their ultimate benefit. That does not mean speakers cannot speak out of personal interest, as long as it isn't personal interest to the denial of audience interests—such as promoting a product or idea that could bring harm to the audience, or that would bring them no benefit and yet cost them money.[4]

Listeners should understand that they too have an ethical responsibility. They must give the speaker a full hearing, laying aside biases and prejudices. They should try to be empathetic, try to understand why the speaker feels as he or she does. Listeners also have an obligation to give the speaker open, honest feedback. Speakers have a right to expect active listeners.

SUMMARY

This chapter on persuasive speeches addresses several important areas not previously discussed. The first section was designed to put the process in proper perspective by looking at your potential persuasive impact. How successful you are likely to be will be determined, in part, by the amount of information available, potential persuasive elements, the likely effect that you can have, and the willingness of audience members to persuade themselves.

In the section on types of persuasive speaking, speech purposes that included to convince, actuate, and stimulate were considered. In the next section propositions of fact, value, and policy were discussed.

Because the whole purpose of persuasive speaking is to influence attitudes, the section on influencing attitudes considered how one determines attitudes as well as how one approaches the audience with this knowledge of attitudes. It is important to remember, however, that despite one's knowledge of attitudes, the process of changing attitudes can be painfully slow.

Four organizational patterns unique to persuasive situations were discussed in the next section. Inductive patterns, deductive patterns, and causal patterns were presented. A special problem–solution order, Monroe's motivated sequence was then discussed. Relationship of these patterns to the Toulmin model was emphasized where appropriate.

The final section of this chapter considered persuasion and ethics. From the speaker's point of view, this means being truthful and informed as well as keeping audience interests in mind. From a listeners' point of view, it means giving the speaker a full hearing and open, honest feedback. Ethical responsibility is clearly both a speaker and a listener function.

Because most of the communication you engage in and listen to every day has an underlying persuasive intent, you must become both an effective user and consumer of persuasion. This chapter has attempted to raise some of the critical issues involved.

NOTES

[1]Keith Jensen and David A. Carter, "Self-Persuasion: The Effects of Public Speaking on Speakers," *Southern Speech Communication Journal,* 46 (Winter 1981): 163–174.

[2]Douglas Ehninger, Alan H. Monroe, and Bruce E. Gronbeck, *Principles and Types of Speech Communication,* 8th ed. (Glenview, Ill.: Scott, Foresman, 1978), Chapter 9, pp. 142–163. Also see Alan H. Monroe, *Principles and Types of Speech,* 5th ed., (Glenview, Ill.: Scott, Foresman, 1962), Chapter 16, "Adapting Speech Organization to the Audience: The Motivated Sequence," and Chapter 17, "Outlining a Complete Speech Using the Motivated Sequence."

[3]David M. Jabusch and Stephen W. Littlejohn, *Elements of Speech Communication: Achieving Competency* (Boston: Houghton Mifflin, 1981), p. 10.

[4]For more information on persuasion and ethics see, Wayne C. Minnick, "A New Look at the Ethics of Persuasion," *Southern Speech Communication Journal* 45 (Summer 1980): 352–362. Also see Richard L. Johannesen, *Ethics and Persuasion* (New York: Random House, 1967); and Richard E. Crable, *Argumentation as Communication: Reasoning with Receivers* (Columbus, Ohio: Chas. E. Merrill, 1976), pp. 223–247.

fourteen

SPEAKING TO CONVINCE

Reasoning Logically

Most persuasive speakers reason with their audiences; reasoning is a natural part of many persuasive speeches. To hear one of your friends say to you, "Hey, don't worry, you're going to pass the course. After all, you're intelligent, you keep up with the class, and you like it," is to hear them use reasoning—in this case causal reasoning—to encourage or persuade you.

In this chapter we will begin with a definition of reasoning. Next, we will examine some basic principles of reasoning. Finally, we will look at some basic kinds of reasoning commonly used. The point of this chapter is twofold: (1) to help you become more comfortable in your use of reasoning, and (2) to help you become more aware of the use of reasoning by others.

DEFINITION

Reasoning is the process of drawing inferences or conclusions from sufficient explanation, justification, or grounds. Suppose, for example, that I go through several days of feeling sluggish, uninspired, and even disagreeable. As I think about how I have been behaving, I say to myself, "I think I need more sleep." This is an example of drawing an inference or conclusion based on sufficient explanation, justification, or grounds—facts that cause one to believe. These, too, are facts available to me.

But what if someone else notices that my work hasn't been up to par, that I tend to argue a lot, and that I no longer crack jokes or make wisecracks. They might say to me, "Are you getting enough sleep?" or if they were parents, they might ask, "What time are you getting to bed?" They are drawing a conclusion based on facts apparent to them; they are reasoning.

PRINCIPLES OF REASONING

With this brief definition, then, let's put reasoning into a familiar context: the Toulmin model. The explanations, justifications, and grounds for the conclusion are the *data*. These provide the basis for an inference. In the above examples, the data would be sluggishness, lack of inspiration, and disagreeableness on a personal level; inferior work, a tendency to argue, and diminished sense of humor in someone else's observation. The inference, conclusion, or *claim*, as Toulmin labels it, is the end product of reasoning: "I need more sleep." A parent would be inclined to say, "Get to bed earlier," or "Stop staying up so late."

The *warrant* in Toulmin's model, as you may recall, is a statement that shows a relationship between the data and the claim. It is the key that indicates how the claim results from the data presented, and it is usually unstated. However, to test the soundness of the reasoning, one must actually state the warrant. If it cannot be stated, what may be implied is that there is no relationship between the data and the claim and, thus, the reasoning is *fallacious*—that is, the reasoning fails to satisfy the conditions of valid or correct inference.

A warrant for the example used above might be stated as follows: "Sluggishness, lack of inspiration, disagreeableness, inferior work, a tendency to argue, and diminished sense of humor are signs of lack of sleep." Can you determine a warrant for the claim that the teachers at this institution are excellent instructors in the classroom if I told you that the teachers all publish a large number of books and articles, attend numerous professional conferences, and serve on many different university committees? What would the warrant be? That publishing attending conferences, and serving on committees are signs of excellent classroom instruction? You and I know better than that! There does not appear to be a strong relationship between the data and claim; thus, this reasoning appears to be fallacious. It is erroneous.

But we *do* have what appears to be a reasonable warrant for our first example regarding the need for sleep. This example could be diagrammed. Again, we will use a *D* for data, a *W* for warrant, and a *C* for the claim. We will follow this labeling throughout this chapter.

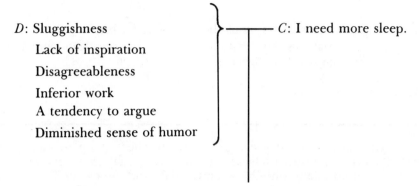

D: Sluggishness

    Lack of inspiration

    Disagreeableness

    Inferior work

    A tendency to argue

    Diminished sense of humor

C: I need more sleep.

W: [These occurrences are important
signs of the need for sleep.]

The warrant is placed in brackets to indicate that it is usually implied and not actually stated.

TRY THIS 1

In the following groups, label the data, warrant, and claim just to get into the practice of recognizing them. Use *D* for data, *W* for warrant, and *C* for claim.

1. a. _____National samples show Americans get most of their news from national network television

   b. _____For millions of Americans, national network news is the only source of national and world news.

   c. _____The samples cited are representative of Americans.

2. a. _____Students have the right, as human beings, to freely select the courses they take in college.

   b. _____Students are human beings; Professor White says they should be free to select their courses.

   c. _____Human beings should be free to make choices; Professor White is a credible source.

3. a. _____The problem of automobile fatalities is serious enough to warrant further safety controls.

b. ____Automobiles should be made safe for human beings.

c. ____Statistics show that the number of fatal accidents caused by faulty or poorly designed automobiles is high.

(See page 312 for answers.)

The example cited previously about teachers at this institution being excellent classroom instructors was determined to be fallacious because the warrant indicated no relationship between the data and the claim. This is one test that can be used to determine the strength of the reasoning. The best way to test a warrant is simply to rephrase it as a yes or no question, such as "Is it true that publications, conference attendance, and committee service are the major determiners of excellent classroom instruction?" If the answer is yes, the reasoning is sound; if it is no, the reasoning is fallacious. In the above case the answer is clearly no.

Another test would be to examine the data. There are numerous tests that can be used in examining data. Some of the important questions that should be asked are:

- Are the data sufficient?
- Representative?
- Accurate?
- Recent?
- From a reputable source?
- Biased?
- Have the data been taken out of context?

Simply laying the argument out and testing the data and warrant does not guarantee that the reasoning is sound. But by doing so, you increase the chances of discovering breakdowns in reasoning. With practice you become more sensitive to and aware of the way that reasoning works.

CONSIDER THIS

Only the time and attention you devote to preparation justifies the time and attention your audience will have to devote to listening. Use *your* time to make *their* time worthwhile.

It has been said that "the reason there are so few good speakers in public is that there are so few good thinkers in private." Thinking takes time. . . .

The point of giving yourself plenty of time to prepare your talk is so that you can think it through. You cannot give birth to a full-fledged speech the first night. A speech and an unborn baby have this in common: they both need considerable development before they are delivered.

Source: Dorothy Sarnoff, *Speech Can Change Your Life: Tips on Speech, Conversation and Speechmaking* (Garden City, N.Y.: Doubleday, 1970), p. 171.

KINDS OF REASONING

Most reasoning falls into several recognizable patterns. And although these patterns can supply many different warrants, familiarity with them and how to test them will help insure soundness in reasoning. In this section, the four major forms of reasoning will be considered: generalization, causation, analogy, and sign.

Generalization

When a speaker argues that what is true in certain circumstances is true in all circumstances (or in at least enough circumstances to confirm the generalization), the speaker is using generalization. One can often find exceptions to generalizations, but these do not always invalidate—weaken or destroy—the generalization. For example, if you generalize that remarried people feel as well-adjusted and as happy as those in first marriages, you could undoubtedly find exceptions: people who experience higher levels of worry and anxiety in their second marriage than in their first. However, if the exceptions prove to be more prevalent than simply rare or isolated instances, they open the generalization to question.

Generalization reasoning could be diagrammed as follows:

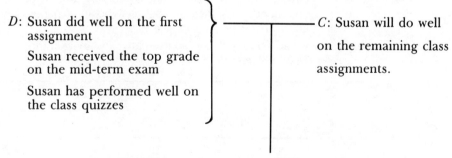

D: Susan did well on the first assignment

Susan received the top grade on the mid-term exam

Susan has performed well on the class quizzes

C: Susan will do well on the remaining class assignments.

W: [What is true in representative instances will be true in all instances.]

To test whether this reasoning is valid, look first at the warrant to make certain the data and the claim are closely related. They are. Then look at the data. Are enough instances cited? Are they true? Are these instances typical of what is likely to come in the course? *Typical* means that the instances cited exhibit the essential characteristics of all the instances that could be cited within this group of data. Finally, are negative instances accounted for? That is, have there been projects or activities on which Susan did not do well? Negative data do not invalidate the claim; however, if there are numerous negative data and they do appear to be typical, then it might be suspected that the speaker is carefully selecting his or her data to make the point or claim, and the claim would be suspect. When the claim is suspect the reasoning may be fallacious.

TRY THIS 2

In the following examples, supply the missing portion, whether it be data *(D)*, warrant *(W)*, or claim *(C)*. Label each. Maintain consistency by making each example fit generalization reasoning:

1. a._____ Science fiction novels are too unreal to be taken seriously.
   b._____ *Strangers from Space, Encounters From Above,* and *Xenobar: An Extraterrestrial Experience* are each an instance that is unreal.
   c._____ _____

   _____

   _____

2. a._____ Thomas and Frank live together as a couple; Lisa and Peter have a "trial marriage" that is working; and Paul lives in a commune. All of these are people who are experiencing different forms of real-life families.
   b._____ What is true in these representative instances is true across the United States.
   c._____ _____

   _____

   _____

Causation

Causation is a special kind of generalization. In using this form of reasoning, a speaker assumes that one or more circumstances always produces a predictable effect or set of effects. If a speaker was talking about becoming a mature person, he or she might use causation in the following manner:

D: If you are self-aware—in touch with your feelings

Centered—aware of your values and priorities

Focused—selective and able to make decisions

Committed—involved and responsible for your actions

Autonomous—thinking for yourself

Secure—fully accepting of the challenge of growth

C: You will become mature.

W: [Self-aware, centered, focused, committed, autonomous, and secure people are mature people.]

Causation can also occur from a single fact; for example, a person might reason (perhaps erroneously!) that an excess of any resource, such as oil, gas, or coal, will bring down the price of that particular resource.

To test this line of reasoning, one could begin, once again, by examining the warrant. In the example immediately above, the warrant that an abundance of any resource causes or results in lower prices is immediately suspect! Based on personal experience, it only *sounds* logical. It would have to depend on the resource as well as on the circumstances; these are *reservations*—simply the recognition that under certain circumstances, the claim may not apply.

The test of the warrant, then, is simply a look at the consistency between cause and effect. Using the previous example, one might ask of the warrant: are self-aware, centered, focused, committed, autonomous, and secure people always mature?

One speaker claimed that "We are moving toward a cashless society." As data, the speaker cited rising interest rates, advances in computer technology, and the easing of government regulations on banking and credit. To test the warrant, we need to ask if rising interest rates, advances in computer technology, and easing of government regulations in banking and credit will result in a cashless society. Are there times when the claim does not follow from these data? Could we get a cashless society without this set of data? Or with an entirely different set of data?

After testing the warrant, one can test the data as well. Will they alone yield the claim? Are the characteristics of being self-aware, centered, focused, committed, autonomous, and secure important enough to result in maturity? If these are important enough, then if we eliminate any of them, we would eliminate the result as well. Also, if the claim can result without the data, then we can also question the causal relationship.

In cause-effect reasoning, one can also question whether some other data that might accompany the data cited could be the real cause of the claim. For example, could maturity result from competence and confidence—factors that are likely to accompany those cited? Or could other factors, such as a person's compassion or creativity, cause maturity? The point is that in using causation, one must be careful about the accompanying data and their importance in bringing about the effect.

TRY THIS 3

In the following examples, label each of the existing portions, then fill in the missing one. Use reasoning from causation. Also, use the labels *D* for data, *W* for warrant, and *C* for claim.

1. a._____ _____

 _____

 _____

 b._____ Your anger will disappear quickly.

 c._____ You express your angry feelings to yourself and others and you indicate how much you really care.

2. a._____ A garden that is planted correctly will yield large dividends.

 b._____ _____

 _____

 _____

 c._____ How crops are planted determines plant yield.

3. a._____ It must be getting warmer outside.

 b._____ I'm getting warmer.

 c._____ _____

 _____

 _____

Analogy

Still another type of generalization is analogy. When speakers reason by analogy, they attempt to show that similar circumstances will produce similar conclusions. Thus, an audience member listening to argument by analogy would likely ask, "If it is true in this one set of circumstances, is it likely to work in another comparable set of circumstances?" An argument by analogy might be diagrammed as follows:

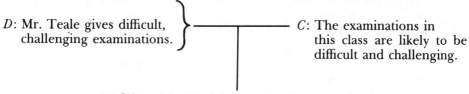

D: Mr. Teale gives difficult, challenging examinations.

C: The examinations in this class are likely to be difficult and challenging.

W: [Since Mr. Teale's examinations are always difficult and challenging, those in this class—since it is taught by Mr. Teale—are likely to be similar.]

Argument by analogy seemed to operate when states originally adopted lotteries: If the lottery worked in state X, it will also work in ours. When states choose to raise or lower the drinking or driving age, they use analogous reasoning, basing the case on successes or failures in other states.

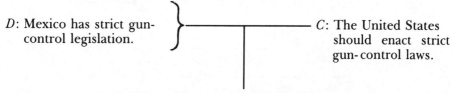

D: Mexico has strict gun-control legislation.

C: The United States should enact strict gun-control laws.

W: [Since gun-control laws are in effect in Mexico, and Mexico and the United States are similar in many key respects, gun-control laws will work in the United States.]

Such reasoning can be tested in several important ways. The first might be to examine the warrant. Considering the warrant in the example above, one would want to know if the gun-control legislation is working there. How well? What is the proportion of deaths resulting from guns in Mexico as compared with the United States?

What about the comparison being suggested? The warrant suggests that Mexico and the United States are similar in many key respects. What are these "key" respects? Are the laws enforced? Do citizens accept the laws? Do citizens consider gun possession to be a fundamental right? Do Mexico and the United States have similar forms of government? If Mexico and the United States are not similar, then they are not comparable and reasoning by analogy breaks down.

Other questions might also be asked. For example, are Mexico and the United States dissimilar in ways important to the outcome: the claim? Are the roots of the issue different? Is the size or the heritage of the country a factor? How about the dissimilarities in the expressed need for guns? If the dissimilarities outweigh the similarities, then the claims drawn from the comparisons are likely to be invalid.

TRY THIS 4

As in the previous "try this" exercises, label and fill in the missing portions using *D* for data, *W* for warrant, and *C* for claim. Use reasoning by analogy as your guideline in each group of items.

1. a._____ One does not need to study for this examination.
   b._____ _____

   _____ _____

   _____ _____

   c._____ Since the instructor gave easy examinations in both of his former courses and since the format of this course is similar, no
   study will be needed for this examination.

2. a._____ _____

   _____ _____

   _____ _____

   b._____ Only students with over a 3.70 G.P.A. (grade point average)
   received the scholarship for the past several years.
   c._____ You should be eligible for the scholarship this year.

3. a._____ Universities and colleges across the nation are tightening their
   standards.
   b._____ Our university (or college) should tighten its standards.
   c._____ _____

   _____ _____

   _____ _____

Sign

Speakers who reason by sign argue that because the presence of certain characteristics, events, or situations usually accompany other unobserved characteristics, events, or situations, then the latter unobserved characteristics, events, or situations can be predicted when the former are observed. Doctors use this form of reasoning when they diagnose a disease. Because a patient exhibits certain conditions, then he or she is likely to have a certain disease. A *sign* is simply something that serves to indicate the presence or existence of something else. Signs may be confused with causes, but signs are simply indicators, not causes. When a doctor diagnoses an illness, the signs are indicators: A high temperature, cough, and congestion may be signs of pneumonia, but they are not causes. The cause of pneumonia is infection or irritants.

Reasoning by sign may be diagrammed as follows:

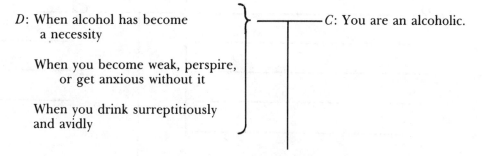

D: When alcohol has become a necessity

When you become weak, perspire, or get anxious without it

When you drink surreptitiously and avidly

C: You are an alcoholic.

W: [A strong need for alcohol, or weakness, perspiration, and anxiousness without it, and drinking that is done surreptitiously and avidly are signs of alcoholism.]

We often reason from sign to draw conclusions about what is happening in the world around us. That a movie does not stay long at a popular theatre *D* indicates that the movie probably is not very good *C* because a short run for a movie is a sign that the public does not like it *W*.

Just as in the other types of reasoning, we have several ways to test reasoning from sign. First, we can look at the warrant. Do these data always (or usually) indicate the claim? When someone needs alcohol, gets weak, perspiry, and anxious without it, and drinks surreptiously and avidly, does this always (or usually) indicate that the person is an alcoholic? When a movie leaves from a certain theatre, does that mean it is no good? If these data can occur with no effect on the claim, then they are not necessarily indicators.

Then one might focus on the data. Are these sufficient signs? Are need, physical signs such as weakness, perspiration, and anxiety sufficient to indicate alcoholism? What about loss of job, friends, and family? Situations and events are often indicated by a variety of signs. If enough are not present, then the claim may not follow.

One further test is to look at the claim. For example, if you were noting that a person was an alcoholic, does the person exhibit signs that contradict signs of an alcoholic? Is the person stable and normal? Is the person a teetotaler? Or, in the second example, do good movies come and go quickly from the popular movie houses? The claim may not be valid if signs that predict different claims can be discovered.

TRY THIS 5

In the following space, using your own substance—whether real or fabricated for this exercise—diagram reasoning by sign:

D:_____   C:_____

_____   _____

_____   _____

_____   _____

_____

_____

W:_____

_____

_____

_____

Now, test your reasoning:

1. Does the warrant clearly connect the data with the claim?
2. Do the data indicate the claim?
3. Are there sufficient signs present?
4. Can you find contradictory signs?

SUMMARY

In this book we have examined the Toulmin model in three different contexts: as part of speech support (in Chapter 5), as part of persuasive organization (in Chapter 13), and, now, as part of reasoning. It is a useful way of looking at the relationship between one's data and the claims one draws from these data.

In this chapter we defined reasoning, examined some of the principles of reasoning, then showed some of the major forms of reasoning: generalization, causation, analogy, and sign.

To use reasoning in a speech is to use argument. Argument is the process of drawing conclusions (claims) from reasons (data). In making an argument, the speaker states the claim first, or the proposition, then cites the data for that claim. Usually, the proposition is part of the introduction to the speech. Then, the major elements of data can become the main heads of the speech:

> Proposition: You are an alcoholic.
> Support: I. Alcohol has become a necessity.
> II. You become weak, perspire, or get anxious without it.
> III. You drink surreptitiously and avidly.

The point of this chapter has been to provide a logical base to speaking. Reasoning gives you a practical way to lay out your data and to see how claims are drawn from the data. If the data or reasons for a claim are sound, and if the warrant that connects the data and claim is sound, then the argument is likely to be logical. If they also satisfy the audience, they can be said to be persuasive.

The speaker, then, must seek to find data that not only prove the proposition but are also likely to be most persuasive—likely to have the greatest impact on the audience. Thus, the speaker should strive to find a variety of material so that the best can be selected for the speech. If you do not have enough material for some points, they may have to be rejected. If some data are unlikely to impress the audience, they, too, may have to be rejected. Most speeches require a minimum of two and probably not more than four supportable, impressive reasons.

With the reasons in hand, concern for the different types of speech support—mentioned in Chapter 5—become relevant. It becomes clear, too, how the various chapters of this book are tied together. The process of public communication is an integrated one that involves a large number of activities at the same time—some obvious, some reinforcing, some subtle and elusive. But it is all of them, working together, that compose the whole: public communication.

SPEAKING TO PERSUADE USING LOGICAL ARGUMENTS[1]

The following speech is offered as an example of a persuasive speech that incorporates logical arguments. The arguments used by the speaker are analyzed as the speech progresses to help you understand how they are incorporated. This speech was given by Alan D. Dufur in his speech class at Oklahoma State University at Stillwater, Oklahoma, on April 5, 1979.

Law School Blues

by Alan D. Dufur

Notice that the proposition of the speech is stated at the very beginning of the speech.

I am sure at one time or another you have heard someone say that lawyers are a bunch of crooks because of the high fees they charge the public; however, some considerations should be made before a statement of this kind is made. Lawyers have to overcome many barriers and spend great sums of time and money in the preparation for the practice of law. Not everyone is cut out for law school, and if you are thinking about it, I hope you really indulge in some soul searching.

This, then, is the claim of the argument.

Approximately one and a half years are needed to prepare for law school. The admission process to law school is certainly one of the largest barriers one must overcome to become a lawyer. To be admitted to law school, a person must meet the following requirements: (1) a four-year college degree, (2) a high grade-point average during undergraduate work, (3) good recommendations from others, and (4) a good LSAT score. The undergraduate degree, which is essential, does not have to be from any certain field or area of study. The grade point average which was merited while earning the degree is of great importance. A G.P.A. of approximately 3.2 on a 4.0 scale is generally needed even to be considered for admission to most law schools. Recommendations from others, not from your mother or friends but from employers, professors, and counselors, may be helpful when applicants are being selected.

This is the specific data for the claim. During the rest of the speech, the speaker explains and extends the data presented here.

The Law School Admission Test, or simply LSAT, is generally what "makes or breaks" the person who is applying for law school. The LSAT is an examination which takes a half day to be administered and is normally taken in the spring or summer semester of one's junior year. Many publications and other materials have been printed as an aid to help study for the exam. *The LSAT Handbook* is one such publication, and I would like to read its opening statement: "The Law School Admission Test probes your capacity to read, understand, and reason logically using a variety of verbal and quantitative material." In other words, it's a bunch of English and math.

This material is more informative than directly persuasive. Although interesting, it could have been omitted without

In order to comply with and make the correspondences required by most schools, an organization has been set up to handle most of the paper work involving grades and test scores. The Law School Data Assembly Service was organized for this purpose. The LSDAS *damaging the arguments.*

works as a liaison between the student and the law school which has been chosen by the applicant. The organization serves practically all of the 163 American Bar Association approved schools in America.

This is the second argument in support of the proposition of the speech.

A considerable amount of money is needed for the tuition and other expenses which are encountered by the law student. Law schools are just like most other institutions of higher learning in that the prices vary a great deal among schools. Of course, the private institutions are more expensive than the public. In addition, the tuition is normally greater than that required of an undergraduate degree.

This is the third argument that the speaker advances in support of the proposition. The sentence beginning with "Another change . . ." begins the fourth argument the speaker advances.

The biggest change for the new law student is to adjust to the work load. A law degree is usually set up on a three-year, ninety-hour program consisting of six semesters of a fifteen-hour schedule. Another change is found in the method of teaching. In most cases, the Socratic method of teaching is used. This method, which inherited its name from the great Greek philosopher Socrates, is where students are given raw, undistilled material, and they are expected to research and reason for themselves. The teacher is there only to make the students probe in the right direction. Library work is the mainstay of the law student, who is allowed very little or even no spare time during the first year of law school. The first-year student is generally introduced into classes of (1) Contracts, (2) Property, (3) Torts, which are cases involving personal injury, (4) Criminal Law, and (5) Civil Procedure. An interesting fact is that the dropout rate of first-year students is between 35 and 40 percent.

This is the fifth and final argument the speaker uses to support his proposition.

The testing procedure is also something a law student must become accustomed to. Usually only one examination is given per semester in each class. This test is normally a simple statement supplied by the instructor; then the student must supply both the questions and answers.

After the first year, things become a little more relaxed. Most courses after the initial year are electives, plus teaching tools like moot court are implemented. Moot court is an exercise which combines a student's research, writing, and speaking skills. A feeling of the court room is actually evident during moot court. During the third year of schooling, most students are able to participate in some sort of internship.

Upon completion of work and graduation, the law student will recieve his Juris Doctor Degree. Then the Bar Admission Test is in line for most students. The admission to the Bar is governed separately by each state, with the state usually administering a test to determine admis-

Now, the speaker states the warrant and restates the claim. Notice how the speaker has relied on a very relaxed, informative approach.

sion. Some states have a diploma privilege, which allows a student who has successfully graduated from an American Bar Association approved school to immediately be eligible to practice law in that state.

I hope from this presentation that you have become aware of the fact that lawyers "don't just get a degree." Maybe next time you hear somebody complaining about the cost of an attorney, you can give them an explanation of the time and work that the attorney had to forfeit in order to practice law.

Answers to Try This 1

1. a. *D*; b. *C*; c. *W*; 2. a. *C*; b *D*; c. *W*; 3. a. *W*; b. *C*; c. *D*

NOTE

[1]William D. Brooks, *Public Speaking* (Menlo Park, Calif. Benjamin/Cummings, 1980), pp. 168–170.

RESOURCES

Anderson, Lynn, and C. David Mortenson, "Logic and Marketplace Argumentation." *Quarterly Journal of Speech,* 50 (April 1967): 143–151.

Brembeck, Winston L., and William S. Howell, *Persuasion: A Means of Social Influence,* 2nd ed. Englewood Cliffs, N.J.: Prentice-Hall, 1976.

Brockriede, Wayne, and Douglas Ehninger, "Toulmin on Argument: An Interpretation and Application." *Quarterly Journal of Speech,* 46 (February 1960): 44–53.

Cronkhite, Gary, *Persuasion: Speech and Behavioral Change.* Indianapolis: Bobbs-Merrill, 1969.

Fisher, Walter R., and Edward M. Sayles, "The Nature and Functions of Argument," in *Perspectives on Argument,* eds., Gerald R. Miller and Thomas R. Nilsen. Chicago: Scott, Foresman, 1966, pp. 2–22.

Freeley, Austin J., *Argumentation and Debate: Rational Decision Making,* 3rd ed. Belmont, Calif.: Wadsworth, 1971.

Kahane, Howard, *Logic and Contemporary Rhetoric,* 2nd ed. Belmont, Calif.: Wadsworth, 1976.

Larson, Charles U., *Persuasion: Reception and Responsibility,* 2nd ed. Belmont, Calif.: Wadsworth, 1979.

McKerrow, Roy E., "Rhetorical Validity: An Analysis of Three Perspectives on the Justification of Rhetorical Argument," *Journal of the American Forensic Association,* 13, No. 3 (Winter 1977): 133–141.

Toulmin, Stephen, *The Uses of Argument.* Cambridge: Cambridge University Press, 1969.

Toulmin, Stephen, Richard Rieke, and Allen Janik, *An Introduction to Reasoning*. New York: Macmillan, 1979.

Windes, Russel R., and Arthur Hastings, *Argument and Advocacy*. New York: Random House, 1965.

Ziegelmueller, George, and Charles A. Dause, *Argumentation: Inquiry and Advocacy*. Englewood Cliffs, N.J.: Prentice-Hall, 1975.

fifteen

SPEAKING FOR SPECIAL OCCASIONS

Some Different Situations

Although you now have the basic components for putting a speech together and material on the two most common forms of speech (speeches to inform and speeches to persuade), you may face a variety of speech situations that have not been considered. Fortunately, most speech situations simply call for speakers to combine the basic elements in new ways. All communication has much in common; thus, a speaker familiar with the fundamentals can successfully and quickly adapt to special occasions.

While it would be impossible to discuss all special occasions in this chapter, several will be considered.[1] These are, among special occasions, some of the most important or, perhaps, frequent and obvious. One must remember that every speech occasion is original. None is exactly identical to any other. The successful speaker not only notices the nuances (differences) but also capitalizes on them. It is often the speaker's success in capitalizing on the differences—building on them and making them obvious—that makes a speech stand out as fresh, original, and exciting.

CONSIDER THIS

The man who may be everbody's favorite doctor never dissected a frog in med school, never made rounds as an intern, never even earned an M.D. degree. No matter. When Actor Alan Alda, 43, known to millions of televiewers as Army Captain Hawkeye Pierce of the Korean War–era 4077th Mobile Army Surgical Hospital (M*A*S*H), spoke at the Columbia University College of Physicians and Surgeons commencement last week, he was absolutely right in telling the class, "In some ways you and I are alike. We both study the human being. We both try to reduce suffering. We've both dedicated ourselves to years of hard work. And we both charge a lot." Alda, named an honorary member of P and S's 210th graduating class, also offered some heartfelt advice to the new doctors as they prepared to pick their way through "the minefield of existence." Excerpts:

Be skilled, be learned, be aware of the dignity of your calling. But please don't ever lose sight of your own simple humanity.

Unfortunately, that may not be so easy. You're entering a special place in our society. People will be awed by your expertise. You'll be placed in a position of privilege. You'll live well, people will defer to you, call you by your title, and it may be hard to remember that the word doctor is not actually your first name.

I ask of you, possess your skills, but don't be possessed by them. You are entering a very select group. You have a monopoly on medical care. Please be careful not to abuse this power that you have over the rest of us.

Put people first. And I include in that not just people, but that which exists *between* people. Let me challenge you. With all your study, you can read my X rays like a telegram. But can you read my involuntary muscles? Can you see the fear and uncertainty in my face? Will you tell me when you don't know what to do? Can you face your own fear, you own uncertainty? When in doubt, can you call in help?

Will you be the kind of doctor who cares more about the case than the person? ("Nurse, call the gastric ulcer and have him come in at three.") You'll know you're in trouble if you find yourself wishing they would mail in their liver in a plain brown envelope.

Where does money come on your list? Will it be the sole standard against which you reckon your success? Where will your family come on your list? How many days and nights, weeks and months, will you separate yourself from them, buried in your work, before you realize that you've removed yourself from an important part of your life? And if you're a male doctor, how will you relate to women? Women as patients, as nurses, as fellow doctors—and later as students?

Thank you for taking on the enormous responsibility that you have—and for having the strength to have made it to this day. I don't know how you've managed to learn it all. But there is one more thing you can learn about the body that only a non-doctor would tell you—and I hope you'll always remember this: the head bone is connected to the heart bone. Don't let them come apart.

Source: "A M*A*S*H Note for Docs," *Time,* May 28, 1979, p. 68. Courtesy of Time, Inc.

Whether or not a speech stands out depends on the speaker's ability to find and use creative material, to develop a warm, informal relationship with the audience, and to put into practice effective speaking techniques and practices. No matter the occasion, this is essential.[2] The following special occasions will be discussed: (1) introductory speeches, (2) presentations, (3) acceptances, (4) tributes, farewells, and eulogies, and (5) the speech of entertainment.

INTRODUCTORY SPEECHES

The speech of introduction is a very common type of speech. It is a special speech situation only because it differs from major types of speeches such as those to inform or persuade. It is often weak. Introducers forget the main purpose of the speech of introduction. Instead of (1) trying to get the attention of the audience, (2) building some anticipation of the speaker and topic to follow, (3) acquainting the audience with the speaker's credibility, and (4) presenting the speaker as a genuine human being, the introducer will try to be clever, demonstrate his or her own wealth of knowledge, embarrass the speaker, or talk for too long. In such cases, the introducer serves as a distraction and becomes counterproductive.

Here are some clear guidelines that will help introducers with their task and help guarantee a favorable audience attitude:

1. Keep your comments brief and to the point. The length of the introduction depends on the speaker and his or her credentials, the nature of the topic, and the demands of the situation. Just the same, thirty seconds to two minutes is the usual range. To keep your comments this short, *try to keep your own interest in talking subordinated to the interest of both the speaker and the audience.*

2. Make certain your comments are accurate. Remember, in many cases you are providing the audience with their first impression of this speaker. Knowing how important first impressions are, make sure you get the speaker's background correct. The kind of information that is usually covered includes:

   a. Present place of residence (and family information if appropriate and relevant)
   b. Present and past positions (jobs or offices held)
   c. Publications, research grants, research findings
   d. Memberships in organizations, clubs, honorary societies
   e. Listings in biographical reference works or references to speaker by other acknowledged experts (e.g., quotations from others)
   f. Personal investigations, travels, and experiences (include any special awards)
   g. Relationship to the audience (Are there some close connections?)

Since this material is highly factual, it is easy to make errors. Check your material carefully. Also, make no errors in pronunciation; check pronunciation of words beforehand. Secure the essential information far enough in advance of the occasion so that you can practice with it. Errors in pronunciation or errors in facts can be embarrassing for you, the speaker, and the audience. Above all else, get the name of the speaker correct.

3. Be sincere and genuine. Avoid any clowning around that might be embarrassing. Also, avoid excessive hyperbole. Praise that is genuine is far more appreciated than that which is overstated. Uncalled-for superlatives can prove very embarrassing for the speaker.

4. A brief reference to the occasion or to the importance of the topic is enough. Attempt to provide a link between speaker and audience without giving the speaker's speech yourself. One reference to the occasion or to the speaker's topic is usually enough. It is often useful, for example, for the audience to know why this person was selected to deliver this talk.

5. Try to plan the introductory remarks so that they build toward a climax—the actual mention of the topic and then, just before the speaker comes forward, the mention of the speaker's name. In this way, a strong mood or feeling of anticipation is created. The audience's curiosity is whetted.

6. Attempt to offer fresh ideas that are uncluttered by clichés and hackneyed phrases. Try to avoid overused phrases such as, "Our speaker tonight needs no introduction . . ." or "and now, without further ado . . ." It is easy to fall into such common phraseology because we hear it so often. Rather than think, people fall back on overused phrasing because it is easier.

7. If you anticipate the possibility of having to thank the speaker after the speech, or having to say a few words about the speech at its conclusion, be alert during the speech. Jot down any relevant ideas so that you can refer back to them. Do not just try to remember them. They are likely to be forgotten.

A speech of introduction may be written out beforehand by the person being introduced and then rewritten by the person doing the introduction. In this way the material the speaker wants in the introduction is certain to be given. This procedure is certainly within the right of the person being introduced and is often welcomed by the introducer.

Because of the highly factual nature of introductions, they are often delivered by manuscript. Pay attention to previous suggestions for the proper use of a manuscript. Remember that statements of praise and phrases designed to reveal your feelings for or attitude toward the speaker lose their potency and effect when read. These must appear to emanate spontaneously, freely, and sincerely.

TRY THIS 1

Plan a speech of introduction. Select some outstanding public figure and prepare an introduction for him or her. You serve as this person's advance agent; you should plan to sell him or her to your audience. Make certain that in your speech you are not only arousing curiosity about the speaker and the subject (you can decide what that subject is to be) but also generate respect for the speaker. Try to make certain that your audience will respond favorably to the message they are going to hear from the speaker. Make certain that your manner of speaking is suited to the nature of the situation you create, to your familiarity with the speaker, and to the speaker's prestige.

PRESENTATIONS

Presentations are another familiar type of special occasion speech. They are designed to accompany the presentation of a gift, award, or prize. They are usually made when a member of an organization is leaving because of a promotion, move, or retirement, or when a member of an organization has accomplished something outstanding: a publication, a new sales record, a high goal or feat, or a perfect attendance record. Presentation speeches usually offer a short, formal recognition of the accomplishment.

When speakers make presentations they usually accomplish three tasks. First, they talk about the nature and history of the award. Who is the donor? What are some of the reasons the award was originated? What are the criteria used for selection? What are the conditions under which the award is made? What are some of the names and accomplishments of other winners? Second, they discuss the qualifications and accomplishments of the recipient. General as well as specific accomplishments that relate to the award should be mentioned. If the award resulted from competition, how the person did in the competition can be discussed as well as how the person met the criteria of the award. Finally, presentations talk about the physical qualities of the award itself.

In preparing to give a presentation, the speaker should follow these suggestions:

1. Find out all you can about the award and the conditions under which such presentations are made.
2. Although an award may have a long history, be careful not to bore your audience with extensive lists of historical detail. Condense the historical material to reasonable length and interest.
3. Be certain to learn all you can about the recipient of the award:

   - What was done?
   - How were the criteria met?
   - How many contestants were there (if a contest was held)?
   - How was the contest judged (if a contest was held)?

4. Again, it is often best to allow the name of the recipient—whether known or not—to be left until last. If it is not known, it will be a surprise—much as the announcement of the winner of a beauty pageant. If known, the speech will still have some climactic building sense.
5. Avoid hyperbole. Excessive use of superlatives may result in a loss of sincerity.

6. When handing the award to the recipient, hold it in your left hand and put it to the left hand of the recipient. This will leave the right hand free for shaking hands and will avoid a great deal of confusion and possible embarrassment.

TRY THIS 2

Select one of the following situations and prepare a speech of presentation that centers on the situation chosen:

- You are the employer and must award a diamond stickpin to an employee who has just completed thirty years' service with your company.
- You are a Scout leader and must award waterproof matchboxes to those Scouts who sold the most products in your latest fund–raising drive.
- You are a university president and must award an honorary degree to an outstanding local citizen at commencement.
- You are a sportswriter and have been asked to present a trophy to an outstanding athlete.
- You are the president of a local civic group and must present a statue of a local luminary to the community.

Make certain your presentation is well–suited to the audience, the donor, the purpose of the meeting, the recipient of the gift, the gift itself, and you as the speaker. Make your talk brief (three to five minutes at most). In your speech tell why the presentation is being made, express the satisfaction felt by the donor in making the presentation, and, finally, make the actual presentation.

ACCEPTANCES

Some speakers take a long time to learn it; others never seem to learn it: the best kind of thank you in the world is a simple "Thank you." When a presentation is made, an acceptance speech is often expected. The speech of acceptance is made in response to a presentation. Brief thanks are appropriate—if they are brief. Not to offer a thank you of any kind may appear rude, discourteous, even self–centered. In any case, a thank you is expected.

The acceptance speech usually has two functions: (1) to thank the person, group, or organization responsible for the award or gift, and (2) to recognize any others who have helped or who share in the honor. The most important key is to keep it short. Brevity is expected with speeches of acceptance. Not to be brief automatically rubs audience members the wrong way because it counters their expectations. Appropriateness may be another problem—particularly when an acceptor uses the opportunity to launch into one of his or her personal crusades. The effective acceptance speech usually shows appreciation, reveals pride and humility, and indicates determination to live up to or fulfill the expectations that accompany the honor.

On occasions where more than a mere thank you is required, the acceptance speaker should consider any of the following additional materials:

1. Admiration of and appreciation for the gift or honor
2. Expression of appreciation for the kindness of friends, associates, or supporters
3. Minimization, though not depreciation, of one's own contribution, service, or merit in the effort
4. Recognition of the cooperation and participation of others who also share in the gift or honor

The brief address could also include reference to personal experience. The difficulties encountered could be described. When possible, however, the speaker should avoid self–glorification. When referring to personal successes, the speaker should attribute those to the assistance obtained from others. Paying tribute to those who assisted is always appropriate.

The acceptance speaker can also refer to the gift or honor itself:

1. What does it mean beyond its intrinsic worth or practical use?
2. Does it inspire him or her to accomplish anything more or new in the future?
3. What does it symbolize with respect to past association, present aspirations, or future ideals?

It is important that speakers in such situations not depreciate the gift, themselves, or the donor.[3]

TRY THIS 3

Prepare a speech of acceptance. Assume you have just received a gift in a public presentation. Now you must appropriately express your appreciation. The gift is a scholarship that fully covers books, living expenses, and tuition for all your remaining years of formal schooling. It was given to you by a benevolent, unknown donor. Adapt your speech to the audience, the occasion, and the gift itself. Think about the nature of a speech of presentation that would be appropriate for presenting this gift to you, and adapt your speech of acceptance to that type of presentation. It is likely that the mood established by the presenter will be solemn and dignified, thus your speech should likewise be solemn and dignified. In your speech, try to express appreciation for the gift, minimize your own accomplishments and magnify those of others who have assisted you (including teachers), pay tribute to the benevolence of the donor, and conclude your acceptance speech by accepting the gift.

TRIBUTES, FAREWELLS, AND EULOGIES

We have grouped these three speeches because they are similar in nature. All three are usually designed to praise another's accomplishments. This occurs when someone has a birthday, takes a new office, leaves for another office, retires, or dies. The only difference between these speeches and a presentation is that in a presentation an award or gift is offered. In the case of a death, the speech given is called a eulogy: a speech of high praise.

In tributes, farewells, and eulogies, the emphasis is not on the content of the effort—as it is in a speech of introduction—it is on the mood or feeling created. The atmosphere is conveyed by the spirit of the speaker. The spirit, in general, should be one of sincerity.

CONSIDER THIS

The speakers, too, seemed to have caught the commencement fever. They spoke as if the ceremony were launching new battleships made out of the new gray matter. They broke their vintage bottles across the brows of the assembled, and allowed their favorite thoughts to bubble over.

With a sense of urgency, they poured last-minute knowledge into the ears of their students, trying to catch them while they were still hot, still thinking, still incomplete.

SOURCE: Ellen Goodman, "Graduation—A Higher Learning Plateau." © 1979, The Boston Globe Newspaper Company/Washington Post Writers Group, reprinted with permission.

These speeches have as their overall function three goals:

1. The speaker should provide praise for the person's qualities and for his or her specific achievements.
2. The speaker should express appreciation for the contribution that the person has made. He or she can also indicate the sense of loss that is felt.
3. Finally, in a tribute or farewell, the speaker can wish the person success in his or her new job or happiness in any future pursuits—perhaps retirement.

Excessive hyperbole can have a negative effect. The speaker should attempt to maintain a sense of objectivity. It is important that a person receive the proper credit for accomplishments and achievements, but it is also important that this be done honestly and sincerely.

TRY THIS 4

Rather than offering a tribute, farewell, or eulogy for someone else, *you* provide a speech of farewell because of your own transfer. You are leaving the employ of this company to move to another company in another locality. You are now to express publicly your regret at leaving. This takes place at a farewell dinner. Your speech should cover the following points:

1. You should express genuine regret about leaving. Tell why you are reluctant to leave. Talk about the enjoyment you have received from your work, and briefly mention your pleasant associations with other members of the group. Recall any happy or outstanding experiences. Indicate that you will take many pleasant memories with you. Do not ramble.

2. You should let the group know that you hold them in high esteem. This is your genuine expression of how much you have profited from your association with a group of such high merit and quality.

3. You should try to predict future cordial relations. Indicate that you plan to maintain contact, that the friendships established in the past will continue, and that you anticipate seeing many of your listeners at conferences and conventions in the future. Invite listeners to visit you when passing through your new community.

4. You should conclude your brief address by wishing the group farewell. Make this step especially brief and to the point. Do not drag out your final expressions of goodbye. Try not to rely on the cliché "Goodbye and God bless you," but if nothing else occurs to you, or if you have nothing else to say, you may use this phrase.

TANK McNAMARA by Jeff Millar and Bill Hinds. Copyright, 1978, Universal Press Syndicate. Reprinted with permission. All rights reserved.

THE SPEECH OF ENTERTAINMENT

The speech that is most often associated with entertainment is the after-dinner speech, a speech that is generally short, genial, and humorous. The after-dinner speech is generally delivered to an audience in a mood to be entertained. It is, as a speech type, a widely used special occasion speech. Since it is one type of humorous speech, I will discuss humor in general. An informative or persuasive speech may make use of humor just as all speeches may have entertaining elements.[4] In these instances, many of the suggestions in this section will be appropriate. The goal of the speech of entertainment is to get the audience to relax in a lighthearted and enjoyable atmosphere. This is accomplished through elaborate and extensive audience analysis. It may be helpful if the reader who is planning a humorous speech goes back and rereads Chapter 4, "Analyzing the Audience: Idea Adaptation," at this time. It provides an approach or process for getting at the kinds of information essential for making an entertaining speech relevant, appropriate, and on the mark.

Certain characteristics are usually associated with the speech to entertain. The first is humor. We suggest that any use of humor be appropriate for the speaker, audience, and occasion, and that it be relevant to the topic and material, that it be fresh as opposed to stale and cliché–ridden. Beyond these suggestions, the entertaining speech should show the following elements.

Energy and enthusiasm. A speaker confined to a manuscript may not be natural and spontaneous. Fresh, enthusiastic animation often results from an extemporaneous style of delivery.

"I don't think a speaker should crack up over his own jokes."

Examples and stories. A speaker using this form of speech should depend on illustrations, humorous anecdotes, and unique experiences. Those that work best result from the personal experiences of the speaker. In this way, there is more assurance that the material will be fresh, original, and well understood.

Organization. The entertaining speech is easy to follow. One commonly used format is simply a string of examples or anecdotes organized or oriented around a central theme.

Brevity. A complex organizational scheme should be avoided. The speaker should develop only one or, at most, two main points. Maintaining control of the organization and number of points to be covered helps attain succinctness. Remember that attention spans are short and audience expectations are often clear: Brevity is much appreciated.

CONSIDER THIS

Far too many after-dinner orations bear out the wry truth of Ambrose Bierce's definition of a "lecturer" as a man "with his hand in your pocket, his tongue in your ear, and his faith in your patience."

SOURCE: From STRICTLY PERSONAL by Sydney J. Harris. © 1979 Field Enterprises, Inc. Courtesy of Field Newspaper Syndicate.

The speaker may want to plan several convenient and possible stopping points for his or her speech. If the program goes on too long or if audience members become restless or bored, the speaker can end the presentation early. Such alertness reflects the competence and skill of the speaker.

Responsiveness. A speaker bent on entertainment should seek an immediate response from the audience. He or she needs to capitalize on the moment. This requires careful listening to audience members before the speech, careful and alert observation to the whole situation, and a sensitivity to current, local issues, and circumstances.

Planning. The after–dinner speech must be thoroughly planned and rehearsed. One cannot allow it to result just from the mood and temperament of the moment. This is true of most humorous speeches. It is through prior thought and planning that charm in the humorous speech is revealed. The speaker does not hesitate or grope for ideas and words. Despite the extensive planning, however, the speaker must also allow for spontaneity. Plans can be made to play off the immediate situation!

Informality. A relationship between the audience and the speaker must be established. This is unlikely to occur in a rigid, formal situation. Thus, the speaker's language and delivery must be easy, comfortable, and relaxed. A successful speech of entertainment is likely to result in a feeling of informality.

Speakers must take care not to transform themselves into entertainers or comics. At this point—when the transformation occurs—speakers sacrifice their position as speakers. Listeners also become more demanding, as they think of speakers who have made such a transformation as entertainers, not speakers. They begin to react as a nightclub or television audience would, demanding polished and clever material. If speakers want to be entertainers, they should get agents and pursue that goal. If they want to be humorous speakers, they should remember to work humor into their speeches and not speech into their humor.

It was stated that humor can be used in any speech situation. It was also suggested that the after-dinner speech is the type of special occasion speech in which humor often assumes a prominent role. We failed to mention that the after-dinner speech may also be serious in nature. A few suggestions may help the speaker who is facing this situation. First, it should be realized that many of the suggestions for speaking outlined earlier in this book become relevant. Second, the nature of the after-dinner audience must be understood. It is usually comfortable and relaxed, just as you often are after completing a big meal. Because of informal conversation and a feeling of conviviality, a friendly ingroup feeling occurs. Also, with the engagement of the digestive system, which functions at peak capacity following a meal, the other mental and physical bodily functions are diminished in their efficiency. Thus, people are often less able to follow a complex, logical argument, a series of serious, rational lines of thinking, or a string of dull, unrelated statistics. Not only do they tend to be mentally inefficient they are often more mentally prepared for a vivid, sparkling, interesting speech with some entertainment inherent in it.

A serious after-dinner speech must not drag. As a matter of fact, the speaker must depend far more on attention-holding devices than in the normal, serious speech. He or she might need:

Additional illustrations and analogies
Relevant and interesting humor sprinkled throughout
Strong enthusiasm and energy to counter sluggishness
Feelings of warmth, closeness, and congeniality
An atmosphere of sincerity and honesty

A speech of this type in this situation must not become heavy-handed, long, and unbearable. To attempt to give a serious speech in an after-dinner format will counter audience expectations as well as cultural prescription; thus, the speaker who plans such a speech begins by facing rather ominous odds.

TRY THIS 5

Prepare an entertaining after-dinner speech. Plan your speech to meet a six-to eight-minute time format. In your use of humor, do not embarrass anyone in your audience, poke a little fun at yourself, avoid off-color humor, be brief, be enjoyable, use only relevant humor, try to avoid stale material, and strive for a variety of materials —stories, puns, anecdotes, and personal experiences. Keep your speech organization sufficiently flexible so that you can be spontaneous—making on-the-spot adaptations as necessary. Be sure that you plan your speech well, rehearse it, and make certain that it is appropriate for you, the audience, and the occasion. Strive to prepare a speech that possesses charm in both content and presentation.

SUMMARY

The chapter began by pointing out that *all* speech occasions contain ingredients that stand out as unusual and relevant to that particular combination of audience, situation, speaker, and material. They are unique in that in no way could that particular combination be re-created. But there are also special speech occasions that have not been previously discussed in this textbook and that do occur rather frequently in society. As a speaker you do not need to begin from scratch to prepare for such occasions; you can build on what you have already learned.

The first special occasion speech discussed was the introductory speech, calculated to get the attention of the audience, build some anticipation of the speaker and topic, acquaint the audience with the speaker's credibility, and present the speaker as a genuine human being. The introductory speaker should keep his or her comments brief, make certain the comments are accurate, be sincere and genuine, make a brief reference to the occasion or to the importance of the topic, try to build toward a climax, offer fresh ideas, and anticipate having to thank the speaker after his or her speech.

The second special occasion speech discussed was the presentation speech, designed to accompany the presentation of a gift, award, or prize. To be able to talk about the nature and history of the award, discuss the qualifications and accomplishments of the recipient, and the physical qualities of the award, a speaker must find out all he or she can about the award and the conditions under which such a presentation is made, keep the historical material brief, know as much as possible about the recipient of the award, try to build to a climax, and finally, avoid hyperbole.

The third special occasion speech discussed was the acceptance speech. Brevity here is essential. Basically, this speech should serve two purposes: (1) to thank the person, group, or organization responsible for the award or gift, and (2) to recognize any others who have helped or who share the honor. But if more than this is necessary, the acceptance speaker can admire and appreciate the gift or honor, express appreciation for the kindness of friends and associates, minimize his or her own contribution, and recognize others who share in the gift or honor.

The fourth section discussed tributes, farewells, and eulogies. These are all designed to praise another's accomplishments. The best praise occurs in situations where the mood is right. Three goals for these speeches were offered: (1) praise for the person's qualities or specific achievements, (2) appreciation for the contribution that the person made, and finally, (3) a wish for the person to succeed in his or her new job or for happiness in future pursuits or in retirement.

The final kind of special occasion speech discussed in the chapter was the speech to entertain. It is the form often used for the after-dinner speech. The speech to entertain should reflect energy, examples, organization, brevity, responsiveness, planning, and informality. The chapter ended by suggesting that the after-dinner speech can also be serious, but that if it is, it should include additional illustrations and analogies, relevant and interesting humor, strong enthusiasm and energy, feelings of warmth, closeness, and congeniality, and, finally, an atmosphere of sincerity and honesty.

Although it is not possible to enumerate all the special occasions that speakers may encounter or to make suggestions to help speakers face all these occasions, if the reader has read and digested the material in previous chapters, it is likely he or she will be prepared to be flexible and able to adapt to meet changing occasions. It is our belief that the more information one has, the more options one has. However, the essential qualities of all public communication should never be forgotten: clearness, distinctness, and easy audibility. Thus, the goal has been to provide a broad, comprehensive base for looking at and understanding public communication.

NOTES

[1]For more information on speeches for special occasions, see W. Hayes Yeager, *Effective Speaking for Every Occasion* (Englewood Cliffs, NJ: Prentice-Hall, 1940); Robert G. King, *Forms of Public Address* (Indianapolis: Bobbs-Merrill, 1969), pp. 58–128; and Ralph Borden Culp, *Basic Types of Speech* (Dubuque, Iowa: Wm. C. Brown, 1968), pp. 59–101.

[2]For sources of sample special occasion speeches, see Goodwin F. Berquist, Jr., *Speeches for Illustration and Example* (Glenview, Il: Scott, Foresman, 1965); Wil A. Linkugel, R. R. Allen, and Richard L. Johannesen, *Contemporary American Speeches: A Sourcebook of Speech Forms and Principles*, 4th ed. (Dubuque, Iowa: Kendall/Hunt, 1978); Glenn R. Capp, *Famous Speeches in American History* (Indianapolis: Bobbs-Merrill, 1963); and Bower Aly and Lucille Folse Aly, eds., *American Short Speeches: An Anthology* (New York: Macmillan, 1968).

[3]Donald C. Bryant and Karl R. Wallace, *Fundamentals of Public Speaking*, 5th ed. (New York: Prentice-Hall, 1976), pp. 378–379.

[4]Research has indicated that if a speaker is thought to be humorless and aloof, using humor may enhance his or her rating of competence. David R. Mettee, Edward S. Hrelec, and Paul C. Wilkens, "Humor as an Interpersonal Asset and Liability," *Journal of Social Psychology*, 85 (October 1971), 51–64. For additional material on humor, the reader should see Dorothy Markiewicz, "Effects of Humor on Persuasion," *Sociometry*, 37 (September 1974), 407–422.

APPENDICES

Sample Speeches

INFORMATIVE SPEECHES

VITAMINS—TAKE THEM OR LEAVE THEM[1]

(I started my speech by popping some vitamins in my mouth. I held up the vitamin samples and asked the class,) How many of you, when cold season comes around, pop a Vitamin C pill or when your sex life seems to be lagging, reach for a Vitamin E with the added hope that it will ward off heart disease? How many take some kind of vitamin because of poor eating habits? Every day, millions of Americans—including my father, friends, and celebrities, whose livelihoods depend on youthfulness and good health—are downing doses far greater than the recommended daily allowances. Foods can and do supply most Americans with adequate nutrients, and consumers should not expect any major physical benefits from multivitamin pills. I want to answer these questions during my speech: (1) What are vitamins? (2) Do we really need to take vitamins? (3) Is there any possible harm in taking excessive amounts of vitamins?

(Transition) Vitamins are essential to human life, but their true role in the body and in nutrition is often misunderstood. So what are vitamins?

According to Dr. Robert Giller in an article from *Mademoiselle,* "Everyone has to determine their vitamin needs according to their own eating habits." One of the reasons that all of us eat good nutritious food is to get the correct vitamins and minerals. Whoever depends on good health should not rely solely on unlimited prescriptions of vitamins. Vitamins are essential for good health, but taking them in excessive amounts is unnecessary and can be harmful.

From the book, *Realities of Nutrition* by Ronald M. Deutsch, "Vitamins are organic compounds necessary in small amounts in the diet for the normal growth and maintenance of life of humans. In today's health-conscious society, how many of us believe that vitamins give you "pep" and "energy"?

Vitamins do *not* provide energy nor do they construct or build any part of the body. Vitamins are needed for transforming foods into energy and for body maintenance. There are thirteen or more of them, and if any are missing, a deficiency disease becomes apparent. Vitamins are similar because they are made of the same elements; carbon, hydrogen, oxygen, and sometimes nitrogen. They are different in that their elements are arranged differently and each vitamin performs one or more specific function in the body.

Did all of you know that the majority of vitamins consumed including all the B vitamins and every bit of vitamin C are the kind that dissolve in water? That means once your body takes out its tiny daily requirements of these expensive chemicals, all the rest goes bubbling out in your urine. On any given day there are more vitamins in the sewers and septic tanks of America than in the drugstores.

Of course, there are a few vitamins that cannot be dissolved in water. They are stored in our body fat for use later. They include vitamins like vitamin A, vitamin D, and vitamin E. These are probably the most promoted, most exploited, most profitable, and least understood of all vitamin substances.

It is possible that some of us here need help in terms of vitamin supplementation, and some of us might need more help than others. But we should not look for good health to happen overnight; modifying our diet and vitamin intake is an ongoing process. *(I held up the poster of U.S. Recommended Daily Allowances of vitamins and then explain the functions of vitamins.)*

How many of you know what function each of the vitamins has for our bodies? When adequately supplied, vitamin A helps to maintain healthy skin, hair, and nails. It is especially crucial to healthy vision. According to *FDA Consumer,* anyone of us could go for at least three months without consuming any vitamin A whatsoever, since a quarter year's supply is already stored in the liver. The average adult needs 5000 IUs [International Units] of vitamin A a day.

How many of you know that vitamin B_1(thiamin) is essential for the proper functioning of the central nervous system? Thiamin also helps in carbohydrate metabolism, growth, maintaining appetite and good digestion. The FDA states that 1.5 milligrams of thiamin per day is the RDA, which is the recommended daily allowance.

Vitamin B_2(riboflavin) helps the body obtain energy from carbohydrates and protein substances. It is necessary for healthy skin and eye tissue. The RDA that we should have is 1.7 milligrams. Milk and milk products contribute about half of the riboflavin consumed in the U.S.

According to *FDA Consumer,* niacin lowers the serum cholesterol in our bodies, but it also tends to keep the blood from clotting too easily and increases the oxygen-carrying capacity of red blood cells. The RDA for an adult is 20 milligrams.

Vitamin B_6 is important in red-blood-cell formation and in production of hormones in the central nervous system. It is also involved in many stages of protein metabolism. The RDA is 2.0 milligrams for an adult.

Do all of you know that a common belief about vitamin B_{12} is that the old "rundown feeling" can easily be overcome by vitamin B_{12} supplements? Vitamin B_{12} is necessary for the normal development of red blood cells and the functioning of all cells. The U.S. RDA of vitamin B_{12} is 6 micrograms.

All of us should know these things about vitamin C: It helps hold body cells together and strengthens blood vessels; it helps heal wounds; it helps tooth and bone formation; and it helps us resist infection. It is also known that vitamin C does not cure or prevent colds. The claim that vitamin C lessens the number and severity of colds remains controversial. The RDA of vitamin C is 60 milligrams per day.

How many of you were told when you were little to drink your milk—that it is good for you? Well, that was because you needed to have your vitamin D. Vitamin D is an important vitamin because it regulates the calcium and phosphorus metabolism of the body. It is also necessary for bone growth. The U.S. RDA of 400 International Units per day is best met by drinking fortified milk. Exposure to sunlight probably ensures vitamin D adequacy for an adult, which I get when I go to Florida for spring break.

How many of you have heard that vitamin E will help you grow hair, cure your skin problems, prevent ulcers, and make you sexually young? These are just a few of the claims made for vitamin E. But there is no scientific evidence that vitamin E will do any of the dramatic things that are being claimed for it. Its chief function is as an antioxidant that helps to prevent oxygen from destroying other substances and thus acts as a preservative. The RDA of vitamin E is 30 International Units for an adult.

Do all of you know that there are two forms of vitamin supplements: synthetic and "natural" vitamins? According to the book, *Mega-Nutrients for Your Nerves,* synthetic vitamins are produced in the laboratory according to formulas exactly the same as found in nature. "Natural" vitamins are derived from their natural sources. The body cannot tell the difference between the two forms of vitamins. Everyone can get the same benefits from either source.

(Transition) Getting enough vitamins is essential to life, although the body has no nutritional use for excess vitamins. Do we really need to take them?

Everybody needs vitamins. They play an indispensable role in millions of everyday chemical reactions that occur in the body. Every important event, from digestion to reproduction to reading to walking, requires one vitamin or another. If all of us were to eat a diet totally lacking in vitamins, our life expectancy would be measured in weeks.

In an ever-changing environment in which our bodies are exposed to smog, radiation, birth-control pills, and alcohol, it is best to supplement our meals with vitamins. A balanced diet which generally meets the U.S. RDA requirements for vitamins A, B_1, B_2, C, and D will nearly always provide the needed amounts of other vitamins.

Do you have high blood pressure? Do you have diabetes or high blood sugar? Do you have a tendency toward depression? Do you have an ulcer or any digestive problem that could be aggravated by large doses of vitamins? Are you taking any drugs (such as antidepressants) that might be affected by your vitamin intake? These questions have to be asked if you are seriously considering taking high dosages of vitamins. Find a nutritionist or knowledgeable doctor with whom you can discuss your medical history and be sure it is safe to take them.

(*Transition*) All of us in search of good health are taking vitamins in ever-increasing amounts. What is the harm?

The dangers of self-medication should be well known to everyone. Self-treatment with large amounts of vitamins may be a risky business. From the book *The Great Vitamin Hoax*, too much vitamin D can cause nausea, weight loss, weakness, excessive urination, and the more serious conditions of hypertension and calcification of soft tissues, including the blood vessels and kidneys. Bone deformities and multiple fractures are also common. Vitamin A can be toxic in high doses and people who self-medicate with this compound risk severe liver damage. The water-soluble vitamins C and B, however, cannot be stored in the body and any excess is simply passed out. So, if any of you are taking vitamins, be sure that you know how much you are taking. Why take excessive amounts of them when you do not need them?

(*Transition*) We owe it to ourselves to learn much more about these vitamins before we accept them as nutrients and/or medicaments.

For those of you who are wasting time, money and energy by popping pills in excessive amounts you should be eating a good nutritious meal instead. Believing that these vitamins can cure "tiredness," "lack of pep," sexual impotence, and a thousand other self-diagnosed conditions by excessive popping is sheer madness!

CAFFEINE[2]

A can of cola, a cup of coffee, and a cup of tea (*Holds each one up*). These three beverages all have one thing in common, they all contain caffeine. Caffeine, as described by H. Leon Abrams in *Consumer Research Magazine*, is a powerful stimulant which acts on the central nervous system and can become habit-forming. Today, I'd like to talk to you about what caffeine does to your central nervous system, show you through examples of why we should cut down on our intake of it, and give you a few possible alternatives to try.

Let's start by looking at where caffeine comes from and what it is doing to your central nervous system.

As stated in *Consumer Research Magazine*, caffeine comes in three forms: the kola bean, the coffee bean, and tea leaves. Kola beans come from a tree native to tropical Africa and are now commercially grown in many tropical regions. People in Africa get a caffeine lift from chewing these beans. Coffee beans are also native to Africa and were introduced into Europe during the seventeenth century. The tea plant originated in China and tea drinking was introduced into Europe during the early sixteenth century. Tea soon became the major stimulating drug beverage in England and America until the time of the Boston Tea Party, when the Americans became so mad at England that they switched from drinking tea to drinking coffee.

Now, before I show you how caffeine affects your system, I'd like to show you how much caffeine is in certain beverages and foods. Coffee and tea each have about 100 to 150 milligrams of caffeine per 8-ounce serving, while cola drinks have 42 milligrams of caffeine per 12-ounce serving. Hot cocoa has 26 milligrams of caffeine per 6-ounce serving, and an ounce of chocolate has between 3 and 19 milligrams of caffeine *(All compared on a chart shown to the class)*. The amount of caffeine in coffee and tea varies with the way in which it is prepared; brewed coffee or tea has more caffeine than instant.

Dr. Melvin E. Page stated in an article in *Consumer Research Magazine* that he has been studying the causes, cures, and preventions of degenerative diseases for over forty years. He has found caffeine to be a factor in causing degenerative diseases such as heart trouble and circulatory disease such as high blood pressure, arthritis, and cancer.

Many people state that they drink coffee for the taste, yet give them some decaffeinated coffee and they say that they don't like the taste. What these people are really saying is that the decaffeinated coffee doesn't give them the lift that regular coffee does. These people have become dependent on a constant intake of caffeine without realizing it. Also, many beverages that contain caffeine also contain either sugar or an artificial sweetener, which is also disrupting to the normal body chemistry. An article in *Consumer Research Magazine* spoke of a lady who drank eighteen cups of coffee a day and suffered from severe swelling in her feet. When she quit drinking coffee the swelling went down. Later she started to drink ice tea and the swelling returned. When she quit drinking the ice tea the swelling went down again. She had suffered severe pain from this swelling for ten years until her doctor finally realized that it was the caffeine she had been drinking that caused her illness.

In an experiment done by the Department of Pharmacology at Stanford University, researchers selected thirty-eight housewives who drank coffee and eighteen housewives who didn't drink coffee. The eighteen who didn't drink coffee were divided into two groups. The first group was given regular coffee; these ladies showed feelings of nervousness, became jittery, and occasionally suffered from an upset stomach. The second group was given decaffeinated coffee and showed no side effects. The thirty-eight housewives who did drink coffee were at first given decaffeinated coffee, they all became very irritable; then when they were given regular coffee they all reported feeling perked up and fine.

Now, in the report given by Dr. Page you've seen that caffeine is damaging to your health and in the experiment with the housewives you've seen how it can upset your central nervous system. Let's now take a look at some possible alternatives.

As far as stimulants go, caffeine is the most harmless; that is, it takes a large dose of caffeine to affect the body, yet in time it will. I feel that Americans should decrease their intake of cola, coffee, and tea, thus reducing their intake of caffeine. In the morning, instead of grabbing that one cup of coffee you need to get you going, why not try getting down on the floor and doing some good old morning exercises. According to Dr. Albert Marchetti, in an article in *Science Digest,* a good way to overcome fatigue or drowsiness is by physical exercise, thereby bringing the energy reserves to a higher level. Later in the day, if you are going to the library to study and feel the need for a can of Coke, why not try going to the Recreation Center for an hour or so and doing a little swimming or running a few laps around the track. Now, if that bit of swimming isn't enough to get you through those long hours at the library, then when you start to feel low again, why not go into the bathroom and splash some cold water on your face. That will wake you up a bit. Granted, it may mess up the make-up a bit, but what the heck are you in the library for, to study or to impress someone?

These ideas can work and we should try them if we want to take good care of our bodies.

To give you an example of how these ideas work, I thought I'd try them myself. Last night at about 2:00 A.M., while I was working on this speech, I started to feel a little tired. Before I came home, I had bought a can of Coke, because I don't drink coffee, and Coke helps me to stay awake. Believe me, many a morning it was that cold can of Coke that got me moving. Instead of drinking my Coke, however, I decided to run around the block a couple of times; I never claimed to be sane. It really did make me feel better. Then this morning, after only four hours of sleep—and believe me, I am the original eight-to-ten-hour sleeper—I got up and before taking my shower I tried some exercises. Besides the fact that I smoke and am totally out of shape, it did make me feel more alert and ready to start my day. My can of Coke is still home in my refrigerator.

I've given you some alternatives to the caffeine crutch. Let's see how we can make them work for us.

Being students here, we are all entitled to use the Recreation Center. Why not stop over there today before you start studying? Or why not try the morning exercises? I think they will help. Tell me, do you want to increase your chances of degenerative disease or do you want to have your central nervous system so messed up that you can't even hold a paper still because of your dependence on caffeine? Americans have enough vices, let's not make it one more, okay? Let's give those poor vending machines a break. Take that can of cola, that cup of coffee, or that cup of tea, and toss them into the nearest waste basket. *(Throws each into the waste basket.)*

NOTES

[1]This speech was given by Joanne Georgy in her speech class at Bowling Green State University, Bowling Green, Ohio, on February 18, 1980, and is used here with her permission.

[2]This speech was given by Kathy Dewenter in her speech class at Bowling Green State University, Bowling Green, Ohio, on February 13, 1980, and is used here with her permission.

B

PROPOSITION OF VALUE

Persuasive Speeches

VIOLENT CARTOONS[1]

Purpose Statement: Excessive viewing of violent cartoons causes increased aggression and confusion between reality and fantasy in children; therefore, parents should set guidelines and offer alternatives for television viewing.

Introduction

ATTENTION I. Every Saturday morning, the average American child sits in front of the television, entranced by cartoons.

      II. Most cartoons that children watch are violent ones, which make up 71 percent of the Saturday morning commercial programs.

STATISTICS   A. In 1971, cartoons had as many as thirty-four violent incidents per hour.

        B. In a typical five-minute cartoon, starring The Roadrunner and The Coyote, seven violent acts occurred.

     III. My purpose is to tell you of two major problems this viewing of violent cartoons has caused and what parents, and we as future parents, should do to counter these problems.

Body

NEED   I. The first major problem is that excessive viewing of violent cartoons causes increased aggression in children.

        A. This is because all children learn to cope with the world through imitation; thus, they naturally imitate the actions of cartoon characters, too.

REASONING   1. For instance, a child may imitate Tweetie Bird, a hero, as he uses violence to obtain goals.

AUTHORITIES   2. Albert Bandura and Gerald Lesser, psychologists, confirmed the fact that by watching televised models children learn socially undesirable and desirable behavior.

        B. The more children are exposed to aggression, the more hostile they become in interactions.

STATISTICS   1. Dr. Stein and Dr. Friedrich (Pennsylvania State University) found a marked difference between effects of violent and nonviolent programs in their study.

STATISTICS   2. In 1970, a government study of TV habits of 400 boys (ages nine to twelve) found that the more violence a boy is exposed to, the more likely he is to resort to violence and to suggest violent solutions to problems.

AUTHORITY   3. Similarly, in 1968, the Eisenhower Commission found that male and female preschoolers can and do learn aggressive behavior from cartoons.

(Besides cartoon violence causing increased aggression, there is another problem.)

NEED   II. Children have difficulty distinguishing between the reality and fantasy of cartoons.

        A. Cartoon violence appears harmless.

REASONING   1. Characters are not permanently damaged.

            2. Grief, pain, and injury are absent.

        B. A child's comprehension and logic are limited.

AUTHORITY   1. Dr. Albert Solnit explained: "Children under the age of six are more vulnerable to being confused because their sense of reality . . . their ability to use what we call orderly causal thinking is not as available to them developmentally until they are about six or seven."

STATISTICS   2. An experiment by Lyle and Hoffman with first-, sixth-, and tenth-grade students revealed the confusion.

            a. 50% of the first-graders believed that the TV characters were "just like" people they knew.

            b. Older children were skeptical but believed that they were alike most of the time.

REASONING   C. The violent means used on fantasy cartoons are contrary to the real world, and unless someone explains the difference, children grow up confused.

(So far, I have shown that viewing violent cartoons increases aggression and distorts reality.)

SATISFAC-III. Therefore, parents must acknowledge these problems and take
TION measures to reduce them.
REASONING A. Select the cartoons with the children, according to their levels of understanding and the amount of violence in the cartoons.
B. Regulate viewing time consistently.
C. Be near the TV in order to answer any questions the children may have about the cartoon.
D. Provide alternatives to viewing that are more realistic, creative, and nonaggressive in nature.
VISUAL- E. Write letters of complaint to the networks, directors, or sponsors.
IZATION IV. Parents should put these suggestions into action.
A. If they do so, the children will be better able to cope with the
REASONING fantasy and aggression of cartoons.
B. If the problems are ignored, children will grow up confused and believe that violence is acceptable and effective.

Conclusion

ACTION I. Cartoons do not have to be banned, but they should not be taken too lightly, either.
II. We, as future parents, need to realize the importance of cartoons.
A. John Murray, Ph.D., stated that "television can be considered a window on the world, a school if you will, through which a child first perceives his society and then learns from repeated examples to cope with the vicissitudes of living."
B. Therefore, if cartoons are making a child's transition into adulthood an unhealthy one by presenting fantasy and aggression, we must counter these problems by setting guidelines and offering alternatives.

SEXUAL HARASSMENT: THE BOSS'S FILTHY LITTLE PREROGATIVE IS FINALLY BEING EXPOSED[2]

In Los Angeles, supermarket checker Hallie Edwards walked into a storeroom to find her manager exposing himself and groping for her breasts. After Edwards complained, the chain promoted her boss and transferred her.

In Cambridge, Massachusetts, college freshman Helene York went to her Harvard professor's office looking for research help. Instead, she found an instructor determined to kiss her.

In New York, typist Doreen Romano's boss offered her a raise if she slept with him. When she refused, he fired her.

It can be as subtle as a look or as direct as a pinch. It can be found in executive offices, in army barracks, or on college campuses. It is primarily a man's problem, an exercise of power, for which women pay with their jobs, or worse yet, their health. Sexual harassment, the boss's filthy little prerogative, is finally being exposed.

I'm not going to ask those of you who have been sexually harassed to raise your hands, although I bet that at least one person in this room has been.

To emphasize the point that sexual harassment is a problem and that even people on this campus are familiar with it, I turn your attention to today's issue of *The B.G. News.* The headline reads "Sexual Harassment." This indicates that the authors of *The B.G. News* regard it as current information.

For us to understand exactly what sexual harassment is I would like to give you a couple of definitions. According to *The Alliance Against Sexual Coercion,* sexual harassment is "any sexually-oriented practice that endangers a woman's job; that undermines her job performance and threatens her economic livelihood." *Working Women United Institute* defines it as "any repeated and unwanted sexual comments, looks, suggestions, or physical contact that you find objectionable or offensive and causes you discomfort on the job." Both these definitions of sexual harassment can occur in other settings. One of these definitions also refers strictly to women, but don't be misled. According to *Newsweek,* in their March issue, men are also victims, although much less often.

Sexual harassment can be of two types—either physical or psychological, or both. Sexual harassment in its milder form can involve verbal innuendos and inappropriate, affectionate gestures. It can, however, escalate to extreme behavior such as rape. Physically, the victim can be the recipient of pinching, leering, brushing against, and touching. Psychological harassment involves a person's being encountered with relentless proposals of physical intimacy beginning with subtle hints which may lead to overt requests for dates and sexual favors.

Everyone is a target for this type of behavior in normal social settings, but when this activity is transferred to the work setting, the victim's vulnerability increases.

One way to prove that sexual harassment is indeed a problem today is to research its frequency. According to a *Working Women United Institute* survey conducted in 1975, of 155 women, 70 percent reported that they had experienced sexual harassment at least once; 92 percent of the respondents considered it a serious problem, even among those who had never experienced sexual harassment. Of the 70 percent who had been sexually harassed, 75 percent ignored it. The harassment only increased. Of those who ignored it 25 percent were penalized by unwarranted reprimands, sabotage of their work, and dismissal. Only 18 percent of those harassed complained through established channels. No action was taken in over half of the reported cases. In one-third of the cases, negative repercussions, such as increased workloads, unwarranted reprimands, and poor personnel reports resulted. In another study, conducted in 1977 by Professor Sandra Carey at the University of Texas, 481 working women replied that they had suffered some form of sexual harassment; 16 percent said that sexual advances by male coworkers or the boss were so disturbing that they resigned. Sexual advances mentioned by these women included leering or ogling, 36 percent; hints and verbal pressures, 37 percent; touching and brushing against, grabbing or pinching, 3 percent. Eighteen percent of these women were asked away for the weekend. Six percent said they were promised rewards for their other-than-business activities. These surveys indicate that sexual harassment is a problem of epidemic proportions. Now we might ask ourselves, who are the sexual harassers and why do they sexually harass?

According to Backhouse and Cohen, authors of *The Secret Oppression*, sexual harassers cannot be defined as psychologically disturbed, perverted, or even immature. Bosses, supervisors, coworkers, clients, and customers can all be perpetrators of sexual harassment. Bosses and supervisors, obviously, have a great deal of power and can threaten with serious employment consequences for failure to comply with sexual demands. Coworkers have an opportunity to poison the working atmosphere and can make working life intolerable.

These sexual harassers can be one-time offenders or relentless repeaters. One-time offenders are often in a crisis such as a death in the family, the approach of middle-age, or divorce.

The repeated offender just assumes that sex goes with the territory. These types of offenders, unfortunately, are in the majority. According to Backhouse and Cohen, in regards to a male, he often starts sexually harassing a woman after he experiences some blow to his manhood at work.

Our society often encourages and tolerates men who take their frustrations out on women. Once a sexual harasser sees that his behavior makes him feel more powerful, that he won't get in trouble, and that in fact may get applause from other men for his actions, he is likely to sexually harass again.

Male sexuality is equated with power, virility, strength, and domination. It is important to know then, that sexual harassment is not an expression of sexual desire. People who sexually harass are simple bullies. It is a demonstration of power, much like rape. Sex goes with the territory in the psyche of a sexual harasser. I have informed you that sexual harassment is alive and well and living in many organizations. It has affected many lives both male and female. Being students that will soon enter the job market, it is important for us to be aware of this growing problem so that we can deal with it constructively, should we ever encounter it.

NOTE

[1]This speech was given by Ann Gordon in her speech class at Bowling Green State University, Bowling Green, Ohio, on May 17, 1978, and is used here with her permission.

[2]This speech was given by Lynn Thies in her speech class at Bowling Green State University, Bowling Green, Ohio, on January 22, 1981, and is used here with her permission.

PROPOSITION OF POLICY

Persuasive Speeches

JUST DON'T SIT THERE—EXERCISE[1]

Do you find yourself becoming lethargic after an hour or two of studying? If so, try exercising. Do you notice the poor responsiveness of your muscles when you want them to perform an activity? If so, try to break up your day with an exercise. Being fat and, in a sense, out of shape is one of the biggest health problems in our country, says Dr. Peter Bennett of the U.S. Public Health Service in the July 1980 issue of the *Saturday Evening Post*. Combined with the 80 percent of men and women in the United States who suffer lower-back pain, a statistic by Paul Martin in the Magazine *Let's Live*, these health problems might be an indication of the large amount of time we spend on our buttocks. Exercising can change flab into toned muscle and with proper stretching exercises, such as the stretches discussed in *Let's Live*, you can live a happier life. If you are not in one of these two categories, you can still improve your health and well-being by exercising.

"Students sit in class and at homework six hours a day" according to the *Saturday Evening Post* article, written by Dr. Polke Mossfeldt and Mary Susan Miller. For us this number is probably an underestimation. Besides sitting in school, most American students spend twenty hours a week sitting and eating. Another forty hours a week is spent watching their favorite TV show. All these sedentary hours are not healthful for us.

If you are not active during the day, chances are good that you spend a lot of time sitting, and what does all this sitting (nonphysical activity) do to our body? Why do we need to exercise? The following information is from Dr. Folke Mossfeldt and Mary Susan Miller's book, *SAS in-the-chair Exercise. (Turn on overhead projector.)* Dr. Folke Mossfeldt describes seven changes that take place when the body is inactive and therefore gives reason why we should exercise.

First, when the body sits, the heart slows down on the job and less work is demanded of it. This causes the heart muscle to become weak and less able to pump strongly when the body starts itself again. This also causes the blood to circulate more slowly through the vessels, enabling blood deposits to form in the arteries.

Second, muscles that, throughout the body, force blood back up to the heart will relax and weaken. Over a period of time gravity takes over, and legs, hands, and feet swell with collected blood.

Third, the supply of oxygen required to feed the body's muscle cells is reduced by the inadequate flow of blood, which carries the oxygen. This makes the muscles stiffen and ache, as I am sure you have noticed after long periods of sitting for an exam.

Fourth, your body's weight is resting on the base of the spine and pressure is exerted incorrectly. Humans are standing animals. You begin to notice the back and stomach muscles sagging, causing all the common lower-back pains (as previously mentioned, 80 percent of the U.S. population has such problems) and poor digestion. Spasms in the lower back can occur from the lack of blood circulation to the spinal muscles.

Fifth, your shoulders and neck are also affected by inactivity. The top four vertebra grow stiff and a typical "dowager's hump" may form. The most typical result of long sitting periods is muscle tenseness, causing a stiff neck and headache, noticeable when you drive a car for long periods of time.

Sixth, the brain receives an insufficient supply of oxygen during inactivity. It thus becomes lazy. A familiar situation I am sure you have experienced is when you suddenly stand after a long sit and become dizzy. This occurs because gravity pulls blood away from your brain and your circulation is too inactive to resist the pull.

The seventh and final reason for exercise is that since the condition of the body reflects that of the mind, and the condition of the mind reflects that of the body, long sitting shrouds both in low-key depression. Your emotional and physical vigor will disappear from your normal routine.

Besides these seven signs of deterioration from sedentary positions, a book called *Health and Fitness Through Physical Activity* offers additional evidence of the need for exercise. Michael L. Pollock, Jack H. Wilmore, and Samuel M. Fox, III, authors of the book, say there is a growing area of knowledge that demonstrates that physical inactivity and the increased sedentary nature of our daily living habits are a serious threat to the body. This threat is causing major deterioration in our normal body functions. Such common and serious medical problems as coronary heart disease, hypertension, obesity, anxiety, depression, and lower-back problems have been directly or indirectly associated with our lack of physical activity. *So don't just sit there—exercise!*

There are a variety of exercises and a variety of exercise equipment available on the market today. This book *(hold up book) Exercise to Live and Live to*

Exercise gives hundreds of exercises. I will cover, first, some exercises you can perform without the use of gadgets. In the September 1980 *Mademoiselle,* Dr. Mildred Bressler-Fiener, a practicing psychotherapist, compiled a group of isometric exercises designed for people who lead sedentary lives. You can do these exercises when you study. The exercises take two minutes for the whole cycle and six seconds each. You do not sweat, you barely move, and because you exericse the muscles as a whole unit you reduce the risk of pulling or injuring anything. *(Turn on overhead to show the eight diagrams.)* These exercises are based on resistance, which means they are a form of isometric exercises. When one muscle is pitted against another, both get exercised. Make the maximum effort for each exercise and hold that position for six seconds. *(Each exercise will be demonstrated.)*

(Diagram 1.) In this simple exercise you clasp your hands behind your head and push your head against the resistance of your hands and arms. This is a good exercise for you head, neck, shoulders, and arms.

(Diagram 2) Here you place the palm of your hand near your temple and push your head against your hand. This is great for your upper arm muscles. You can repeat the exercise with your other hand.

(Diagram 3) This is the same exercise as in Diagram 1 except you clasp your hand over your forehead and press your head forward.

(Diagram 4) You can do this exercise sitting or standing. Clasp your right wrist with your left hand then push your right hand up against the resistance of your left grip. You should feel this all the way up your arm.

(Diagram 5) Find a desk and grab hold of it, keeping your elbows bent, tense your arm muscles, and try lifting from underneath. If you can lift it, find an immovable counter somewhere. You can feel the chest and arm muscles being exercised.

(Diagram 6) Grab anything handy, a telephone receiver, a bottle and squeeze. Remember to hold for six seconds. This exercises your biceps.

(Diagram 7) You can do this in a sitting position. Place your hands on the inside of your thighs and resist the closing of your legs. Your whole body is being exerted here.

(Diagram 8) Plant your feet firmly on the floor and try to lift the chair while sitting on it. Here both your back, arms, and legs are exercised.

The exercises I just have covered are ones you can do at your desk while studying without disturbing anybody. Dr. Feiner suggests doing these exercises once a day when you are feeling low. If you do your muscle strength will improve 5 percent a week. You should not, however, depend on isometric exercises as the only form of exercise.

Exercise can also involve isotonic training, which is the actual movement or lifting of a constant resistance through the range of motion of joints or joints involved. A basic example is lifting weights or doing push-ups. People prefer using exercising equipment or doing exercises involving isotonics because of the direct feedback, as in how many push-ups or military presses you can do.

Exercising equipment can be stored right in your room. *Mechanics Illustrated* has listed a variety of gear for keeping fit. Gear ranges from the simple jump rope to complicated contraptions such as a universal weight machine that exercises your whole body. The jump rope can be used to tighten and firm the stomach, leg, and arm muscles and build endurance and coordination. Exercycles can be used year round if your budget allows. There is a cycle that tells you how many calories you are burning as you use it. Carrying concealed weights that slide into slots in your clothing is another method used to keep in shape. A chinning bar is a piece of equipment you can take wherever you go and install in the doorway. You can do pull-ups or chin-ups or simply stretch by hanging. An item you can use at your desk or while driving is a handgrip. *(Show the gadget.)* You squeeze the two handles, which work against a spring. Favorite items gaining attention on the market are the spring and pulley gadgets you use by pulling them apart and contracting them. DJ's, a local health store in town, sells an item called a Whirl-A-Sizer. *(Show everyone the brochure.)* Men and women can use this product to keep in shape. These are just a few kinds of exercise equipment available to you.

Exercising either physically or with exercise equipment is beneficial to the mind and body. An article in *National News,* "All Work and Enough Play Keeps Employees Fit," discussed a study showing that workers who took part in regular exercise were in better general health, were absent less, and produced more while on the job. Some of the programs used nothing more than regular routines and short periods of rhythmic exercises for employees, such as the ones I described to you. Brian J. Sharkey, a Ph. D. and director of the Human Performance Laboratory at Montana State University, was quoted in *Vogue* magazine as saying, "When you feel yourself getting firm and strong, you have greater confidence about everything. It's gratifying." Another supporter of exercise and its effects is Dr. William P. Morgan, a sports psychologist. Dr. Morgan says individuals who participate in a vigorous exercise program consistently report that they "feel better" as a result of vigorous exercise. The sensation of feeling better appears to represent an alleviation of anxiety and tension. Being in better health, feeling better, having a sense of greater confidence, and reducing the tension and anxiety all can improve our performance at school and allow us to enjoy life instead of wasting away while sitting on our "cans."

Now what are you going to do—sit around and be sluggish and nonenergetic? Why not practice some of the exercises I have discussed or purchase an exercise gadget. These exercises can make you feel better, look better, keep your muscles toned, and alleviate the anxiety and stress that can build up during school. *So don't just sit there—exercise!!!!!*

OFF-CAMPUS HOUSING[2]

Title: What a student should know before committing himself or herself to off-campus housing.

Introduction: Sometime during the college years almost every student considers moving out of a dorm and into an off-campus apartment. They want the freer life of renting their "own place." However, much more is involved than simply paying the rent each month. If you are not aware of the many other considerations, you are liable to find yourself in a very undesirable situation. First, I will propose some things to consider before deciding to move into an off-campus apartment. Second, we shall explore the things required of you, the tenant. Finally, we shall look at the other half of this business venture: the landlord.

    I. So, you are thinking about moving off-campus into an apartment?

        A. First, you must consider roommates.

            1. How many, if any, are compatible with your individual life style?

                a. What do you and your roommates expect of one another?

                    (1) Do your attitudes on the subjects of smoking, drug use, pets agree?

                    (2) Will overnight visitors be allowed?

                b. Do you have compatible sleeping, study, and partying habits?

                c. How will the housekeeping responsibilities be divided up?

            2. Next, you must agree on a location, with neighbors and local conveniences satisfactory to everyone.

        B. Another major consideration before moving off campus, naturally, is money. Is your budget comparable to that of your roommates?

            1. For example, how much are each of you willing to spend on rent, food, and utilities?

                a. Will you buy food together or separately?

                b. Are you aware of the average price range for utilities and rent?

                    (1) Rent and utilities are usually paid monthly or quarterly.

                    (2) Monthly gas bills can range from seventeen to forty dollars, according to *Consuming Sense,* published by the Student Consumer Union, and electric bills from ten to seventy dollars.

            2. Initially, you must realize that security deposits are required for both rent and utilities.

                a. For this reason, you should be aware of the Ohio Revised Code, taken from Baldwin's Fourth Edition, that if a security deposit is in excess of one month's rent and is also in excess of fifty dollars the landlord must pay 5 percent annual interest unless the tenant lives in the unit less than six months.

                b. Security deposits are required for phone services, and electricity and can run as high as fifty and sixty-five dollars respectively.

Transition: Now that you and your prospective roommates have worked out the finer points of your proposed relationship, found your apartment, and settled all disputes about money, you're all set, right? Well, sorry to disappoint you, but there are some legal aspects required of you as a tenant.

    II. There are things that are required of you, and that you should be made aware of as a tenant in an off-campus housing unit.

        A. Usually, every tenant is required to sign a lease, but you must fully understand it, for it is a legal document.

       1. A lease will usually state how much your rent is per month or quarter, and when it must be paid.

       2. It should also include, in clauses, any special requirements made of you.

         a. These may be requirements for pets, lawn care, or possibly pool restrictions.

         b. There may also be some stipulation on the condition of your unit, with periodical check-ups by the landlord.

   B. It would be wise for you to make yourself familiar with the landlord-tenant bill, which came into effect November 1, 1974, as Senate Bill 103.

       1. Under this bill you must keep your premises safe and sanitary, and dispose of all waste.

       2. You must also take proper care of all fixtures and keep them in good working order.

   C. As a tenant, you have some legal rights protecting you.

       1. If the landlord fails to fulfill his or her part of the lease, you can put your rent money in *escrow.* This means placing it in a municipal court until the landlord fulfills his duties; according to the Student Consumer Union.

       2. You also have Tenant Insurance (Home Owner's Policy #4) available to you, according to Martin Partington, author of the case studies, *Landlord and Tenant.* This will protect your property from all named perils and cover anyone injured on your property.

Transition: Therefore, as a tenant, you are now familiar with lease requirements, the landlord-tenant bill, the tenant's legal rights, escrow, and tenant insurance when renting off campus. But, as I said before, you are only one half of this business venture. It is necessary to understand what is required of the landlord, and what his or her rights are.

III. A landlord, who is in some cases the resident manager, has as many things required of him as the tenant.

   A. The landlord must also abide by the landlord-tenant bill.

       1. He or she must keep all areas of the premises safe and sanitary, in accordance with health standards.

       2. He or she must provide fixtures in good working condition, running hot water, and garbage receptacles.

       3. He or she must also give twenty-four-hour notice for entry into the tenant's unit.

   B. I had the opportunity to interview the resident manager of the Village Green Apartments, Christopher Meyer. He gave me some helpful hints to make landlord-tenant relationships run more smoothly.

       1. Mr. Meyer informed me that, when signing a lease, be aware that there is no law that states that you *must* pay rent on the first of every month.

       2. He stated that, for both party's protection, during check-in

Conclusion:

and out, it is a good idea for both landlord and tenant to go through the apartment and assess its condition.

Now that you have been exposed to some of the complications that may arise when deciding to move off campus into an apartment, it is wise to keep the old warning in mind, *caveat emptor*—let the buyer beware. However, with good planning and knowledge of the rights and responsibilities of both the tenant and landlord, and of course good relationships with your roommates, you can safeguard yourself against any major problems arising with off-campus living. Just remember—what you don't know *may* hurt you!

NOTES

[1] This speech was given by Kerr Wargo in his speech class at Bowling Green State University, Bowling Green, Ohio, on February 19, 1981, and is used here with his permission.

[2] This speech was given by Leigh Greaser in her speech class at Bowling Green State University, Bowling Green, Ohio, on January 24, 1980, and is used here with her permission.

SPECIAL OCCASION SPEECHES

COMMENCEMENT SPEECH

Carl Bernstein of the writing team of Woodward and Bernstein, was graduated in 1961 from Montgomery Blair High School in Silver Spring, Maryland—barely. He became a reporter at nineteen and joined the Washington Post in 1966. After his fame in the Watergate epic, his old high school invited him back for the honored role of commencement speaker in 1977. His speech was enthusiastically received by students and parents. [1]

The ultimate revenge in this life, I think, is to come back to your high school as its commencement speaker. Imagine. Me. Not the president of my class, not the former chairman of the Latin Scrabble Club, not the head of the Keyettes (I think it was Nancy Immler, who would never go out with me). Not Goldie Hawn, with whom I once rode to the Hot Shoppe after the Bethesda–Chevy Chase game in the back seat of Pete Oldheiser's chopped-and-lowered Buick. Not Bob Windsor, the football player. But me, from the very bottom of my class.

So it would be presumptuous of me to preach at you from the usual list of topics for graduation speeches—patriotism, national service, leadership, these are the best years of your life, etc. I'd rather get back to basics. Which is to say that I'd like to share with you some of my feelings about Montgomery Blair, about high school, about the educational process in this country, and about the "real world" that is something quite apart from what most teachers and parents would have you believe.

I think the best way to do this is to tell you about my own stay at Blair now that—after some 15 years—I seem to have overcome the pain.

My own graduation from Blair is a memory so vivid that I continue to have nightmares about it. I was never able to send out invitations and those little white cards with your name engraved in script because Mr. Adelman, with good reason, had refused to pass me in chemistry. And I was also flunking gym. The explanation had less to do with my scores on tests or physical dexterity than with the fact that I wasn't in class very often.

I was also working evenings at the time—I started as a copyboy at the Evening Star in my junior year—and working for a newspaper seemed to me a lot more interesting than doing homework at night.

So when it came time to order caps and gowns in 1961, Mr. Shaw, then the principal of Blair, told me not to bother. There followed some intense lobbying by me and my parents. And there was a big discussion among members of the faculty, who finally reached a decision to get me out of Blair rather than put up with me for another year.

Then came the University of Maryland, which, despite my hopeless grades, accepted me on probation because I scored reasonably well on the essay exam—the major part of Maryland's entry test in that era.

That didn't last for long, however. I started working at the paper five days a week, stopped showing up for classes unless there was an exam, and flunked out the next semester. It went on like that for a couple of years—readmitted on probation, middling grades, up and down—and then came the final straw. The university suspended me for having too many parking tickets. I never went back.

I concentrated on my work at the Star and became a reporter. I started to find a satisfaction in my life that had been lacking at school. And I tell you this not to recommend that anybody here follows the same course or to extol the virtues of starting at the bottom, but to make a slightly different point—and it's the only thing I want to pass on to you today.

Your life isn't over if you're not at the top of this class. You've been graded and you've been tested and you've been ranked and I'm here to tell that it really doesn't mean a thing. The die isn't cast yet; the final scores aren't in. And that goes for the top of the class, too. The fact is that easy passage through Blair, through high school, doesn't mean that the wheels of success are somehow permanently greased.

One of my most intense memories is of my 10th reunion of the class of '61. For reasons that sociologists and educators and psychiatrists could spend lifetimes analyzing, what happened to that class contradicts all the old myths about success in high school. A disproportionate number of those judged in our yearbooks and in the hallways of Blair as "most likely to succeed" seemed to have had the most difficult time of it—trouble adjusting to college, to professional life, to personal relationships.

And, to generalize again, many of those who had the roughest time at Blair—the kids regarded as troublemakers by the faculty, the students with obvious difficulties of social adjustment, the ones who often seemed so aimless—a disproportionate number of them seemed to have moved on in their lives to real satisfaction—professionally, educationally, emotionally.

Which brings me finally to the idea rattling around in my head since I first received your invitation to speak. Quite simply: The real world is a lot more tolerant, a lot more interesting, a lot more fun, a lot more sensible really than the cocoon that is high school.

Wherever you stand in this class, you've gotten through the worst part —high school—and you deserve to feel really good about that. Now come the opportunities, whether you're headed for university, a job, the military, marriage. Now you get to be your own person, not what your teachers want you to be, not what your parents expect you to be. At last you're not going to be compelled by others to do anything. And that really is what that piece of paper—that diploma —is all about. It's a ticket—out of this place and into life.

NOTE

[1]Carl Bernstein, "High School Diploma Ticket To Real World, Writer Tells Students," *Times-Post News Service, The Blade* (Toledo, Ohio), June 17, 1979.

GLOSSARY

Acceptances: speeches made in response to a presentation.

Accurate language: words that convey exactly what the speaker means; that is, words that will stir up meaning in the listerners' minds that are as close to those the speaker's mind as possible.

Action step: the fifth and final step of the Monroe motivated sequence; designed to indicate to the audience the kind of action that is necessary to bring about the change being requested in the satisfaction step.

Active language: words that add the force that causes the message to have an effect. Words, for example, used to depict someone doing something: activity.

After-dinner speech: usually a short, genial, humorous speech delivered to an audience in a mood to be entertained.

Analogy reasoning: when a speaker attempts to show that similar circumstances will produce similar conclusions.

Antithesis: placing two opposing ideas side by side.

Anxiety: apprehension or fear, often marked by physiological signs such as sweating, tension, or increased pulse, that results from a perceived threat or from self-doubt regarding one's capacity to cope with a situation.

Appearance: how a speaker looks.

Appropriate language: words designed for a specific audience, not for just any listener, but for the listener who is to hear the speech.

Argument: the process of drawing conclusions (claims) from reasons (data).

Articulation: the distinctness with which words are spoken.

Attention step: the first step of the Monroe motivated sequence; designed to call attention to the topic or situation.

Attitude: a tendency or predisposition to behave in a certain way.

Audience: the recipients of the speaker's message, or at least those with whom the speaker is speaking.

Audience analysis: the process of discovering audience needs, wants, interests, beliefs, knowledge, and desires.

Axioms: widely accepted propositions or truths.

Belongingness and love needs: needs that include sense of family or group cohesiveness, love of mate, and acceptance by others.

Causal pattern: a persuasive organizational pattern that moves from the cause to the effect or from the effect to the cause.

Causation reasoning: when a speaker assumes that one or more circumstances always produces a predictable effect or set of effects.

Channel: that through which a message or feedback must pass to get from speaker to listener.

Claims: the conclusions drawn from the evidence.

Clarity of language: when the words the speaker uses are immediately meaningful to the listeners; that is, when there is a close correspondence between the speaker's meaning and the meaning stirred up in the minds of audience members.

Classification: a form of proposition of definition that sets out the boundaries of a word.

Commonalities: things with which the audience can immediately identify.

Competence: having requisite or adequate ability or qualities.

Complementary relationship: when there are differences between the speaker and audience.

Concepts of communication: broad generalizations regarding human communication behavior.

Concurrency: when the verbal and nonverbal communication of a person agree.

Connotative meaning: words that suggest meaning as a result of the emotional attachments people have for them. Connotative words are subjective because the meaning is suggested apart from the thing it explicitly names or represents.

Coordination: following parallel headings under a topic order indicates coordination. In outlining, using headings equal in value.

Credibility: the speaker's status or image with reference to this audience, on this topic, and at this time. The speaker's believability.

Data: the evidence used in a speech.

Deductive pattern: persuasive organizational pattern that moves from the general to the specific.

Delivery: the process of communicating with the audience.

Demographics: vital information about or characteristics of a given group of people. Demography is the science of determining (finding out) this vital information.

Denotative meaning: words that fairly accurately or directly refer to the objects they represent.

Descriptive speech: one designed to provide a clear, vivid impression through accurate and informative material. To be descriptive is to create a mental image of something one has experienced —a scene, person, or sensation.

Dissonance: an unresolved feeling or discordant note.

Distraction: anything that takes a listener's attention away from the speaker's intended message.

Dynamic language: words that are vivid and impressive; that is, ones that enhance the content through emphasis and imagery.

Dynamism: speaker enthusiasm, energy, force, or intensity.

Editorial opinion: opinion that is drawn from editors—those who write or deliver editorials. A speaker would use editorial opinion if he or she used data from the media that give the opinions of the editors or publishers.

Elaborated specific purpose: includes specific purpose of the speech plus the major points or assertions in the speech.

Elements of communication: basic, essential parts of the communication process.

Emblems: nonverbal words.

Emphasizing: the process of giving some points of more importance than others.

Empty words: words that have *no* meaning.

Entertaining speeches: speeches designed to get an audience to relax in a lighthearted and enjoyable atmosphere.

Esteem needs: needs that include having respect and admiration of others, exercising power and influence, and acquiring self-respect by advancement and effort.

Ethics in persuasion: principles of conduct governing speakers and listeners.

Ethos: the character of the speaker in the eyes of the audience.

Etymology: a form of proposition of definition that provides an account of the history of a word.

Eulogies: speeches designed to offer high praise of another's accomplishments.

Evaluative language: words that introduce an evaluation (severity, mildness, importance) into a description of something.

Examples: instances or cases in point.

Expert opinion: data taken from someone who has acquired special skill in or knowledge of a particular subject—an authority.

Extemporaneous speaking: the ideal style of delivery; it allows the speaker to prepare and practice thoroughly but allows the exact wording of the speech to be determined at the moment of utterance.

Extended conversation: recommended form of public-speaking delivery—as if a speaker is talking to just one person, but extended to the number in the audience.

Extrinsic ethos: credibility that is established external (really prior) to a speech occasion.

Facts: bits of truth that we know to exist and that can be checked against reality.

Fallacious reasoning: reasoning that fails to satisfy the conditions of valid or correct inference; erroneous reasoning.

Farewells: speeches designed to praise the accomplishments of one who is leaving.

Feedback: the response a speaker gets from an audience and the adaptation he or she makes in the message to compensate for or acknowledge that response.

Fidelity: accuracy in understanding of a message by audience members.

Figures of speech: forms of expression (as a simile, metaphor, antithesis, personification, or hyperbole) used to evoke meaning or heighten the speaker's effect.

Function: a form of proposition of definition that explains the use of a person, idea, or thing—its function.

Generalization reasoning: when a speaker argues that what is true in certain circumstances is true in all circumstances (or in at least enough circumstances to confirm the generalization).

General purpose: to inform, persuade, convince, or entertain. A general or broad, overriding goal for a speech.

Gestures: the use of the arms or hands as means of expression.

Halo effect: the effect created when, because the audience agrees or disagrees with the speaker in one or two areas, the audience projects agreement or disagreement (respectively) in other areas.

Heterogeneous audience: an audience made up of people of dissimilar characteristics.

Hierarchy of needs: Abraham Maslow's list of common human needs arranged with the strongest (most pressing or important) ones first.

Homogeneous audience: an audience made up of people with the same or similar features.

Hostile audience members: those who are strongly opposed to the speaker's essential message.

Hyperbole: exaggeration or overstatement. Example: the majesty of argument.

Hypothetical examples: instances or cases in point that are created by the speaker for a specific purpose.

Identification: the speaker's attempt to achieve sameness or unity with the audience or vice versa.

Illustrations: a longer, more detailed, or extended example told in narrative, storylike form.

Illustrators: gestures used along with the oral message—to accompany and complement it.

Impromptu speaking: a form of delivery that involves no previous, specific preparation and that is accomplished on the spur of the moment.

Incongruency: when the verbal and nonverbal communication of a person do not agree; also known as *mixed message*.

Inductive pattern: a persuasive organizational pattern that moves from the specific to the general.

Inferences: conclusions, judgments, predictions, or interpretations. Leaps from a fact or group of facts into the unknown and unobserved. In audience analysis inferences are part of the process of finding out about the needs and desires of the audience.

Inflection: changes or variances in pitch.

Informative speaking: oral communication designed to increase or secure audience understanding.

Initial partition: when speakers show what they intend to cover in the speech initially—at the beginning of the speech—and before beginning to cover it.

Intended meaning: the interpretations that reside in the speaker's mind.

Intrinsic ethos: earned credibility—that impression (or character) a speaker creates during a speech.

Introductory speech: a speech designed to formally or officially announce and present a person to an audience.

Jargon: technical language.

Kinesics: facial and bodily movements.

K.I.S.S.: *K*eep *I*t *S*imple and *S*traightforward

Listening: the physical, emotional, and intellectual process of receiving and interpreting the speaker's messages—both verbal and nonverbal.

Logistics: in a speech situation, logistics would include the size and seating of the audience, use of or need for a microphone and PA system, type of hall or room, lighting, reason audience is assembled, degree of formality, time, other speakers, potential noise, lectern availability, etc.

Main heads: those statements or issues that provide the structure of a speech.

Manuscript speaking: a form of delivery that involves writing the speech out in full and then reading it aloud.

Meaning: the interpretation a person assigns to a symbol; the many associations that are aroused or evoked when you conceive of ideas.

Message: that element of the communication situation that carries the essential freight—idea substance. Can be both verbal and nonverbal.

Metacommunication: communication about communication. Comments made by people engaged in communication about the communication they are engaged in.

Metaphor: a comparison between two unlike things. Example: curtain of fear.

Minor cue: something that we (as speakers) might throw off unconsciously or consciously with little thought or concern.

Mixed message: when the verbal and nonverbal communication of a person do not agree. Also known as incongruency.

Model: the manner in which the various elements of communication are interlocked with or related to each other in a visual depiction or representation.

Monotony: sameness in tone or sound.

Monroe's motivated sequence: a organizational pattern for persuasive speeches that distinguishes the five steps: attention, need satisfaction, visualization, and action.

Needs: the underpinnings for warrants; needs are conditions that require supply or relief.

Need step: the second step of the Monroe motivated sequence; designed to explain the audience needs being addressed.

Noise: physical or external distraction is one kind of noise; psychological, or internal (within the mind) distraction is another kind of noise.

Nonverbal communication: communication through posture, gestures, facial expression, voice inflection, or rhythm.

Norms: principles of right action that guide, control, and regulate acceptable behavior.

Opinions: views, judgments, or appraisals about facts, events, or beliefs.

Paralanguage: vocal nonverbal communication; how words are said (not the words themselves).

Parallelism: when the exact same sentence structure is used repeatedly.

Perception: one's awareness of the various elements of one's environment as a result of physical sensations that are interpreted in the light of one's experience.

Periodicals: newspapers, magazines, and other publications with fixed intervals between the issues or numbers.

Personal experience: what speakers themselves bring to the data of the speech from their own knowledge and background.

Personification: attributing human characteristics to inanimate (things with no life) objects. Example: Good fortune smiled on her.

Persuasive speaking: oral communication designed to secure a change of commitment in either belief or action.

Physiological needs: needs that include hunger, thirst, health maintenance, and sexual gratification.

Pitch: a speaker's vocal key—determined by the vibration of the vocal folds; technically, the difference in the relative vibration frequency of the human voice.

Plagiarism: passing off the ideas or words of another person as if they were your own—without crediting the source; literary theft.

Posture: the position or bearing of the body as a whole.

Presentation: a type of special occasion speech that accompanies the presentation of a gift, award, or prize. Short, formal speeches designed to recognize someone for his or her accomplishments.

Presentness: a speaker's ability to be himself or herself in a speech situation—to be a genuine, sincere, unique person; allowing your real self to be revealed. Also refers to one's mental set as one conceptualizes the "being" of the speaker-audience relationship.

Principle: a unifying factor.

Problem-solution order: an organizational pattern in which the main heads develop first the problem, then the solution.

Pronunciation: the correctness with which words are spoken.

Proof: the evidence of a speech; determines the truth and strength of the speaker's ideas.

Proposition of definition: a form of factual proposition that alleges the essential nature of a person, idea, or thing.

Proposition of fact: a form of proposition that alleges (suggests) the existence of something.

Proposition of policy: a form of proposition that proposes a course of action; a speaker who uses this form argues that something should or should not be done.

Proposition of value: a form of proposition that contains a value judgment; a speaker using this form maintains that something is good or bad, beneficial or detrimental, justified or unjustified, worthwhile or worthless.

Public communication: the attempt by a communicator to evoke in receivers (the audience) the same meaning for a message as that intended by the communicator.

Public opinion: data taken from polling or sampling.

Qualifier: statement regarding the degree of probability inherent in the claim.

Quality: peculiar, inherent, and distinguishing attributes of a person's voice.

Rapport: a relationship a speaker establishes with audience members characterized by harmony, conformity, or affinity.

Rate: how fast a speaker chooses to speak.

Reasoning: the process of drawing inferences or conclusions through the use of sufficient explanation, justification, or grounds.

Received meaning: the interpretations evoked or called forth in the receiver's or listener's mind by the speaker's message.

Refinement: improvement in language made by introducing subtleties or distinctions; that is, to avoid pomposity, confusion, and ostentatiousness.

Refrain: a sentence or phrase that occurs at regular intervals in a passage or speech.

Regulators: gestures used to encourage or discourage the participation of others.

Repetition: restating a point or word using exactly the same language.

Reservation: recognition of possible extenuating circumstances or exceptional contexts in which the claim may not apply.

Satisfaction step: the third step of the Monroe motivated sequence designed to show how the needs (developed in the need step) can be met.

Security needs: needs that include freedom from physical danger, avoidance of emotional disturbance, and protection from environmental dangers (heat, cold, aridity).

Selective perception: choosing (either consciously or subconsciously) from the various elements of one's environment just those particular elements one wants to sense; seeing what one wants to see or hearing what one wants to hear.

Self-actualization needs: needs that include full development of capabilities and ambitions and opportunity for growth.

Sign: something that serves to indicate the presence or existence of something else.

Sign reasoning: when a speaker argues that because certain characteristics, events, or situations usually accompany other unobserved characteristics, events, or situations, then the latter unobserved characteristics, events, or situations can be predicted when the former are observed.

Simile: a comparison between two unlike things announced with the words *like* or *as*.

Simple language: the short, familiar words that are readily understood by listeners.

Situation: where a speech occurs. A location in both time and space.

Slang: harsh, coarse, or vulgar language; often peculiar to a particular group; usually informal and nonstandard.

Space order: an organizational pattern in which each of the main heads reveal a spatial relationship.

Speaker: the originator of the public communication message.

Speaker's character: how a speaker is viewed by audience members; Sometimes referred to as *ethos*.

Specific purpose: includes general purpose (to inform, persuade, convince, or entertain), plus the mention of the audience and a *specific* statement of the topic, or thesis. It serves as a summary statement of what the speaker wants from the audience as a result of the speech.

Speech of explanation: speech designed to tell others how to do something, how to make something, or how something works.

Speech to actuate: presentation designed to move audience members to action.

Speech to convince: presentation designed to secure the audience's agreement with each of the speaker's main points.

Speech to stimulate: presentation designed to reinforce audience feelings or rejuvenate them; a speech that heightens, sharpens, or brings to the fore audience feelings.

Spotlighting: as a speaker, turning your attention and eye contact toward individual members of your audience.

Stage fright: nervousness felt at appearing before an audience.

Statistics: numerical representations of groups of examples or facts.

Strength of language: words that evoke an impressive (strong) mental picture of what you want to communicate in the minds of listeners.

Style: the language—words—the speaker chooses to use in a public communication.

Subordination: following a system whereby one point occupies a lower class or rank than the previous point.

Superpurpose: all speech should serve to maximize human potential: to help others become what they can become. Also see *transcending purpose.*

Suspending judgment: trying to make certain we fully understand the speaker's message before we respond to it. Also, trying to listen to what other people are *really* saying, and not to what we want them to say.

Symbols: things with communicative value. Verbal and nonverbal elements are symbols. In speech, they are those elements designed specifically to evoke in an audience the same meanings the speaker has for those symbols. A word is a symbol because it represents something else (an object, idea, concept, or feeling).

Symmetrical relationship: when speaker and audience mirror each other's behavior; neither is considered better than or stronger than the other—only equal.

Target audience: the specific, relevant, and identifiable audience before which you plan to deliver a speech.

Testimony: data taken from witnesses under oath in response to interrogation by lawyers or authorized public officials.

Thesis: the rallying point for speech material; the position you are advancing and willing to support in your speech.

Time order: organizational pattern in which each of the main heads follows a chronological (or time) sequence.

Topic order: organizational pattern in which each of the main heads develops part of the specific purpose.

Toulmin model: model of reasoning that emphasizes a logical relationship between the specific evidence one gathers for a speech effort and the conclusions one draws from that evidence.

Transaction: that unique interaction that occurs between speaker and audience as each constructs images of the other and responds to those impressions.

Transcending purpose: helping others to maximize their potential or to help people become what they can become; also referred to as the superpurpose.

Transitions: links in a speech that indicate to listeners where a speaker has been, is, and is going in the speech. Transitions are words or phrases that tell the listener that the speaker is moving to the next idea.

Tributes: speeches designed to praise another's accomplishments.

Trite language: overused and overworked words and phrases.

Trustworthiness: the quality or state of being worthy of confidence.

Variables: those aspects that are subject to change.

Verbal clutter: verbal interference; that is, sounds or words that are uttered by the speaker as unnecessary filler material.

Verbal communication: communication using words.

Visual aid: an instructional device (such as a chart, map, or model) that appeals chiefly to vision; used to amplify or expand a speech.

Visualization step: the fourth step of the Monroe motivated sequence; designed to indicate the improvements or changes that will result once the solution is implemented.

Warrant: the reason why a claim follows from the data.

NAME INDEX

Alda, A., 315
Allen, R. R., 116, 237
Aly, B., 327
Aly, L. F., 327
Andersen, K., 115, 116, 253
Anderson, L., 312
Anderson, R. C., 165
Argyle, M., 215
Aristotle, 70
Aronson, E., 215
Asch, S., 66
Auer, J. J., 91
Ausubel, D. P., 165
Ayres, J., 90

Bachner, J., 220, 248
Baird, J. E., Jr., 166
Banaka, W. H., 137
Barker, L. L., 65
Barnlund, D. C., 47, 115
Bassett, R. E., 166, 275
Bast, B., 57
Beavin, J. H., 47

Beighley, K. C., 253
Bem, D. J., 91
Berg, D., 275
Berkowitz, L., 66
Berlo, D. K., 275
Berlyne, D. E., 275
Berquist, G. F., 327
Birdwhistell, R. L., 214
Bittner, J. R., 190
Blankenship, J., 191
Bohn, E., 65
Boies, S. J., 115
Bombeck, E., 228
Bostrom, R. R., 65
Bowers, J. W., 191
Bradac, J. J., 191
Brady, J., 137
Brembeck, W. L., 312
Brockriede, W., 312
Brooks, R. D., 65, 115, 116
Brooks, W. D., 191, 312
Brothers, J., 59, 247
Brown, R., 47

Bryant, C. L., 65
Bryant, D. C., 327
Burgoon, M., 116, 191

Calero, H. H., 190, 214
Campbell, S. K., 116
Cantril, H., 65
Capp, G. R., 327
Carrel, S. P., 275
Carter, D. A., 296
Carter, J., 116
Cash, W. B., Jr., 137
Christensen, J. A., 103
Clevenger, T., Jr., 90, 115, 116, 253
Coakley, C. G., 65
Colburn, C. W., 65
Conklin, F., 215
Cook, M. G., 137
Cooper, G. L., 219
Cooper, L., 90
Crable, R. E., 296
Craig, R., 275
Cronkhite, G., 166, 312
Culp, R. B., 327

Dale, E., 275
Dause, C. A., 313
Davies, R. A., 191
Davis, F., 214
Davitz, J. R., 215
Dean, J., 215
DeHaan, H., 166
DeVille, J., 210
Donaho, M. W., 137
Downs, R. B., 137
Dyer, W. W., 233

Eagly, A. H., 90
Edgar, E. E., 218
Egan, G., 47
Ehninger, D., 115, 116, 191, 296, 312
Ehrensberger, R., 91
Eisenberg, A., 214
Eisenson, J., 91
Ekman, P., 214, 215
Ellis, D. S., 215
Emmert, P., 191

Farb, P., 190
Farson, R., 65
Fast, B., 209
Fast, J., 209, 214
Fisher, W. R., 312
Ford, G. R., 116
Fortinberry, A., 275
Foss, K., 65
Freeley, A. J., 312

Freeman, J. L., 90
Freshley, D., 65
Friedman, M., 116
Friesen, W. V., 214, 215
Fulbright, J. W., 200

Gardner, H., 189
Geeting, B., 65
Geeting, C., 65
Gelman, D., 179
Genua, R. L., 137
Gibson, J. W., 90, 91
Goodman, E., 321
Goranson, R., 66
Gordon T., 48, 54–55, 65
Greenberg, B. S., 191
Gronbeck, B. E., 296
Guthrie, R. D., 214

Haiman, F. S., 115
Hanna, M. S., 90
Harris, S., 8, 25, 31, 42, 55, 86, 171, 177, 191, 255, 324
Harrison, R. P., 214
Harte, T. B., 115
Hastings, A., 313
Hastorf, A. H., 65
Hawkins, G. J., 253
Hayakawa, S. I., 190
Hazen, M. D., 90
Hewgill, M. A., 253
Higbee, K. L., 253
Holtzman, P. D., 90
Hooker, Z. V., 137
Hopper, R., 90
Hovland, C. I., 116
Howell, W. S., 312
Hrelec, E. S., 327
Huff, D., 116
Hurt, H. T., 233
Huseman, R., 65

Insko, C. A., 116
Irwin, J. V., 91

Jabusch, D. M., 296
Jackson, D. D., 47
Janik, A., 313
Jensen, K., 233, 296
Jewell, T., 137
Johannesen, R. L., 116, 296, 327
Johnson, A., 166
Johnson, L. B., 166
Jones, E. E., 65
Jones, J. E., 232
Jones, J. L., 116
Jones, S. B., 191

Kahane, H., 312
Kamenetsky, J., 166
Katz, D., 275
Keller, C. D., 137
Kiesler, S. B., 90
King, L. B., 191
Knapp, M. L., 214, 215
Kohler, R., 65
Konsky, C. W., 191
Kramer, E., 215

Lamport, F., 191
Landers, A., 36
Langer, E., 116
Larson, C. U., 312
Leathers, D., 214
Leavitt, H. J., 253
Leeper, R., 65
Lesly, P., 139, 184, 186, 242
Linkugel, W. A., 116, 275, 327
Littlejohn, S. W., 253, 296
Logue, C., 65
London, H., 253
Lorayne, H., 253
Lucas, J., 253
Lynch, M. D., 191

Manis, M., 66, 90
Marsh, C., 275
Maslow, A. H., 105–8, 109, 116
Maslow, C., 253
McCabe, C., 133
McClung, T., 165
McCroskey, J. C., 115–16, 166, 233, 253
McEwen, W. J., 191
McGuire, W. J., 116
McKerrow, R. E., 312
McQuown, N. A., 191
Medley, A., 137
Mehrabian, A., 214, 215
Mehrley, R. S., 166, 253
Mettee, D. R., 327
Metzler, K., 137
Meyer, J. L., 137
Miller, G. A., 165
Miller, G. R., 191, 253, 312
Mills, J., 215
Minnick, W. C., 296
Monaghan, J. P., 238
Monroe, A. H., 291, 296
Mortensen, C. D., 47, 312
Mueller, R. A. H., 253
Mulac, A., 191
Murphy, G., 65
Murray, F. S., 115

Narramore, C., 164
Nelson, B., 42

Newman, D. R., 115
Newman, R. P., 115
Nichols, R. G., 65, 66
Nicholson, H. E., 191
Nierenberg, G. I., 190, 214
Nilsen, T. R., 312

Osborne, M. M., 191

Pearce, W. B., 215
Petrie, C. R., Jr., 275
Pfeiffer, J. W., 232
Pinson, W. M., Jr., 116, 137
Pittenger, R. E., 191
Pollock, T., 286
Porter, R. E., 65
Posner, M. I., 115
Prichard, S. V. O., 166

Richardson, F. C., 222
Richmond, V. P., 233
Rieke, R., 313
Rivers, W. L., 137
Rogers, C., 61, 65, 66
Rosenberg, M. J., 116
Rosnow, R. L., 166

Samovar, L., 65
Sayles, E. M., 312
Schafer, R., 65
Scheidel, T. M., 115, 116
Schwartz, T., 105
Schweitzer, D. A., 253
Scott, M. D., 233
Seiler, W. J., 275
Seinberg, S. B., 65
Sereno, K. K., 47, 253
Shamo, G. W., 190
Sharp, H., Jr., 165
Sheehan, G., 225
Sheehy, E. P., 137
Sheehy, G., 90
Shopper, M., 102
Sifford, D., 239
Smith, H. L., Jr., 191
Smith, R., Jr., 214
Smith, R. G., 165
Snell, F., 157
Snyder, J., 215
Spence, M., 137
Spicer, C., 166, 275
Starkweather, J. A., 214, 215
Stephen, B., 199
Stevens, L. A., 66
Stewart, C., 137
Stewart, D., 191
Stone, J., 220, 248

Stone, M., 170
Strunk, W., 176, 191

Tannenbaum, P., 166
Thistlethwaite, D. L., 166, 275
Thompson, E., 165, 166, 275
Thomson, D. S., 175
Thourlby, W., 195, 213
Toulmin, S., 93–96, 115, 288, 292, 295, 298, 309,
    312, 313
Trager, G. L., 215

Ullmann, S., 191

Vick, C. F., 190, 275
Vickrey, J. F., Jr., 166

Wallace, A., 22
Wallace, I., 22
Wallace, K. R., 327
Wallechinsky, D., 22

Watzlawick, P., 47
Weaver, C. H., 65
Weaver, R. L., II, 66, 91
Webster, B., 215
Weitz, S., 214
White, C., 137
White, E. B., 176, 191
Widgery, R. N., 215
Wilke, W., 215
Wilkens, P. C., 327
Williams, F., 191
Windes, R. R., 313
Wolvin, A. D., 65
Wood, R. V., 190, 191, 275
Woolfolk, R. L., 222

Yamanchi, J. S., 191
Yeager, W. H., 327
Yoselson, K., 253
Young, T. J., 115–16, 253

Ziegelmueller, G., 313

SUBJECT INDEX

Acceptances, 316, 319–20, 326
Accept givens, as a way of focusing energy, 218, 220–21
Accurate language, 175, 177–78, 262, 274
Active language, 182–84
Actuating, as a type of persuasive speaking, 280
Adaptation in nonverbal communication, 213–14
Age of audience. *See* Audience
Analogy, as a kind of reasoning, 301, 305–6, 309
Analyzing the audience, 3–6, 67–90
Animation, 206, 247, 323
Answering questions, 255, 271–73, 274
Antithesis, 180
Anxiety, 217, 218–28
Appropriate language, 175, 178–79, 262, 274
Argument, 297–309
Arrangement, 138–65 *See also* Organizational patterns; Organizing the material; Outlining
Articulation, 18, 207, 211
Assertion, 151
Attention, as an aspect of the speech introduction, 153
Attitudes, 45, 46, 52

Audience, 27, 34–38, 45, 67–90
  adaptation, 68
  age of, 78
  analysis of, 68–75
  analysis checksheet, 78–79
  apathetic, 73, 79
  demographics, 69–75
  educational level of, 72
  education of, 78
  favorable, 73, 79
  hostile, 73–74, 79
  how to analyze, 76–79
  how to determine success of analysis, 88–89
  knowledge background of, 72–75
  knowledge level of, 78
  logistics, 75–76
  neutral, 73, 79
  sex of, 72, 78
  strongly opposed, 73–74, 79
  what to do with information from analysis of, 79–87
  what to analyze regarding, 69–76
Audience analysis, 106–7
Axioms, 24–27

Being impressive, as an aspect of the conclusion, 156–57
Belongingness needs, 105–8
Bias, removing it from our speeches, 62
Big words, 185
Bodily movement, 192, 202–5, 206
Body, 139–52, 192–214
  appearance, 202–3
  as an aspect of nonverbal communication, 192, 202–5, 206
  gesture, 202, 205
  language, 192–214
  movement, 202, 203–4
  of the speech, 139–52
  posture, 202, 204–5
Body of the speech, 139–52
  finding main heads, 140–43
  ordering main heads, 143–48
  supporting main heads, 148–52
Brevity, as an aspect of the entertaining speech, 324
Building credibility, 246–49

Card catalog, 124–27
Catalog of needs, 105–8
Causal pattern, 288, 289–90, 295, 301, 302–4, 309
Causation, as a kind of reasoning, 301, 302–4, 309
Chalkboard, as a visual aid, 266
Changing attitudes, 276–95
Channel, 39
Charts, as visual aids, 266
Checklist for main heads, 148
Choosing the language, 3, 15–16, 96, 157–90, 262
Chronological order, 143, 145–146 *See also* Time order
Chronological pattern, 12 *See also* Chronological order; Time order
Claims, 93–96, 288–89, 292, 298–309
Classification, as a type of proposition of definition, 282
Clear language, 175–76, 262, 274
Commonalities, 36
Communication as a transaction, 43–46, 169, 173
Communication skills, 45, 46, 56–63, 187–89, 212
Competence, 113, 246
Complementary communication, 26
Complex relationship between verbal and nonverbal symbols, 201
Concepts of communication, 23–47
Conclusion, 14, 155–58
Confide your feelings, as a way of focusing energy, 219, 226
Confidence, 247
Conformity, as a motive, 109
Confront the task, as a way of focusing energy, 219, 223–24
Connotative meanings, 173–74
Content, 10

Content, as an aspect of audience analysis, 80–81
Content, leading into, as an aspect of the speech introduction, 153, 154–55
Content aspects of communication, 24–25, 26
Control, 3, 17, 31, 197, 198, 202, 222, 247–48, 270, 272
Conversational speaking, 15–16, 19–20, 176, 229, 236
Convincing, as a type of persuasive speaking, 279–80
Coordination, as an aspect of outlining, 151–52
Creativity, 50–51
Credibility, 45, 92, 111–14, 241, 246–49, 252, 292
Cross-checking, 171

Data, 93, 96–104, 288–89, 292, 298–309
Deductive pattern, 288, 289
  figure, 290, 295
Definition, proposition of, 282–83
  classification, 282
  etymology, 282
  function, 283
Delivery, 3, 18–20, 214, 216–32, 234–53
  anxiety and, 217, 218–28
  as an aspect of audience analysis, 86–87
  building credibility through, 217, 246–49, 252
  memory, as part of, 217, 250–51, 252
  preparation and practice in, 217, 229–32, 252
  problems in, 217
  styles of presentation, 217, 234–53, 252
Demographics, 5, 69–75, 78
Denotative meanings, 173–74
Descriptions, 255, 261–62, 274
Descriptive speech, 6
Desires, 3–4
Diagrams, as visual aids, 266
  sample, 269
Different perceptions of words, 172–73
Differing interpretations of nonverbal cues, 199–200
Directions, 255–58, 273
Dissonance, 292
Distraction, 28, 195, 211, 244
Distractions in language use, 184–85, 211
Don't plan too grandly, as a way of focusing energy, 218, 222
Double message, 17
Dynamic language, 175, 180–81, 262, 274
Dynamism, 113, 206, 246–47, 323

Editorial opinion, 102
Educational level of audience, 72 *See also* Audience
Education of audience. *See* Audience
Effectiveness in speaking, how do you measure it? 88–89
Elements of communication, 23–47
Emotional considerations, 104–11
Emphasis, as an aspect of language use, 85–86

Emphasizing, as a way to increase understanding, 263, 265
Empty words, 185, 186–87
Energy, 323
Engage in self-analysis, as a way of focusing energy, 219, 226–27
Entertain, 121
Entertaining speeches, 316, 323–25, 327
Enthusiasm, 113, 206, 246–47, 323
Equality and difference in communication, 26–27
Esteem needs, 105–8
Ethics, 294–95
Ethos, 111–14, 246
Etymology, as a type of proposition of definition, 282
Eulogies, 316, 321–22, 326
Evaluative language, 181–82
Evidence, as an aspect of audience analysis, 82–83
    See also Data; Examples; Facts; Illustrations; Opinions; Personal experience; Speech Support; Statistics
Examples, 5, 9, 36, 96, 98–100, 149, 292, 324
Expert opinion, 102, 151, 292
Explanations, 255–58, 273
Extemporaneous speaking, 229, 234, 239, 244–45, 252
Extended conversation, 176, 247
Extrinsic ethos, 112
Eye contact, 3, 18, 206

Face, as an aspect of nonverbal communication, 192, 205–6
Fact, propositions of, 280–83
Facts, 5–6, 9, 96, 97–98, 149
Fallacious reasoning, 298
Farewells, 316, 321–22, 326
Fear, 217, 218–28 See also Anxiety
Feedback, 27, 41–43, 46, 175
Fidelity, 27, 30
Figures of speech, 180–81
Finding appropriate material, 3, 6–10
    appropriateness to audience, 8–9
    appropriateness to message, 9–10
    appropriateness to self, 6–7
    appropriateness to situation, 8
Finding main heads, 140–43
First impressions, 16
First speech, 1–21
    analyzing audience, 3–6
    choosing language, 15–16
    finding material, 6–10
    organizing material, 10–14
    presenting the message, 18–20
    using nonverbal communication, 16–18
Focusing, 121
Focusing on principles, as a way to increase understanding, 263–64
Focusing your energy, delivery, 216–32

Focus on a better world, as a way of focusing energy, 218, 221
Focus on the here and now, as a way of focusing energy, 219, 225
Frame of mind, 39
Function, as a type of proposition of definition, 283

Generalization, as a kind of reasoning, 301–2, 309
General purpose, 121–22
Gestures, 18 See also Nonverbal choices
Getting started, 1–21
Glibness in speaking, 93
Government documents, 132–33
Graphs, as visual aids, 266
    samples, 268–69

Halo effect, 37
Hearing, 51
Heterogeneous audiences, 36
Hierarchy of needs, 105–8
Homogeneous audiences, 35, 73
Humor, 316, 323–25, 327
Hyperbole, 180

Identification, 36–38, 44, 45, 114
Identifying appropriate material. See Speech support; Finding appropriate material
Illustrations, 5, 9, 36, 96, 98–100, 149
Immediacy, 82
Immediate speech results, 88
Impact, persuasive, 276–79
Impression, leaving one, as an aspect of the conclusion, 155, 156–57
Impression control, 25
Impromptu speaking, 229, 234, 240–43, 252
    anticipate for, 241
    be positive, with respect to, 243
    control yourself, with respect to, 242
    listen carefully, to prepare yourself for, 241
    organize your thoughts, in anticipation of, 242–43
Improving our langauge use, 187–89
Improving our listening skills, 56–63
Improving our nonverbal communication, 212
Increasing understanding, 255, 263–65 See also Informative speeches
Inductive pattern, 12, 288–89
    figure, 289, 295
Inference process, 197–98
Inferences, 98, 197–98
Influencing attitudes, 285–87, 295 See also Persuasion
Inform, to, 121, 122 See also Informative speeches
Informality, as an aspect of the speech to entertain, 324
Informative organizational patterns, 140, 143–48 See also Organizational patterns, informative
Informative speeches, 254–74
    descriptions, 255, 261–62, 274

directions, 255, 261–62, 274
explanations, 255–58, 274
lectures, 255, 258–61, 274
reports, 255, 258–61, 274
Initial partition, 154
Intended meaning, 32
Intended versus received meaning, figure, 33
Interesting, meaning of, as an aspect of topic or material choice, 149
Internal summaries, 158–60
Interviews, 119
Intrinsic ethos, 112–13
Introduction, 139–40
minimum functions, 14
of speech, 14, 152–55
Introductory speeches, 316–17, 326

Jargon, 185

Kinds of informative speeches, 255–63
Kinds of reasoning, 301–8
analogy, 301, 305–6
causation, 301, 302–4
generalization, 301–2
sign, 301, 307–8
Kinesics, 202, 203–4
K.I.S.S. (Keep It Simple and Straightforward), 9–10, 243
Knowledge, 45, 46
as a motive, 110
level of audience, 78

Language, 3, 15–16, 96, 157–90
choices, 175–87
emphasis, 85–86
improving it, 187–189
nature of, 168–74
skills, 187–189
Language choices, 175–87, 262
accuracy, 177–78, 262
appropriateness, 178–79, 262
clarity, 175–76, 262
dynamism, 180–81, 262
simplicity, 177–78, 262
Learning, ways to increase it, 255, 263–65, 274
Learning-forgetting curves, 53
Lectures, 255, 258–61, 274
Library, 117–36
card catalog, 124–27
how much use is enough, 134–36
periodicals, 127–31
usage, 117–36
Listeners, 173
Listening, 3, 48–65
implications of, 173
a model, 52
skills, 46, 56–63
to a speech, a form for use, 64–65

Loaded language, 181
Locating sources, 3, 6–10, 117–36
Logical support in speeches, 96–104, 292
Long-range speech results, 88
Loudness, 96, 207, 210, 211
Love needs, 105–8
Low awareness level, of nonverval cues, 199

Magazines, 127–29
Main heads, 140–43
checklist, 148
Manuscript speaking, 229, 234, 237–40, 252
Many uses of words, 171–72
Meaning, 3
Meaning is in people, 32, 174
Memorized speaking, 229, 234–36, 252
Memory, 250–51, 252, 262
Message, 27, 30–33
Messages, 46
Metacommunication, 25
Metaphor, 180
Methodology, 10
Mind set, 39
Minor cues, 195–97
Mixed message, 17, 26
Model of communication, 43–46
Models, as visual aids, 266
Modes of communication, 25–26
Monroe's motivated sequence, 290–94, 295
action, 291, 293–94
attention, 291
need, 291, 292
satisfaction, 291–92
visualization, 291, 293
Motivating, as a way to increase understanding, 263, 264–65
Motives, 108–10
Movies, as visual aids, 266

Narrative speech, 6
Narrowing topics, 7
Needs, 3–4
Nervousness, 217, 218–28. See also Anxiety
Newspapers, 130
Noise, 27, 40–41
physical, 40–41
psychological, 40–41
Nonverbal choices, 201–11
body, 202–5
face, 202, 205–6
voice, 202, 206–11
Nonverbal communication, 3, 16–18, 25–26, 193–212
choices, 201–11
improving, 212
nature of, 193–201
skills, 212
Norms, 46

Notetaking and note usage, 125–26, 244–45

Object language, 169
Objects, as visual aids, 266
Opinions, 5, 9, 96, 101–2, 149
Ordering main heads, 140, 143–48 *See also* Organizational patterns
Organization, 3, 10–14, 256–58, 324
  as an aspect of audience analysis, 83–84
  why do it?, 12
Organizational patterns, informative, 140, 143–48
  problem-solution order, 143, 147–48
  space order, 143, 146–47
  time order, 143, 145–46
  topic order, 143–45
Organizational patterns, persuasive, 288–95
  causal pattern, 288, 289–90, 295
  deductive pattern, 288, 289, 295
  inductive pattern, 288–89, 295
  special problem-solution order, 288, 290–94, 295
Organizing the material, 3, 10–14, 256–58, 324
  as a way to increase understanding, 263, 264
  body of the speech, 139–52
  conclusion, the, 155–58
  introduction, the, 152–55
  outlining, 139–65
  transitions and internal summaries, 158–60
Outline, sample, 160–64, 257
Outlines, 138–65 *See also* Organizing the material
Outlining, 139–65, 256–58
  causal pattern, 288, 289–90, 295
  deductive pattern, 288, 289, 295
  inductive pattern, 288–89, 295
  problem-solution order, 143, 147–48
  space order, 143, 146–47
  special problem-solution order, 288, 290–94, 295
  time order, 143, 145–46
  topic order, 143–45
Overhead projector, as a visual aid, 266

Pacing, 96
Paralanguage, 18, 169, 192, 206–12
Parallelism, 183
Perception, 51–52
Periodicals, 127–31
Personal considerations, 111–14
Personal experience, 96, 102, 149, 151
Personal opinion, 151
Personification, 180
Persuade, to, 121, 122
Persuasion, 276–95
  ethics and, 294–95
  impact through, 276–79
  influencing attitudes through, 285–87
  organizational patterns in, 288–94
  propositions in, 281–84
  types of, 279–81
Persuasive impact, 276–79, 295
  amount of information available, 276–77

likely effect you can have, 276, 278
  potential persuasive elements, 276–77
  where persuasion takes place, 276, 279
Persuasive organizational patterns, 288–95 *See also* Organizational patterns, persuasive
Persuasive speeches, 276–95
Physical noise, 40–41, 46
Physiological needs, 105–6
Pitch, 96, 207, 209, 211
Plagiarism, 104
Planning, as an aspect of the speech to entertain, 324
Policy, propositions of, 280–81, 283–84
Potential persuasive impact, 276–79, 295
Power, as a motive, 109
Practicality, as a motive, 109–10
Practice, as an aspect of delivery, 229–32
Practicing speeches, 229–32
Preparation, as an aspect of delivery, 229–32
Presentations, 316, 318–19, 326
Presenting the message, 3, 18–20, 214, 216–32, 234–53 *See also* Delivery
Presentness, 19–20
Principles of reasoning, 298–300
Problem-solution order, 143, 147–48 *See also* Special problem-solution order
Problem-solving speeches, 143, 147–48, 280–81, 283–84
Process of communication, 23–47
Process of drawing conclusions, 197–98
Projections, 37
Pronunciation, 211
Propositions, 280–81, 281–84, 309
  definition, 282–83
  fact, 280–81, 281–83
  policy, 280–81, 283–84
  value, 280–81, 283
Psychological noise, 40–41, 46
Public opinion, 102
Purpose of speech, 120–24 *See also* Propositions

Qualifiers, 94–96
Quality, as an aspect of language, 96, 207, 211

Rapport, as an aspect of the speech introduction, 153–54
Rate, as an aspect of language, 3, 207, 208–9, 211
Reasoning logically, 297–309
  definition of, 297–98
  kinds of, 301–8
  principles of, 298–300
Received meaning, 32
Redundancy, 175
Refinement, 176
Refrain, 183
Rehearsing a speech, 230–31
Relationship aspects of communication, 24–25, 26
Relevant, meaning of, 149

Repetition, 183
Reports, 255, 258–61, 274
Reservations, 95–96, 303–8
Resonance, 18
Responsiveness, as an aspect of the speech to
 entertain, 324
Reward yourself, as a way of focusing energy, 219,
 228
Rhythm, 18

Security needs, 105–8
Seeking understanding, 254–74
Selective perception, 52
Self-actualization needs, 105–8
Self-analysis, 219, 226–27
Self-image, 45, 46
Set goals, as a way of focusing energy, 218–20
Sex, 72
Sex of audience. See Audience
Sheer wealth of nonverbal cues, 193–95
Short-term speech results, 88
Sign, as a kind of reasoning, 301, 307–8, 309
Significant, meaning of, 149
Simile, 180
Simple language, 175, 177–78, 262, 274
Situation, 27, 38–40, 46
Slang, 185, 186
Slides, as visual aids, 262
Some different speaking situations, 314–27
Space order, 143, 146–47, 262
Speaker, 27–29, 45
Speaking for special occasions, 314–27
 acceptances, 316, 319–20, 326
 eulogies, 316, 321–22, 326
 farewells, 316, 321–22, 326
 introductory speeches, 316–17, 326
 presentations, 316, 318–19, 326
 speech of entertainment, 316, 323–25, 327
 tributes, 316, 321–22, 326
Speaking to convince, 297–309
 definition, 297–98
 kinds of reasoning, 301–8
 principles of reasoning, 298–300
Speaking to persuade, using logical arguments,
 309–12
Special-occasion speeches, 314–27
 acceptances, 316, 319–20, 326
 eulogies, 316, 321–22, 326
 farewells, 316, 321–22, 326
 introductory speeches, 316–17, 326
 presentations, 316, 318–19, 326
 speech of entertainment, 316, 323–25, 327
 tributes, 316, 321–22, 326
Special problem-solution order, 288, 290–94, 295
 action, 291, 293–94
 attention, 291
 need, 291, 292
 satisfaction, 291–92

visualization, 291, 293
Specific purpose, 120–24, 140–43
Speech of definition, 6
Speech purpose, 140–43
Speech support, 92–116, 309
 argument structure, 93–96
 data, 96–104
 definition, 92
 emotional considerations, 104–11
 examples, 98–100
 facts, 97–98
 illustrations, 98–100
 logical, 96–104
 opinions, 101–2
 personal considerations, 111–14
 personal experience, 102–4
 public opinion, 102
 statistics, 100–101
Speech to entertain, 316, 323–25, 327
Stage fright, 217, 218–28 See also Anxiety
Starting out, 1–21
Static nature of words, 171
Stating the purpose, as an aspect of the conclusion,
 155, 156
Statistics, 9, 96, 100–101, 151, 292
 sources for, 131–32
Stimulating, as a type of persuasive speaking,
 280–81
Stories, 5, 9, 36, 96, 98–100, 149, 292, 324
Strength of language, 180–81
Style, 157–90
 as an aspect of audience analysis, 84–85
Styles of presentation in delivery, 96, 217,
 234–53
Subordination, as an aspect of outlining, 151–52
Success, 249, 252
Summarizing, as an aspect of the conclusion,
 155–56
Superpurpose, 21, 83
Support, speech. See Speech support
Supporting main heads, 140, 148–52
Supports from language, 183
Suspend judgment, 61–62
Symbolic interaction, 168–71
Symbolic nature of words, 168–71
Symbolic reality, 169
Symmetrical communication, 26–27

Take time off, as a way of focusing energy, 219,
 225–26
Target audience, 10, 35, 69, 71, 72
Testimony, 102
Thesis, 9
Time order, 143, 145–46
Topical pattern, 12, 262 See also Ordering main
 heads; Outlining
Topic order, 12, 143–45, 262
Topic selection, 120–24

Transaction, communication as a, 43–46, 82, 90, 169, 173
Transcending purpose. *See* Super purpose
Transitions, 13, 14, 158–60
Tributes, 316, 321–22, 326
Triteness, 185
Trustworthiness, 113, 246
Types of persuasive speaking, 279–81, 295
   actuating, 280, 295
   convincing, 279–80, 295
   stimulating, 280–81, 295
Typical, as a test of data, 301–2

Using the body, 96, 192–214

Value, propositions of, 280–81, 283
Variable, 2–3
Variety, 202, 210
Ventilation, as a way to alleviate fear, 223
Verbal clutter, 185
Verbalizations, 209
Verbal mode of communication, 25–26

Visual aids, 255, 265–71, 274
   samples, 268–69
   types, 266–67
   uses, 267–70
Vocal action, 96, 192, 206–12
Vocalized pauses, 209, 248
Vocal variety, 206, 208–11
Voice, as an aspect of nonverbal communication, 192, 206–12
Volume, 3, 96, 207, 210, 211

Warrants, 93–96, 292, 298–309
Ways speakers have to increase understanding, 255, 263–65
Wealth, as a motive, 108
We cannot not communicate, 24
Word, as symbol, 32
Words are perceived differently, 172–73
Words are static, 171
Words are symbolic, 168–71
Word selection, 157–90
Words have many uses, 171–72